Kansas a[illegible]ns in W[illegible]rld War I

Kansas and Kansans in World War I

Service at Home and Abroad

Blake A. Watson

University Press of Kansas

Published by the University Press of Kansas (Lawrence, Kansas 66045), which was organized by the Kansas Board of Regents and is operated and funded by Emporia State University, Fort Hays State University, Kansas State University, Pittsburg State University, the University of Kansas, and Wichita State University.

Library of Congress Cataloging-in-Publication Data

Names: Watson, Blake A., 1956– author.
Title: Kansas and Kansans in World War I / Blake A. Watson.
Other titles: Kansas and Kansans in World War One
Description: Lawrence, Kansas : University Press of Kansas, 2024 | Includes bibliographical references and index.
Identifiers: LCCN 2024003029 (print) | LCCN 2024003030 (ebook)
ISBN 9780700637409 (cloth)
ISBN 9780700637416 (paperback)
ISBN 9780700637423 (ebook)
Subjects: LCSH: World War, 1914–1918—Kansas. | World War, 1914–1918—Social aspects—Kansas. | World War, 1914–1918—War work—Kansas. | World War, 1914–1918—Regimental histories—United States. | Kansas—History, Military—20th century. | Kansas. National Guard—History—20th century. | Kansas—Biography.
Classification: LCC D570.85.K2 B53 2024 (print) | LCC D570.85.K2 (ebook) | DDC 940.3/781—dc23/eng/20240301
LC record available at https://lccn.loc.gov/2024003029.
LC ebook record available at https://lccn.loc.gov/2024003030.

British Library Cataloguing-in-Publication Data is available.

For my great-uncle Private Ralph Nichols (1899–1929) and my mother,
Barbara Nichols Watson (1930–2023)

We'd go forward, about ten feet or so between us. If someone was killed, or wounded, we'd fill up the space and continue to advance. We'd go over or under barbed wire strung to slow us down—some fellows used wire cutters. We kept low, crouching, then when it sounded safe, we'd get up and run a distance, guns in position all the time.

—Theodore Roosevelt Blevins, 139th Infantry, 1979

I sometimes wonder if we realize what these boys did for us.

—Kansas governor Henry Allen, March 4, 1923

Contents

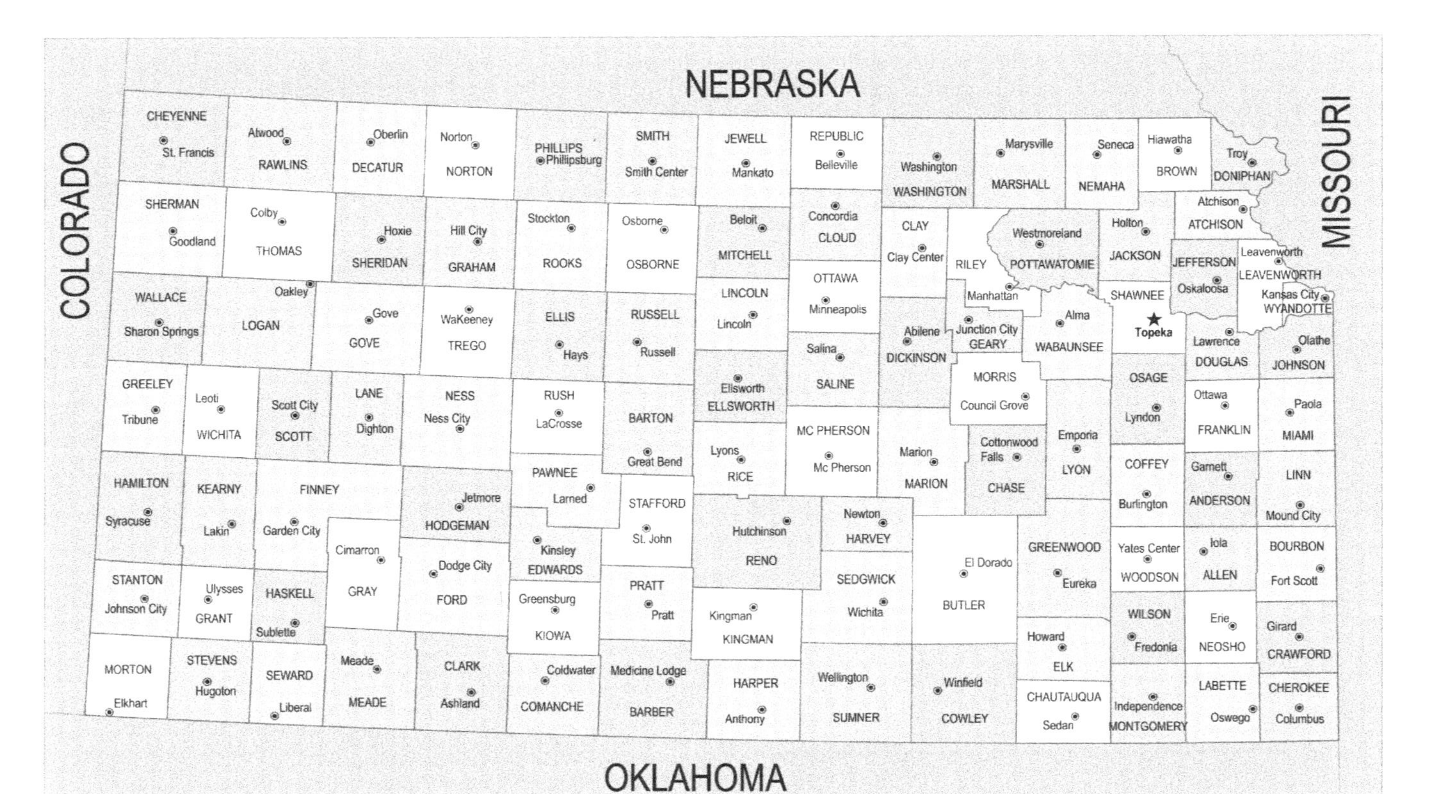

Photo 0.1: Kansas counties and county seats. Courtesy of Getty Images.

Preface

On the morning of July 13, 2018, my wife, Pam, and I traveled northeast from Paris to Rheims. Our express train sped by the winding Marne River and the town of Château-Thierry. In this part of France, several momentous and bloody battles were fought during World War I. In the First Battle of the Marne (September 1914), the French army—transported in part by taxi drivers—stopped the Germans within thirty miles of Paris. In the last year of the war, the German army attacked repeatedly along the western front in hopes of achieving victory before the United States could fully mobilize its soldiers. In May and June 1918, the fledgling American Expeditionary Forces (AEF) experienced modern warfare at Cantigny, Château-Thierry, and Bois de Belleau (Belleau Wood). Shortly thereafter at the Second Battle of the Marne (July 15–August 6), American and French forces stopped the final German offensive in what has been described as "the turning point of the Great War."[1]

Exchanging the train for an automobile at Rheims, we headed east to Verdun, stopping at several points to visit World War I sites. We first toured restored trenches near the village of Massiges. With the site to ourselves, we viewed dugouts containing vintage tables, beds, canteens, and wine bottles, while taking care to avoid strands of rusted barbed wire. As Vova Pomortzeff demonstrates with photographs and commentary, this "ground of bloody battles has turned into a stunning open-air museum through the efforts of local enthusiasts." Although some distance north of the Autoroute de l'Est (A4), the chalk-filled trenches of La Main de Massiges are well worth the detour.[2]

Our next destination was the Argonne Forest, where the "Lost Battalion" of the Seventy-Seventh Infantry Division was surrounded and attacked for six days in October 1918. After leaving the forest, we passed through Apremont, crossed the Aire River, and turned onto a narrow road (D242) that continues east through open spaces and cultivated fields. On this road, within sight of Chaudron Farm, we stopped again at the crest of a small hill. In the distance to the north is Montrebeau Wood. On the other side of this

Photo 0.2: La Main de Massiges, France, 2018. Courtesy of Blake Watson.

thicket is the village of Exermont and to the north and east is Romagne-sous-Montfaucon, the site of the Meuse-Argonne American Cemetery and Memorial.

On September 28, 1918, nineteen-year-old Ralph Nichols of Oskaloosa, Kansas, was shot in the cheek somewhere near or in Montrebeau Wood. Ralph wrote to his father, Reverend Townsend Nichols: "The Germans began to give us a barrage. Well, I was lucky enough to get through the barrage, but about 11 a.m. a machine gun bullet got me thro the face." The young man narrowly avoided death, recovered fully, and returned to Oskaloosa in 1919 to finish high school. He thereafter attended Kansas State Agricultural College, was a captain on the 1923 Aggie football team, and worked in South America and Texas as a petroleum engineer.[3]

Other Kansas soldiers were not as fortunate on the twenty-eighth of September. Eighty-four men from the Sunflower State were killed in action on that fateful day. All but one (Lieutenant Wade Priest of Greenleaf) were members of the Thirty-Fifth Infantry Division, tasked with attacking German machine-gun positions and other fortifications in the Aire valley east of the Argonne Forest. The Thirty-Fifth advanced beyond Montrebeau Wood as far as Exermont before falling back to a defensive line near Chaudron Farm. After its relief on the first of October, the division was scheduled to return to battle in mid-November, orders that were canceled when the armistice went into effect at the eleventh hour of the eleventh day of the eleventh month. The Meuse-Argonne offensive remains the largest and most costly battle in U.S. military history, lasting forty-seven days, involving more than 1.2 million American soldiers, and resulting in the loss of over 26,000 American lives.[4]

Ralph Nichols, my great-uncle, was the impetus for this book. His two older brothers also served during the Great War: Arvil, who went to France as a machine gunner and returned as a member of the military police, and Charles, who was training in Louisiana as an aviator when the war ended. On the other side of my family, grandfather Thomas Watson was stationed in 1918–1919 at Camp Funston, Kansas, during the height of the Spanish flu epidemic. Due in part to the fact that Townsend Nichols was an itinerant Methodist minister, my relatives have lived in Brown, Chase, Chautauqua, Cherokee, Dickinson, Elk, Franklin, Jefferson, Johnson, Leavenworth, Lyon, Morris, Neosho, Osage, Ottawa, Riley, Saline, Wabaunsee, Wallace, and Wyandotte Counties. My parents grew up in Oskaloosa and Overland Park, and our family lived for a time in Olathe, Kansas. As a Boy Scout, I spent time in Wyandotte County at Camp Naish, named for a man who perished at sea when the *Lusitania* was sunk in 1915.

The initial plan was to write about the Ralph Nichols's National Guard unit, which during the war became Company B, 139th Regiment, Thirty-Fifth Infantry Division. Thanks in part to increased internet access to Kansas newspapers, there is a wealth of information about the organization of Company B as well as its training, movements, and engagements. This book includes several chapters that describe the lives of eight guardsmen: William Davis of Winchester, William Smith of Valley Falls, and Theodore Blevins, Melvin Dyson, Samuel Gutschenritter, William Kimmel, Ralph Nichols, and Victor Segraves of Oskaloosa. These Jefferson County men, who in April 1917 ranged in age from seventeen to twenty-nine, were both ordinary and extraordinary. One had been abandoned by his parents as a child and rode the "orphan train" to Kansas and a new life. Two were killed in action, three were wounded, and one became a prisoner of war. The German-born parents of one of the wounded men were required to register as alien enemies. One of the men who died was awarded the Distinguished Service Cross, while the other man who did not return is the subject of a famous painting. After the war the survivors took on new roles: Chief Justice of the Kansas Supreme Court, offensive tackle in the National Football League, and beloved teacher and namesake of a junior high school.

This book, however, covers much more ground. Although my research began with Nichols and the Oskaloosa National Guard, "one thing led to another" while seeking context and perspective. Consequently, the stories that follow not only feature the aforementioned guardsmen but also describe famous generals and obscure privates, bravery and shameful behavior, altruistic patriotism and xenophobic hysteria, and heroism and racism. The primary points of focus are the Kansas home front, the three components of the wartime U.S. Army (the state-based National Guard, the permanent Regular Army, and the conscripted National Army), and the wartime experiences of African Americans in Kansas and from Kansas.

When President Woodrow Wilson spoke in Topeka on February 2, 1916, in favor of a stronger military, he faced skepticism and outright opposition from many residents, including Governor Arthur Capper and Frank Strong, chancellor of the University of Kansas. But when war against Germany was declared two months later, virtually everyone joined forces to lend support, in terms of both money and manpower. Fueled in part by "Uncle Sam" posters ("I Want YOU for U.S. Army"), George M. Cohan songs ("Over There"), and government-sponsored "four minute" speeches, many Kansans chose to enlist in the armed forces, contribute to relief organizations, participate in "meatless Mondays" and "wheatless Wednesdays," and purchase Liberty Loan bonds. College students joined the Reserve Officer Training Corps (ROTC) or the short-lived Student Army Training Corps (SATC) as well as the Red Cross and the Young Men's Christian Association (YMCA). Newspapers prominently displayed military service "honor rolls" and printed letters that passed along the news—good, bad, and occasionally erroneous—from "somewhere in France." When a Kansan was commended, promoted, wounded, killed, or captured, the entire community experienced corresponding pride or sorrow.

Yet in addition to patriotic sacrifice and support, there was also xenophobia, hysteria, and suppression. Kansans, like citizens in other states, were conditioned by silent movies and the printed word to dehumanize Kaiser Wilhelm ("the Beast of Berlin") and his soldiers ("demoniac Huns seeking to slay and spoil"). This resulted in some abusing German Americans, both verbally and physically, while noncitizens of German ancestry were required by federal law to be fingerprinted and registered. Members of Mennonite religious groups in Kansas, committed to pacifism, were subjected to particular scrutiny, forced to kiss the U.S. flag and buy war bonds, and in some instances drafted and then jailed for refusing to engage in activities related to the war effort. Anti-German sentiment devolved into hysteria: Americans were convinced that spies were putting glass in their food, and in one instance federal

Photo 0.3: *Food Will Win the War* poster, American Lithographic Company, 1917. Courtesy of the Library of Congress.

officials in Topeka investigated suspicious loaves of Butter Krust bread (and determined that the ground glass threat was groundless). With the passage by Congress of the 1917 Espionage Act and the 1918 Sedition Act, numerous Kansans were prosecuted, either for uttering "disloyal, profane, scurrilous, or abusive language" about the United States or the military or for making speeches that intended to "incite insubordination, disloyalty, mutiny, or refusal of duty." There was only muted opposition in the state (and elsewhere) to this abridgment of civil liberties, and newspapers across the Sunflower State reported other acts of suppression—banning of the German language in schools and churches, for instance—with disturbing frequency. There is no question that the war in Europe had a significant and lasting effect on Kansans who remained home.[5]

National Guard units were an important part of the AEF. In order to understand the role of Kansas guardsmen in the Great War, I briefly outline how the state militia was organized, supported, and deployed prior to 1917. The two most important events, discussed in chapters 1 and 3, were the strengthening of the U.S. Army–National Guard relationship and the deployment of Kansas guardsmen to the Mexican border.[6]

Partly in reaction to lessons learned during the Spanish-American War (1898), Congress enacted legislation in 1903 and 1908 that made National

Guard soldiers available for duty beyond state borders and outside of the United States. Guardsmen were henceforth trained according to federal requirements, provided equipment purchased with federal funds, and organized in conformity to the units and command structure of the "Regular Army." Kansas welcomed this opportunity to improve its militia. Led by its adjutant general, Charles I. Martin (who later commanded a brigade in the Thirty-Fifth Division), the Kansas National Guard grew in size and benefited from training opportunities for officers, engineers, and signalmen at Fort Leavenworth and Fort Riley. Martin was a strong proponent of the National Guard and effectively lobbied against alternative proposals to strengthen military preparedness, such as compulsory "universal training" and the creation of an auxiliary "continental army" of trained men subject to call in time of need. The National Defense Act of 1916, described by one historian as "essentially a political victory for the National Guard," confirmed that the Guard would continue to serve as the nation's primary reserve force. Congress provided funds to encourage enlistment, authorized increased control by the War Department to ensure uniform training and equipment, and empowered the president to draft Guard units directly into federal service in time of war.[7]

President Wilson immediately exercised his new power by calling out the National Guard to protect the Mexican border. Approximately 2,800 Kansans were sent to Texas in 1916 to oppose Pancho Villa and possible invasion. Although little action ensued, the Guard units drilled and trained, learned invaluable lessons, and returned home better prepared for actual warfare. Chapter 2 describes the formation of the Oskaloosa National Guard, and chapter 3 looks at its deployment to Texas.

The border crisis with Mexico did not change the fact that, when the United States entered World War I, it was not prepared to fight. On April 1, 1917, there were 5,791 officers and 131,797 enlisted men in the U.S. Army, which ranked seventeenth in the world behind Portugal. Without additional resources, one army officer opined that an American offensive war in Europe would be more futile than the medieval Children's Crusade. Consequently, to supplement the existing soldiers, new enlistments, and future draftees, the War Department created several army divisions based on state National Guard organizations. When President Wilson drafted the Guard into federal service, all but one unit from Kansas joined the newly created Thirty-Fifth Division; the sole exception was the First Ammunition Train, which became the 117th Ammunition Train of the Forty-Second (Rainbow) Division, one of the first four divisions to arrive, train, and fight in France. As discussed in chapter 6, these men—mostly from the Kansas City area and small towns in southern Kansas—joined guardsmen from twenty-five other states and the District of Columbia to form an effective fighting force that was eventually commanded by Douglas MacArthur, the future five-star general.[8]

The remaining Kansas guardsmen were sent to Camp Doniphan, Oklahoma, where they joined with Missouri guardsmen to form the Thirty-Fifth Division. Kansas supplied infantry, artillery gunners, engineers, signalmen, military police, ambulance drivers, and medical personnel. The Jefferson County men featured in this book—Blevins, Davis, Dyson, Gutschenritter, Kimmel, Nichols, Segraves, and Smith—found themselves in Company B, First Battalion, 139th Infantry Regiment, Seventieth Brigade. Their experiences provide insight into the role of the Kansas National Guard in World War I.

Kansans, of course, also served in the regular forces of the U.S. Army. The Regular Army divisions were numbered one through twenty, the National Guard divisions were numbered twenty-four through forty-two, and the National Army divisions (of draftees) were numbered seventy-six through ninety-three. Some divisions were never formed, and others were assigned to noncombat roles. At first the Regular Army divisions consisted entirely of career soldiers and enlisted men. But over time both they and the National Guard forces were replenished with transfers and draftees, blurring the distinctions between the three components of the wartime U.S. Army.[9]

This book looks at a number of career soldiers and volunteers from Kansas who, with one exception, served with honor. Chapter 10 focuses on three privates from the First Division: Charles Orr, the “first American hero” in World War I; Clyde Grimsley, one of the first doughboys to be captured by the Germans, and Frank Cadue, the first American soldier hanged in France for criminal behavior. Chapter 11 looks at two lieutenants from Emporia, Charles Avery and Harry “Buzz” Martin, and a captain from Bushton, Clarence Huebner, who in May 1918 helped the First Division capture and hold the village of Cantigny. Throughout the ensuing month of June, the Second Division fought relentlessly—and famously—in Belleau Wood. In an unusual arrangement, half of the division’s infantry were U.S. Marines, commanded at the time by James Harbord, a graduate of Kansas State Agricultural College, army brigadier general, and former chief of staff for General John J. Pershing. In another unusual arrangement, the members of the Sixth Marine Regimental Band, from Holton and neighboring towns in northeast Kansas, exchanged their musical instruments for stretchers and helped carry the wounded from the field of combat. The Kansas contribution to the Battle of Belleau Wood is the subject of chapter 12.

Ulysses Grant McAlexander, born in Minnesota but raised on a farm near McPherson, Kansas, earned the nickname "Rock of the Marne" for himself and his regiment, the Thirty-Eighth Infantry, Third Division, by repulsing a three-sided attack by numerically superior German forces. Chapter 13 makes the argument, however, that Captain Thomas Reid, who grew up in Columbus, Kansas, also stood like a rock and rallied his men at perhaps the most critical juncture of the battle.

With the exception of Cadue, all the men mentioned above were heroes, but none was awarded the Medal of Honor. Chapter 20 looks at four volunteers with Kansas connections—John Balch, Erwin Bleckley, George Mallon, and George Robb—who earned the nation's highest military decoration.

The final component of the wartime U.S. Army was the National Army. Whereas less than 8 percent of the Union army was drafted during the Civil War, over 70 percent of the American soldiers in World War I were conscripted. Eligible Kansas men were required to register at 113 local draft boards (one for each of the 105 counties and eight additional districts covering Kansas City, Topeka, and Wichita). When Secretary of War Newton Baker initiated the draft by selecting the capsule containing number 258, it meant that the individual holding that number (if his county had 258 registrants) would be first person selected for military service (unless exempted or discharged or if the county had met its quota). Chapter 5 describes the implementation of the Selective Service Act and tells the stories of a handful of the Kansans who held number 258 in their county or district. Some of the disqualified men were greatly disappointed, such as Laird Archer, a Wichita newspaper reporter who was both underweight (because of an appendicitis operation) and vision impaired (due to a childhood encounter with lightning). Other men unsuccessfully sought exemption, such as Levi Matson of Cloud County, whose overwrought reaction was sympathetically described by one newspaper and lampooned by another. At least two Kansans first selected in their county were killed in action, and several were gassed or wounded. The 258th registrant in Decatur County, George Washington Gardner, became a sergeant in the 353rd Infantry and was awarded the Distinguished Service Cross.[10]

The 353rd, part of the Eighty-Ninth Division, was known as the "All Kansas" Regiment because it was initially composed of Jayhawk draftees. Chapter 7 focuses on the formation and training of the Eighty-Ninth Division at

Photo 0.4: Secretary of War Newton Baker selecting the first draft number on July 20, 1917. Courtesy of the Library of Congress.

Camp Funston, while chapters 15 and 17 describe the critical role played by the 353rd Infantry—and George Gardner—at the Battle of Saint-Mihiel and during the final phase of the Meuse-Argonne offensive.

This book also examines the wartime experiences of African Americans in Kansas and from Kansas. Chapter 7 describes the treatment of African Americans who trained in the state, and chapter 19 looks at the wartime experiences of Black soldiers from Kansas. The Ninety-Second Division, one of two segregated infantry divisions, was organized at Camp Funston and included Black soldiers from across the United States. Because no separate cantonment was provided for the division, however, the various units of the Ninety-Second were sent to seven different camps out of state, and only the Division Headquarters, Headquarter Troops, the 349th Machine Gun Battalion, and divisional trains were stationed in Kansas. At the direction of the War Department, the men of Eighty-Ninth and Ninety-Second Divisions were kept apart, and a "Negro zone" was built at the east end of Camp Funston, with "separate amusement places and [postal] exchanges." The Black soldiers at Camp Funston were instructed by their white commander to "avoid every situation that can give rise to racial ill-will. Attend quietly and faithfully to your duties, and don't go where your presence is not desired."[11]

With the approval of General Pershing and the War Department, the "Buffalo Soldiers" of the Ninety-Second Division and the "Harlem Hellfighters" and "Black Devils" of the Ninety-Third Division were assigned to the French army. Among their ranks were Kansans selected—based on prior performance as soldiers or educational achievements—to attend an officers' training camp for African Americans at Fort Des Moines, Iowa. Chapter 19 recounts some of the war experiences of black men from Kansas, including Lieutenant William Bly, a career soldier from Leavenworth who was gassed during an attack the day before the armistice, and Lieutenant Wesley Jamison of Topeka, a graduate of both Washburn College and the law school at Northwestern University, who described in a letter an encounter with a shell that "threw a plank across my nose, knocked my helmet off, and otherwise stirred me up." Another graduate of Washburn College, Sherman Scruggs Jr., was awarded the Croix de Guerre by the French government for "securing under heavy shell fire the liaison with contiguous units." Lieutenant Scruggs returned to Kansas; earned master's and doctoral degrees from the University of Kansas; was an educator in Kansas City, Kansas; and served eighteen years as president of Lincoln University in Jefferson City, Missouri.[12]

Not every soldier, of course, was a combatant, and the War Department created both white and Black regiments to build roads, repair bridges, and provide other labor services. James Henry Irwin of Oskaloosa served in the 803rd Pioneer Regiment, while George "Never" Sweatt of Humboldt, a star athlete at Kansas State Normal School (now Emporia State University), served in the 816th Pioneer Regiment. As Chad L. Williams relates in his book on African American soldiers, Black men in the pioneer regiments "built cemeteries and reinterred dead soldiers in varying states of decomposition for several months after the war." Irwin—his last name is sometimes spelled "Irvin" or "Erwin"—was the first African American male to graduate from Oskaloosa High School. He attended Western University, served in the army, and died of disease in France. Sweatt was more fortunate, returning to Kansas to complete his education and become a well-respected teacher. He also excelled at baseball: Sweatt is the only person to appear in the first four Negro World Series and is in the Kansas Sports Hall of Fame and the Kansas Baseball Hall of Fame.[13]

* * *

According to the American Battle Monuments Commission, of the approximately 80,000 Kansans in the U.S. armed forces during World War I, about 8 percent (6,480) were lost to combat, accidents, or disease. Interest in the Great War increased in the years leading up to the one-hundredth anniversary of the armistice. Chapter 26 describes how Kansas and Kansans have honored the men and women who gave their lives, both at home and overseas, in connection with the Great War. Both Kansas State University and the University of Kansas held commemorative events. In Manhattan "the Fallen 48" were honored (and an oversight corrected) when the limestone Memorial Stadium was officially dedicated on April 21, 2017. "If you are a K-Stater, this has to be meaningful to you," remarked university president Richard B. Myers. "If you've been in the military," he added, "this is meaningful to you because we're finally bringing to a close a chapter that was open but never officially closed." On November 11, 2019, the University of Kansas rededicated its Memorial Union. "We have engraved in the arch canopy 129 stars representing each of the fallen," explained David Mucci, director of the building. "This Veterans Day seemed the appropriate time to do that, and we are happy to honor those who served and sacrificed so dramatically on behalf of the nation."[14]

The National WWI Museum and Memorial in Kansas City, Missouri, honors all Americans who took part in the Great War, as does the World War I Memorial in Washington, DC. This book has a more limited scope but a similar purpose: to honor Kansans who served and sacrificed in World War I and to commemorate the role played by Kansas and Kansans both at home and abroad.

1916

Photo 1.1: *Anxious Moments*, by Clifford Kennedy Berryman, published in the *Washington (DC) Evening Star*, November 7, 1916. Courtesy of the Library of Congress.

CHAPTER ONE

The President Comes to Topeka

Woodrow Wilson and the "Preparedness" Debate

"WILSON IS COMING.—THE PRESIDENT WILL VISIT TOPEKA WEDNESDAY, FEB. 2—WILL DISCUSS HIS POLICY OF PREPAREDNESS AND DEFENSE." This headline, on page one of the January 22, 1916, edition of the *Topeka State Journal*, was a surprise announcement since Kansas was not part of President Woodrow Wilson's scheduled tour. Under his revised itinerary, however, Wilson would make a brief stop at the train depot in Lawrence and then spend five hours in Topeka. He had visited the state capital twice before—in 1911 as a prospective presidential candidate and in 1912 during the closing weeks of that year's election campaign. Wilson would now return on February 2, 1916, as the twenty-eighth president of the United States.[1]

Most Kansans were proud and excited to host the president, his new bride, and the rest of his entourage. The day, replete with marching bands, the firing of cannons, and an overflow audience at the city auditorium, would be long remembered. But as the *State Journal* noted on January 27, the "big and spectacular reception that Topeka is to give to President Wilson is not, of course, an endorsement of his preparedness program." Kansas was considered one of the states least receptive to the military proposals of the Wilson administration regarding the war then raging in Europe and elsewhere.

Opponents fell into two camps: those who feared that any buildup would push the United States into the ongoing conflict, and those who supported preparedness but disagreed with the War Department's plan. Representing the first camp were Republican governor Arthur Capper and Frank Strong, chancellor of the University of Kansas, who both participated in a meeting of the Kansas Peace and Equity League just three days before Wilson's visit. The most influential person in the second camp was Charles I. Martin, adjutant general of the Kansas National Guard, who favored a stronger military but opposed the creation of a separate "Continental" reserve force.[2]

When Kansas helped elect Wilson to the White House in 1912, war was not on the horizon. But when the president came to Lawrence and Topeka in 1916, the world was a very different place, with the real possibility that the United States could be drawn into armed conflicts in both Mexico and Europe.

* * *

Kansas had approximately 1.7 million inhabitants in 1917, up from 1.4 million in 1900. In 1910 there were three cities having over 40,000 residents (Kansas City, Wichita, and Topeka) and nine cities with populations of over 10,000 but less than 20,000 (Leavenworth, Hutchinson, Atchison, Pittsburg, Coffeyville, Parsons, Lawrence, Independence, and Fort Scott). The 2,444 enumerated Native Americans composed 0.1 percent of the state's inhabitants, while African Americans (54,030) were 3.2 percent of the population. Of the foreign-born white population residing in Kansas in 1910, the majority had immigrated from Germany (25.5 percent), while others came from Russia (11.3 percent), Sweden (9.8 percent), Austria (8.9 percent), or England (8.3 percent). Nearly five-sixths of the state's land was devoted to farming, with corn and wheat being the leading crops. Industrial activities included mining (salt, coal, lead, and zinc), flour milling, meat packing, cement manufacture, and most significantly, oil and gas production. On October 6, 1915, a Wichita company discovered "the oil field that won World War I" in Butler County. By 1918, the El Dorado Oil Field was the largest single producer in the United States, responsible for nearly 13 percent of national oil production and 9 percent worldwide.[3]

The predominant theme in Kansas at the beginning of the twentieth century was progress, both at home and in government. On November 17, 1912, citizens of Topeka watched the mayor's son, Philip Billard, fly over the capital in a plane built by Albin Longren, who with Clyde Cessna helped make Kansas a center of aviation. In a span of eighteen months in 1913 and 1914, owners registered over ninety thousand cars in Kansas, and Walter Chrysler—born in Wamego and raised in Ellis—began his career in the automotive industry. There were 250,000 telephones in Kansas, a concrete highway in Allen County, and nearly ten thousand miles of railroad. The Kansas State Agricultural College won twenty-four prizes at the 1910 Livestock Show in Chicago, and farmers increasingly used new varieties of seed and fertilizers as well as steam and gasoline tractors and threshing machines. Progress in education was also being made, although only seventeen of one thousand Kansans went to college, and only fifty-three of every thousand entered a high school. As of 1914, there were thirty-two denominational schools and nine state institutions of higher learning: the University of

Kansas in Lawrence; the State Agricultural College in Manhattan; three normal (teacher) schools at Emporia, Hays, and Pittsburg; schools for the blind and deaf in Kansas City and Olathe respectively; and two "colored" schools, the Topeka Industrial and Educational Institute and Western University at Quindaro. Native Americans were educated by the federal government and attended the Haskell Institute in Lawrence or the Pottawatomie Boarding School at Nadeau.[4]

Political milestones included leadership in the national Prohibition movement, completion of the Kansas State Capitol in 1903, approval of state suffrage for women in 1912, regulation of railroads and public utilities, enactment of laws pertaining to public health and child labor, creation of primary elections, and the increased adoption of the new "city manager" system of local government. Kansas had been a Republican stronghold since the Civil War, but there were a few exceptions: two Populists (Lorenzo Lewelling, 1893–1895, and John Leedy, 1897–1899) had served as governor as had two Democrats (Washington Glick, 1883–1885, and George Hodges, 1913–1915). Democrat William Jennings Bryan of Nebraska carried the state in the 1896 presidential election but was unable to duplicate the feat in 1900 or 1908. To date, the 1896 election is the only time a Republican candidate (William McKinley) has won the presidency without Kansas.[5]

Wilson in 1912 became the first of three Democratic presidents to prevail in Kansas (the others being Franklin Delano Roosevelt and Lyndon Johnson). He won that year despite garnering less than 42 percent of the popular vote. Many Republicans at that time switched their allegiance to the Progressive "Bull Moose" Party headed by Theodore Roosevelt, drawing votes away from President Howard Taft, the Republican nominee. Wilson carried Kansas despite being favored by just 39 percent of the voters. A fourth candidate, Eugene Debs of the Socialist Party of America, was chosen by 7 percent of Kansans (and finished first among all candidates in Crawford County).

Congress enacted progressive legislation during the first term of the Wilson administration, including the Federal Reserve Act, the Federal Trade Commission Act, and the Federal Farm Loan Act, which increased the availability of credit to rural farmers. The success Wilson enjoyed as president, however, was tempered by the declining health of his wife, Ellen, who was eventually diagnosed with Bright's disease in July 1914 and died at the White House on August 6.[6]

Prior to the European war, the "Mexican problem" was the focus of U.S. foreign affairs. The month before Wilson assumed office, President Francisco

Madero was deposed, arrested, and subsequently killed. The United States refused to recognize the new government, and Venustiano Carranza of northern Mexico proclaimed himself provisional president. In April 1914 a shipment of weapons from Germany to Mexico prompted the American occupation of Vera Cruz, which Major General Frederick Funston of Kansas then administered for the next seven months. Wilson and his advisers considered calling up the National Guard in the spring of 1914, and Adjutant General Martin announced that two infantry regiments and an artillery battery were ready to depart "at a moment's notice" from Kansas. Yet despite receiving an order from the War Department in May regarding inoculation against typhoid (a prevalent disease in Mexico), National Guard units from interior states were not mobilized at this time.[7]

Mexico no longer dominated the headlines when, on June 28, 1914, Archduke Francis Ferdinand of Austria-Hungary was assassinated in Sarajevo. The Austro-Hungarian Empire declared war on Serbia, triggering a series of escalating responses by the major powers of Europe. The German army provoked outrage by invading neutral Belgium and Luxembourg and created panic by advancing toward Paris, before being pushed back by the French to the Aisne River. In the weeks and months that followed the First Battle of the Marne, both sides constructed trenches along a "western front" extending through Belgium and France from the North Sea to the Swiss border.

On December 8, 1914, President Wilson reaffirmed his commitment to neutrality but acknowledged the need for a strong National Guard: "We must depend in every time of national peril, not upon a standing army, nor yet upon a reserve army, but upon a citizenry trained and accustomed to arms. . . . [T]he National Guard of the states should be developed and strengthened by every means which is not inconsistent with our obligations to our own people or with the established policy of our government." Despite his assurance that the nation was "at peace with all the world," the war in Europe soon touched the lives of Americans, including Belle Naish. Her husband, Theodore, originally from England, attended the University of Kansas and worked as the city engineer of Kansas City. In 1915 the couple booked passage on the British ocean liner *Lusitania* in order to visit Theodore's family. Germany had declared the waters around the United Kingdom to be a war zone, but the Naishes did not learn of the warning until they were crossing the Atlantic. On May 7, 1915, the *Lusitania* was torpedoed by a submarine off the southern coast of Ireland, killing nearly 1,200 passengers and crew members, including 128 Americans. According to Theodore's brother, "the ship broke in half just where they stood and parted them." Belle survived the icy waters, but her husband did not. She later donated land near Edwardsville in Wyandotte County known today as the Theodore Naish Scout Reservation.[8]

Soon after the *Lusitania* sinking, Wilson directed Secretary of War Lindley Garrison to prepare an adequate program for national defense. As reported by the *Topeka Daily Capital*, Garrison's proposal advised "augmenting the regular army to 140,000 men (an increase of more than 50,000) and the creation of a new continental army of 400,000 men." The relegation of the National Guard to a third line of defense was due in part to a lingering dispute over whether the federal government was empowered to order guardsmen to serve overseas. As historian John Patrick Finnegan observes, the preparedness plan did not sit well with the Guard's supporters: "By coming out for a Continental Army, the War Department was forced to scrap the Organized Militia as a first-line reserve. This was a fateful decision, deliberately made by the secretary of war and his senior advisers. It would irretrievably alienate the National Guard lobby and states' rights congressmen." On December 7, 1915, in his third annual message to Congress, Wilson acknowledged that the "Continental army" plan depended not only on "the patriotic feeling of the younger men of the country" but also on whether their employers would give them leave to complete their required training. He made no mention of the Guard in his speech but elsewhere made the dubious claim that "none of this would be done in such a way as in the slightest degree to supersede or subordinate our present serviceable and efficient National Guard."[9]

Kansans immediately questioned the need to enlarge the military. Stating that "great expenditures for armament invite war," the agriculture-based Kansas State Grange resolved to "go on record as taking a firm stand against preparedness." The Kansas State Teachers' Association protested "the present tide of militarism of the European fashion," while Democrat Joseph Taggart of Wyandotte County argued that "preparedness talk is dictated by commercialism." Everyday citizens, such as John H. Bryan of Moline, Kansas, held similar views, as evident by his letter published in the *Capper's Weekly*: "The man with a gun in his pocket is the man who gets into trouble. What can be applied to an individual in this case can be applied to a nation."[10]

The leading opponent of the Wilson-Garrison preparedness plan in Kansas was Governor Capper, a Quaker Republican who owned *Capper's Weekly* and the *Topeka Daily Capital*. Capper, who was born in Garnett, served as president of the Board of Regents of Kansas State Agricultural

Photo 1.2: James Montgomery Flagg's *Uncle Sam* on the cover of *Leslie's Illustrated Weekly Newspaper*, July 6, 1916. Courtesy of the Library of Congress.

College (later Kansas State University) from 1910 to 1913. He would serve as governor from 1915 to 1919 and thereafter represent the state in the U.S. Senate until 1949. The new governor, at a peace convention in Topeka, urged Kansans to "protest against the lapse into barbarism which will for all time disgrace the twentieth century of the Christian era." A year later, on January 15, 1916, Capper published an editorial in the *Daily Capital* that argued that the Wilson policy constituted "a reversal of the century-old policy of the United States." He did not disagree with preparedness "in the true meaning of the word," but he strenuously objected to a hasty adoption "of that policy of militarism which has demonstrated so tragically its futility and wickedness in Europe."[11]

Capper's editorial was published one week before Wilson added Kansas to his speaking tour. The news of the presidential visit, however, did not change the governor's strident rhetoric. As the leader of the Kansas Peace and Equity League, he spoke at an antimilitarism rally on January 30, just three days before Wilson's arrival. "Our present war scare," the governor told the

Photo 1.3: Arthur Capper. From *Honor Roll, Shawnee County, Kansas* (Kansas City, MO: Burger Engraving, 1920).

audience at the Topeka First Baptist Church, "is largely due to the carefully worked up propaganda of the men and interests that make great profit out of war and preparedness for war." Several other prominent Kansans spoke in favor of peace, including Chancellor Strong of the University of Kansas, who read from the Beatitudes, "Blessed are the peace makers; for they are the children of God," then declared: "Civilization depends upon what the United States does in this emergency. The crisis of Christianity is upon us." The Peace and Equity League concluded the meeting by adopting a lengthy resolution, which states in part: "We recommend the establishment of peace societies in every community of our state to reverse the old sentiment so it shall read 'In time of war prepare for peace.' . . . We pledge ourselves to work for universal peace because we believe it is possible to get it." The resolution, in its entirety, was published in the *Topeka Daily Capital* under the headline "DOCTRINE OF LOVE BETTER THAN GUNS TO PREVENT WARS."[12]

It is not known how many Kansans in January 1916 agreed with the Peace and Equity League. It is certain, however, that the league's position was not

Photo 1.4: Charles Martin. From *Honor Roll, Shawnee County, Kansas* (Kansas City, MO: Burger Engraving, 1920).

endorsed by the state's adjutant general, who certainly did not attend the meeting. Martin wholeheartedly concurred with the need to improve military preparedness but objected to the new continental reserve army. His viewpoint was shared by many Kansas politicians. Republican congressman Daniel Read Anthony Jr. of Leavenworth said that the Wilson-Garrison plan was "doomed for the junk pile" and presciently declared that Congress would instead enact an army bill that would "build up our national guard." Democrat Guy Helvering of Marysville agreed, arguing, "we should link the national guard more closely to our regular establishment and . . . training should be done regularly, instead of sporadically by army officers."[13]

* * *

To better understand the role of the National Guard in World War I, it is necessary to briefly describe how the Kansas militia evolved since statehood and how Adjutant General Martin effectively promoted the National Guard at both the state and national levels.

Article I of the Constitution authorizes Congress to provide for "calling forth the Militia to execute the Laws of the Union, suppress Insurrections and repel Invasions" as well as for "organizing, arming, and disciplining, the Militia." The right to appoint officers, however, is reserved to the states. Article II provides that the president "shall be Commander in Chief of the Army and Navy of the United States, *and of the Militia of the several States, when called into the actual Service of the United States*." The Second Amendment declares that a "well regulated Militia [is] necessary to the security of a free State" and provides that "the right of the people to keep and bear Arms, shall not be infringed."[14]

According to Article VIII of the 1861 Kansas Constitution, all "able-bodied white citizens between the ages of twenty-one and forty-five years" were members of the state militia unless exempted by state or federal law or were "citizens of any religious denomination whatever who from scruples of conscience may be adverse to bearing arms." During the Civil War, Kansas supplied twenty thousand men to U.S. forces, including two African American regiments and one African American artillery battery. The men, however, did not fight as state militia but rather as federal volunteers. For example, Jennison's Jayhawkers joined the Union cause as the Seventh Kansas Volunteer Cavalry under the command of the notorious Charles "Doc" Jennison. One of his men, Private William F. Cody, would later become known as "Buffalo Bill," the famous bison hunter and showman.[15]

The state government in 1885 officially designated the militia as the Kansas National Guard. For the next decade, guardsmen were mobilized infrequently, usually to maintain order during labor strikes. When President McKinley sent troops to Cuba and the Philippines, he did not mobilize the National Guard but instead relied on volunteer units such as the First Volunteer Cavalry, otherwise known as the Rough Riders. Kansas supplied four volunteer units during the Spanish-American War and was one of only eight states to raise a regiment (the Twenty-Third Kansas) comprising Black officers and troops. The Twentieth Kansas Volunteer Infantry, led by the irrepressible "Fighting Fred" Funston, established its stellar reputation in 1899 at Caloocan in the Philippines. Major General Arthur MacArthur, the father of Douglas MacArthur, complimented Funston's men by sending the following message to headquarters: "Caloocan taken. Kansans a mile in advance of the line. Will stop them if I can." Shortly thereafter, during a counterattack, Kansans shouted "Rock Chalk! Jay Hawk!" as they faced their foes. A reporter for the British Associated Press, who most likely had never been to the Sunflower State, wrote that the soldiers "jumped into that jungle as many a time they had done in their great Kansas rows of 12-foot corn, and they went through it with a mighty shout."[16]

Beginning in 1894, National Guard officers were trained at Fort Leavenworth and Fort Riley by members of the U.S. Army. According to one account, "at least three-fourths of the officers and two-thirds of the men of [the Twentieth Kansas] had attended the officers' schools and encampments." Three officers (all University of Kansas men) and one soldier are worth mention. Wilder S. Metcalf enlisted in 1888 as a private in the Kansas National Guard. While in the Philippines, Metcalf was wounded twice and promoted to colonel. Future adjutant general Charles Martin joined the Kansas National Guard in 1880 at age nineteen and attained the rank of major while in the Philippines. The third officer, Clad Hamilton of Topeka, served as a captain in the Twentieth Kansas before returning to his law practice. All three men would play prominent roles when the federal government mobilized the Kansas National Guard in 1916 and 1917. The soldier, Derwood Eugene "Stub" Quakenbush, served as an orderly in the Philippines for Colonel Metcalf, taking care of his horses. He would later be instrumental in securing a National Guard company for the town of Oskaloosa.[17]

Congress in 1908 authorized state militias to serve beyond the borders of the United States and for the duration of hostilities. The legislation was questioned by Attorney General George Wickersham, who opined that this was unconstitutional. In response National Guard proponents suggested that men could simultaneously enlist in the national army and their state militia. Congressman James Hay of Virginia, chairman of the House Committee on Military Affairs, endorsed the dual enlistment "work-around" and supported a federalized National Guard. Consequently, Adjutant General Martin received a friendly reception when he appeared before Hay's committee and argued for a stronger National Guard. His testimony came just one day after Wilson's visit to Topeka. Unbeknown to Martin, the president was already thinking about dropping the continental army idea from his preparedness plan.[18]

* * *

On February 2, 1916, just after nine o'clock in the morning, President Wilson's train pulled into the Santa Fe station at Lawrence. The ground was covered with snow, and it was extremely cold. A large crowd nevertheless had gathered to greet the president and the First Lady, Edith Bolling Galt Wilson, a widow from Virginia whom Wilson had met in March 1915 and married that December. Native American children from the Haskell

Institute formed an honor guard complete with a marching band, and morning classes at local grade schools and Lawrence High School were canceled. When the First Couple stepped onto the train's rear platform, students from the University of Kansas yelled "Rock Chalk, Jay Hawk, K.U.!" Observing the multitude of winter hats, Wilson remarked, "I see you believe in preparedness." After making a few more unsubstantial remarks (for example, "How's the thermometer this morning?"), the train departed for Topeka. According to the *Topeka Daily Capital*, the visit lasted ten minutes, while the *Lawrence University Daily Kansan* reported that it was "exactly three minutes and forty-five seconds."[19]

The next stop was the state capital. As reported in the *Topeka State Journal*, "necks were craned from every available window, thousands of small American flags waved, thousands of hats were thrown into the air in the near zero weather and from the thousands of good American throats issued lusty American cheers as the president and his beautiful bride passed up the street." A cannon on the statehouse grounds was fired to signal the start of the president's motorcade, escorted by numerous groups, including veterans of the Civil War and Spanish-American War, National Guard soldiers and band members, firemen, Rotarians, the Topeka Rifle Club, students from the Boys' Industrial School, and the Boy Scouts. The *Topeka Daily Capital* noted that "interest in business and common pursuits of Topekans ceased," and spectators "who could find standing room on pavement or sidewalk pushed and shoved to gain a vantage point as the parade crawled slowly up Fifth street and south on Kansas avenue."

Every seat was occupied at the Municipal Auditorium, with thousands of people turned away. The audience was entertained with music, and when Marguerite Gohlke of Topeka sang a song with a peace message, she received a volley of applause. The crowd also reacted when Wilson and Capper arrived, although the *State Journal* noted that the "mild welcome" lasted "for a brief minute." Matters did not improve with the governor's introduction. Although praising Wilson for maintaining neutrality—"He has sat undismayed on the hottest lid that has seated any president since Lincoln"—Capper also observed that many Kansans were "not in accord with the program of vast armament, *with all its hazardous consequences*." When the governor sat down and the president rose to speak, hundreds of small silk flags were dropped through trap doors by Boy Scouts hidden in the auditorium attic. The crowd listened attentively as Wilson made his case for a stronger military. There was applause, but it was described as "spasmodic and scattered."

What is most perhaps most noteworthy is what the president did *not* emphasize in his speech. There was little discussion of the proposed continental army, most likely because Wilson was beginning to realize the political ramifications of insisting on a proposal that was unpopular with both the public and Congress. He did point out that, under current laws, the National Guard was "a body of state troops and not a body of national reserves." For most of the speech, however, Wilson appealed to the patriotism and pocketbooks of Kansans. "It may be necessary," he declared, "for the United States to use force to vindicate the rights of Americans everywhere to enjoy protection under international law." One of those, the president told the audience, was the right to sell agricultural products to other countries: "The world needs the wheat of Kansas fields and we have a right to supply those demands."[20]

The immediate reaction was mixed, as evident by articles, editorials, and speeches in nearby Jefferson County. The *Oskaloosa Independent* noted, "Kansas turned out in fine style to greet the President of the United States and cheered him loyally," but then wrongly predicted that Kansans would "turn out next November and swat Mr. Wilson and his mistaken doctrines and policies." The *Independent* also reprinted an editorial from the *Lawrence Gazette* that complained, "President Wilson, for a time sane and level, has been driven off his feet by the howlings of the men with guns to sell." On the other hand, the *Oskaloosa Times* and several other newspapers ran a story headlined "A Splendid Speech to Which All Can Subscribe," followed by "President Wilson denies any Attempt to Prussianize America—Asks only a Sufficient Army and Navy to Protect Rights of Citizens." Eight days after the president's speech, a student from the Oskaloosa High School, Theodore "Ted" Blevins, attended the Jefferson County Democratic Banquet in Perry and gave "an exceptionally well constructed" talk on Wilson, "whose name was received with thunderous applause."[21]

As Congress moved toward a final resolution of the preparedness issue, Kansas businesses used the debate to promote their products. The *Olathe Register* announced, "while Preparedness is still an uncertain issue, WE ARE PREPARED to fill your orders for letter heads, envelopes, stationary . . . or anything else in the printing line." The Kansas Lumber and Supply Company warned the readers of the *Harveyville Monitor* not to wait until an enemy attacks: "Everywhere we hear people talking about Preparedness. Are you prepared for the worst enemy of the summer season—General FLY and his vast army of disease spreaders? . . . Come in now and let us quote you prices on window and door screens."[22]

On March 6, 1916, the House Military Affairs Committee reported out a promilitia bill that authorized the president to federalize the National Guard. Three days later Mexicans under the leadership of Pancho Villa raided the border town of Columbus, New Mexico, killing American civilians and eight U.S. soldiers. Submarine attacks in the Atlantic also continued, prompting President Wilson to warn Germany that such conduct was unacceptable. Given these circumstances, the immediate availability of trained militia likely contributed to the Senate abandoning the continental army plan, and on June 3 the National Defense Act of 1916 became law. In terms of manpower, it authorized a near doubling of the Regular Army over five years (with further additions in time of war) and a potential expansion of the National Guard to a force of approximately 450,000 men. It established the army's first air division (with 375 airplanes) and created the Reserve Officer Training Corps (ROTC) to enable colleges and universities to produce additional officers. Congress empowered the War Department to impose requirements on Guard organizations for drilling, fitness, equipment, summer encampments, and commissioning of officers. The act did not contain provisions for conscription, however, and did not authorize an army sufficient in size to enter the war in Europe.[23]

As the legislative actions played out in Washington, DC, the town of Oskaloosa, Kansas, largely through the efforts and connections of "Stub" Quakenbush, was granted the right to form a National Guard infantry company. On Wednesday evening, April 19, 1916, sixty-one men from Jefferson County were mustered in to service by Colonel Metcalf after giving oaths of allegiance to Kansas and the United States. Two months thereafter—just sixteen days following the enactment of the National Defense Act—President Wilson called out the militia of every state for service on the Mexican border. Consequently, in the summer and fall of 1916, Ted Blevins, Sam Gutschenritter, William Kimmel, Vic Segraves, Bill Smith, and the rest of the Jefferson County guardsmen found themselves in Texas defending the interests and security of the United States.

CHAPTER TWO

Oskaloosa Forms a National Guard Company

Oskaloosa, the county seat for Jefferson County, is located approximately fifteen miles north of Lawrence and forty miles northeast of Topeka. The 1910 census recorded 15,829 Jefferson County residents (a number that was not exceeded until the 1990 census), with Valley Falls (1,129), Oskaloosa (851), Nortonville (638), and McLouth (571) as the four largest communities at that time. Founded in 1856, Oskaloosa was built around the county courthouse, described in 1883 as "a fine two story brick building . . . situated in the center of the public square, which is finely ornamented by a grove of tall maple trees, so thickly set as to shade all over the square, and make one of the finest of parks." There were two railroad stations in the first decades of the twentieth century: the Oskaloosa Station northeast of town, transporting passengers through McLouth, Dunavent, and Valley Falls, and the Oskaloosa Depot west of town, servicing the Leavenworth-Topeka Railroad, which went past McLouth, Oskaloosa, Ozawkie, and Meridan before turning south to the state capital.[1]

Its history contains elements of humor, ingenuity, and progressive politics. Several newspaper articles, going as far back as 1875, describe the formation of a "Lazy Man" club, which supposedly expelled members who were found to have performed any type of work. A more verifiable story concerns Samuel Peppard, who in 1860 rigged a sail over the center of the front axle of his wagon and headed west, attaining a maximum speed of fifteen miles per hour. He and three companions got within one hundred miles of Denver before a storm demolished the wagon and injured the occupants.

Peppard's "wind wagon" gained regional notoriety, but national attention was focused on Oskaloosa in 1888 when the town elected women to all five city council positions and the mayor's office. Mary Lowman ran for mayor because she believed "the city would only be improved when the power was placed in the hands of the women." The all-female city government widened and graded the streets, installed gasoline street lamps, enforced a previously ignored prohibition law, and banned "expectorating on the sidewalks."[2]

Oskaloosa had contributed two companies of men to the Fourth Regiment of the Kansas State Militia, which was organized in Jefferson County to defend against pro-Confederates and "bushwhackers" from Missouri. The companies were disbanded after the Civil War. In order to organize a new National Guard unit, the state legislature had to authorize its need, the town had to provide sufficient men, and the Kansas Military Board had to give its approval. With apparently one exception (Smith Center), all Kansas towns with state-sanctioned militia between 1885 and 1915 were larger than Oskaloosa. Consequently, when it became one of twelve communities competing in 1916 for two new companies (one infantry and one artillery), its chances appeared slim, given that only one town (Severance) was smaller, one (Cottonwood Falls) was comparable size, and the remaining ten ranged from twice the size of Oskaloosa (Liberal) to ten times its size (Leavenworth). But Oskaloosa had a singular advantage: "Stub" Quakenbush, a man of small stature but with a larger-than-life personality.[3]

Born in Missouri in February 1873, Derwood Eugene Quakenbush spent much of his youth in Baldwin City, Kansas, south of Lawrence. The *Lawrence Daily* reported on March 2, 1899, that Private Stub Quakenbush of Company H, Twentieth Kansas Volunteer Regiment, "takes great pride in caring for the team and carriage owned by Col. Funston and Major Metcalf." By serving as an orderly for the officers and caring for their horses, Quakenbush forged a connection with two of the most important men in the regiment. It did not hurt that "the comical-est man in the Twentieth" was also well regarded, as evident by a 1903 newspaper article describing his visit to Ottawa, Kansas:

> The presence of Mr. Quakenbush in town is something of an event. . . . His service was with the Twentieth Kansas, and it is a part of the unwritten history of that regiment that Quakenbush could start more different things in less time than any other man who went from Kansas to the Philippines. Not all the discipline of the whole army system was sufficient to depress Mr. Quakenbush, who never permitted a dull moment while he was awake.

Stub Quakenbush was living in Oskaloosa in January 1916 when Adjutant General Martin, who also served with the Twentieth Kansas, announced that the state military board would consider petitions from communities seeking to form a National Guard company. As it happened, Stub's old company held a reunion in February in Lawrence, where he met with Colonel Wilder Metcalf and discussed the possibility of forming an artillery battery in Oskaloosa. Metcalf suggested that Quakenbush "get busy" and start a membership roll to gauge interest. The forty-three-year-old veteran returned to Jefferson County and, according to the *Oskaloosa Independent*, "enrolled 37 men, with a dozen to 20 in sight." One of the men who expressed interest was Rhudean "Dean" Peppard, the son of the "wind wagon" inventor, Samuel Peppard.[4]

* * *

Seventeen-year-old Theodore Roosevelt "Ted" Blevins and eighteen-year-old Victor Segraves were also among the first to sign up. The Blevins family established roots in Kansas prior to statehood. Ted's grandfather William Blevins had left Ireland in 1848 and by 1850 was employed by the U.S. government at Fort Leavenworth. As a wagon master, he traveled all across Kansas and as far west as Utah, delivering supplies to forts, assisting in topographical surveys, and helping build army barracks at Fort Riley. In 1860 William married Martha Chandler and purchased a farm near Oskaloosa that featured a large apple orchard. He died in 1886, but Martha lived until age eighty-seven and was able to tell her grandchildren about her husband's adventures and their life together. They had five children, including Ted's father, James C. Blevins (1863–1958).

James married Jessie Meeker and moved to Colorado, where two daughters, Martha and Cenith, and a son, Jesse James Blevins, were born. (Family members disagree on whether Jesse was named for the infamous outlaw who died in 1882). After trying his hand as a newspaper publisher, James brought his family back to Oskaloosa, where four more sons were born: Paul, Ted (in September 1898), Charles, and Frank. Two of Ted's siblings lived short lives: Paul died in April 1918 at age twenty-three, and Martha died in 1931, when she was burned after using gas to clean clothes in her basement. One of Ted's uncles, John M. Blevins, lived in Missouri but sent his children to Oskaloosa for schooling after his wife passed away. His three sons—Beeler, William "Ed," and Fred— served during World War I; Ed Blevins fought alongside his cousin Ted in France.

James and Jessie must have encouraged their children's education, as Martha, Cenith, Jesse, and Ted became teachers. In the fall of 1913, the three oldest children were employed at Kansas schools, while Ted was entering his freshman year of high school. He was elected class president and reelected his sophomore year. Throughout high school, Ted was active in

Photo 2.1: Theodore Blevins (left, seated), brother Jesse Blevins (center, standing), and cousin William "Ed" Blevins (right, seated). Courtesy of Scott Pattee.

drama, debate, and sports. He played football, was the center on the basketball team, and was a hurdler in track. It was during his junior year that he spoke at the Democratic Party's county banquet at Perry on February 10, 1916, delivering a tribute to Woodrow Wilson ("Our Chief") with the "grace and assurance of a practical orator." That same month Ted and his younger brother Charlie helped Oskaloosa's basketball team win the county championship. He also read the following notice in the *Oskaloosa Independent*: "Want to Enlist? Any physically fit man between the ages of 18 and 45 who will join the military company now being formed at Oskaloosa should inform 'Stub' Quakenbush at once and then sign the roll as soon as convenient." Both Jesse and Ted, who would not turn eighteen until September, immediately signed up as potential members.[5]

Victor Lewis Segraves was born in January 1898, the second youngest of eleven children. His parents moved to Kansas from Tennessee between 1878 and 1880 and settled near Perry in south-central Jefferson County. The family rented a farm near Oskaloosa in 1914 and lived there for a while, Victor attending high school there. Two of his brothers, Al and Joe, joined the military prior to World War I, while three more, George, John, and Pat, enlisted during the war. Al, his oldest brother, signed up with the U.S. Army in 1898 and was sent to Manila. While in battle, a blood vessel in one of his lungs burst, which developed into tuberculosis, eventually causing his death in 1900. Victor would have had little or no memory of Al, but his second-oldest brother, Joe, undoubtedly made a strong impression. Twenty years older than Victor, Joe served with the Kansas volunteers in the Philippines, became a sergeant, and was described as "one of the most daring soldiers in the Twentieth Kansas." In 1905 he became captain of the police force in Cristóbal Colón, a coastal city on the north side of Panama. In April 1914 sixteen-year-old Victor likely read an article in the *Perry Mirror* describing his brother's most recent occupation: a naval gunner stationed on the dreadnought USS *Pennsylvania* at Vera Cruz, Mexico. Another article, in November 1915, reported that Joe was a gunner's mate first class on the USS *San Diego* and acknowledged "as the best diver on the vessel." It is not surprising, therefore, that Vic seized the first opportunity to join the military.

Although eight months older, Vic Segraves was one class behind Ted Blevins at Oskaloosa High School. They played together on the football team, with Ted anchoring the offensive line as center and Vic as one of the guards. It is likely that the two boys talked at school about joining the town's new National Guard company. Ted later recalled why he and his brother Jesse joined: "We thought we'd spend the summer in Yellowstone Park on

Photo 2.2: Victor Segraves. Courtesy of Jane Hoskinson.

maneuvers, so of course we joined. We'd get off the farm for the summer, too! Things didn't quite work out that way."[6]

* * *

On March 8, 1916, Adjutant General Martin accepted Stub Quakenbush's invitation to speak to a capacity crowd in the courtroom of the Jefferson County courthouse. After joking that it was actually Quakenbush who "ran the regiment" and was boss of the Twentieth Kansas, Martin spoke about the process of forming a company and the requirements for serving in the National Guard. The townspeople had decorated the room with flags and bunting and placed chairs inside the bar railing for the men who had enrolled in the proposed company. Martin was impressed and remarked that nowhere had he seen such a demonstration of public interest. Three days later—the day after Pancho Villa's forces killed nineteen Americans in New Mexico—Quakenbush went to Lawrence to confer with Colonel Metcalf, one of the five members of the Kansas Military Board. On March 30 eight automobiles transported thirty Oskaloosa businessmen to Topeka to appear at the board's hearing. It was apparent that the town was not in the running for the artillery battery, but it hoped to land the infantry company. The next morning Quakenbush called from Topeka with the news: while Eureka was given the artillery battery, Oskaloosa was awarded the infantry company. Cherryvale, Cottonwood Falls, Kingman, Leavenworth, Liberal, Manhattan, Olathe, Ottawa, Sabetha, and Severance would have to wait for another opportunity.[7]

A triumphant Quakenbush returned to Oskaloosa with a provisional commission as lieutenant. He remarked, in jest, that the women in town were "up in arms" about his recruitment efforts: "Why it's gotten so bad," he said, "that when I pass a woman on the street she'll remark to another, 'there goes the man who's trying to get all our boys in the army.'" Sixty-five men were needed to form the company, and by April 7, Quakenbush had secured seventy-five names on the membership roster. Two of them were Samuel Gutschenritter and William Kimmel.[8]

Sam Gutschenritter and Billy Kimmel were born on the same day—July 23, 1897—but led very different lives. Sam's paternal grandparents were born in the Alsace region at the foot of the Vosges Mountains in southeastern France, about thirty-five miles from Basel, Switzerland. As a result of the French defeat in the 1870 Franco-Prussian War, Germany took control of most of Alsace and parts of neighboring Lorraine, transforming the Gutschenritters into German citizens. Sam's father, John Charles "Charley" Gutschenritter, was born in 1865; as a young man, he was required to serve three years in the German infantry. He came to the United States in 1892 and four years later married Mary (Martha) Blockwicz, who was born in 1878 or 1879 to parents who spoke Polish but had lived in Germany. Her family immigrated in 1880 and settled in Kansas, first near Leavenworth and then on a farm northwest of Oskaloosa. Charles and Martha, who purchased a farm southwest of town, had five children—Sam, Tommy, John, Mary, and Francis—between 1897 and 1916. According to the *Oskaloosa Times*, in May 1910 Charles declared his intention to become a U.S. citizen. It was not until 1915, however, that he filed a petition in the Jefferson County District Court for naturalization. The hearing was set for June 1916, but at that time a motion to dismiss the petition without prejudice was issued. Not much is known about Sam Gutschenritter's youth other than the following newspaper notice published in November 1913, when he was sixteen: "To Whom it May Concern—I will not be responsible for any debts or contracts by my son, Sam Gutschenritter. Charles Gutschenritter."[9]

Photo 2.3: Birt Blockwicz (left), Charles "Tommy" Gutschenritter (center), and Samuel Gutschenritter (right). Courtesy of Debra Gutschenritter Freeman.

Photo 2.4: William Kimmel. From *Honor Roll, Shawnee County, Kansas* (Kansas City, MO: Burger Engraving, 1920).

William James Kimmel was born William James Potthoff, younger brother of Anna May Potthoff of Staten Island, New York. Their parents were unable to care for them, and in 1911 at ages fourteen and sixteen, they became part of a "placing out" program commonly known as the "orphan train," although many of the children were abandoned by living parents. Their journey to Kansas was organized by the Children's Aid Society, and their arrival on January 23, 1911, was reported on page one of the *Oskaloosa Times*: "Fourteen little folks from the orphanages of New York City arrived at Oskaloosa [today] and will be placed in homes in and around Oskaloosa. . . . They are well behaved and look very clean and very decent. Adoption is not demanded. . . . Should the child prove unsatisfactory it will be taken back by the society."[10]

After being presented on the stage of the Oskaloosa Opera House, William and Anna were taken in by Louis and Margaret Kimmel, who had two young children and would have three more between 1912 and 1921. Louis was a prosperous farmer and grain merchant, with a large concrete silo and "the finest barn in Jefferson County." Anna left soon thereafter, marrying at age nineteen, divorcing shortly thereafter, and then remarrying and living a contented life surrounded by children and grandchildren. Her younger brother, however, adapted more readily to life with the Kimmels and soon took their surname, although there is no evidence of a formal adoption. William was in the same high school class as Vic Segraves and on the debate team with Ted Blevins. When he signed up for the National Guard in the spring of 1916, Kimmel was only a sophomore but, like Segraves, was eighteen years old.[11]

* * *

Their enlistment was not official for the Oskaloosa recruits until they were "mustered in" by taking a double oath of allegiance to the State of Kansas and the United States of America. On April 19, 1916, sixty-one young men were sworn in as members of the First Separate Company of the Kansas National Guard. According to the *Oskaloosa Independent*, the ceremony was conducted by Colonel Metcalf (in full regimentals) at the county courthouse. Later that evening two of the men seeking to become the company bugler "kept [the town] awake by . . . persistent efforts to blow the various calls." As reported by the *Valley Falls Daily Reporter*, "not a single member was wearing eye glasses," although several men were later discharged due to defective vision.[12]

The company held its first drill the following week. Equipment soon arrived, including tools, stoves, mess kits, blankets, cots, conical tents, rifles, drill manuals, "dress up" uniforms, fatigues, shoes, shirts, leggings, and broad-brim hats. Drilling was a part-time requirement, so the boys in high school attended classes and continued to participate in extracurricular events, such as the Jefferson County High School Literary Field and Track Meet. On Decoration Day (Memorial Day), the National Guard marched in a body to the Methodist church, listened to a talk by Reverend Townsend Nichols, and then escorted veterans to the city cemetery and placed flowers on graves.[13]

Even before the Oskaloosa National Guard was mustered in, events in Mexico were escalating tensions and raising the possibility that President Wilson would call out the militia. Brigadier General John J. "Black Jack" Pershing, commander of the Southwestern Department's cavalry, was ordered to mount a punitive expedition into Mexico to catch Pancho Villa. In May, after two Texas border towns were attacked, Wilson mobilized guardsmen from Texas, New Mexico, and Arizona to supplement the U.S. soldiers on American soil under the overall command of Major General Funston. On the third of June, the National Defense Act was signed into law, giving the president additional authority to make use of the National Guard. On June 18 and 19, Secretary of War Newton Baker and President Wilson acted to mobilize guardsmen for the limited purpose of border defense from the District of Columbia and every state (except Nevada, which had no National Guard). In light of these developments, Will Smith of Valley Falls, who had unofficially signed up with the National Guard in May, hurried down to Oskaloosa to be sworn in.[14]

William Amos Smith was born on December 31, 1888, the youngest of three children, and grew up in Valley Falls, the largest city in Jefferson County and located twenty miles northwest of Oskaloosa. Smith went by the name "Will" prior to World War I but thereafter became known as "Bill." He was the only male among the four high school graduates in 1910 and poked fun at his classmates by declaring himself "the one rose among three thorns." With financial help from his uncle, Smith went to Washburn College in Topeka, where he played football, studied law, and was "the stand pat leader of the class, and adviser for all, when advice is needed." Returning to Valley Falls in 1914 with a law degree, he immediately announced his candidacy for county attorney but lost in the Republican primary to an Oskaloosa lawyer. Apparently well regarded despite his inexperience, Smith was appointed the city attorney of Valley Falls. He continued his private practice as well, and in one of his first cases, the future Chief Justice of the Kansas Supreme Court convinced two neighbors to settle a dispute over ten turkeys by each accepting half of the flock.[15]

Will's father, Henry M. Smith, was a Civil War veteran, a farmer, and a justice of the peace. He passed away in January 1916, survived by his wife, Lucy, who as a widow would live many years with her only son. In the following month Will announced that he was once again running to become the Republican nominee for county attorney. In May, prior to the primary election, he went to Oskaloosa to sign up with the National Guard. Smith was not officially sworn in until June 19, just four days before the guardsmen left Oskaloosa and just after he presided at a banquet for Jefferson County Republicans attended by Governor Capper. The educated lawyer, who was older than most of his fellow soldiers, would soon rise to leadership positions within the Kansas company.[16]

* * *

Once the guardsmen came under federal control, they were fed at local restaurants at the government's expense. The Jefferson County soldiers received

Photo 2.5: William Smith. From *Honor Roll, Shawnee County, Kansas* (Kansas City, MO: Burger Engraving, 1920).

orders on Wednesday, June 21, to load their equipment at the train depot west of Oskaloosa and prepare to depart on Friday for Fort Riley. Kimmel came home from Topeka. A farewell dance was held at the Opera House, and when the time came to leave, a large crowd gathered to wave American flags and say goodbye. When the Oskaloosa company arrived at Fort Riley, it was merged with the unit from Holton, which upset both towns until they were told it was a temporary arrangement. A Holton man was named captain, Quakenbush was appointed first lieutenant, and the consolidated unit became Company B, Second Kansas Regiment. After camping several days in tents and receiving typhoid shots, the men of Company B were put on trains for their journey to the Texas border. They first passed through Topeka, greeted by friends and relatives and given ice cream by the Topeka Commercial Club. Crowds in Oklahoma and Texas also gathered to cheer the troops. On Monday, July 3, the Kansans arrived at Eagle Pass, Texas, a border town on the Rio Grande about 140 miles west of San Antonio. "My Dad had to sign up for me," recalled Ted Blevins. "Mother didn't even want me to go, but the family thought Jesse would take care of me."[17]

CHAPTER THREE

The Kansas National Guard at the Mexican Border

The Kansas National Guard provided 2,800 soldiers for federal service on the U.S. southern border to guard against invasion from Mexico. With over one hundred men, the combined Holton-Oskaloosa company was the largest in the Second Kansas Regiment, although some men were subsequently transferred to another unit. Commanded by Colonel Perry M. Hoisington of Newton, the Second Kansas sent to the border a total of 1,100 men from Emporia, Great Bend, Holton, Hutchinson, Independence, Larned, McPherson, Minneapolis, Newton, Oskaloosa, Topeka, Salina, Wichita, and Winfield. The First Kansas Regiment, headed by Colonel Metcalf, comprised companies from Burlington, Fort Scott, Fredonia, Garnett, Hiawatha, Horton, Humboldt, Kansas City, Lawrence, Manhattan, and Paola. The two Kansas infantry regiments, along with Battery A of the Field Artillery and the Signal Corps Company, were among the first soldiers from nonborder states to arrive along the Rio Grande. Although it has not been definitively established, some historians argue it was in Texas where the name "doughboys" was given to American soldiers. According to Laurence Stallings, the marching infantrymen became powdered white with the dust of the adobe soil and called "adobes" by the cavalrymen; the term was shortened to "dobies" and soon transformed into "doughboys."[1]

The Kansas tent camp, named Camp Shafter, was on a hill a mile from the Rio Grande and about a mile and a half north of the town of Eagle Pass. Ted Blevins described the area to his mother as two acres of "cactus, sage brush, scorpions, etc." and later recalled the frequent dust storms that would blow down their tents. Guardsmen from Vermont and Maryland camped farther from the river on the other side of a railroad line, as did two regiments of "regular" soldiers. Consumption of alcohol in camp was forbidden, as the *Oskaloosa Times* reassured its readers ("No Booze Will Reach Men on Fighting Line"). Mexican troops were visible from the river bluffs, but the men obeyed orders and never left Texas. (Decades later, in 1964, Jesse Blevins did cross the Eagle Pass International Bridge with his wife). According to Private Frank Gibson of Winchester, the men on guard duty had little difficulty detecting Mexican raiding parties: "They wear white uniforms, [and it is] sure easy to see them on dark nights."[2]

Letters home, many of which were published in local newspapers, focused on weather, insects, reptiles, and the monotony of camp life. Jefferson County residents learned from Rue Jenkins: "Ted Blevins said today he would never tell anyone to go to H— again. He'd simply tell them to go to Eagle Pass, Texas." Jenkins also noted, "everything that grows down there has horns and stickers on it, even the toads." At night "one has to take their bed out and shake it," explained Frank Henderson, "so as to be sure there are no rattle snakes, lizards, or tarantulas in it." Stub Quakenbush came up with an idea to raise funds for families of the soldiers by sending home "curios" (centipedes, scorpions, lizards, tarantulas, armadillos, and cacti) that could be viewed for a fee at the Holton and Oskaloosa fairs. Instead of attacking Mexican soldiers, the men drilled each day and went on five-mile hikes with increasing amounts of equipment. "I joined the army to fight," complained Sam Gutschenritter, "but they have made me put up ten wagons." Will Smith remarked that soldier life "is about what I expected but I haven't seen Carranza yet." The men "sure do earn our $15.60," said Jesse Blevins. Perhaps the most memorable complaint came from Merle Trapp, a high school classmate of Ted Blevins: "They make me wash once a month," he wrote, "whether I need it or not."[3]

Frank Gibson wrote in mid-August, "everyone is anxious to go home." In a long letter published in the *Winchester Star*, he described the daily routine of the Kansas guardsmen:

> We have to get up at five forty-five. . . . We then go out for about thirty minutes exercise before breakfast. Breakfast is at six thirty. After breakfast, we have sick call, all the sick line up and are marched up to the hospital. Then we clean up our camp, we have to even pick up the matches that are on the ground. At eight we go out for drill. We drill forty minutes and come back to our tents and get ready for inspection. After inspection we go back and drill till eleven thirty and we return to camp for the day. Dinner is ready at twelve. . . . After dinner if you are not on any detail you can sleep or anything you want to pass the time away till supper. We have a large building now where we can go and write our letters, it is called the enlisted Men's club. Chaplain [Alexander] McKeever rented a piano for us and so we have plenty of music in the evening. Supper is at five. At six

we go out on regimental parade. Then we have the rest of the evening to ourselves.[4]

Army chaplains not only administered to the religious needs of the soldiers but also endeavored to make camp life enjoyable and wholesome. The chaplain for the First Kansas Regiment was Dr. James Naismith of the University of Kansas. While teaching at the YMCA Training College (now Springfield College) in Massachusetts, Naismith attached peach baskets to opposing walls and invented the game of basketball. He thereafter received his medical degree in Denver and in 1898 came to the University of Kansas (where he remains the only men's basketball coach with a losing record). His remarkable career includes several months of border service at age fifty-four with the Kansas National Guard after his appointment as the First Regiment's chaplain on March 18, 1915. With the rank of captain, he was mustered into federal service on June 18, 1916, and sent to Texas in July. "Chaplain Naismith has a hard row to cultivate at Eagle Pass," the *Fredonia Daily Herald* reported in July, "for there are numerous dives and saloons here and they reap the harvest of young men." Accepting the challenge, he joined with Chaplain McKeever of the Second Kansas to stop the construction of a large dancehall in Eagle Pass, then provided a wholesome alternative by forming an inter-regiment baseball league. The inventor of basketball also took time in Texas to modify the dimensions and rules of his game for the soldiers:

> The court . . . consists of a large oval . . . [and the] baskets are set inside the bounds of the court at least ten feet from the ends. . . . The basket has no backstop and it is possible to throw the ball into it from behind as well as from the front. The reason given for the spread of the new game is that the court is larger and the ball seldom gets out of bounds. Throwing baskets from all angles also speeds up the game.

In September University of Kansas dean Olin Templin appealed directly to Major General Funston to allow Naismith to return to the school. In a letter written in August, Naismith acknowledged the "hard fight to keep out some of the evils of army life" but gave assurances that he and his assistants "have succeeded even beyond our expectation." The *Lawrence Daily Journal-World* agreed, noting that the sports program on the border helped the boys "from the state of cyclones and no booze" show themselves "to be gentlemen in every respect." Ted Blevins considered the overall experience a positive one:

Photo 3.1: Dr. James Naismith, 1917, chaplain, First Kansas Infantry. Courtesy of the Kenneth Spencer Research Library, University of Kansas.

"Company B was made up of friends, our Mothers sent food and letters—we were well taken care of. It was an adventure we enjoyed, and I don't remember ever getting homesick."[5]

At the beginning of September, seven married men from Jefferson County were discharged. The other men were anxious to return to Kansas, including Will Smith, who was seeking the Republican nomination for county attorney. In July he had placed the following notice in the Valley Falls newspaper:

> To the voters of Jefferson County—I have been unable to continue my campaign for the nomination for County Attorney on account of being called to the Mexican border. Some people seem to think that if elected, I will be unable to serve. I have been promised that if I am elected, an application for discharge will be honored. Hoping that you will remember me at the Primary, I remain, Yours very respectfully, Will Smith.

The novice lawyer was endorsed by the paper—"if you believe in rewarding patriotism go to the polls and vote for Will Smith"—and won the primary election, which ensured victory in November, as the Democrats did not field a candidate.[6]

Gutschenritter also wanted to go home. When the soldiers of the Maryland National Guard left Eagle Pass on September 7, they were escorted by a Kansas regimental band to the railroad station and cheered as their train pulled out. "That made the tears come in my eyes," Gutschenritter was said to have remarked, "to see them boys leaving and I have to stay here." The Kansas guardsmen remained and took part in the army's first experiment with large-scale motorized troop movements. The first leg of the journey for Gutschenritter and his comrades was by truck from Eagle Pass to San Antonio, a distance of about 140 miles. In his letters written during this trip, Ted Blevins told his family that there were "142 trucks loaded with soldiers, one right after the other," and that at one point they rode for three hours "without seeing a single house." Once in San Antonio, the Kansas guardsmen joined units from Wisconsin, Illinois, Missouri, and Texas to march as a division to Camp Mabry, near Austin, a distance of 80 miles. Over fourteen thousand men participated, with 165 motor trucks and 5,750 horses and mules. The men slept in pup tents when it rained and on the ground by the road when it was dry. The *Oskaloosa Independent* described the hike with a mixture of pride and disgust:

> The march of the troops from San Antonio to Austin was hard on most of the boys. . . . [I]t was too much of a hardship when there was nothing in the world to gain except to satisfy officers that the march could be made without killing the boys off. . . . We haven't heard how many of the officers marched on foot with the boys. . . . One [Oskaloosa soldier] wrote that when they marched from 7 to 3 without a halt for a meal he grew so hungry that he took a strip of raw bacon from his kit and ate it as he marched.

Ted Blevins, as usual, provided a more lighthearted account in a postcard dated September 21: "We are about eighteen miles from Austin, we go eleven miles tomorrow and 7 Saturday and that's the end of it. . . . We are seeing lots of country and if it wasn't for walking I might enjoy it."[7]

The Kansas National Guard performed its duties well; in fact, perhaps too well. Brigadier General Tasker Bliss, assistant chief of staff of the U.S. Army, told Adjutant General Martin in July that the two Kansas regiments were among the four best on the border. General Funston also assured Martin that the Kansans "are topnotchers" and rated the Second Kansas Regiment as the best of six regiments at Eagle Pass in "drill discipline, appearance, and general efficiency." The high marks may have contributed to its longer stay in Texas. September turned to October, and while the rest of the country reflected on the baseball exploits of Babe Ruth (as a pitcher), Grover Alexander, Walter Johnson, Tris Speaker, and Ty Cobb, the guardsmen from Kansas waited for weeks for their turn to go home. Most were still in Texas on Election Day (but not candidate Will Smith, who was given a two-day leave to go back to Jefferson County). Although Ted Blevins was only seventeen, he voted for the first time: "The Captain called us out and told us we were going to vote. I said, 'No, some of us aren't old enough.' The Captain answered, 'The hell you aren't! If you're old enough to fight, you're old enough to vote!'"[8]

Finally, on November 13, 1916, parts of the Second Kansas Regiment—among them Company B—were cheered, fed, and welcomed home with a parade in Topeka. After a chicken dinner with pie and ice cream in the Scottish Rite dining hall, Governor Capper stood and said, "You have justified the faith of the people in citizen soldiers, and have proved that the people will respond to the call to arms when needed." Ted Blevins and Vic Segraves returned to Oskaloosa High School in time to play in the last two football games of the season. The town held a banquet at the Methodist church, where a large crowd listened to Colonel Metcalf and Private Will Smith, who spoke for Company B at the request of Lieutenant Quakenbush. There was a violin solo and orchestral music, and American flags adorned each table, with flag napkins at each plate and tricolor bunting and larger flags placed throughout the room. In December Smith moved his office fixtures and law books by wagon to Oskaloosa, where he took up residence with his widowed mother. Louis Kimmel sold his farm to go into the grain-elevator business, and the new owners hired Quakenbush to manage the farm and the stock. The threat of war, and with it the need for the Kansas National Guard, had seemingly passed.[9]

Was the National Guard required on the border in 1916? General Funston said it was "absolutely necessary." On the other hand, Major General Leonard Wood, an advocate for universal training, told Congress that the Guard mobilization was a military failure, and that if the guardsmen had met good troops, they "would never have known what hit them." Kansas congressman Daniel Read Anthony Jr. (a nephew of suffragist Susan B. Anthony) responded by accusing the Regular Army of putting the Guard on "discouraging police duty" with the premeditated view of causing its disintegration. Adjutant General Martin agreed with Anthony, arguing that "the conduct of the regular army officers in Washington and elsewhere will make it almost impossible to maintain the guard in the future, unless Congress takes a hand in behalf of the states." One thing is certain: with minimal loss of life (only one Kansan died, Herbert Adams of Emporia, who drowned in the Rio Grande), the guardsmen who served on the border received more valuable training than would have been possible in their home states. The divisional march from San Antonio to Austin helped prepare the troops for similar movements required in France, as shortcomings were identified and lessons learned.[10]

* * *

On February 19, 1917, Frederick Funston died unexpectedly at age fifty-one, succumbing to a heart attack at the St. Anthony Hotel in San Antonio, Texas. His family had moved to Iola, Kansas, when he was two years old. After failing the entrance exam for the U.S. Military Academy, Funston attended the University of Kansas but did not graduate. He held a series of jobs before joining Cuban insurgents in 1896 in their revolt against Spain. He was captured but avoided execution, returned home, and was appointed by Governor Leedy to command the Twentieth Kansas Volunteer Infantry Regiment. While in the Philippines in 1901, he personally led a raid that captured rebel leader Emilio Aquinaldo, for which he received the Medal of Honor and a commission as brigadier general in the Regular Army.

Returning to the United States a national hero, Funston was stationed in California, where he helped maintain order after the 1906 San Francisco earthquake. During the troubles with Mexico, he served as military governor of Vera Cruz and later was in charge of maintaining security along the U.S. southern border. As Funston was Pershing's superior officer, some speculate that "Fighting Fred" of Kansas would have been the War Department's choice to command the American Expeditionary Forces in France. According to William Allen White, the Emporia newspaper editor and nationally regarded pundit, "only a breath of wind, the flutter of a heart, kept Funston out of Pershing's place in the World War."[11]

1917

The Wichita Daily Eagle.

VOLUME LXIII. PRICE TWO CENTS WICHITA, KANSAS FRIDAY MORNING, APRIL 6, 1917 PRICE TWO CENTS. NUMBER 119

HOUSE ACTS EARLY THIS MORNING; WAR IS ON

WHEELS OF AMERICA'S GIANT WAR ENGINE NOW IN MOTION

MAY TAX INCOMES OF $1,500

Law Probably Will be Amended So as to Furnish Government With Increased Revenues During War.

RICH MEN WOULD BE HIT HARDEST

One Congressman Would Limit Incomes to $100,000—Need $33,562,317,000 to Finance War One Year.

Fire Destroys Entire Block

Flames Do Great Damage in Asbury Park, N. J.—Several Hotels Are Burned.

BLEAKLEY GIVES UP SEAT

ANOTHER U. S. SHIP IS SUNK

American Steamer Missourian, Unarmed, Is Torpedoed Without Warning.

ENTIRE CREW OF 53 IS REPORTED SAVED.

TO RAISE 2 MILLION MEN IS AIM

One Million Within First Year, Second Million in Second Year, Program Outline.

THREE BILLIONS TO BE SPENT FIRST YEAR

First 500,000 of Young Men to be Drafted Into the Service Very Quickly.

GIGANTIC MACHINE IN ACTION

Mobilization of Actual and Potential Resources Never Before Equaled by Any Nation Are Planned.

AMERICA'S DESTINIES ARE NOW SECURE

This Government Is Now on Defense Basis Not Even Hoped for Two Years Ago, It Is Asserted.

THE STEP

IS THIS GERMAN THREAT?

WAR IS OPPOSED BY FIFTY

Resolution Passes House at 3 o'Clock This Morning With 373 Congressmen Favoring It.

REJECT ALL AMENDMENTS WITHOUT ROLL CALLS.

Gives President Wilson Power to Send Troops to Europe Without Congressional Authority.

Wilson's Speech

Photo 4.1: United States declares war on Germany. From *Wichita Daily Eagle*, April 6, 1917.

CHAPTER FOUR

"Today We Stand behind the Nation's Chosen Leader"

Kansas Supports War with Germany

Ted Blevins cast his ballot for Woodrow Wilson in November 1916 because "he kept us out of the war." The president won a surprising victory in Kansas—and was narrowly reelected—in large part due to his commitment to neutrality. In the first three months of 1917, however, Germany's resumption of submarine warfare made it impossible for the United States to stay out of the conflict in Europe. When Congress voted for war on April 6, Kansans embraced the intense patriotic fervor sweeping the country. Public and private organizations mobilized the home front, as institutions of higher education, such as Washburn College, Kansas University, and Kansas State Agricultural College, experienced changes in enrollment, curriculum, and student life. At the same time, ethnic Germans encountered increased hostility, while National Guard units—in Jefferson County and elsewhere—competed with the Regular Army for recruits and drilled with greater purpose.

* * *

"The people of the United States," President Wilson noted in August 1914, were drawn "chiefly from the nations now at war." At the beginning of World War I, approximately nine million people in America spoke German, and "a further 15 million, almost a quarter of the population, were of Germanic stock." Germans were the largest group of continental Europeans to settle in Kansas, residing on farms and in towns such as Bern, Bremen, Humboldt, and Stuttgart. The National German-American Alliance, which sought to preserve German culture, had over two million members in the United States. Its Kansas chapter met at Great Bend in January 1915 and urged the national government to "withdraw from the contending powers all aid and assistance of the Republic." Four months later, when the *Lusitania* was sunk by *Unterseeboot* (U-boat) torpedoes, the Deustcher Club of Kansas City pointed to prior warnings given by Germany as well as rumors (which proved true) that the ship carried munitions and argued, "England, and

England alone, is responsible for the loss of the lives of the Americans." Most people in the United States disagreed. In June the Boston Committee of Public Safety commissioned a poster depicting a mother holding her infant, both dead and suspended in water below the ocean's surface. The poster's message—"Enlist"—clearly encouraged citizens of the United States, a neutral nation, to fight with the Allied powers. And when President Wilson in December condemned individuals "who have poured the poison of disloyalty into the very arteries of our national life," it was widely assumed that he was referring to ethnic Germans.[1]

Public opinion, however, remained strongly opposed to war. The popular song "I Didn't Raise My Boy to be a Soldier" proclaimed, "It's time to lay the gun and sword away, there'd be no war today, if mothers all would say, 'I didn't raise my boy to be a soldier.'" Governor Capper, Kansas University chancellor Strong, and other prominent Kansans participated in a meeting of the Peace and Equity League on January 31, 1916, just three days before President Wilson's visit to Topeka. "I look upon all attempts toward militarism among us with great apprehension," Strong told Charles R. Van Hise, his counterpart at the University of Wisconsin, "and believe that colleges and universities should be the very last agencies in our civilization to further, by compulsion and official action, the military idea."[2]

When a U-boat torpedoed and damaged the *Sussex*, a French ferry carrying Americans, President Wilson extracted an agreement from the German government to stop the indiscriminate and unannounced sinking of nonmilitary ships. The so-called *Sussex* pledge of May 4, 1916, temporarily stopped the U-boat scare and gave the Democrats a boost in the fall elections. As the Battle of the Somme continued from July to November, claiming more than one million casualties, the Democratic National Committee announced that the campaign slogan for the party would be "Wilson and Peace or Hughes and War." The *New York Tribune* predicted that Charles Evan Hughes, the Republican candidate, would prevail in both California and Kansas on his way to narrowly defeating Wilson in the election. The newspaper was correct in one respect: it was an extremely close race, one that Hughes did not concede until more than two weeks after the polls closed. But Wilson carried both California (by less than four thousand votes) and Kansas (where Governor Capper, a Republican, was easily reelected). As historian Lewis Gould notes, Hughes "had little idea of peace sentiments in normally Republican Kansas" and elsewhere, losing the women's vote in ten of the twelve states where women could vote. "We Republicans gave the women of Kansas the ballot," said W. J. True of Pittsburg, and they "used it against us

Photo 4.2: 1916 campaign button (reproduction). Courtesy of Blake Watson.

Tuesday." It was the last presidential election (as of 2020) in which Kansas voted more Democratic than the nation at large.[3]

Wilson's promise to keep America out of the war was not absolute and unconditional. On January 31, 1917, the German ambassador informed the United States that his government had renounced the *Sussex* pledge and resumed unrestricted submarine warfare. Diplomatic relations were severed, and U-boats proceeded to sink two American vessels: the SS *Housatonic* (after the crew abandoned ship) and the *Lyman M. Law* (also without injury to the crew). On February 28 President Wilson informed the public of the intercepted "Zimmerman Telegram," in which German foreign minister Arthur Zimmerman outlined a proposal to ally with Mexico to "make war together" and support the recovery of "lost territory" in the southwestern United States. Three weeks later, on March 18, Wilson learned of the boarding, plundering, and bombing of the oil tanker *Illinois*, which sunk in the English Channel with a large pair of American flags and "U.S.A." painted on its side. The president issued a call for Congress to meet on April 2, when he then requested a declaration of war against Imperial Germany. "It is a fearful thing to lead this great peaceful people into war," Wilson acknowledged, but "the world must be made safe for democracy."[4]

The Senate adopted the resolution for war on the fourth of April, with eighty-two senators in favor, six opposed, and eight not voting. Both Kansas senators, William H. Thompson, a Democrat, and Charles Curtis, a Republican (and a future vice president), voted with the majority. Two days later, after much debate, the House of Representatives concurred by a vote of 373 to 50. Six of the eight Kansas congressmen cast affirmative votes, including Guy Helvering, despite receiving a telegram on behalf of two thousand Riley County residents who opposed the resolution. The two representatives who voted against war were Democrat John R. Connelly of Thomas County and Republican Edward C. Little of Kansas City. Little had been a lieutenant colonel with the Twentieth Kansas Volunteers during the Philippine-American War (1899–1902). "I found it a whole lot easier to fight for my country on the battlefield," he explained, "than to sit in congress and vote to send other people to war."[5]

The declaration of war had an immediate effect in Kansas. The *Topeka Daily Capital*, owned by Governor Capper, acknowledged that the Senate vote in favor of war marked the beginning of a new era:

> Until yesterday America was divided into many groups on the solemn question how best to meet the issues raised by attacks persistently made in defiance of the laws of nations upon American rights and lives at sea. Today we stand behind the nation's chosen leader in his weighty responsibility and in his reluctant decision to meet war by war. . . . The nation . . . will give him unstintedly the co-operation and support that he requires.

President Wilson, on the same day that Congress declared war, addressed the issue of "alien enemies," defined as "natives, citizens, denizens, or subjects of Germany, being male, of the age 14 years and upwards, who shall be within the United States and not actually naturalized." Relying in part on the 1798 Alien Enemy Statute as precedent, he proclaimed that, among other restrictions, such individuals could not publish attacks or threats against the United States, give aid or comfort to U.S. enemies, or enter into prohibited areas. Violators would be subject to arrest and confinement "in such penitentiary, prison, jail, military camp, or other place of detention as may be directed by the President." Furthermore, if deemed necessary at some point, "all alien enemies will be obliged to register."[6]

During his reelection campaign, Wilson appealed to voters by stating that disloyalty "must be absolutely crushed." In response, the Kansas German-American Alliance charged the federal government with being "unneutral" and claimed that "certain elements within this great nation of ours have been willfully and maliciously misjudged." Shortly thereafter, however, German agents set off a series of tremendous explosions at a freight terminal on Black Tom Island, an artificial promontory connected to Jersey City, New Jersey. On the night of July 29–30, 1916, some two million pounds of munitions destined for the Allied powers were destroyed. As described in the *Salina Semi-Weekly Journal*, the fire also "set blazing ammunition barges adrift to bombard the statue of liberty and the Ellis Island immigration station with shells and shrapnel." The act of sabotage mesmerized Americans and reinforced notions of Teutonic depravity. In the 1916 poster entitled *Destroy This Mad Brute*, Germany is represented by a giant gorilla with a spiked helmet. As described by Zachary Smith, "the most significant aspects of the poster are that the wild-eyed, salivating beast carries a bare-chested damsel in distress (denoting defilement of civilized culture), that he has left Europe in ruins behind him, and that he is standing on the shore of 'America,' where the brute presumably would turn his attention after he had finished his decimation of the Old World."[7]

Kansans were not immune from the prevalent anti-German sentiment. Prior to the declaration of war, the *Wichita Eagle*, in a front-page article entitled "Spy Ruins Wichita's Hyphenated Saloon," reported that a German-American Alliance club was raided based on a tip that "profits from the sale of the foamy pale stuff, $500 in all, were being sent to Germany." In March residents of Jefferson County were enthralled by two silent films that warned of misguided pacifism and duplicitous enemies. The Golden Belt Theatre in Perry showed *If My Country Should Call*, an apparent tragedy (that in the end turns out to be a dream) involving a well-meaning mother who incurs the hatred of her son after she puts drugs in his drinks that causes the army to declare him unfit to enlist. At about the same time, Kansans filled the Electric Theater at Valley Falls to watch *The Nation's Peril*, in which Oswald Dudley, a conniving foreign spy, induces Ruth Lyons, a pacifist, to hand over plans for a wireless aerial torpedo created by Lieutenant Sawyer, her fiancée. The United States is thereafter attacked, but in the end all is well: the chastened Ruth kills Oswald with a sword, the enemy is annihilated, and the dashing lieutenant eludes his captors and takes Ruth into his arms under an American flag. Inspired by the silent film, thirteen-year-old Marjorie Sterrett of Brooklyn sent a dime to the *New York Tribune* as the first donation for a new battleship. Newspapers across America, including the *Ottawa Herald* and the *Wichita Daily Eagle*, publicized the cause, with readers providing over $20,000 in donations.[8]

When the United States declared war, fear of foreign intrigue intensified. On the same day as the vote in Congress, the front page of the *Newton Evening Kansan Republican* included an advertisement from the First National Bank,

Photo 4.3: Propaganda poster, by Harry R. Hopps, circa 1917. Courtesy of the Library of Congress.

announcing that it will resist "any attempt to abrogate American Freedom, Justice and Honor." Appearing directly above the announcement is a news item from Birmingham, Alabama, stating, "federal agents say they have evidence of a widespread movement on the part of agents of the imperial German government to incite Negroes to rise against the United States government." (No such widespread movement took place.) On April 13, the same day the *Oskaloosa Independent* advised German sympathizers, "you have nothing to fear if you obey the law and keep your mouth shut," President Wilson by executive order established the Committee on Public Information, which has been described as "America's first and only ministry of propaganda." Led by George Creel, a former reporter for the *Denver Rocky Mountain Press*, the committee used a variety of methods to influence public opinion, including the dissemination of a "loyalty leaflet" entitled Friendly Words to the Foreign Born. In his remarks given in April 1917 to naturalized citizens, federal judge Joseph Buffington stated, "The crux is not the fact of the hyphen, but whether the man's heart is at the American end of the hyphen." The committee also recruited local residents for the purpose of giving patriotic speeches. Known as "Four Minute Men," they would speak at movie theaters for four minutes, the approximate time needed to change film reels on a projector. The Creel Committee was advised to avoid "hymns of hate" but nevertheless sanctioned a poster that declared "Halt the Hun!" and depicted a U.S. soldier restraining a German who stands over a terrorized mother and child.[9]

The Four Minute Men were employed in Kansas and elsewhere to encourage (and cajole) Americans to buy Liberty Loan bonds. Rather than increase personal income taxes to pay for the war effort, Congress in April 1917 passed the Emergency Loan Act, which enabled citizens to provide a cash infusion to the government by purchasing interest-bearing bonds. Governor Capper designated "Liberty Days" for the sale of bonds, including June 5, the day that American men signed up for the draft. "I urge that registration day be made also a day of popular subscription to the Liberty Loan," he proclaimed, to "show the Nation that the people of Kansas are willing and glad to contribute from their bounty to the sustenance of our armies and the support of our allies across the sea." The governor also helped create the Council of Defense (to coordinate war work), the Committee on Agricultural Production (to discourage hoarding and promote food conservation), and the Committee on Public Relations (to induce immigrants to use the English language). Private groups and relief organizations also made significant contributions, including the Women's Liberty Loan Committee, the Red Cross,

Photo 4.4: Government-bond campaign poster, by Harry P. Raleigh, circa 1918. Courtesy of the Library of Congress.

the Knights of Columbus War Work Council, the Young Men's Hebrew Association War Work Council, the Rotary Club War Work Committee, the Fatherless Children of France Society, and the Belgian Relief Commission. Kansans deemed unfit for military service could find other forms of service, such as employment with the YMCA War Work Council.[10]

On October 15, 1918, the outgoing president of the Kansas Historical Society, George Morehouse, gave a speech entitled "Kansas as a State of Extremes, and Its Attitude during This World War." With the tremendous benefit of hindsight, he belittled prewar "peace-at-any-price pacifists" in Kansas and stated—without evidence—that state antiwar organizations "were financed by German gold." In particular, he expressed contempt for the Peace and Equity League, which he said delayed the day when the Sunflower State finally "about-faced from her utopian dreams of a warless world." He concluded on an optimistic note, arguing, "our good old fighting Kansas of heroic days is running true to form once more." He did not discuss, however, some of the extreme measures taken in connection with this shift in attitude, such as the harassment of conscientious objectors, the burning of schools and churches in German American communities, and the suppression of basic civil liberties.[11]

* * *

The advent of war and its consequences for young adults was keenly felt at educational institutions. Washburn College in Topeka responded with a "preparedness-for-war" plan that provided for compulsory training, abolition of athletics in favor of military drills, the training of coeds in Red Cross work, and a continuation of the effort to secure an officer training school. Forty-nine "Ichabods"—a nickname based on benefactor Ichabod Washburn—enlisted for military service by June 1917, prior to the compulsory draft. The War Department authorized the volunteer Washburn Ambulance Corps, which eventually became the 347th Ambulance Company, Eighty-Seventh Infantry Division. The company was headed by Dr. Charles Henry Lerrigo, a founder of the Society for the Study and Prevention of Tuberculosis, the forerunner of the American Lung Association. When the 119 men departed for Camp Pike, Arkansas, their mascot, a collie puppy named Ichabod, or "Ich," refused to board the train. The unit eventually served in France, where the company bugler, Private Lyman Rice, was the first of these men to die, succumbing to pneumonia on October 8, 1918.[12]

When news of the decision to go to war reached Lawrence, people all across town sounded bells and whistles, including the foghorn blast of the steam whistle at the Kansas University's power plant. Chancellor Strong assured the public and President Wilson that the university would fully support the war. "It has always been loyal to the country and the flag," he said, "and always will be." The school, however, faced challenges: in the spring of 1917, nearly 40 percent of the enrolled men (764 of 1,929) withdrew to enlist, enter training camps, or return to farms to increase food supplies. According to Jayhawk historian Clifford Griffin, faculty members with military experience organized four voluntary companies of trainees, which included over three hundred students, while other faculty members offered courses in military engineering, military science, mapping, electrical signaling, and explosives. On May 4, 1917, Chancellor Strong appeared before the National Council of Defense in Washington, DC, and explained how his university was "attempting to make itself fully available for the service of our common country." He noted that students called into service "in any way," including farm labor, would receive credit for the semester on the basis of their current work. Strong further reported that "sixty students have received endorsements to join the Officers' Reserve Corps . . . , six students have joined the Medical Corps of the United States Navy . . . , one hundred twenty-six have enlisted in the Kansas National Guard . . . , [and] thirty one [have joined] the Kansas Engineering Corps." He also discussed military training on campus, curriculum changes, contributions of faculty members, and collaboration with the American Red Cross. With respect to the last point, women from the university and the town of Lawrence established a local chapter of the Red Cross and took part in "a two-month program consisting of ten lessons on first aid, fifteen lessons on hygiene, and an additional fifteen lessons on 'care of the sick.'"[13]

Some eighty miles to the west in Manhattan, more than three thousand people listened to patriotic songs on April 9 and heard from former governor Edward Hoch that it was "time for differences to cease" because "every American citizen should help lick Germany." The State Agricultural College's cadet band offered its services to the federal government; after some hesitation, the War Department accepted. On June 11 bandmaster Burr Ozment, twenty Aggie band members, and eight additional recruits left Manhattan by train for the East Coast. They were supposed to go to France but were instead stationed at the Philadelphia Navy Yard as the First Marine Regiment Band. Martin Bruner of Concordia later reported that there were numerous parades, "and our Band has had the misfortune to lead every one them." In a letter published in the *Concordia Blade-Empire*, he told of playing for Mrs. Woodrow Wilson and being directed by Charlie Chaplin and Douglas Fairbanks at an event to sell war bonds. The band also appeared at Madison Square Garden in New York City with Geraldine Farrar, the noted opera singer and movie actress. After eighteen months of stateside service, the First Marine Regiment Band finally received orders to sail to France. The trip, however, was canceled due to the armistice, and the band instead toured Cuba and Haiti.[14]

Although the Aggie musicians never set foot in France, more than 1,200 classmates and alumni took part in the fighting in Europe, including four major generals, seven colonels, and five lieutenant colonels. At home, the Home Economics faculty published recipes and menus for "wheatless" and "meatless" days, and the Division of Agriculture faculty focused on increasing food production. Given its proximity to Camp Funston and Fort Riley, the college instructed detachments of draftees (who were lodged in the main

Kansas State Band

B. H. Ozment .... *Director*
A. M. Butcher .... *Principal Musician*
Chas. Zimmerman .... *Drum Major*

Photo 4.5: Kansas State Band. From *The Royal Purple 1916* (yearbook of Kansas State Agricultural College), courtesy of the Morse Department of Special Collections, Kansas State University Libraries.

gymnasium) on how to be mechanics, blacksmiths, electricians, radio operators, and carpenters.[15]

* * *

Although not yet incorporated into the U.S. Army, the Kansas National Guard took immediate steps to prepare for war. In many ways life had returned to normal for the men in the Oskaloosa National Guard at the beginning of 1917. Will Smith, the new Jefferson County attorney, moved into an office in the southeast corner of the courthouse. He also was commissioned as a second lieutenant after Stub Quakenbush resigned to go to Idaho, where he had spent some time after returning from the Philippines. Ted Blevins led the Oskaloosa basketball team to victory over Holton and likely faced players who had served with him on the Texas border. The junior-class play, *The Dear Boy Graduates*, featured two other guardsmen, Merle Trapp and Victor Segraves. It was performed at the end of March, just days before the war declaration.[16]

Once the United States was at war, however, Lieutenant Will Smith was

Photo 4.6: Ralph Nichols. From *The Royal Purple 1923* (yearbook of Kansas State Agricultural College), courtesy of the Morse Department of Special Collections, Kansas State University Libraries.

tasked with the job of persuading Jefferson County men to join the National Guard. Starting in his hometown of Valley Falls, Smith pointed out that, with a few more recruits, "we will be able to have our own company and our own officers." He also spoke in Nortonville and Winchester, where the "good sized crowd" that gathered likely included twenty-one-year-old William Davis, the son of a local farmer. Smith's efforts were successful, and the *Oskaloosa Independent* reported "several additions to the local company of National Guards," including Ralph Nichols, a junior at Oskaloosa High School.[17]

Ralph Nichols was born on August 2, 1899, the third of five boys. His paternal grandfather, James Nichols, who died when Ralph was twelve, served with the 117th Ohio Infantry in the Civil War. James moved his family to Kansas and settled in Dunlap, where Ralph's father, Townsend, married Charity "Alice" Kidd. As a Methodist minister, Townsend preached in several small towns in the state, including Galesburg, where Ralph was born. In the spring of 1916, the Nichols family moved to Oskaloosa, with Ralph joining the high school's sophomore class. While Ted Blevins, Sam Gutschenritter, Billy Kimmel, Vic Segraves, and other high school boys spent the summer in Texas, sixteen-year-old Ralph worked on his uncle's farm in Lyon County. When Oskaloosa celebrated the return of the guardsmen with an elaborate dinner and speeches at the Methodist church, he was likely in attendance. It is not surprising, therefore, that when the country decided to send soldiers to France, young Nichols jumped at the chance to enlist.[18]

* * *

The eight weeks prior to draft-registration day, June 5, was exciting for everyone but particularly memorable for Blevins. As a corporal in the combined Holton-Oskaloosa company, he instructed Nichols and other "rookies" to the military, as people from all over Jefferson County came to Oskaloosa to watch the drills at the courthouse square. In May the Adjutant General's Office authorized Oskaloosa to form its own company as part of the new Third Regiment, with Will Smith as first lieutenant and the captain to be brought in from another unit. In the middle of May, Blevins graduated first in his class (of twenty) despite having missed two months of his senior year. He also excelled at the combination County Track and Literary Meet, winning the high hurdles, shotput, and oratory contests. His winning essay, printed in the *Oskaloosa Independent*, argued that "right must conquer might" and that Germany's day (*der tag*) was fast fading into night (*die nacht*): "After the turmoil of this great war has subsided we can look forward to the day of world peace, when . . . nations shall be satisfied with what they have and shall use all their energy and influence to improve and better that which they possess. And in that day the United States of America will stand as an inspiration for freedom, liberty, and right."[19]

As the day to register for the draft approached, most young men in Kansas and across the United States were uncertain about their future. In contrast, Blevins, Gutschenritter, Kimmel, Nichols, Segraves, and Smith knew where they stood. They were all members of Company B, Third Kansas Infantry.

CHAPTER FIVE

The Army Draft and "Fatal Number 258"

"Where is it written in the Constitution," Daniel Webster asked the House of Representatives in 1814, "that you may take children from their parents, and parents from their children, and compel them to fight the battles of any war in which the folly or the wickedness of the government may engage it?" Congress did not enact a conscription law during the War of 1812, so Webster's question went unanswered, but the issue resurfaced when the Pennsylvania Supreme Court considered the legality of the 1863 Enrollment Act. The court declared this national law to be "an unauthorized substitute for the militia of the states" but then reversed course (following a change in personnel) and vacated the decision. The Civil War conscription laws enacted by both sides in that conflict were unpopular, the U.S. draft helping incite four days of widespread rioting and racial violence in New York City in July 1863.[1]

Although the United States relied on volunteers during the Spanish-American War, "between 1870 and 1914, virtually every European nation except Britain . . . adopted variations of the successful Prussian emphasis upon mass conscript armies." After war with Germany was declared, President Wilson, who wished to avoid a reincarnation of the volunteer Rough Riders by political rival Theodore Roosevelt, immediately requested a "National Army" raised by conscription. Representative Daniel Anthony and Senator Charles Curtis preferred to rely on volunteers before resorting to a draft but joined the other Kansas legislators in voting for the Selective Service Act on May 18, 1917. This law, which did not repeat the Civil War practices of substitutions and purchased exemptions, required men between the ages of twenty-one and thirty to register for selection by lottery and subsequent examination by local boards. "The whole Nation must be a team," President Wilson proclaimed, "in which each man shall play the part for which he is best fitted." With tortured logic, he contended the law was "not a conscription of the unwilling" but instead a "selection from a Nation that has volunteered in mass."[2]

Reaction across Kansas was mostly positive. Governor Capper immediately proclaimed the fifth of June—the nationwide day of registration—a "public holiday within this state" and urged Kansans "to observe it with the patriotic fervor and the solemnity befitting the momentous importance of occasion." Young men were encouraged to "Be a Went—Not a Sent" and enlist with the National Guard or the Regular Army. Lieutenant Will Smith signed a prominent advertisement in the May 18 edition of the *Oskaloosa Independent* that featured an American flag and the headline "Don't Wait for Draft—ENLIST IN THE THIRD KANSAS." Jefferson County men who volunteered with the Guard, Smith pointed out, "will be among friends and neighbors, backed by the sympathy and support of the home communities; whereas, under conscription, the men may be sent they know not where and be scattered among strangers, and perhaps with undesirable associates."[3]

Not everyone, however, was on board. On May 31, 1917, six Kansans, including a University of Kansas professor, were charged with conspiring at a Unitarian church meeting to obstruct the operation of the draft law. Nearly a year later in a federal courtroom in Topeka, the defendants admitted distributing handbills critical of militarism but denied knowing that three individuals from Kansas City were going to talk against the draft at the meeting. After an hour's deliberation, the jury acquitted the defendants, in contrast to the successful prosecution in Missouri of the Kansas City residents. But most resistance to the draft in Kansas came from conscientious objectors affiliated with the Mennonites and other religious groups. It was difficult (and dangerous) for anyone to maintain a conscientious objection to conscription during World War I. "What I am opposed to," declared President Wilson, "is not the feeling of the pacifists, but their stupidity. My heart is with them, but my mind has a contempt for them." Exhibiting a similar lack of sympathy and understanding, Governor Capper refused to assist a resident of Alton, Kansas, who had been targeted for his views: "I know that you have conscientious objections to war, but now that we are in war, it seems to me . . . it is a time when we should lay aside our conscientious objections until we get out of war." Meanwhile, at the national level, legal objections to the draft were put to rest when the U.S. Supreme Court in January 1918 held that conscription was sanctioned by the power of Congress to "declare war" and "raise and support Armies" and did not violate either the First Amendment's protection of freedom of conscience or the Thirteenth Amendment's prohibition of involuntary servitude.[4]

Over 9.6 million men registered for the draft on June 5, 1917. The registration cards were numbered and contained information relevant to the selection decision. For example, the registration card for George Herman Ruth states his age as twenty-three; his residence as Boston; his status as a natural-born citizen from Baltimore, Maryland; his employment as a baseball player (at Fenway Park by the Boston American League Baseball Company); that he was married with no children; that he was without prior military service and not claiming exemption from the draft; and his racial status as Caucasian, providing his physical details as being six feet two inches tall with a medium build, brown eyes, and dark hair. Printed in the lower-left corner of each registration card was the following instruction: "If person is of African descent, tear off this corner." In Kansas registrants appeared at 113 draft boards, 1 for each of the 105 counties, 4 for Kansas City, 2 for Topeka, and 2 for Wichita. In Baldwin registration day coincided with commencement week at Baldwin College, and out-of-town visitors and local residents joined together to form a parade that included five girls dressed in the colors of the Allied nations, veterans, a drum corps, numerous automobiles, and an estimated one thousand school children holding flags. Registrants were given priority seating in the college chapel, where they listened to speeches and wore badges of honor pinned on their chests by women of the Red Cross. An even larger parade took place in Topeka, with fifteen thousand people, five bands, a bugle corps, a drum corps, and horse-drawn caissons that passed in review before an estimated thirty-five thousand onlookers. Severe weather cut short celebrations in several locations, including Jefferson County, where a tornado combined with hailstones larger than a man's fist tore a destructive path and killed a man near Meridan. Men received a certificate to indicate they were duly registered. In Leavenworth eighteen men who celebrated after signing up for the draft were charged with drunkenness and fined.[5]

The next step was the lottery. On July 20 at 9:45 A.M., Secretary of War Baker announced that the "solemn and historic moment" had arrived and, after removing his glasses and being blindfolded, drew a capsule from a large glass bowl containing 10,500 numbers (the largest number in any registration district). The number selected was 258. At some point in the early hours of the following morning, the last of the numbers was drawn, although it was unlikely that men holding any number drawn after the first 2,000 would be called for examination. According to the *Washington Post*, over 1.3 million men were selected, more than enough to secure the first increment of

REGISTRATION CERTIFICATE.

To whom it may concern, Greetings:

No. 7

(This number must correspond with that on the Registration Card.)

THESE PRESENTS ATTEST,

That in accordance with the proclamation of the President of the United States, and in compliance with law, Urban Brownell, Rosedale

(Name) (City or P. O.)

Ward 2 Precinct 2 County of Wyandotte, State of Kansas

has submitted himself to registration and has by me been duly registered this 5th day of June, 1917.

3—4227

R. Olson
Registrar.

Photo 5.1: Registration certificate for Urban Brownlee of Rosedale, who served with the 117th Ammunition Train, Forty-Second (Rainbow) Division. Courtesy of the National WWI Museum and Memorial, Kansas City, Missouri, USA.

687,000 draftees. Number 13 did not prove unlucky: it was not drawn until 7,889 other numbers had been selected.[6]

Newspapers across the country fixated on the number 258 and the men who would be called first in the draft. Numerologists pointed out that it was approximately 258 miles from Paris to the Rhine and that the sum of the numbers 2, 5, and 8 equals the fifteen letters in the following phrases: "General Pershing," "Democracy upheld," and "Defeat the Kaiser." No mention was made of the fact that it was also approximately 258 miles from the Rhine to Paris or that there are fifteen letters in the phrase "America must lose." Charles Holland Kidder—at age eighty, he was not eligible for the draft—published a poem directed to the men holding number 258:

> You had hoped it would come to another
> But now, like a bolt from the blue,
> The lot has fallen, my brother,
> And the summons is meant for you.

In Savannah, Georgia, a traveling salesman holding "the fatal Number 258" killed himself. Will Bradley of Covington, Louisiana, went into the woods "heavily armed" and declared that "he would not return alive." Perhaps the oddest conscription-related story occurred twenty-three years later, when the number 158, the first selected in the 1940 draft, was held by three men whose fathers had held number 258 in 1917. The notoriety associated with number 258 eventually disappeared, although it was briefly revived in November 1917 when the silent film *Draft 258* was released. Part of its complicated plot concerns a character named George, who holds the fateful number but refuses to report until he is shamed into action by his sister's offer to go in his place.[7]

In Kansas only 108 men held number 258 because in five counties—Greeley, Hamilton, Haskell, Wallace, and Wichita—there were fewer than 258 registrants. By canvassing newspaper articles and other records, it appears that about half of these men actually served in the military: fourteen of the first registrants enlisted, and forty were either immediately drafted or drafted after receiving a deferment. Fifty-three did not serve because they were discharged or exempted, including number 258 from Jefferson County, Floyd Gragg of Valley Falls, who had flat feet and a weak heart and lungs. Five were Mexican aliens, and one was transferred to Texas, where he was a resident. Two men—Timble Massey of Osborne County and Brades Garret of Wilson County—were drafted in lieu of being prosecuted for failing to appear when called. Kansas was required to furnish 17,764 of the 687,000 men in the first draft (about 2.6 percent), but the number was reduced to fewer than 7,000 in light of credits awarded for men who had enlisted in the Regular Army or were serving in the National Guard. According to one account, the reduction was proportionally the largest in the country. When credits were factored into the quotas for each registration district, it turned out that nine counties—Allen, Chase, Douglas, Ford, Kearny, Montgomery, Ottawa, Woodson, and Wyandotte—and the city of Topeka had already furnished 770 more men than required and were not presently required to draft additional men. Cherokee County in southeast Kansas had the highest remaining quota at 268 men.[8]

The examination process began in late July and continued into September until the new training camps were filled with the first wave of draftees. Men were called in to their local draft board for physical examination and for discussion of requests for exemption or discharge. The grounds for exemption were based on status: government officials, ordained ministers, students preparing for the ministry in recognized theological or divinity schools, members of the military or naval services, German citizens, and "resident aliens" who had not taken out naturalization papers were not subject to the draft. If not within one of the aforementioned categories, a registrant could seek a discharge based on specified grounds, the most commonly invoked involving marital and family status: husbands with dependent wives or children; sons of dependent widowed mothers; sons of dependent aged or infirm parents; fathers of dependent motherless children under sixteen; and brothers of dependent orphan children or children under sixteen. In addition, discharges were granted to men "engaged in industry, including agriculture found to be necessary to the maintenance of the military establishment, the effective operation of the military forces, or the maintenance of national interest during the emergency." Decisions by local draft boards could be appealed. For example, Thomas Watson of Merriam claimed exemption on two grounds: as the son of a dependent widowed mother and as a person engaged in agricultural labor essential to the war effort. The Johnson County board denied his claims, which were also dismissed by the First District Appeal Board in Topeka.

Some men were inducted, some were deferred, and others were excused. Eventually, a classification system was developed, although as it turned out, only men in Class I were drafted: unskilled workers; workers engaged in nonessential industrial or agricultural enterprises; husbands and fathers who either habitually failed to support their wives and families or who were not usefully employed; and bachelors. In May 1918 the War Department issued its "work or fight" order, providing that any deferred registrant who was unemployed or engaged in a nonproductive occupation would lose his deferment and be inducted. The theater, opera, and motion-picture industries were deemed productive, but amusement parks and professional sports were declared nonessential. The classification of baseball as a nonessential occupation caused an uproar, forcing the Wilson administration to bow to public pressure and postpone implementation of the new policy until after the 1918 World Series.[9]

According to the *Bonner Springs–Edwardsville Chieftain*, in response to the registration question "Are you an alien citizen?," one potential draftee replied in the affirmative, stating, "I am not a well man." When Grace Shuck of Topeka learned that her husband, Clarence Shuck, had been exempted by a Minnesota draft board on the grounds of being the sole support of his wife and children, she signed an affidavit that stated he was only supporting himself. According to the *Topeka Daily Capital*, "slacker" marriages were dealt a blow in January 1918, when the War Department announced that marriages after May 18, 1917, of draft-eligible men would be presumed to be attempts to evade conscription. This issue had surfaced shortly after the draft was announced: noting that a new record of 187 marriage licenses were issued in June 1917 in Wyandotte County, the *Daily Capital* commented, "whether 'slacker' marriages are responsible is not known."

Some of the Kansans holding number 258 sought exemptions but were denied. Levi Matson, a recently married twenty-three-year-old farmer from Cloud County, unsuccessfully sought to be excused on religious grounds. His reaction to the news is described at length in an article on the front page of the *Concordia Daily Blade* entitled "No. 258 Feels Tragedy of War." If the article is an accurate depiction of events, it is fair to say that Levi and Dela Matson were upset:

> A dark cloud seemed to envelope his vision, and with a loud shriek he fell backwards out of the seat of the sulky plow. How long he lay there he could not tell, but he knew he must break the news to his wife. The two had often talked of the possibility of his going to war and it haunted them. If it came, it would tear their very souls and each tried to buoy up the other with the hope that it could not be. They are religious people and they prayed long and earnestly that they would not have to bear this burden, but with the letter came the fact that it must be.
>
> No. 258 turned for the house, and crying out with the agony of one whose mind is tortured with horrible visions caused by fear, he staggered on. His wife was working in the kitchen and the first shriek she heard made her clutch her heart. . . . She went to the door and saw her young husband stumbling along with his head bowed down. With almost every step he would lift his face to the heavens and give a loud wail as if he were railing at the fate which an erstwhile Kind Providence had thrust upon him. . . . She threw herself into his arms and moaned and sobbed as if her heart was broken. Together they gained the house and fell prostrate on the floor, where they bewailed their great sorrow until both were utterly exhausted.
>
> A visitor witnessed the whole circumstance and he tried as best he could to cheer these two young people who believed that the sunlight of the whole world had disappeared. He talked to the young man and tried to tell him that it wouldn't be so bad as was imagined, and finally No. 258 came to himself and weakly promised to recover his self possession and help his wife withstand the blow. Whether this young man will ever recover from the first real tragedy that has entered his life is problematical for he has been crushed.

After quoting from the article and ridiculing its overwrought tone, another local newspaper—the *Jamestown Optimist*—offered the following advice:

> Drafted man No. 258 in Cloud county should take a good wet elm club in hand, visit the office of the *Daily Blade* in Concordia, and then and there give some reporter the job of writing up the story of Cloud county's first war casualty. . . . The *Blade* . . . pulls out the tremolo stop and brings out the sob stuff and big gobs. . . . To be drafted into the army is a hard blow to the average man who must leave a family behind, but to be the subject of such a senseless, mushy, lying sketch as this is infinitely worse than the horrors of the battlefield. If Mr. Matson, who is probably a decent, law-abiding and peace-loving citizen, would turn the *Blade* office into a shambles and shoot the fellow who wrote the stuff on the spot . . . , it would be impossible to secure a jury in the county that would convict him of having committed a serious crime.[10]

Levi Matson did not assault anyone at the *Daily Blade*. He reported to Camp Funston and was discharged from the army in April 1919 without going to France. Dela died in 1951, while Levi passed away in 1977 at age eighty-three.

Whereas Levi Matson was devastated to be drafted, Laird Archer of Wichita was deeply disappointed to be turned away. When Archer was a young man, he was blinded in his right eye by a lightning shock. Although an operation restored sight in the eye, he was required to wear glasses to correct his impaired vision. When Kansans were called to the Mexican border in 1916, the young reporter for the *Wichita Beacon* tried to enlist but was rejected. Just a month before his number was the first drawn in the national lottery, Archer was weakened by an operation for appendicitis. When he appeared before the local draft board, the reason given for his rejection was that he was underweight. Archer then asked to be admitted to the Red Cross but was turned down. Undaunted, he applied for war-service work with the YMCA and, with the help of Henry Allen, publisher of the *Beacon* and a future governor, Archer was selected and sent to Fort Sill, Oklahoma, where he fell ill following a typhoid inoculation, and then to France, where his thumb was almost amputated after poison infected a laceration caused by a kicking horse.[11]

Approximately 40 of the 113 Kansas registrants called first by their draft boards were inducted. Like all draftees in World War I, some did not go overseas, some went but did not see action, some fought and survived, and others were killed. One of the first to be called, George Washington Gardner of Traer, earned the Distinguished Service Cross for his leadership and heroism on November 2, 1918 (see chapter 18). Two of the men holding number 258 died on the battlefield: Lyndon's Albert Beskow of the Third Division in July 1918 and David Fawcett of Norcatur in October 1918, while fighting with the Twenty-Sixth "Yankee" Division. Several of the "258 club" were gassed or wounded, including Herman Fred Christ Volkening of Belvue, who entered the service only after President Wilson denied his appeal from the rejection of his exemption claim. Volkening, who fought with the Third Division, was severely wounded in May 1918 when an aerial bomb struck the railroad car transporting him to the front. The resulting skull fracture eventually healed, and he returned home, married Ida Laging of Wabaunsee, and lived a long life before passing away in 1977 at age eighty-four, one year after the death of his wife.[12]

* * *

On August 10, 1917, the War Department announced that the Regular Army was at full wartime strength and that Kansas had filled its quota. As the war progressed, there were additional registrations and inductions. After the first draftees were sent to camp, draft boards examined another 3 million men, certified 1 million for military service, and inducted 516,000 of them. In March 1918 Congress amended the Selective Service Act to permit conscripted men to be furloughed to work on farms, a measure greatly appreciated by Kansas wheat producers. By war's end, draftees made up more than half of the American Expeditionary Forces in France. Many drafted Kansans trained at Camp Funston and served in the 353rd (All Kansas) Regiment of the Eighty-Ninth Division.[13]

As for Archer, his rejection by the Wichita draft board led to a career in public service. By September 1918, the earnest Kansan was the YMCA's regional business officer in Nevers, France, where he helped provide a variety of essential services for U.S. soldiers. He came home after the war but soon returned to Europe, where he worked for the International War Work Council and the American Near East Relief organization. Archer would survive a train attack by bandits in Italy, employ packhorses to deliver silver to starving Armenians, fall into the Tigris River, travel across the Syrian desert, and help Americans leave Greece before and during the Nazi occupation. In 1939 Archer was made a Knight Commander of the Royal Order of the Phoenix of Greece, one of the highest honors to be accorded an American relief worker. He spent much of his life in Greece and eastern Europe, writing

Photo 5.2: Fern and Laird Archer, circa 1950s. Courtesy of Jane L. Archer.

two books about the Balkans. The introduction to his first book, *Balkan Journal*, describes Archer as possessing a "zestful Kansas curiosity about every aspect of public affairs."[14]

Archer retired in 1952 and settled in Fayetteville, Arkansas, where he passed away in 1981. His family scattered his ashes around sites in Greece that he loved: the Acropolis, Mount Lycabetus, Olympia, Sparta, Mycanae, Tyrins, Delphi, Marathon, and in the sea off Cape Sunium.[15]

CHAPTER SIX

Kansas "Rainbow" Guardsmen

The 117th Ammunition Train, Forty-Second Division

Even before Congress tasked Secretary Baker with implementing the Selective Service Act, the War Department was taking measures to beef up and organize the National Guard. In Kansas, Adjutant General Martin was told to increase the militia to a "full war strength" of approximately 10,500 men and 450 officers. In order to form an army division of 28,000 soldiers, the Kansans would be combined with the Missouri National Guard. Lieutenant Will Smith was instructed to seek additional infantrymen in Jefferson County. Another Guard officer, Captain Frank L. Travis of Iola, was authorized to enlist men throughout Kansas to form an ammunition train, an essential divisional component responsible for supplying the artillery and infantry with the shells, bullets, and other equipment needed to perform their jobs.[1]

The forty-nine-year-old Travis, a businessman who had served on the Mexican border with the First Kansas Regiment, proceeded to recruit a large number of men—six of the regiment's twelve companies—from Rosedale; Kansas City, Kansas; and Kansas City, Missouri. He also secured enlistments in Wichita, Topeka, and Manhattan as well as towns in southeast Kansas (such as Buffalo, Chanute, Chetopa, Coffeyville, Independence, McCune, Oswego, and Parsons) and southwest Kansas (including Bucklin, Dodge City, Ensign, Hugoton, Pratt, and Spearville). The opportunity to enlist with friends in this new noncombatant unit was appealing:

> In Dodge City, Kansas, Calvin Lambert had decided to enlist in something, but the infantry did not appeal to him. While drilling with a volunteer home guard unit he decided to enroll in a new company—a mule-drawn ammunition train that, to his delight, was changed to a motor truck company to haul ammunition. There was a problem: The company had no troops and no vehicles. Consequently, Lambert and a few stalwart ammunition-train men went on the road like a traveling medicine show

to recruit members. . . . "We promised them," Lambert recalled, "there would be no drilling [and] no loading and unloading."[2]

On July 10, 1917, President Wilson proclaimed that the soldiers in the National Guard would, on August 5, become soldiers in the U.S. Army. Pursuant to the National Defense Act, the guardsmen would be discharged from their state militias and drafted into federal service, thus avoiding the constitutional issue of deploying the Guard outside of the country. The Guard units would form divisions and train at camps under construction in a number of states. Consequently, Travis, now a lieutenant colonel in command of the First Ammunition Train of the Kansas National Guard, expected to be part of a combined Kansas-Missouri army division. He learned otherwise on August 14, when the War Department announced that a new division would be created by selecting parts of National Guard units from twenty-six states and the District of Columbia. The four infantry regiments would come from Alabama, Iowa, Ohio, and New York; a field signal battalion would be supplied by Missouri; and Kansas would be represented by its ammunition train. Because the numbers twenty-six through forty-one were reserved for other Guard-based divisions, the new command became the Forty-Second Division, headed by Major General William A. Mann of Pennsylvania. His chief of staff was thirty-seven-year-old Colonel Douglas MacArthur, who would take command by war's end. According to some sources, MacArthur was responsible for his unit's nickname, the "Rainbow" Division, by noting that its composite formation would be seen by the public to "stretch over the whole country like a rainbow."[3]

The Rainbow Division was a public-relations coup: due to its geographical disparity, it could be selected by the War Department as one of the first units sent to France without offending any particular state or region of the country. It also managed to project an image of being an "elite" command. Secretary Baker intimated that the Forty-Second Division comprised the best of the National Guard units, and the *Manhattan Mercury* described the Jayhawk unit—now the 117th Ammunition Train—as "the cream of Kansas young manhood." With a great deal of local press coverage, the men mobilized at Topeka, camped a few days at the fairgrounds, and departed at the beginning of September for New York. Their six weeks of training at Camp Mills on Long Island received national attention, although readers were not informed that the Alabama and New York troops disliked each other or that Iowa's fighting men sparred with soldiers from other states.[4]

While at Camp Mills, Lieutenant Harold Stanley Johnson compiled and

Photo 6.1: Officers of the Rainbow Division (Forty-Second Division), January 8, 1919. Courtesy of the Library of Congress.

published a roster of the Rainbow Division. At that time there were 968 soldiers in the 117th Ammunition Train, with a surprisingly high number (362) from places other than Kansas. But the 169 soldiers from Kansas City, Missouri, and the 606 Kansans comprised 80 percent of the unit. Besides Kansas City, Missouri, the towns contributing the most men were Chanute (81); Parsons (34); Kansas City, Kansas (28); Pratt (22); Manhattan (21); and Rosedale (21). Almost a quarter of the soldiers were from the Kansas City metropolitan area. Jefferson County contributed seven men, including three from Oskaloosa: Private Chauncey "Chan" Hargrave, Private Samuel Patrick "Pat" Segraves, and Stable Sergeant Quakenbush. Pat Segraves, an older brother of Vic Segraves, was working as a bookkeeper in Pratt, Kansas, when he enlisted. Quakenbush, who had resigned from the National Guard in March to go to Idaho, returned home after war was declared and enlisted with another unit in the Third Kansas Regiment. "When a fellow's been in as long as I have," he later said, "it's in his blood—even if he does have to enlist as a private." Soon thereafter, following the formation of the Rainbow Division, Quakenbush requested and received a transfer. "I want to get over to France," the forty-four-year-old bachelor told the *Leavenworth Post*. With his experience caring for horses, Quakenbush was put in charge of the stable of a caisson company.[5]

The Rainbow Division was the fourth American combat unit to arrive in France, the other three being the Twenty-Sixth "Yankee" Division, a National Guard–based unit from New England, and the First and Second Divisions of the Regular Army, containing both career soldiers and recent volunteers. The Forty-Second's composite units dispersed to different training areas, but the 117th Ammunition Train was hampered by the lack of motorized vehicles. In February 1918 the division was reunited in eastern France and put under the operational command of the French army. A month later the Americans were assigned to a quiet sector of the western front. The men were subject to artillery bombardment, however, and Private Everett King of Harris, Kansas, was killed when a shell landed on the company commissary. In a letter received home after his death, King wrote of his father: "I never will forget the day I left home, when he told me he never expected to see me again." He also reported candidly about life as a soldier. "I don't like this job," he wrote, "even though I'm willing to stick to it," adding, "the happiest moment of my life will be when I get on a west-bound ship, or more so, when I tumble down the U.S. gang plank."[6]

Germany in the spring of 1918 began a series of attacks that initially overwhelmed the British and French forces. In response the 117th Ammunition Train helped move the Forty-Second Division into the Champagne region of north-central France to bolster defenses there. In a letter dated May 12, Sergeant Quakenbush noted, "We see a great many things over here we can't write about, but one thing is sure, this is a real war." In July and August the Rainbow soldiers suffered many casualties in both the German-initiated Champagne-Marne offensive and the Allies' Aisne-Marne counteroffensive. In a letter to his brother, Corporal Gordon May of Kansas City, Kansas, described the fierce fighting from the perspective of a soldier in the ammunition train:

> Of course our line of work in no way compares with infantry or artillery, but we have to undergo many exciting events. Our first experiences started at midnight on July 14th when we were suddenly awakened by the roar of gun fire beyond human imagination and the whizzing of shells over our heads and bursting all around us. . . . It is interesting to see the big shells explode at a distance but when they start lighting close enough to throw shrapnel all around you, it has the inclination to make you shake a wicked foot.

On the last day of July, three members of Company D, 117th Ammunition Train were killed near the Soissons-Rheims front when a German airplane made a direct hit on their truck. Howard Gotschall, a farmer, and Charles Ernest Scott, who owned a pool hall at the time of his enlistment, were both from Ford, a town of less than three hundred people near Dodge City. The other occupant of the truck was Hewitt Swearingen of Kansas City. To honor their memories, the Ford County American Legion named its post after Scott, the Ford County Veterans of Foreign Wars post carries the name of Gotschall, and American Legion Post 201 in Kansas City honors Swearingen.[7]

Stub Quakenbush managed to avoid the German shells and remain alive, but he did not shirk his responsibilities. On August 17, 1918, Captain Max Payne, the commanding officer of Company F, 117th Ammunition Train, commended the stable sergeant for his devotion to duty while under fire. Noting that his company had "been under severe bombardment by the enemy, causing many casualties to both men and animals," Captain Payne praised Quakenbush for his actions on July 28 and August 7: "your devotion to duty, the fearlessness with which you performed that duty and the care you gave to both wounded men and animals is highly commended."[8]

The 117th Ammunition Train continued to support the infantry and artillery when the Forty-Second Division went into action during the Battle of Saint-Mihiel (September) and the Meuse-Argonne offensive (October–November). The services of the unit in the final operation drew particular praise from the chief of staff of the Forty-Second Division, Colonel William N. Hughes: "In the Argonne Meuse, night and day it toiled; heart-rending, muscle-breaking toil. Men were in the saddle for days at a time. Trucks went where trucks were not expected to go. A measure of endurance was demanded that would have been thought impossible before. Aeroplane bombs and enemy shells did not stop it." On the day of the armistice, the Rainbow Division—MacArthur, now a brigadier general, in charge—was at Sedan near the Belgian border. After the fighting ended, the men went through Belgium and Luxembourg and across the Rhine River into Germany. On May 2, 1919, the *Topeka Daily Capital* reported the arrival in the United States of the "Sunflower state's crack war organization, the 117th ammunition train." The city of Rosedale honored the returning soldiers by renaming a major north–south street Rainbow Boulevard and by completing, in September 1924, the World War I Memorial Arch in Mount Marty Park.[9]

* * *

The *Kansas City Star* reported in May 1919 that the 117th Ammunition Train "was the first Kansas National Guard unit to go and the last unit to come home," and while its men were in France, "not a single arrest for misconduct was made." There may not have been any arrests, but there was misconduct. According to Colonel Travis, Sergeant Quakenbush "borrowed" his car at one point and toured for two days in northeastern France. When asked how he "got away with it," Quakenbush said that when he ran out of gasoline, he went to a station and ordered the vehicle's tank filled because it was a headquarters car. When he was discharged, the veteran soldier told a Kansas newspaperman that he would not serve in another war, "at least, until it comes." As it turned it, Quakenbush stayed home during World War II and died at age seventy-three in 1947.[10]

CHAPTER SEVEN

Camp Funston

White and Black Men Form the Eighty-Ninth and Ninety-Second Divisions

Fort Riley currently covers over one hundred thousand acres between Junction City and Manhattan in Geary and Riley Counties, where "the 1st Infantry Division as well as National Guard and Reserve units from several states use the modern training facilities . . . to gain skills necessary to defend our nation." The fort is home to the U.S. Army's First Division (the Big Red One), formed in 1917, but previously it housed infantry and cavalry that protected the Oregon, California, and Santa Fe Trails. It also hosted an officers' training camp during World War I as well as a training center for army doctors and other medical personnel.[1]

From 1917 to 1924, Fort Riley was the site of Camp Funston, a hastily constructed cantonment named for Major General Funston, a Kansan who had died six weeks before the United States entered World War I. Captain Francis Gilman Blake—later dean of the Yale Medical School—did not describe his stay in Kansas with fondness in a letter written in August 1918: "No . . . cool days, no cool nights, no drinks, no movies, no dances, no club, no pretty women, no shower bath, no poker, no people, no fun, no joy, no nothing save heat and blistering sun and scorching winds and sweat and dust and thirst and loud and stifling nights and working all hours and lonesomeness and general hell—that's Fort Riley Kansas." The barracks and buildings of Camp Funston were dismantled after the war; all that remains today are a few limestone foundations, a sign that reads "Camp Funston—World War I Headquarters of Major General Leonard Wood," and a stone obelisk that honors "The Men Who Trained at Funston for the Great War." During its day, however, Camp Funston rivaled Topeka in population, "covered more than two thousand acres, contained fifteen hundred buildings constructed with more than forty-seven million feet of lumber, [and] had twenty-eight miles of paved streets."[2]

The Eighty-Ninth Division of the U.S. Army formed at Camp Funston. General Pershing ranked the division as one of his top-four fighting units,

Photo 7.1: Camp Funston, 1917. Courtesy of the Kenneth Spencer Research Library, University of Kansas.

in part due to the men of the 353rd Infantry, the so-called All Kansas Regiment. The Eighty-Ninth also included the 342nd Field Artillery, known for its famous collegiate and professional athletes. The African American Ninety-Second Division also organized and trained at Camp Funston. The Ninety-Second, one of two segregated infantry divisions, was formed with Black draftees and commanded in part by Black officers. Residents of Junction City and Manhattan, including the acting president of Kansas State Agricultural College, protested the decision to bring thousands of African Americans to Camp Funston. The white soldiers of the Eighty-Ninth Division trained separately from the "Buffalo Soldiers" of the Ninety-Second Division, who were told to refrain from "doing anything, *no matter how legally correct*, that will provoke race animosity."

Congress in May 1917 authorized the construction of camps—or "cantonments"—for the National Guard and for draftees comprising the new National Army. While the National Guard tent camps were concentrated in the southern and southwestern regions of the United States, the National Army camps were more evenly dispersed across the country. Camp Funston, built on bottomlands of the Kansas River about three miles east of Fort Riley, was the largest of the sixteen National Army cantonments. During the summer of 1917, "a vast wooden city was . . . built, capable of housing over

50,000 men." In addition to barracks, shooting ranges, and training facilities, the camp provided most of the amenities found in towns and cities, such as infirmaries, libraries, schools, general stores, social centers, and theaters. One area, known as "the Zone," offered numerous commercial establishments, an amusement hall, a Jewish center, and buildings for the YMCA and Knights of Columbus.[3]

The Eighty-Ninth Division was officially activated in August. American infantry divisions in World War I were large, approximately twenty-eight thousand men in all, with headquarters, four infantry regiments, machine-gun battalions, field artillery and trench mortar units, signalmen, engineers, military police, medical personnel, and ammunition, supply, and sanitary trains. Divisional command was given to Major General Leonard Wood, who was considered a rival by Pershing and—as a Republican ally of Teddy Roosevelt—persona non grata by Wilson. The former U.S. Army chief of staff (under President Taft) needed to be placed somewhere, however, and the middle of Kansas was viewed by his military and political opponents as an excellent choice.

Wood's first task was to assemble the leaders of the division, a combination of career soldiers, men from the Officer Reserve Corps, and recent graduates of the first officer training camp. The first 5 percent of the drafted men were scheduled to arrive on September 5, 1917, followed in two weeks by another 40 percent. The majority of inductees who formed the Eighty-Ninth Division came from seven states—Arizona, Colorado, Kansas, Missouri, Nebraska, New Mexico, and South Dakota—and an initial contingent of 2,974 Jayhawks formed the 353rd Infantry, which consequently became known as the "All Kansas" Regiment. To get the new divisions off to a good start, draft boards were instructed to give preference, if possible, to men with past military service or those with experience in cooking.[4]

Twenty-eight-year-old Harlan Deaver, the 258th registrant and first person drafted from Nemaha County, was among the men who arrived at Camp Funston on September 20. Due to a clerical error, Deaver had been initially told his exemption request was granted. The mistake was corrected only a short time before his scheduled departure. On the appointed day Deaver and five other men from Sabetha boarded a train for the short journey to Seneca, where thirty-nine other inductees joined them for a group picture and an elaborate farewell:

> The children of St. Peter and Paul's parochial school marched down town and stood in line, [and] public school teachers and students, business men

> and busy housewives quickly joined the company of relatives and friends around the band stand. The Seneca band, always ready to respond, played as the people assembled. Rev. A. J. Morton gave the invocation. Judge W. I. Stuart of Hiawatha made an eloquent appeal for the "undivided allegiance." A procession was formed, led by the band, followed by the veterans of the Civil War, the new recruits, school children, relatives, and friends. The train approached the depot slowly, goodbyes were fondly said, the boys boarded their private car, the roll was called and in a few minutes they were on their way to Camp Funston, the band playing "The Star Spangled Banner" as the train pulled out.

Deaver would return home from France, but three of his fellow travelers to Camp Funston did not: Corporal Clare Sparling (Oneida) of the 353rd Infantry Regiment and Privates John Meyer (Sabetha) and Delbert Moyer (Centralia), who were transferred to other units. Each man was killed in action.[5]

In order to minimize interference with regular railroad service, most of the trains bringing recruits to Camp Funston arrived in the evening or early morning. There was a palpable sense of excitement. For example, Colorado's initial quota of 164 men, after leaving Denver on the evening of September 5, were fed breakfast in Ellis, Kansas, and received "a hearty reception and dinner" in Abilene. When their train stopped at Camp Funston, the men "were warmly welcomed, assigned to their regiments, given a bath, a change of clothing, a medical examination and by 10 o'clock they were in bed getting ready to drill tomorrow." Kansas draftees had similar experiences. "We got to Camp about 11:30 P.M.," wrote Benjamin Harrison Gilmore of El Dorado, "and marched about a mile to our bunk house. The next thing we did was to take a cold shower bath. You can imagine how it felt to strip out doors and take a cold shower about midnight."[6]

At first there was a shortage of uniforms and equipment. Soldiers wore denim overalls or in some instances their own shirts, pants, and shoes. Surplus civilian clothing was sent home or donated to the Belgian Relief Commission. Draftees who arrived in the morning were on the drill field in the afternoon, and evening arrivals were put in the line the following morning. Inductees were inoculated upon arrival and quarantined when ill, but the spread of communicable diseases in camp remained a constant problem, such as the outbreak in March 1918 of what would soon be known as the "Spanish" flu. When permitted to drill, infantry carried wooden rifles, while men assigned to the field artillery practiced without actual guns. To perform cavalry maneuvers without horses, saddles were strapped to barrels mounted on wooden legs.[7]

An extensive system of trenches was laid out near the camp, and French and British officers shared their expertise in conducting modern warfare. Men were instructed on the use of grenades and required to spend time in a "gas house" to test their ability to use gas masks. They also engaged in traditional forms of training, such as general physical-fitness drills, marching, bayonet maneuvers, and marksmanship. Sandra Reddish describes the training regimen at Camp Funston in detail and summarizes the results of tests taken by the draftees:

> Farm boys seemed to have made the best soldiers even though they had the least education, required a longer period of training, and were not as familiar with recreational games, which enabled the men to work in teams. Although these "boys" lagged behind in formal education and teamwork skills, their physical fitness could not be denied. According to Colonel Leonard P. Ayres's postwar statistical summary, the highest percentage (70 to 80 percent) of men passing their physical examinations came from the Central Plains.

Some of the men were at Camp Funston from September 1917 until May 1918, whereas others arrived shortly before the Eighty-Ninth Division departed for France. Holiday passes were limited, and during the winter, many were quarantined due to disease or illness. Visitors were mostly unregulated at first, but time and place restrictions were mandatory by the end of 1917. Soldiers on leave would often visit Topeka; in February 1918 a squad of military police from Camp Funston went to the state capital and told fourteen Kansas City women, who had just arrived by train, to return home.[8]

One sanctioned form of recreation was organized sports. The Eighty-Ninth Division fielded a football team that featured Roy "Pete" Heil, a regimental dentist described by the *University Daily Kansan* as "one of the greatest field generals and open field runners in the history of football at Kansas." Two future Jayhawk coaches, George "Potsie" Clark and Adrian "Ad" Lindsey, were also standout players. But the division was best known for its baseball squad. It was not a coincidence that several professional baseball players who were drafted ended up in the 342nd Field Artillery. The major leaguers trained for their combat mission but were also encouraged to play baseball, both in the United States and in France. Winfield "Win" Noyes (Philadelphia Phillies), Clarence Mitchell (Brooklyn Dodgers), and Lloyd Waite and

Charles Ward (both with the Pittsburgh Pirates) participated in numerous exhibition games. They were joined by Otis "Otie" Lambeth, a six-foot right hander from Berlin, Kansas. Dubbed the "Kansas Cyclone," he played in Topeka, where he recorded a no-hit game, before becoming a member of the Cleveland Indians in 1916. Primarily a sidearm pitcher, Lambeth was praised by the *New York Tribune* for his "deceptive delivery" and ability to throw at "a marked change of pace." He appeared in two games in 1918 before being ordered by his draft board to report to Camp Funston in late April.[9]

The most prominent baseball player to come to Kansas was Grover Cleveland Alexander. Nicknamed "Old Pete" and "Alexander the Great," the Nebraska native finished his career with 373 victories, more than all pitchers except Cy Young (511), Walter Johnson (417), and Christy Mathewson (also 373). In 1917 Alexander won thirty games for the Philadelphia Phillies, who nonetheless traded him to Chicago, due in part to the possibility that he would be drafted. Alexander told the Cubs he expected to be placed in Class 3 because his mother was dependent on him, but the draft board denied his exemption request and listed him as Class 1-A. While other stars, including Babe Ruth, Rogers Hornsby, and "Shoeless" Joe Jackson, avoided induction by taking jobs with shipbuilding yards, Alexander reported for duty at the beginning of May, ending his 1918 season with a 2-1 record and a 1.79 earned run average. "Hard boiled veterans of six months training regarded him with awe," reported the *Manhattan Mercury*, and "organization commanders busied themselves bidding for this altogether unusual recruit." It was more or less a foregone conclusion that Alexander would end up in the 342nd Field Artillery, although the *Sporting News* said several other units tried to "secure him as if he had been a new type of machine gun or the latest invention in long range cannon."[10]

Alexander only spent a few weeks at Camp Funston, although he did find time to marry his high school sweetheart in a ceremony performed in Manhattan by a Riley County probate judge. The Eighty-Ninth Division learned in mid-May that it would go to France, boarding trains for Camp Mills, New York, at the end of the month. Recently drafted men received little or no training, and some never had the opportunity to practice marksmanship at the rifle ranges. With regard to the 353rd (All Kansas) Regiment, the "strictest secrecy was enjoined upon all" of the Kansas troops, but nevertheless "crowds were at the stations to cheer the soldiers" on what was "the first trip across the country for many of the men." Just prior to the overseas departure of the Eighty-Ninth Division, its commanding officer, Major General Wood, was ordered by the War Department to return to Camp

Photo 7.2: Grover Cleveland Alexander, 1918. Courtesy of the National Baseball Hall of Fame and Museum.

Funston, where he trained the Tenth Division, which did not leave Kansas before the war ended.[11]

* * *

The African Americans of the Ninety-Second Division at Camp Funston were neither welcomed nor treated in the same manner as the men of the Eighty-Ninth. On August 31, 1917, Junction City filled its community building to capacity for an evening reception on behalf of General Wood upon his arrival to command the Eighty-Ninth Division. The subsequent influx of draftees in September was greeted with enthusiasm. On September 11 the residents of the neighboring city of Manhattan—by more than a two-to-one margin—approved a bond issue to build its own community building to entertain soldiers. The response was much different, however, when the War Department announced that some of the Black soldiers of the new Ninety-Second Division would be stationed at Camp Funston. "We are all writing our representatives at Washington," stated an October 16 editorial in the *Riley County Chronicle*, "to keep thousands of negro soldiers out of this state." Junction City officials, in a telegram sent to the War Department and members of the Kansas congressional delegation, declared that the town "shall not dare to keep open the community house heretofore built and since maintained by our citizens, if a large number of negro troops are sent to Camp Funston." A similar telegram was signed by the mayor of Manhattan, two city commissioners, the county and city attorney, the president of the local commercial club, and J. T. Willard, acting president of the Kansas State Agricultural College:

> Influx of large number of negro troops into parks, streets and places of amusement of small cities near Camp Funston would evidently result in race conflicts which the civilian authorities would be unable to control. The State College at Manhattan includes more than one thousand young women students who reside throughout the city and their welfare is gravely threatened by the proposed action. The whole moral situation of the town and country adjacent to the camp would be greatly disturbed.[12]

Despite suggestions to the contrary, the presence of Black soldiers in Kansas was not new. As historian Roger D. Cunningham notes, during the Civil War the state raised two African American infantry regiments and an artillery battery for Union service. The men of the First Kansas Colored Infantry in October 1862 became the first Black soldiers to engage Confederate forces. A *New York Times* correspondent described the skirmish at Island Mound, Missouri, as "a complete victory" and reported that the enemy "had at first a most contemptible idea of the negroes' courage, which their engagement speedily changed." Between 1867 and 1885, the Ninth Cavalry and Tenth Cavalry of the U.S. Army—the troops called Buffalo Soldiers by Native Americans—were garrisoned at Fort Riley. In 1887 the Kansas Constitution was amended to permit African Americans to participate in the state militia, and ten Black companies were organized between 1875 and 1894 in Kansas City, Lawrence, Leavenworth, Olathe, Topeka, Wichita, and Wyandotte. Although the Kansas National Guard refused to incorporate these units, many of their members helped form the Twenty-Third Kansas Volunteer Infantry Regiment, which during the Spanish-American War assisted in the occupation of Cuba.[13]

African Americans in the military at the beginning of World War I served in the Ninth and Tenth Cavalry, the Twenty-Fourth and Twenty-Fifth U.S. Infantry Regiments, and Black National Guard units in New York, Illinois, and a few other states. The vast majority of African Americans who served did so in the army: the Marine Corps and U.S. Army Air Corps did not accept Black men, and the U.S. Navy refused to enlist or employ them for jobs other than steward or mess-hall positions. The War Department decided early on to keep its existing all-Black regiments out of France but was unsure how to deploy the Black National Guard units and large number of African American draftees. (Thirteen percent of all conscripts were African American, though they were just 10 percent of the population.) The army's initial plan—to use the first seventy-five thousand Black draftees to create sixteen combat regiments—was discarded after members of the Twenty-Fourth Infantry responded to police misconduct by marching into Houston and killing eleven civilians and five policemen. The perpetrators of the "Camp Logan Mutiny" of August 23, 1917, were given sentences of death or life imprisonment, but the growing concern over arming tens of thousands of African Americans led officials to create a single Black infantry division in the Regular Army—the Ninety-Second (Buffalo Soldiers) Division—and place the remaining African American draftees in service and supply positions. A second segregated division—the Ninety-Third Infantry—was created by combining several Black National Guard units.[14]

The Ninety-Second Division was organized at Camp Funston in October 1917. Unlike other Regular Army divisions, the drafted men were put in seven separate camps, a decision that greatly undermined training but prevented the concentration of Black soldiers in one location. For example, the four infantry regiments (the 365th, 366th, 367th, and 368th) were sent to Iowa, Illinois, Maryland, and New York. The units stationed in Kansas included the division headquarters, the 349th Machine Gun Battalion, the military police, and the ammunition, supply, engineer, and sanitary trains. Black female nurses were also assigned to base hospitals at Camp Funston. Despite the dire warnings of local residents, when the Buffalo Soldiers arrived, there were few reported problems, due in part perhaps to having established a "negro zone" at the east end of camp, with "amusement places and exchanges" that were built to keep the Black soldiers "entirely separate" from the white soldiers. As reported by one African American who visited Camp Funston in March 1918, the Eighty-Ninth Division and the Ninety-Second Division were kept apart "by an imaginary line, yet a thoroughly distinct one."[15]

White senior officers and a large number of Black junior officers commanded the units of the Ninety-Second Division. After the war started, fourteen camps were established to train prospective white officers, but none were set up for African Americans. Partially in response to pressure from the Black community, the army established an officer training camp for African Americans at Fort Des Moines in Iowa. It was commanded by Colonel Charles C. Ballou, a West Point graduate (class of 1886) who would be promoted to brigadier general in August 1917 and major general in November. Of the 1,250 candidates, one-third came from civilian life, while the remaining two-thirds had been noncommissioned officers. An initial group of 639 men received commissions in October 1917 as second lieutenants, first lieutenants, and captains and then assigned to the seven training camps of the Ninety-Second Division. One hundred of the junior officers went to Camp Funston, where they joined General Ballou, recently named commander of the Ninety-Second Division. Among the 639 officers were twelve Kansans: three from Lawrence and Topeka, two from Leavenworth, and the other four from Baldwin, Fort Scott, Kansas City, and Ottawa. One of the officers, First Lieutenant Johnson Whittaker of Lawrence, was the son of Johnson Chestnut Whittaker, the victim of a brutal attack in 1880 by his fellow West Point cadets, who slashed him with a razor and knocked him unconscious. The elder Whittaker, who at the time was the only African American at the U.S. Military Academy, did not receive a commission and was instead court-martialed and expelled for allegedly faking his injuries, although the verdict was later overturned. In all, 1,200 African Americans received commissions, representing less than 1 percent of the officer strength of the U.S. Army.[16]

In 1879 several Kansas newspapers reprinted a poem (of sorts) published in the *New York Tribune*, in which "Uncle Sam" concludes that Black families would prefer Kansas over Kentucky and Mississippi based on the Sunflower State's supposed promise to African Americans:

> A home for every man and woman.
> A school for every child;—a field to labor.
> The guarantee that to every right that's human;
> Respect that sees in every man a neighbor.
> The richest soil a farmer ever saw,
> And equal rights to all before the law!

The suggestion that Kansas was colorblind is certainly fanciful. Nevertheless, Randall Woods contends that the "rigid system of Jim Crow" was not implemented in the Sunflower State because African Americans "did not constitute enough of a political or economic threat to warrant total ostracism." In contrast to Missouri, in 1894 over 40 percent of the Black members of the Grand Army of the Republic in Kansas belonged to integrated posts. In December 1915 the State Board of Review of Motion Pictures banned *The Birth of a Nation*, which portrays African Americans in a negative light, and as a consequence the most popular movie of the era was not shown in Kansas until 1924. African Americans generally fared better than Native Americans in nineteenth-century Kansas, in large part because the continued indigenous presence was an impediment to expansion.

Kansans, however, were not immune from taking actions to establish and enforce white supremacy. According to Brent Campney, while racist violence was most common in urban areas, "it also occurred in municipalities where whites implemented and enforced sundown practices." He identifies Augusta, Beloit, Caney, Frontenac, Hays, Hoisington, Liberal, and Mulberry as communities that either excluded African Americans or restricted their nighttime activities and movements. In December 1916 an estimated 250 Black residents were forced to leave the boomtown of El Dorado. Under the headline "It's White Man's Town Now," the *Arkansas City Daily Traveler* reported that "a race riot between oil workers and the negro populace . . . ended with the majority of the colored inhabitants being given floaters' tickets for the other lands."[17]

Emmett Jay Scott, a Black journalist and educator, chronicled the treatment of African Americans at Camp Funston. The forty-four-year-old Texan was an associate of Booker T. Washington at the Tuskegee Institute. Scott was appointed in October 1917 as a special assistant to Secretary of War Baker, a position he described as requiring him to "advise in matters affecting primarily the interests of colored draftees and colored soldiers, as well as render counsel and assistance in those matters." He later described two events that illuminate the treatment of Black soldiers at Camp Funston. The first was the issuance of a statement by General Ballou that received national attention and generated intense criticism from the Black community, while the second concerned the general's attempt to overcome the army's racist policies and promote an African American officer to a "whites only" position.

In March 1918 a Black sergeant of the Ninety-Second Division was asked to change seats at the Wareham Theatre in downtown Manhattan. When a similar incident had occurred the previous year in Iowa, the theater manager backed down when he was reminded of Colonel Ballou's threat to impose martial law if residents discriminated against the Black men at Fort Des Moines. In contrast, now-General Ballou did not threaten martial law or other dire action in Kansas. On March 28, 1918, he had his chief of staff issue the following remarkable document:

Bulletin No. 35, Headquarters, 92d Division, Camp Funston, Kans., Mar. 28, 1918

1. It should be well known to all colored officers and men that no useful purpose is served by such acts as will cause the "color question" to be raised. It is not a question of legal rights, but a question of policy, and any policy that tends to bring about a conflict of races, with its resulting animosities, is prejudicial to the military interest of the 92d Division, and therefore prejudicial to an important interest of the colored race.

2. To avoid such conflicts the Division Commander has repeatedly urged that all colored members of his command, and especially the officers [and] non-commissioned officers, should refrain from going where their presence will be resented. In spite of this injunction, one of the sergeants of the Medical Department has recently precipitated the precise trouble that should be avoided, and then called on the Division Commander to take sides in a row that should never have occurred had the Sergeant placed the general good above his personal pleasure and convenience. This Sergeant entered a theatre, as he undoubtedly had a legal right to do, and precipitated trouble by making it possible to allege race discrimination in the seat he was given. He is strictly within his legal rights in this matter, and the theatre manager is legally wrong. Nevertheless the Sergeant is guilty of the greater wrong in doing anything, no matter how legally correct, that will provoke race animosity.

3. The Division Commander repeats that the success of the Division, with all that success implies, is dependent upon the good will of the public. That public is nine-tenths white. White men made the Division, and they can break it just as easily if it becomes a trouble maker.

4. All concerned are again enjoined to place the general interest of the Division above personal pride and gratification. Avoid every situation that can give rise to racial ill-will. Attend quietly and faithfully to your duties, and don't go where your presence is not desired.

5. This will be read to all organizations of the 92d Division.

By command of Maj. Gen. Ballou.
Allen Greer,
Lieutenant Colonel.
U.S.A. Chief of Staff

The clear message from the white commanding officer was that "the success of the Division . . . is dependent upon the good will of the public," and consequently, the sergeant and all Black soldiers must compromise their civil rights.[18]

The theater incident and the issuance of Bulletin No. 35 do not appear to have been reported in the local newspapers. Strong protests, however, appeared in Black newspapers such as the *Topeka Plaindealer* ("Bulletin at Funston Request Blacks to Yield to Segregation; The Request Is Cowardly and a Disgrace to the Cause for Which They Are Fighting"), the *New York Age* ("'Don't Insist on Legal Rights,' Ballou Tells Colored Soldiers; Policy Is Put above the Law"), and the *Richmond Planet* ("Soldiers in the Black Division Advised to Accept Color Insults"). The *Kansas City Sun* printed a statement of protest that could be cut out, signed, and sent to the War Department describing the bulletin as "vicious in principle, unjust in operation in an army of democracy, and un-American in suggestion." In a subsequent edition the same newspaper declared, "if Negro men are good enough to die for their country they are good enough to be treated like human beings while making the sacrifice." The National Association for the Advancement of Colored People condemned Ballou's statements as "unjust, humiliating and inexpedient," while the National Equal Rights League in Boston requested that President Wilson take action to countermand the bulletin.[19]

When Emmett Scott, in his official capacity, asked Ballou for an explanation, the general responded with a letter. He explained that, after being told by the division judge advocate that the theater manager had violated the law, the general requested prosecution and thereafter counseled his soldiers to avoid race troubles. Mentioning the East St. Louis race riots and the "Houston troubles," Ballou said the officer candidates in Iowa "achieved a glorious success" by "following precisely the advice that was repeated to the 92d Division in Bulletin No. 35." One of his Black soldiers, "Lieutenant T. T. Thompson, assistant personnel officer of the Ninety-Second Division," wrote a long letter to the *New York Age*, noting that General Ballou took immediate action against the theater owner and that a similar policy was successful at Fort Des Moines. Thompson pointed out that all training camps forbid soldiers from "frequenting places of which would be subversive to the best interest of the army" and praised his commander for going "much farther than the white commanding officer usually goes to protect his soldiers against mistreatment." The *Nashville Globe* reported that the conviction of the theater manager—he was fined ten dollars and ordered to pay court costs—"will serve to prevent a repetition of the offense, and will deter other theater owners and managers from making discrimination on account of color." Adam Wilson has observed that Ballou "lost the respect of his black officers and troops," while Scott, in his 1919 book, declares that the general never did "regain the confidence of the colored masses, with whom he had been immensely popular prior to this episode."[20]

The second story concerns Lieutenant Toliver T. Thompson—the same man who defended General Ballou when he issued Bulletin No. 35. Scott describes in detail how the army's racist policies ended Thompson's military career. When the Ninety-Second Division was organized in October 1917, the War Department commanded that certain officers of the division "will be white," including "all officers attached to Division Headquarters, except the Lieutenants of the Headquarters Troop, [and] all Regimental Adjutants." Ballou nonetheless recommended that Lieutenant Thompson be promoted to captain and assigned as an assistant adjutant. "This officer," the general wrote, "has been in charge of the Personnel work of this Division practically from the time of its organization and his work has been found to be thoroughly satisfactory, and his promotion is therefore recommended so that he may continue on his present duty with adequate rank." When Thompson learned his promotion was denied because he was not white, the despondent Texan requested to be discharged from the service because he could no longer "work with the same spirit as an officer who feels that he is getting a square deal." Ballou reluctantly concurred with the request and made a point to inform his superiors that the army's policy was the cause of "the discouragement and lessened efficiency of an officer of considerable promise, who has much justice on his side in alleging race discrimination." In his letter to the *New York Age* defending his commanding officer, Thompson had written —prophetically—"it is expecting too much to demand that any part of the army turn aside from the main purpose [of the war effort] to fight out the race question."[21]

CHAPTER EIGHT

Camp Doniphan

Kansas and Missouri Guardsmen Form the Thirty-Fifth Division

In the fall of 1917, Kansas "regulars" and volunteers were training in army camps all across the country, while draftees remained in state at Camp Funston. The First Ammunition Train of the Kansas National Guard was sent to Camp Mills, New York, where it became part of the Forty-Second (Rainbow) Division. The rest of the Kansas National Guard went to Camp Doniphan in Oklahoma, where it joined with the Missouri National Guard to form the Thirty-Fifth Infantry Division. In the span of one year—May 1917 to May 1918—the guardsmen of Jefferson County were transferred from Company B, Second Kansas Regiment to Company B, Third Kansas Regiment; discharged from the National Guard; drafted into the U.S. Army; reorganized as Company B, 139th Regiment; stationed in Oklahoma for six months; sent to Camp Mills; and then transported by ships to England and France. A few of the men could draw upon their service in 1916 on the Mexican border to help with this transition, but most had no prior military training to fall back on.

The combined Holton-Oskaloosa company as part of the Second Kansas Regiment was not a satisfactory arrangement, and consequently the formation of the new Third Kansas Regiment was a boost to the recruiting efforts of Lieutenant Will Smith. "We now have a company of our own," he announced in the May 25, 1917, edition of the *Jefferson County Tribune*, "with our own officers." The commanding officer, Captain Guy Walling, was not from Jefferson County, electing to remain at his residence in nearby Lawrence and drive to Oskaloosa to drill the men. Crowds would gather to watch as the young soldiers proudly marched through the streets and around the courthouse square. The distant war in Europe became more real on July 10 when President Wilson announced that all guardsmen would be discharged on August 5 and drafted into the army. Ralph Nichols and Ted Blevins left Oskaloosa—presumably with official permission—and spent the last three weeks in July harvesting wheat on a farm in McPherson County (for room and board and three dollars a day). When they returned at the end of the month, Company B had increased to about 125 men, and planning was underway for mobilization and transport of the Kansas National Guard to a training camp in Oklahoma.[1]

With the exception of three men who could not convince their wives to sign a release, the men of Company B gathered in Oskaloosa on August 5, a Sunday morning, to be mustered in to the U.S. Army. The soldiers were now fed at federal expense, and the restaurants in town filled to capacity. A company glee club was organized, vaccinations and inoculations were administered, and a shower bath was installed in the building at the rear of the State Bank. Enrollment soon increased to 145 soldiers with the addition of men from Emporia, Salina, and Kansas City. Uniforms, shoes, and rifles remained in short supply. The *Oskaloosa Independent* advised readers that the best time to observe the unit was at six in evening, when "the corporal on top of the armory takes down the flag while the whole company, officers and men, stand at salute." On August 14 several wagonloads of socks, shoes, underwear, pants, and coats arrived. On the twenty-second Nichols celebrated his eighteenth birthday. By this time, William Davis and Melvin Dyson had joined Company B.[2]

* * *

William Louis Davis was born on June 7, 1895, in Jefferson County. He was five feet ten inches in height and had blue eyes, light hair, and a fair complexion. His maternal grandfather was an acquaintance of Abraham Lincoln, and his father, John W. Davis, was a prominent stockman and farmer who owned land northwest of Winchester. William's mother died in 1906 prior to his tenth birthday, and his father twice remarried, first in 1907 and then in 1928 after his second wife died. William was the second oldest of six children, two years younger than his sister Grace.

Davis listed his occupation as "farm hand" on his 1917 registration card and did not claim an exemption. Rather than wait to see when his number would be selected in the draft lottery, the twenty-two-year-old enlisted on June 16 with Company B. Ten other men from Winchester also signed up, including two second cousins, Lester and Lewis Davis.[3]

* * *

John Melvin Dyson, who went by his middle name, was born on July 3, 1899. When he was seven, his midnight cry of alarm alerted his parents that their attic had caught fire from the kitchen stovepipe. Marion, Anna, and Melvin escaped through a window, but most of the house was destroyed. The *Oskaloosa*

Photo 8.1: William Davis. Courtesy of the National WWI Museum and Memorial, Kansas City, Missouri, USA.

Independent reported that "little Melvin Dyson, whose best clothes, shoes, and cap were all burned, was called down to the Cash Clothing store by Ed Trapp and fitted out from head to foot in nice new clothing." Over the next several years, his father apparently took jobs in Colorado, Texas, and New Mexico. At some point his mother left the family, and Marion remarried and moved with his new wife and Melvin to Fort Worth, Texas. In the summer of 1910, Dyson went missing at age eleven for at least three months. It is not known when and where he was found, but by 1915, Melvin and his father were back in Oskaloosa. The next newspaper mention of the family came that same year, when his mother, Anna, was charged in Topeka with keeping a disorderly house and being drunk. A jury returned a guilty verdict, no doubt because the police found a whiskey glass on her clothing as well as a bottle containing whiskey. According to the *Daily Capital*, one of the people who was at her residence at the time of the arrest was the secretary of the state temperance union, who said he did not know it was a disorderly place.

Having turned eighteen the previous month, Melvin Dyson enlisted on August 16, 1917, after Company B had been mustered in to federal service. A majority of the men in Company B were under twenty-one at that time, including Dyson, Nichols, Ted Blevins, Vic Segraves, Sam Gutschenritter, and Billy Kimmel.[4]

* * *

On September 1 the men of Company B donned their soft indented hats with wide circular brims and posed for a photograph on the west side of the Oskaloosa town square, in front of the courthouse and bandstand. Several weddings took place at this time, including the union on September 18 of Lieutenant Smith and Ada Walker, a classmate at Washburn College and now a teacher in Valley Falls. The federalized guardsmen were ready to serve, but the movement orders from the War Department did not please most of the Kansans. One objection concerned Camp Doniphan, which was viewed as an undesirable location:

> This is a big country and there are innumerable localities in it suitable for military training camps where clouds of dust borne by high winds are not daily occurrences and where the water is abundant and pure. It certainly is too bad, therefore, that Camp Doniphan should have been located at a place where the best that can be said of the water is that it is "not so bad as gypsum water, or alkali water," and where the sun is obscured for days at a time by the dust.

The second complaint concerned the consolidation of the Kansas National Guard with the Missouri National Guard. Because the Third Kansas Regiment had only been recently formed, when the Kansas Guard was combined with its Missouri counterpart, many of its officers lost their positions. "The proposal . . . is unjust to Kansas," declared Governor Capper. "It subordinates the Kansas troops and is not satisfactory to either state." In response, Secretary Baker said the decision was made in light of the War Department's plan to deploy larger companies, regiments, and divisions, which would require fewer officers and enable the fighting units to remain in the field for longer periods.[5]

Company B departed Oskaloosa on September 24, a Monday evening. Jefferson County schools were dismissed to allow teachers and students to attend the farewell ceremonies. By midafternoon, a crowd estimated at three thousand people enjoyed music provided by bands from Valley Falls and Winchester, then listened attentively as the Reverend Dr. Bernard Kelly of Topeka, a Civil War veteran, spoke about ridding the world of "Kaiserism." Following a half-hour drill on the west side of the square, soldiers and families sat together and enjoyed "all the good things that go to make up a Jefferson County, Kansas, U.S.A. picnic dinner." The Rexall drugstore served refreshments and—perhaps a gentle reminder—distributed bars of soap. The men then regrouped in front of the armory and stood at salute while the national flag was lowered and presented to the mayor. The time had come to leave, and the soldiers marched in their suits to the train depot west of town. The young soldiers, who passed by veterans holding flags along their route, were followed by people in automobiles and on foot; the parked vehicles "stretched up the hill and around the bend nearly a quarter of a mile from the depot." The train slowly pulled out from the station, then passed through Ozawkie and Meridan, where crowds gathered in the twilight to add their cheers and good wishes.

The emotional day was the subject of commentary by editor Frank Roberts in the September 28 edition of the *Independent*:

> The ring of martial feet on our paved streets is no longer heard. The shouts of command are stilled. No longer do the cheery notes of the bugle thrill the heart—no more the hurrying feet speed to company formation amid laugh and jest. . . . How we miss the boys! It hurts to have them go. But it would have hurt worse to have them refuse to go when their country needed them and called for their stout arms.

The short trip ended in Topeka, where most of the soldiers slept on the floor at Hamilton Hall, on the corner of Quincy Street and Sixth Avenue, although some went to the homes of friends or to hotels. The next morning Company B marched down Kansas Avenue to the Rock Island depot at Second Street, endured a brief thunderstorm, waited several hours, and then departed in the early afternoon with the regimental band and the supply company. On board were First Lieutenant Will Smith, First Sergeant Jesse Blevins, Sergeant Ted Blevins, Corporal Vic Segraves, Privates First Class Sam Gutschenritter and William Kimmel, and Privates William Davis, Melvin Dyson, and Ralph Nichols. Joe Douglas of Oskaloosa, age fifty-three, and his son John, age nineteen, were also members of Company B, as were Lawrence Robbins of Perry and Robert Austin of Oskaloosa, who were both sixteen. Ted Blevins noted years later the contrast with his previous departure to Texas: "This time there was more seriousness with us all. We didn't know if we'd be coming back."[6]

The guardsmen joined their Missouri counterparts in Oklahoma to form the Thirty-Fifth Division. Kansans who feared unfair treatment may have pointed out that their shared camp was named for Colonel Alexander William Doniphan, a soldier and politician from Missouri. Although state officials were displeased, and some Kansas officers were reassigned, the

Photo 8.2: Parade in Oskaloosa, Kansas, September 24, 1917. Courtesy of the Kansas State Historical Society.

consolidation was accomplished without major difficulties. To achieve the army's new requirement of 250 men, Company B, Third Kansas joined with Company B, Fourth Missouri, which resulted in a surplus that caused the transfer of men to other units. "They seem to be a nice bunch," noted Ted Blevins, who also observed that a few of the men from the Missouri "boot heel" region could not read or write. The *Oskaloosa Independent* reported, "contrary to prophecies that Missourians and Kansans could not get along, the 139th is as near a camp of brotherly love as it is possible for one to be." It is not known whether Jesse Blevins shared this view, especially after being reduced to supply sergeant and then transferred to the ammunition train. Dyson was also transferred, going to the Supply Company along with Joe and John Douglas and a few other men from Jefferson County. By March 1918, there were fewer then ninety men from Jefferson County in the consolidated Company B, and Lieutenant Smith was the only remaining commissioned officer from Kansas. Nichols tried to join his older brother Charles in the aviation corps, but his transfer request was denied. Gutschenritter and Kimmel were promoted to corporals, Vic Segraves became a sergeant, and Ted Blevins was made acting first sergeant. Frank Roberts, the son of the editor of the *Independent*, received an appointment to West Point, while Ted took the academy's entrance exam but was not accepted, perhaps because, as he later explained, "they gave us a lot of European history stuff and I never had any of it."[7]

Of the eight National Guard regiments sent to Camp Doniphan, five were from Missouri and three were from Kansas. The 137th Regiment was another all-Kansas unit, comprising the First and Second Kansas Infantry. The 138th and 140th Infantry were formed with four regiments of Missouri guardsmen. The only "mixed" unit was the 139th Regiment, which consisted of men from the Third Kansas Infantry and the Fourth Missouri Infantry. The 137th and 138th were grouped with the 129th Machine Gun Battalion to form the Sixty-Ninth Infantry Brigade, and the 139th and 140th joined with the 130th Machine Gun Battalion as the Seventieth Infantry Brigade. The First Kansas Field Artillery was part of the Sixtieth Artillery Brigade, which also included the First and Second Missouri Field Artillery. One of the Missouri gunners was Harry S. Truman. The future president enlisted at age thirty-three as a private, became a first lieutenant in a newly formed artillery unit, trained at Camp Doniphan and in France, and then as Captain Truman of Battery D, 129th Field Artillery, commanded two hundred men in the Vosges Mountains and during the Meuse-Argonne offensive.[8]

The auxiliary units of the Thirty-Fifth Division were either mixed or allocated to one state. For example, the supply train, trench mortar battery, and machine-gun battalions were from Missouri; the engineer (transport) train and the field signal battalion were from Kansas; and guardsmen from both states served as engineers and medical personnel. In order to bring the 8,500 Kansans and the 14,765 Missourians up to full divisional strength (27,000), draftees were added where needed in November. In terms of overall command, the Thirty-Fifth Division was led by Major General William M. Wright, a soldier greatly respected by General Pershing and with whom he roomed at West Point before Wright left the academy. When General Wright was sent to France in the fall of 1917 to tour the trenches, temporary command at Camp Doniphan went first to Brigadier General Lucien Berry, Sixtieth Field Artillery Brigade, and then to Charles Martin, who had resigned his position as Kansas adjutant general to become a brigadier general in charge of the Seventieth Infantry Brigade.[9]

Camp Doniphan was located at Fort Sill, a few miles north of Lawton, Oklahoma (and not far from the grave of Geronimo, the Apache leader who died as a military prisoner there in 1909). This tent camp, which occupied twelve hundred acres, was virtually devoid of trees or vegetation. It was laid out in the form of a horseshoe, opening to the east, with Company B, 139th

Regiment assigned to its western edge, closest to the Wichita Mountains. Camp construction was not yet completed when the men from Kansas and Missouri arrived. Over the next two months, wooden floors and side walls were placed in tents, stoves were issued (and placed in boxes filled with sand), and warm water was provided for bath houses. "We are real folks now," Ted Blevins wrote on November 21, with "electric lights in our houses." Each tent housed eight men and their canvas cots. A trolley line went to Lawton, and taxis could also be hired, although drivers may have been reluctant to make the return trip. When soldiers came back to camp, Blevins recalled, "they'd jump out of the taxis, run and scatter, rather than pay, and the poor taxi driver couldn't collect."[10]

In their letters and other historical accounts, Kansans at Camp Doniphan focused on the physical environment, health concerns, and contact with the outside world. At the same time, the men were kept busy training to fight in the trenches and learning the craft of modern warfare.

Concerns about camp conditions, expressed even before the National Guard units left their respective states, were warranted. Charles Hoyt, who published his history of the Thirty-Fifth Division one year after the war concluded, observed, "Camp Doniphan, from a soldier's point of view, lacked everything but dust." When Governor Capper reviewed the Kansas troops on October 25, the *Oskaloosa Independent* reported that "it was so dusty and so windy that no one could see or hear." Strong winds hurled pebbles "as big as peas" into the faces of men and blew away tents, which were never found. "I enlisted to fight for my country," cracked Walton Priest, a corporal in the 137th Regiment, "not to eat it." To add to the soldiers' misery, the water was bad and the winter of 1917–1918 was cold. According to a letter from "one of the Company B boys," when water from a lake was stored overnight, "a layer of mud and moss settles to the bottom of the bucket." As for the lack of heat, Ted Blevins remembered needing "six or so blankets over us to keep warm at night. Sometimes we'd put two cots together and share blankets so we'd have more over us."[11]

Whereas battling the physical conditions at Camp Doniphan was a challenge, maintaining good health was a matter of life and death. Both Davis and Ted Blevins wrote about the strict measures imposed to prevent outbreaks of disease and illness. "They had our tent quarantined for 18 days for the measles," Davis told his father in January 1918. "It was a boy from Oskie. He is still in the hospital." The "boy from Oskie" was Private Charles Thomas "Tommy" Gutschenritter, the younger brother of Sam Gutschenritter. Their father, Charley, registered as an alien enemy on February 4, 1918.

Three days later he and his wife, Martha (who would register as an alien enemy in June), received a telegram from a medical officer at Camp Doniphan. Their son was seriously ill and not expected to recover. Martha's brother, John Blockwicz, went with Charley by train to Oklahoma, but the two men discovered upon arrival that Tommy had died on the seventh, four hours after the telegram was sent. The young man, who was described as quiet in nature, had seemingly recovered from the measles when he contracted a fatal case of pneumonia. A Roman Catholic priest, a military band, and a group of friends accompanied the body to the train station, where a firing squad provided the traditional volley of three shots. Sam served as an additional escort back to Jefferson County, where Tommy was buried in his uniform. For the Gutschenritters, it was a traumatic month because of the war.[12]

Governor Capper in January demanded that medical care at Camp Doniphan be improved, noting that soldiers were telling their families that they refused to respond to sick call because they did not want to be sent to the hospital. Homer Lillie of Winchester was sent back to Company B after he first went to the hospital, and when he was finally admitted for treatment, it was too late to prevent his death on February 22. Private Lillie had purchased a soldier's life-insurance policy of ten thousand dollars, naming his widowed mother as the beneficiary. Over 90 percent of the men at Camp Doniphan were insured, including Davis, who told his father, "I think I will take out that Insurance," and Ted Blevins, who purchased a policy in January, a month before the February 12 deadline. In a letter written on November 2, 1917—the day before the first Americans were killed in action in France—Ted told his parents that he would "see about [cousin] Ed's insurance," adding, "we will come back. I've never doubted that." It is not known whether Ed Blevins was insured, but he died in battle on September 28, 1918.[13]

A third point mentioned in letters and newspaper articles about life at Camp Doniphan was the desire for contact with the outside world. "I sure am lonesome," Corporal Kimmel wrote in November 1917, "to see Old Oska." To remind the boys of Jefferson County, the Oskaloosa and Winchester "Military Sisterhood" shipped over twenty barrels of red apples to Company B in the fall and sent dish towels and "boxes of Christmas good things" in the winter. Some family members traveled to Oklahoma, including Lillie's sister and mother, who were present at his death; Jessie Blevins, mother of Jesse and Ted Blevins; John Davis, father of William Davis; and Lucy Smith, mother of Will Smith. A few soldiers, including Melvin Dyson and Smith, were able to obtain furloughs and return home, but most could not leave camp. Jesse

Blevins was able to obtain a seven-day furlough in February 1918 to marry his fiancée, Marie Peterson, at the Manhattan home of her parents.[14]

A surprising number of Company B soldiers (at least fifteen) simply went home, which Ted Blevins called "French leave"—in contrast to the French, who used the phrase *filer à l'anglaise* ("to leave English style") to describe a soldier leaving his post without authorization. In a letter written on Christmas Day, 1917, Davis told his father that he had thought about taking "a dutch furlough" but was concerned about being fined and sent to the guardhouse. Ted Blevins, who was denied a furlough, went home for a different reason: to retrieve his classmate, Merle Trapp, and two other soldiers who had been arrested and put in jail after using fake documents to leave camp. The *Oskaloosa Independent* reported that nine boys from Atchison and seven from Hiawatha were also arrested, noting that the Oskaloosa boys were not overly concerned: "Trapp's bugle rings out daily from the jail." As it turned out, Sergeant Blevins followed his orders, handcuffed Trapp and his comrades, and returned them to Camp Doniphan, where they each paid seventy-five dollars in fines and costs and worked after drill hours for sixty days. "I took their handcuffs off on the train 'till we got to Fort Sill," Ted told his parents. "There hasn't been a single a.w.o.l. this payday in the Company, something new."[15]

Robert Ferrell has argued that one reason the men fared poorly in France was because their training did not prepare them for the type of fighting that took place in the Meuse-Argonne offensive. While it is true that the Thirty-Fifth Division at Camp Doniphan initially focused on trench warfare instead of open-field tactics, the "well-trained" and heralded Eighty-Ninth Division received similar instruction at Camp Funston. But many factors besides training affected the performance of the Thirty-Fifth Division (as discussed in chapter 17).

Sergeant Dean Trickett of Company A, 139th Regiment described his experience at Camp Doniphan years later near the end of another world war:

> During the first four months the training program was based on trench warfare as practiced on the Western Front. The boys spent weeks digging trenches [that were] pulverized by high explosives. On the bayonet course . . . the boys lunged savagely at dummy Boches, but it is doubtful if any member of the division ever stuck a bayonet into a German. Trained from youth to throw baseball fashion, they wrenched their shoulders mastering the windmill style of lobbing hand grenades. . . . In midwinter the

> army junked the trench-warfare program and reverted to the traditional American system of training for open warfare. The trench fighters unhooked their bayonets and tried out their Springfields on the rifle range.

The focus on constructing trenches seems odd in retrospect, given that the fortifications were already in place in Europe. The men would use picks and shovels for ten minutes, then rest ten minutes. "I don't blame the Germans for hanging on to a trench," said Sergeant Segraves, "if the ground over there is as hard as it is here." Lieutenant Smith received high praise—"Bill can't be beaten"—for his willingness to take part: "He is studying and working hard every day," reported a letter in the *Valley Falls Vindicator*, "and he goes out into the trenches with a pick and shovel just like the rest of the men."[16]

In addition to bayonets and grenades, the men were instructed on the use of gas masks. "One must remember to breathe thru the mouth when wearing the mask," one soldier explained in a letter. "Some of the boys forgot this and had quite a time until they got used to it." Another novel experience for many were airplanes. According to Virgil Willis of Iola, the men "sunburned the roofs of our mouths looking at the aeroplanes when we first came down here." What was not new was the food, described as "plain but plenty," with "bacon or beef, three times a day, with one vegetable always and usually two, plenty of bread, coffee or tea, oatmeal or some other breakfast food in the morning and cooked fruit or pudding of some sort with one or two of the meals every day." Ted Blevins, when asked about rations, agreed that the food "was generally good there at Fort Sill," adding that the sergeants lived together, "and our supply sergeant would often bring us steaks for a special mess."

Officers, both commissioned and noncommissioned, received separate instruction. Lieutenant Smith spent many hours in officer training courses, and Sergeant Blevins informed his parents in October that he drilled during the day and went to "non-com school" in the evenings. In November Ted reported that he was "busy as a cranberry merchant at Xmas time," with "bayonet school in the morning and school of musketry in the p.m." Time was also set aside for physical fitness. "We hiked 4 miles until noon," he wrote in October, "had 2 bacon sandwiches for dinner and then dug [trenches] this afternoon, and hiked back 4 miles." In March 1918, at the end of their time at Camp Doniphan, the men of Company B went on a six-day hike.[17]

On March 21 the German army began its spring offensive, hoping to divide the French and British armies and push the British Expeditionary Force

Photo 8.3: Uncle Sam postcard sent by William Davis to John Davis, April 9, 1917. Courtesy of the National WWI Museum and Memorial, Kansas City, Missouri, USA.

into the sea. At about the same time, the Thirty-Fifth Division was preparing to leave Camp Doniphan. Company B, 139th Infantry left on April 8, taking a train that went through Kansas on its way to New York. John Davis received a patriotic postcard that was dropped off a train at Topeka by his son, William, who had not been able to tell his family he would be traveling near Jefferson County. Ted Blevins was able to send information about the trip and visited family members at stops in Topeka and Kansas City. Both Davis and Blevins sent letters from Camp Mills, Long Island, where they were stationed for about two weeks. Blevins recounted the trip, which included a boat ride down the Hudson River, described sightseeing in New York City, and related how he and the other Kansas soldiers were questioned about Indians and buffalos: "We gave them a good line—how we had to be on guard constantly to protect ourselves. They took it all in." Davis asked his father about the farm, said he was in good health, and promised to "write more the next time and sooner."[18]

On April 26 Lieutenant Bill Smith—as he was now referred to in the *Oskaloosa Independent*—sent a telegraph with one word: "goodbye." Company B left New York on the RMS *Caronia*, a British ocean liner that had been converted to a troopship. Sergeant Dean Trickett described the trip as "cold and windy, with high seas running":

> To avoid submarines, the convoy was routed far to the north, reaching at one time the latitude of the southern tip of Greenland. Near the Scottish coast it turned southward into the Irish Sea. The *Caronia* docked at Liverpool on the morning of May 7. Late in the afternoon the company entrained for southern England, where it went into quarantine. Thousands of Britons lined the streets of Liverpool through which the regiment marched to the railway station.

Reverend and Mrs. Nichols received a cablegram from England sent by their son Ralph that simply said, "Arrived safe." In a letter written to his high school teacher (that was censored by Lieutenant Smith), Nichols asked about the county track meet and provided a snapshot of England: "The country has the prettiest scenery that I have ever seen. The trees are swell. The fields are kept as clean and neat as a pin." On May 16 the 139th Infantry boarded cattle boats, with soldiers bunked in the stalls, that then charted a zigzag course across the English Channel. After disembarking at Le Havre, the men of Company B were billeted in a British camp on the high bluff overlooking the port. They were in France.[19]

* * *

When the Kansas National Guard was sent to Camp Doniphan in September 1917, many soldiers seeking female correspondents handed out slips of paper at train stops that included their name and address. Arbie Langley, a twenty-one-year-old private from Oskaloosa, was one of the members of Company B who threw such a paper slip from a railroad-car window. Sixteen-year-old Ida Thierstein of Whitewater, a town northeast of Wichita, selected Langley's slip because it had the "best handwriting." They wrote to each other during the war and were married in Wichita on February 1, 1921. Sixty-five years later, retired automobile mechanic Arbie Langley died at age ninety in Whitewater, survived by his wife, four children, and nine grandchildren. Ida passed away in 1991, also at age ninety.[20]

CHAPTER NINE

The Kansas Home Front, 1917

Support, Suppression, and Suspicion

When war against Germany was declared in April 1917, most Kansans who favored neutrality immediately changed course. Governor Capper worked closely with the federal government to mobilize citizens, agriculture, and industry. Colleges and universities changed their educational programs to help train students for military service. In communities all across the state, young men said goodbye to their friends and families, and the towns of Manhattan and Junction City experienced a dramatic influx of soldiers at Camp Funston. Kansans prepared for war but did not experience its full effects—except in a few instances—until the following year.

Although the topics overlap to some degree, a discussion of the 1917 Kansas "home front" can be divided into four parts: positive patriotism, abridgement of civil liberties, treatment of conscientious objectors, and anti-German sentiment. Kansans created a "Council of Defense" and increased food production, reduced food consumption, purchased Liberty Bonds, and responded enthusiastically to patriotic speeches, books, and films. They also suppressed opposing viewpoints and disparaged and mistreated "slackers" and pacifists. The enemy was dehumanized as "Huns" and "the Boche," and anti-German sentiment in some instances bordered on paranoia and hysteria.

Most Kansas residents actively engaged in positive patriotism. On March 15, 1917, Governor Capper held a conference in Topeka to discuss the need to increase agricultural production in the state. "The world needs every pound of foodstuffs that we can produce," he said, "and the world is ready to pay for it; so, patriotism aside, business sense says, 'Produce it!'" Due to the fighting in Europe and elsewhere, the world's food supply was below normal, and over half of the previous wheat crop in Kansas had failed. The farmers, bankers, businessmen, and academic experts who attended the conference were among the very first in the country to recommend the creation of a federal commission to regulate the storage and distribution of food products. They also resolved that residents in cities and towns grow garden "truck crops" for table use and "preserve by canning or in storage all surplus products for winter use." Dr. Henry J. Waters, president of the Kansas State Agricultural College, pointed out that farmers seeking to grow more crops would be hard pressed by the scarcity of labor. Dr. William A. McKeever, professor of child welfare at the University of Kansas, promoted "backyard gardening" by boys, noting, "Kansas has [between] 50,000 and 200,000 half-grown boys who should be mobilized into an army of food producers." The *Wichita Eagle* summed up the suggestions as follows: "A vegetable garden in every backyard in the cities. A potato patch on every vacant lot possible in the cities. An extra half acre of potatoes on every farm possible in the state. More common sense in expenditures in Kansas homes." The *Topeka Daily Capital* declared it was time to reverse the advice of populist Mary Elizabeth Lease and "raise more corn and less hell."[1]

The Topeka food conference was the origin of the State Council for Defense, created in April and charged by Governor Capper with "the safeguarding of property, the promotion of production, the conserving of foodstuffs, the care of dependents, and a general mobilization of the resources of Kansas in the defense of the country." The council was headed by Dr. Waters and included Adjutant General Martin, newspaper editor William Allen White, and academic officials from the University of Kansas, Kansas State, and the colleges at Emporia, Hays, and Pittsburg. Work assignments were allocated to twenty committees, including agricultural production, finance, labor, manufactures, public defense, publicity, and social hygiene. In both 1917 and 1918, the Defense Council published a series of circulars providing practical advice to farmers (seed selection), families (canning instructions), and teachers (suggestions for instructing "City Boys" regarding work horses, farm machinery, and dairy cows). The council also urged Congress to adopt national prohibition as a war-emergency measure, pointing to the annual waste of one hundred million bushels of valuable grain in making whisky and beer. Just two weeks earlier, on February 23, 1917, 150 legislators sang Irving Berlin's "How Dry I Am" as Governor Capper signed the "bone dry" law, which made it illegal for anyone to possess intoxicating liquors other than wine for communion purposes.[2]

The campaign to increase the production of wheat and other food products was largely successful. The Committee of Agricultural Production helped ensure a bountiful harvest by assisting farmers in locating available seed, employing school children to conduct germinating tests, and facilitating the extension of credit to pay for labor and equipment. Beginning in July, over twenty-three thousand people watched *Winning with Wheat*, a movie produced by the Kansas State Agricultural College. This silent film, according to the *Wichita Beacon*, was "made under actual Kansas conditions, with actual Kansas farmers as principals, with a Kansas girl to fill out the love plot." The *Leavenworth Post* enticed its readers by describing the movie as "intensely interesting" and by providing the following plot summary: "A young man gets interested in the appeal of the Kansas Council of Defense for more and better wheat and tries to get his father to get into the game. The old man ridicules the idea, but allows his son to try out his 'fool notions.' The son raises 36 bushels of wheat per acre to his father's 15 and he marries the girl and all goes well." In one of its circulars, the Defense Council declared that Kansas farmers "have a duty to perform no less than that of the man in the trenches." After the war ended, Governor Capper proudly reported that Kansas "put in the greatest acreage of crops ever recorded in the state" and "did more than her full share in feeding our own troops, our allied troops, and the homeless and destitute of a war-ridden continent."[3]

On August 10, 1917, President Wilson established the U.S. Food Administration. Herbert Hoover became food administrator, and Dr. Waters was put in charge of conservation efforts in Kansas. As reported in the *Oskaloosa Independent*, Hoover declared, "an average saving of two cents on each meal every day for each person will save to the Nation for war purposes 2 billion dollars per annum." To avoid rationing, Americans refrained from eating certain foods and "Hooverized" on meatless Mondays and wheatless Wednesdays. Recipes for "Victory Bread" were distributed, enabling families to bake "John Pershing Bread" and "Leonard Wood Bread" (1 1/4 cups mashed potato or sweet potato packed solid; 1 1/2 teaspoons salt; 1/8 to 1/4 yeast cake softened in 2 tablespoons lukewarm water; and 2 1/4 cups flour more or less). As noted in her diary, Arthusa "Nettie" Crandall of Oskaloosa made "barley and oatmeal bread" and "pie with barley crust." Some Topeka bakers stopped making cakes and other confections altogether, and several Kansas newspapers reprinted a story about a hotel that urged its customers to use only one lump of sugar in their coffee or tea and "stir like hell." The Council of Defense went beyond its food-thrift campaign and counseled students to reduce expenditures "in entertainment, dress, and especially in social eating and drinking." It requested that women to abstain from "anything showy or elaborate" and asked "all people, as a patriotic duty, to seek simpler standards of living, and to avoid ostentation and display." Such entreaties were apparently successful since there is no indication of an overabundance of showy and ostentatious Kansans during the war.[4]

The Council of Defense also cooperated with the federal government's efforts to sell war bonds. Pursuant to the Emergency Loan Act of April 24, 1917, the Treasury Department issued $1.9 billion in bonds, followed by an additional $3.8 billion under the Second Liberty Loan Act of October 1. William McAdoo, the secretary of the Treasury (and son-in-law of President Wilson), appeared on May 25 at the Topeka city auditorium, receiving a "rousing reception" and securing a pledge from twelve hundred bankers to do all in their power to sell war bonds. At the same time, Governor Capper urged residents to "show the Nation that the people of Kansas are willing and glad to contribute from their bounty to the sustenance of our armies and the support of our allies across the sea." The Berkson Brothers' department store in Topeka designated May 31, 1917, as Liberty Loan Day, announcing that the day's receipts would be used to purchase bonds. On June 2 Pastor M. L. Wickman of the Concordia Methodist Church read from Judges 5:23, in which an angel curses the village of Meroz because its inhabitants "came not to the help of the Lord . . . against the mighty." In the *Arkansas City Daily Traveler* on the sixth, readers were cajoled to buy bonds after being reminded, "You've got money for clothing, and money for hats; for building new houses and furnishing new flats; . . . for races and banquets and lodges and clubs; for boosting the Giants and backing the Cubs." To cap off the bond campaign, famed aviator Ruth Law Oliver included Hutchinson and Wichita as part of her nationwide tour. Flying under her maiden name, "Miss Law" dropped bomb-shaped leaflets that read "A Liberty Bond in Your Home or a German Bomb on Your Home—Which Is Your Choice?"[5]

Beginning in September, the purchase of Liberty Bonds was encouraged by local Four Minute Men in the cinemas. As reported in the *Topeka Daily Capital*, their four-minute talks were "serious, thoughtful propaganda that . . . cause the patriotic blood of this state to boil." According to one report, Kansas led the nation in this program, with 155 Four Minute Men chairmen—six more than New York and almost four times as many as Missouri. In addition to speeches, Kansans also responded enthusiastically to patriotic music, films, and books. The lyrics to "Over There" by George M. Cohan were printed in the *Wichita Daily Eagle*, and a local woman, Emma Strode LaPaz, wrote a war song, "I'm Dreaming of You, Sweetheart," in which a soldier recalls "the smile that gave me courage to respond to Duty's call." Many Kansans went to the theaters in 1917 to watch *The Slacker*, produced by Metro Pictures and released on July 16, just four days before the national draft lottery. In the story, when Margaret learns Robert married her to avoid induction, she calls him a slacker and a coward. Fortunately, after

Photo 9.1: Music sheet title page, *Your Lips Are No Man's Land But Mine* (Jos. W. Stern). Courtesy of the National WWI Museum and Memorial, Kansas City, Missouri, USA.

a series of patriotic flashbacks—one shows Francis Scott Key writing "The Star-Spangled Banner"—Robert stands up to a German who has insulted the American flag, decides to enlist, says goodbye to his wife, and marches off to war. The *Parsons Daily Sun* gave *The Slacker* high marks, saying, "no American can see it without feeling a deeper love and appreciation for his country," and the *Coffeyville Daily Journal* declared that "every alien" who watches the movie will "regret he isn't allied with the Stars and Stripes."[6]

The most influential book of the year was Arthur Guy Empey's *Over the Top*, a personal war narrative that achieved best-seller status. Empey left the United States in 1915, enlisted with the British Army, served in the trenches as a sergeant, and was wounded at the Battle of the Somme. His book sold over 350,000 copies in 1917 and more than 1 million copies by war's end. Kansans embraced Empey's book because his stories, as noted by the *Williamstown News*, "are grim, but they are thrilling, and they are lightened by a delightful touch of humor." The multitalented Empey—he also wrote lyrics to songs such as "Your Lips Are No Man's Land but Mine" and "Our Country's in

It Now, We've Got to Win It Now"—brought the war home to America. As Kimberly Lamay Licursi points out: "His book and lectures portrayed the war as thrilling, justified, and patriotic and encouraged other men to follow in his adventurous footsteps. The highly jingoistic tale was pure war boosterism. He coyly told American boys that the war was not all death and destruction, that there was a lot of fun to be had. The government could not have invented a better war propagandist than Empey."

Serial excerpts from *Over the Top* were published in newspapers in over twenty-five Kansas towns, including Kansas City, Manhattan, and Salina, as well as in tiny hamlets such as Gaylord, Kincaid, and Meridan. The *Independence Evening Star* declared in November 1917 that it was "the most talked of book . . . at Case's Book Store," and in that same month, Caroline Medlicott, a Topeka librarian, reported, "our greatest call is for '*Over the Top*' by Empey." President Wilson and his wife in March 1918 attended the premiere of the movie adaptation, which was advertised as the "Greatest Production in the History of Motion Pictures" and described in the *Parsons Daily Sun* as a "marvelous picturization of Empey's famous book." In what appears to be either a misprint or an extremely generous estimate, the *Pittsburg Sun* declared that "300,000,000 Americans" had read the book.[7]

* * *

Acts and expressions of patriotism were balanced by an abridgement of civil liberties. The Espionage Act of June 15, 1917, provides in part that individuals who "wilfully cause or attempt to cause . . . disloyalty . . . in the military or naval forces . . . or . . . wilfully obstruct the recruiting or enlistment service of the United States . . . shall be punished by a fine of not more than $10,000 or imprisonment for not more than twenty years, or both." Herbert Pankratz states that this federal law could have been narrowly interpreted to apply to enemy agents, spies, and traitors, but instead it "became a means of suppressing any criticism of the government, the President, or the conduct of the war, and of limiting freedom of speech, press, and assembly." On June 16, the day after Congress passed the Espionage Act, a railroad brakeman named Irving T. Boutwell was arrested at the Topeka Union Pacific train depot for passing an antiwar tract through the windows of a troop train. Boutwell admitted that he distributed the leaflet, which condemned blind obedience to military authority, in order to influence soldiers to lay down their arms. Despite a recommendation of clemency from his jury, Boutwell was fined $500 and sentenced to five months in jail. With the exception of twenty-eight members of the Industrial Workers of the World union (who were charged with hampering oil production), Boutwell was the only Kansan convicted of espionage during the Great War. The act was also employed, however, to restrict the circulation of the *Appeal to Reason*, a prominent socialist newspaper published in Girard, and to imprison Kate Richards O'Hare for an antiwar speech. The native Kansan, known as "Red Kate" due to her hair color and politics, unsuccessfully ran as a candidate for Congress on the Socialist ticket in 1910.[8]

When the *Topeka Daily Capital* in September suggested that Americans should not be "especially afraid of free speech," the editor of the *Oskaloosa Independent*, Frank Roberts, took offense and offered up the following rejoinder: "This country will have to get over such namby-pamby, wishy-washy ideas as that if the war is to be prosecuted successfully. . . . The copperheads who try to discourage war preparations should have their jaws slapped shut by police instanter. The *Capital*'s mollycoddle talk to the contrary notwithstanding." Shortly thereafter, the pastor of the Altamont Methodist Episcopal Church complained to Governor Capper about a local farmer who had criticized the government. "Is there no one who has the power to shut his mouth effectually?," wrote H. W. Todd, adding, "He has a boy subject to the draft." In November students at Bethany College in Lindsborg threatened to stop attending classes unless Professor Gustav Peterson was dismissed. "I'm pro-American," said Peterson in response, "I don't remember saying anything that could be construed as un-American." Peterson, who later enlisted in the Student Army Training Corps (SATC), was not dismissed, but suppression of civil liberties where he lived entered a new phase when a McPherson County newspaper on November 29 called out W. B. Kirkpatrick for refusing to "give a cent" to the YMCA or Red Cross. Americans were not only being punished in courts of law for their speech, but they were now also being punished in the court of public opinion for what they did not do and for what they believed.[9]

Another controversial issue in 1917 was the treatment of individuals who held beliefs that conflicted with active military service. Most of the conscientious objectors in Kansas during World War I were Mennonites, members of the Anabaptist faith who did not believe in engaging in war or in any activity that would result in the taking of human life. Eleven separate Mennonite sects existed in Kansas in 1917, with a total membership of 9,411 adults. Mennonites from western Europe and Russia were drawn to the Kansas frontier in part due to a state law passed in 1865 that exempted from military service persons holding a conscientious belief against bearing arms. They purchased large amounts of land north of Wichita in McPherson, Marion, Reno, Harvey, and Butler Counties and were, in the words of Sara Keckeisen, "careful, thrifty, and successful farmers, . . . known as good neighbors and good farmers—an upstanding, God-fearing people." Kansas wheat farmers are indebted to the Mennonites, who brought their superior Turkey Red grain to the Central Plains. But these immigrants were different: they dressed differently, lived separately, and many spoke German in church and at home. Some Mennonites retained strong ties with Germany, such as Abraham Schellenberg, editor of the *Hillsboro Vorwaerts*, who collected funds for the German Red Cross in 1914.[10]

When war was declared in 1917, four Mennonite leaders—Tabor College professor H. W. Lohrenz of Hillsboro, Reverend P. H. Richert of Harvey County, Reverend P. H. Unruh of Goessel, and Reverend J. M. Just of Fairview, Oklahoma—traveled to Washington and presented a petition to the Kansas congressional delegation that pledged support but requested that their creed of not carrying arms be respected. Lohrenz, Unruh, and Just returned to Washington in late June, along with D. E. Harder of Hillsboro and H. P. Krehbell and J. W. Kliewer of Newton, to confer with Secretary of War Baker and Major General Enoch Crowder, who was in charge of the registration, classification, and induction of men into the armed services. As reported in the *Topeka Daily Capital*, the Mennonites emphasized that "they have at no time had any thought of shirking their duty toward the government in any way, but only have asked that they be assigned to service consistent with the long-established principles of non-resistance of their church." The War Department in August determined that Mennonites would not be exempt from service because of their religion but would be assigned to noncombatant roles such as engineer or medical personnel.[11]

On August 29, 1917, at the conclusion of the Old Mennonite Church conference held in Goshen, Indiana, delegates advised drafted members to "present themselves to the authority and meekly inform them that under no circumstances can they consent to service, either combatant or non-combatant, under the military arm of the government." Most Mennonites in Kansas, however, were willing to serve as noncombatants, so there were only a few arrests for refusal to report—two men in McPherson County, for example, were taken into custody during religious services at their homes. In September, as the first contingent of drafted men reported, Secretary Baker ordered the segregation of conscientious objectors in training camps. Some men—Sergeant Alvin York of East Tennessee for one—were convinced to abandon their pacifism, whereas other conscientious objectors had to decide what type of service (if any) was permissible given their beliefs. The largest single group of imprisoned conscientious objectors in the country were held at Camp Funston. Some of the Mennonites assigned to the Eighty-Ninth Infantry Division wore uniforms and worked in the hospital or camp kitchens, whereas others believed that such activities violated their religious beliefs by helping train men who would go on to fight and to kill. Major General Wood, the camp's commandant, was concerned that military discipline among the "fighting" men would be undermined unless conscientious objectors were treated harshly. Consequently, the "COs" lived in soft-sided tents during winter, were required to cook their own meals, and were not permitted to see their families. As noted in the *McPherson Weekly Republican*, "the officers are not at all in sympathy with the view point of the conscientious objectors, and their lot is a hard one compared with that of the men who are willing to shoulder rifles."[12]

Sarah Keckeisen describes the mental and physical abuse at Camp Funston and elsewhere for these men:

> There were reports of . . . COs being forced to take cold showers, having their skin scrubbed with a wire brush or with lye, being assigned "exercises" such as holding a spoon at arm's length for extended periods of time, having to transfer water from one bucket to another with a spoon, or standing on one foot for an hour with the other foot tied up behind were some of the common forms of abuse, which one government official described as "good-natured hazing." Before Camp Funston completed a stockade to house them, any COs who refused to help pick up trash were required to stand outside in any weather while others picked up trash, and the COs were limited to two meals a day.

On October 14, 1917, noncommissioned officers repeatedly struck five Kansas Mennonites who refused to haul trash on a Sunday. The NCOs were "fined and severely reprimanded," but their actions reflected general attitudes. Theodore Roosevelt, prior to the nation's entering the war, denounced opponents of conscription as "professional pacifists, poltroons, and college sissies," later suggesting in 1918 that conscientious objectors should clear minefields. General Wood described conscientious objectors in a letter as "enemies of the Republic, fakers, and active agents of the enemy." The harassment of Mennonites, in the military or in their Kansas communities, accelerated greatly in 1918 once Americans were wounded and killed in Europe.[13]

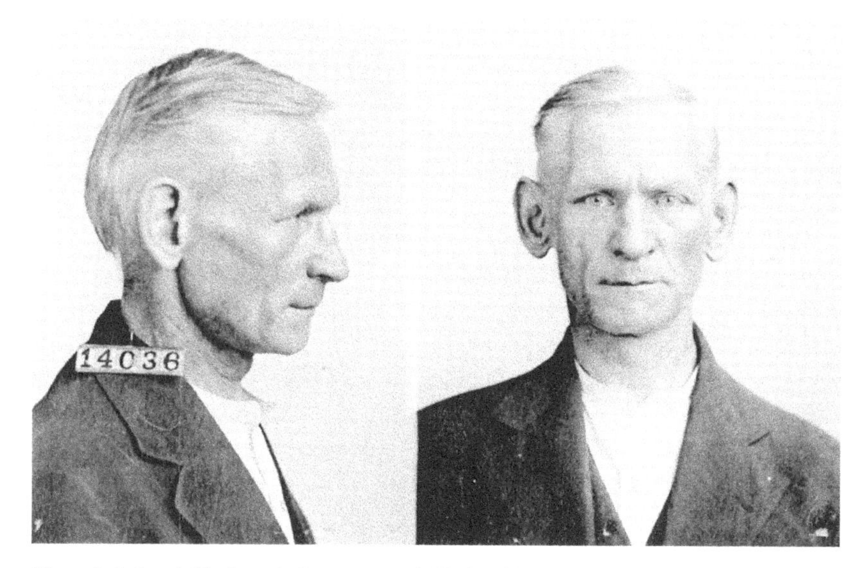

Photo 9.2: Jacob Frohwerk, Leavenworth Federal Penitentiary, 1919. Courtesy of the National Archives and Records Administration, Kansas City, Missouri.

Closely connected to the abridgement of civil liberties and the condemnation of conscientious objectors was the palpable rise in anti-German sentiment. When the state convention for the German-American Alliance was held in Leavenworth in July 1916, Jacob Frohwerk of Kansas City was reelected as president and Fred Zutavern of Great Bend was named the state's delegate to the national convention. The members of the alliance proclaimed their willingness to defend the United States "where the honor of this country and the unquestioned right of its citizens are involved," but they expressed displeasure that German Americans "have been willfully and maliciously misjudged and held up to ridicule and scorn." Less than two years later, the National German-American Alliance was defunct, having disbanded after being accused of spreading "Hun dope" by those commenting in congressional hearings on a bill to revoke its charter. Frohwerk, who wrote newspaper articles opposing American involvement in the war, was convicted of attempting "to cause insubordination, disloyalty, mutiny, [or] refusal of duty, in the military or naval forces." His First Amendment challenge to his conviction was rejected by the U.S. Supreme Court (in a decision written by Justice Oliver Wendell Holmes), and in June 1919 he entered the federal prison in Leavenworth, where he served seven months of a ten-year sentence. His compatriot, Zutavern, who had been twice elected to the Kansas House of Representatives prior to World War I, felt compelled on November 13, 1917, to defend his own loyalty. "I am sorry my patriotism has been doubted," he said in a speech to the Barton County Business Men's Association. "Some friends of forty years have looked at me with suspicious eyes. I have never expressed myself publically before, but it was unreasonable and uncalled for anyone to doubt my citizenship of my adopted country."[14]

Anti-German sentiment in 1917 was less pronounced than what followed in 1918, but the fear of the "enemy within" provoked strong responses from the federal government, the state government, and private citizens. The Espionage Act, in addition to criminalizing antiwar speech and written statements, also empowered President Wilson to restrict entry into areas "in which anything for the use of the Army or Navy is being prepared or constructed or stored." Pursuant to this, "forbidden zones" were established around Kansas factories and establishments holding government contracts, and "alien enemies" were required to obtain permits from the local U.S. marshal in order to enter the areas. In July a Topeka tailor named F. Ulrich and two German members of the Ringling Brothers' Circus, Max Label and Alfons Francois, where charged with unauthorized entry in forbidden zones. In the case of the circus employees, the off-limits area was the state fairgrounds. Not coincidentally, all three men were also accused of making strong assertions against the United States.[15]

Two committees created by the State Council of Defense dealt with the presence of ethnic Germans and German Americans in Kansas. The Committee on Public Defense was charged with "seeking out centers of disloyalty or lack of enthusiasm over our participation in the war." The Committee on Public Relations was organized to facilitate "the complete Americanization of all the foreign elements in the state" as well as "the adoption of the English language as the common language of our country for the transaction of all public business." In June 1917 the Committee on Public Defense submitted a plan and bylaws for a home-guard organization that would, among other tasks, "promote, develop and foster loyalty and patriotism for flag and country." Described by one historian as "a cross between a civic club and a sheriff's posse," Home Guard companies were organized at the county level and served without compensation. The Home Guard was abolished in February 1918 and replaced by the State Guard, which took a more active role in ensuring that Kansas was "100 percent loyal."[16]

Some citizens allowed prejudice and fear of the unknown to blur the lines between positive patriotism and vigilance and negative paranoia and vigilantism. As noted by William Allen White, Germans were commonly called "the Boche, . . . Fritzie and the Hun, that diabolic trinity of evil." The derogatory term "Boche"—the favored French term for Germans—is based in part on the French word *caboche*, slang for both "cabbage" and "blockhead." Fritz was a common German name, and the connection between Germans and Huns was based on a speech given in 1900 by Kaiser Wilhelm urging his soldiers to emulate "the Huns under King Attila" and take no Chinese prisoners during the Boxer Rebellion. In reaction to atrocities in Belgium (both real and imagined), the British depicted Germans as savage "Hun" barbarians, and Kansas newspapers likewise included articles about the bloodthirsty, brutal, devilish, murderous, savage, and treacherous "Hun hordes." The threat posed by German agents within the United States was real, as evidenced by the successful act of sabotage in 1916 that destroyed munitions and damaged the Statue of Liberty, but was vastly exaggerated. Wary Kansans suspected enemy treachery when, on October 16, 1917, a fire in the Kansas City stockyards killed over thirteen thousand cattle and hogs and released livestock that ran through downtown streets. "The burning of nearly half of the Kansas City stockyards," said the *Oskaloosa Independent*, "is believed to have been the work of German agents. This suspicion would seem to be unreasonable if it were not for the many, many acts of deviltry of all kinds." A German formerly employed at the stockyards was arrested, but it appears that no one was convicted in connection with the tragic incident. Two months later the *Meriden Ledger* reported that, because "the alien enemy in our midst [is] so generally recognized," guards were posted at the state's printing and heating buildings in Topeka.[17]

Many Kansans sent letters to Governor Capper reporting incidents of alleged disloyal conduct, which were forwarded to federal officials for further investigation. On April 13, 1917, Capper informed Fred Robertson, the U.S. district attorney for Kansas, that Mrs. George Barker suspected Dr. John Rudolph of Lawrence of being disloyal. The governor's office also passed along a letter from Otis Warrenburg of Centralia, who reported that "several strangers were seen here who nobody seemed to know" and suggested that, "in times like these, it seems that a little looking into would not be out of place." In most cases the decision to investigate or prosecute was left to the district attorney, but in some instances members of the governor's office took a more active role in advising Robertson:

> I believe you could do a powerful lot of good by sending a secret service man out to Wilson, Kansas, to round up one or two German sympathizers. There are many of them out there and if you could get one or two and

> soak them, it would have a most wholesome effect. . . . I was out at Wilson not long ago and was told by several parties that patriotism was very low among a certain class of German sympathizers.

The accusations of disloyalty contained in such letters proved in most instances to be unfounded. Fear and paranoia fueled by propaganda caused Kansans to be overly vigilant in 1917, but there were few reported instances of harassment and physical abuse. In contrast, the Kansas home front in 1918 would become less tolerant and more violent. Ethnic Germans in the state that year were subjected to new restrictions, such as fingerprinting and registration. In some parts of Kansas, citizens suspected of less than absolute fidelity to the United States (such as Mennonites) were called out publically, coerced into purchasing bonds and making donations, and subjected to threats and acts of violence.[18]

* * *

Subscribers to the *Hutchinson News*, including Reverend M. L. Kain of the Grace Episcopal Church, were informed on November 25, 1917, that the upcoming program for the third annual charity concert would include grade-school students singing "The Beautiful Blue Danube," "America the Beautiful," and "The Star-Spangled Banner." Reverend Kain immediately objected to the selection of a "Teutonic waltz" as "an insult to patriotic America," pointing out that the Danube River "traverses only enemy country" and "can no longer be the 'Beautiful' Danube to us." Not wishing to appear disloyal, the Mother's Club—the organization responsible for the charity concert—voted that the rendering of the song by the school pupils would be unwise. Because there was no time to prepare another musical selection, the children who had been practicing the allegedly pro-German song were excluded from the program.

Whereas the residents of Hutchinson took action to protect themselves from the evil influence of composer Richard Strauss (an Austrian who died in 1899), the residents of Wichita failed to act with equal vigilance. As reported in the *Daily Eagle* on January 21, 1918, "The largest crowd that has yet attended the Midian Shrine band concerts at the forum was unusually appreciative yesterday afternoon, and became almost wildly enthusiastic over 'The Beautiful Blue Danube,' rendered by Misses Helen Hastings, Mary Collins, and Eva Hussey, billed as The Columbia Ladies Trio."[19]

CHAPTER TEN

First in France

Charles Orr, Clyde Grimsley, and Frank Cadue of the First Division

When General Pershing and his staff arrived in Paris on June 13, 1917, the French army had just experienced a series of "mutinies," breakdowns of military discipline that included looting, desertion, and the refusal to enter the trenches. French civilians were also tired and demoralized. Pershing was greeted with fanfare and cheers, but he did not bring any combat units with him. Two weeks later, however, a detached battalion of marines and the first four American army regiments arrived at the port of Saint-Nazaire. The Sixteenth, Eighteenth, Twenty-Sixth, and Twenty-Eighth Infantry Regiments were part of the First Division, which combined career soldiers with recent volunteers. Charles Orr, Clyde Grimsley, and Frank Cadue were three Kansans from the First Division who became, respectively, the "first American hero" in World War I, one of the first doughboys captured by the Germans, and the first American soldier hanged in France for criminal behavior.[1]

Of these three men, Charles Lindsey Orr was the youngest. He was born on January 22, 1899, in Rice County, Kansas. His father had left the family (according to the census) prior to June 1900 and his mother thereafter married Fred Regnell, a local farmer. The family in 1915 was living near Bushton—also the hometown of Clarence Huebner, who would rise through the ranks of the First Division to become its commander during World War II. Charles Orr, who was eighteen when he enlisted, was sent to Fort Logan, Colorado, and then to Fort Bliss, Texas, becoming a private in Company F, Sixteenth Infantry.[2]

Clyde Grimsley was also a private in Company F. He was born on February 24, 1889, in Emporia but spent most of his youth in Stockton in north-central Kansas. As a cornet player, Grimsley performed in the city band and eventually became its leader. He married at age twenty and managed the Farmers Union cooperative store in Stockton until 1914, when he and his brother opened up their own general store. They had to sell their business, however,

Photo 10.1: Charles Orr. From *St. Louis Post Dispatch*, January 4, 1918, 19.

Photo 10.2: Clyde Grimsley. Courtesy of Kelly and Toni Holzman.

when Clyde went to Texas for treatment of tuberculosis. According to the *Salina Evening Journal*, after he departed his wife sold his property and belongings and "decamped with the proceeds to Topeka." Upon returning (apparently cured), he made Salina his home and sued for divorce. In May 1917, at the same time the divorce was granted, Grimsley enlisted in the army as a musician. Yet when told that in that capacity he would remain in the United States indefinitely, the twenty-eight-year-old said, "I want to get to France," and was assigned to the Sixteenth Infantry. Grimsley nevertheless continued his role as a musician throughout the war, both as a soldier and as a prisoner.[3]

Frank Cadue was born in either 1891 (according to his headstone) or 1893 (according to the Indian census rolls). He was a member of the Potawatomi, an indigenous people who lived in the upper Midwest prior to removal in the nineteenth century to the Prairie Band Potawatomi Indian Reservation in Jackson County, Kansas. In connection with his arrest in Topeka for drunkenness in March 1915, the *Daily Capital* reported that Cadue spent three years at the Haskell Institute in Lawrence and "deserted" on fourteen occasions. On March 8, 1917, Cadue enlisted at St. Joseph, Missouri. He was a private in Company E, Twenty-Sixth Infantry Regiment.[4]

Orr, Grimsley, and Cadue were among the first American doughboys who saw "Gay Paree." The Second Battalion, Sixteenth Infantry—including Company F—was selected to represent the U.S. Army in a parade through Paris on July 4. Beginning at the Tomb of Napoleon, the effusive celebration was followed by a march of several miles to the tomb of the marquis de Lafayette, who fought alongside George Washington during the American Revolutionary War. "The first appearance of American combat troops in Paris," Pershing later wrote, "brought forth joyful acclaim from the people." The Sixteenth Infantry's regimental band, presumably led by Grimsley, participated in the parade, which ended when Captain C. E. Stanton exclaimed in French, "Lafayette, we are here!" Soldiers were given leave for the evening and then sent by train to eastern France, where they joined the rest of the First Division at training camps near Gondrecourt.[5]

American soldiers were billeted in local villages and put to work building barracks and other buildings; as Grimsley later recalled, "I built Y.M.C.A. huts all summer." The Forty-Seventh French Division—the "Blue Devils"—assisted in training the new arrivals in conjunction with selected French and British instructors and helped establish schools for officers. Infantrymen practiced in trenches with rifle grenades, mortars, and machine guns, then after receiving gas masks participated in gas-attack drills. At the end of the training period, battalion and regimental commanders took over supervision of the men. It appears that while he prepared for trench warfare, Grimsley continued to act as a bandleader. The movie *Under the Stars and Stripes in France* was filmed by the Cinematographic Division for the French army and released in the United States in October. At one point Grimsley, while leading a band, turns and bows. When his four-year-old nephew in Iowa City, Iowa, attended a viewing and saw this, he remarked, "Why there's Uncle Clyde."[6]

At the end of October, the First Division was assigned a "quiet" sector of the western front between Lunéville and Nancy. On the twenty-first the first battalion of each regiment became the initial American occupants of the trenches, with the Sixteenth Infantry positioned between other U.S. regiments. The highest American officer in the sector was a company captain, although officers of higher rank were permitted to visit and observe the troops. During this first rotation, a few men were wounded but none killed. On the second night of November, the second battalions of the four regiments relieved their comrades.[7]

Charles Orr became the "first American hero" soon after taking his position on the front line. The Germans had learned that units of inexperienced American soldiers would be manning the trenches on the night of November 2 and prepared a trench raid against these new arrivals. The attack began at three in the morning on the third, when German artillery executed a "box barrage" that surrounded Company F, Sixteenth Regiment. The shelling directly in front of the trenches was halted to allow some two hundred soldiers from the First Bavarian Landwehr Division to move forward. In what Nick Lloyd describes as "a furious fifteen minutes of cutting, slashing and firing," the Germans engaged their foe in hand-to-hand combat and achieved their twin objectives of welcoming the United States to the war and securing men for interrogation. Three Americans were killed in this action: Corporal James Gresham and Private Merle Hay, both shot dead, and Private Thomas Enright, who was slashed and punctured by bayonets.[8]

One of the men wounded during the raid was Orr. His story received national attention when it was included in an article published in the *Saturday Evening Post* on December 27, 1917. In this account war correspondent George Pattullo describes how Orr refused to leave his bunkmate, George Box of Oklahoma. The story begins with an unnamed Kansas lieutenant who orders Orr, a "black-haired, eighteen year-old country boy, also from Kansas," to leave the trench for a safer place. The officer was Willis Edwin Comfort, who held a degree in civil engineering from Kansas State Agricultural College. According to Pattullo, Private Orr disobeyed the order—"No sir,

I can't. . . . Don't you see my bunkie's wounded?"—and continued with his bare hands to dig out Private Box, who was unconscious with a head wound and partially buried. Lieutenant Comfort repeatedly urged Orr to leave—"You'll be killed here!"—but the young man refused. Utterly spent, Orr finally went into a dugout, and Box was extracted and sent to a hospital, where he spoke with correspondent Pattullo: "'So he wouldn't leave you, hey?' Box closed his eyes and did not answer for a minute. At last: 'That's the kind of bunkie to have,' he said weakly." Pattullo's description of Orr's role in "the first raid" ends with the following sentences: "Young Orr seemed to view the whole affair as a matter of course. He and George were friends; so what else was there for him to do? But the nurses at the hospital have christened him F.A.H.—First American Hero."[9]

Both Orr and Box survived the war. Comfort, however, was not as fortunate. Promoted to captain, he died on July 18, 1918, during the Battle of Soissons. His posthumous Distinguished Service Cross citation states that, after being severely injured, he "refused to be evacuated, but energetically led his company forward to its objective and maintained it there until he was mortally wounded." In a letter to his parents, Comfort wrote, "If it should happen that I should receive that highest of decorations, one of the little wooden crosses which now dot the fields of France, I want you to meet it as cheerfully as I shall." Willis Comfort, who grew up in Westmoreland, is buried in the Sunset Cemetery in Manhattan.[10]

During the raid in which Orr became America's initial hero in World War I, a fellow Kansan was taken into captivity as one of the first American prisoners of war. Clyde Grimsley spent six hours on the front lines and the remainder of the war in German prisons. After returning home, the Kansas native recalled how he became one of eleven Americans captured in the early hours of November 3:

> The Germans came in a close mass, bunching up to get around the mass of barbed wire. . . . We fired as fast as we could, and laid out a good many of them; they were so close together. Five of us were at the left of the line in a bend of the trench. They scattered and went around behind us and threw hand grenades from the rear. Two of our five were knocked out, one being left in the trench for dead and the other, wounded in the shoulder, was taken along when we were captured. A grenade struck the parapet in front of us, and a young fellow with me at this point and I were upset and so stunned by the concussion we could do nothing more, though not wounded.

Photo 10.3: American prisoners of war, November 1917. Courtesy of Blake Watson.

At first it was not known whether Grimsley had been killed or captured. "If Clyde is missing, we hope he hasn't been captured by the Huns," said his sister Verna Grimsley. "We would rather see him killed or wounded." Grimsley himself may have shared this surprising view. As noted by Robert Jackson, "propaganda piled atrocity after atrocity on the heads of the Kaiser's armies," and consequently "thousands of Allied soldiers went to war fully believing that [*Schrecklichkeit*] 'frightfulness' was all they might expect if they were captured."[11]

On November 17 the *St. Louis Star and Times* reported that a Berlin newspaper, gloating over the capture of the first American prisoners, sarcastically remarked: "We shall be able to provide quarters for these gentlemen. However, we cannot promise them doughnuts and jam." Shortly thereafter, the Red Cross was able to report that Grimsley was not among the dead, perhaps based on a photograph of some of the prisoners that appeared in German and Swiss newspapers. Several of the men are shown, including Grimsley, who stands without a helmet clenching his left hand and holding a coat with his right arm. To his right in the photograph is Sergeant Edgar Halyburton of North Carolina, who would take charge of American prisoners and write a book about the prisoner-of-war experience. The photo was printed in the January 1, 1918, edition of the *Salina Evening Journal* with the statement: "The man to the left at the bottom is Clyde Grimsley of Salina. His parents reside at Stockton, Kan."[12]

The Stockton community learned in February that Grimsley was at a prisoner-of-war camp near Tuchel in northern Prussia. Later in the same month, G. E. King, a friend who lived in Salina, received an upbeat letter from him: "I am feeling fine and dandy, am in good health and spirits. Don't worry about me, for I am all right and treated good." In fact, the American prisoners were neither in good health nor well treated. "Tuchel was a first class hell hole," Grimsley said in March 1919. "There was practically no food, we had one poor blanket apiece and it was terribly cold all that winter. The treatment given us was simply awful—inhuman in the worst degree."[13]

* * *

In contrast to Orr and Grimsley, Private Frank Cadue was a mistaken hero. Initial reports failed to describe accurately the circumstances surrounding his death. Consequently, the *Topeka Daily Capital*, on November 23, 1917, published a laudatory article with the headline "Frank Cadue First Full-Blooded Indian and First Kansan to Fall at the Front." Six days later his hometown of Mayetta, north of Topeka, proudly acknowledged "the honor of furnishing the first Kansas man to give his life in defense of his country in the present conflict." Other state newspapers reported that Cadue died from shrapnel or gunshot wounds while serving in the trenches.[14]

Cadue died on November 5, 1917, just two days after Orr saved his bunkmate and Grimsley was taken prisoner. But he was not killed in action. Cadue was, instead, the first American soldier to be executed during military service in the Great War. On October 20, 1917, Cadue brutally raped and killed a seven-year-old French girl near the village of Givrauval, located about fifty miles south of Verdun. The child's body was found at a barn building on top of a manure pile intermixed with garbage, bearing physical signs of assault, rape, and murder (finger bruises appeared at the base of her throat). Although several newspapers did eventually report his crime and execution, other published accounts, including two books on the history of Kansas, perpetuated the erroneous story that Cadue died honorably on the battlefield.[15]

The army held a court-martial on October 22 and rejected Cadue's defense that he did not know what he was doing because he was under the influence of alcohol. The sentence of death was approved by General Pershing, and the hanging occurred at a public place in Givrauval. The American Expeditionary Forces would execute 10 other men for war crimes in the next eighteen months, a rather small number considering that, in just over four years of conflict, the French military executed 918 men. Two months after Cadue's execution, an article appeared in a newspaper in Kansas, where statewide prohibition existed from 1881 to 1948, that characterized him as a victim. A "Methodist temperance organization" argued in the *Burlingame Enterprise* that Cadue "was murdered by the United States government which had done nothing to protect him from the diabolical excitations of French wine." The prohibition group noted that Cadue had "expressed deepest regret for his crime" and blamed the U.S. Army for failing to forbid American soldiers in France from consuming alcohol. It is not known if the organization knew the details of Cadue's actions. Regardless, in 1921 his sister, as next of kin, requested repatriation of his remains, which were transported across the Atlantic by the *Cantigny*, a ship named for the May 1918 battle in which many members of the First Infantry Division lost their lives. Cadue's remains were reinterred in the Shipsee Cemetery on the Potawatomi Reservation. (As recently as 2015, a flag-adorned marker was mistakenly placed next to his headstone to indicate it as the gravesite of an honorably discharged veteran.)[16]

Cadue's aberrant behavior stands in contrast to other Native doughboys from Kansas, who served with distinction. Three Native Americans, for example, fought together in Company B, 137th Infantry, Thirty-Fifth Division. Two of the men did not return home. Private Charlie Speer (Pip-ko-kuk) was fatally wounded during the Meuse-Argonne offensive in late September 1918, and Private Lyman Tapsee (Op-tuck Tap-see) was gassed in October and died at age nineteen in February 1919. The survivor was George Masquat, a "big Kickapoo Indian corporal" described as "one of the worst wounded men from this community." Masquat downplayed the severe shrapnel wounds he received to his shoulder, abdomen, forearm, and wrist. It was reported that he said that if there were another war, he would take part, as the government would need good men, and he was one such man because the enemy could not kill him.[17]

Of the 11,803 Native Americans who registered for the draft prior to September 1918, over 55 percent (6,509) were inducted, and a similar number enlisted for service. In 1917 over one-third of all Native Americans in the United States were not citizens. With the support of Kansas senator Charles Curtis, a member of the Kaw Nation, the federal government extended the right of citizenship in November 1919 to honorably discharged Native veterans of the Great War, five years before citizenship was granted to all Native Americans.[18]

* * *

Although it can be difficult to determine when something takes place for the first time during World War I, military records and newspaper accounts sometimes provide the necessary information. We know that Frank Cadue was the first American soldier to be hanged for a crime in France and that Clyde Grimsley was the first Kansan to be captured by German ground troops. Other apparent "firsts" include Walter Knapp, the first Kansan to die in the Great War; Walter Perkins, the first Kansan captured at sea; William Fitzsimons, the first Kansas officer killed in France; Edgar Rayburn and Algen Guttridge, among the first Kansans in the U.S. Navy to perish; Cecil Rowan, the first Kansan to die overseas as a member of a U.S. Army division; and Donald Hudson, the first Kansan to become an "ace" aviator. It also appears that Delphis Chaquette was the first Kansas soldier to be the victim of a homicide, and Rudolph Negrete from Topeka was the first Mexican alien to enlist in the American army. Finally, Lottie Hollenback of Kansas was the first Red Cross nurse to die at Fort Riley and, according to one newspaper at least, the first in her field to die during World War I.

Walter "Pearl" Knapp of Iola was killed on January 1, 1917, while serving with the Royal Artillery. The telegram received by his mother was the first time she learned that he was a soldier. Knapp was about thirty-eight years old at his death and is buried in Ypres, Belgium. Three months later, on March 10, 1917, Walter Perkins of Wichita became the first Kansan to be captured at sea, after the British steamship *Esmeraldas* was sunk by the German ship *Moewe*. Perkins was employed by the British government to care for a cargo of mules, and the steamship was returning to the United States. He was imprisoned in Brandenberg, Germany, and forced to work outside of the prison camp repairing railways.[19]

William Thomas Fitzsimons was the first American officer killed in France, losing his life on September 4, 1917, when German airplanes bombed Base Hospital No. 5 near Calais. Fitzsimons was born in Burlington in Coffey County. He initially attended college in St. Mary's, Kansas, but transferred and graduated in 1910 from the University of Kansas. Two years later the twenty-three-year-old completed his studies at the university's School of Medicine at Rosedale (now part of Kansas City, Kansas). When war broke out in 1914, Fitzsimons volunteered with the Red Cross and performed surgery for two years in both England and France. In 1916 he came home and settled in Kansas City, but in March 1917 he joined the Medical Reserve Corps and entered active duty in April. First Lieutenant Fitzsimons returned to

Photo 10.4: William Fitzsimons. Courtesy of the Kenneth Spencer Research Library, University of Kansas.

France in August and was working in a hospital for British soldiers when two bombs landed within a few feet of his tent, killing him instantly. The death of Fitzsimons received national attention. Theodore Roosevelt wrote an editorial for the *Kansas City Star* that praised a "fine and gallant life" and condemned the "horror of Germany's calculated brutality." President Wilson signed a bill to posthumously promote Fitzsimons to captain. In 1922 a large crowd assembled at The Paseo and Twelfth Street to witness the dedication of the William T. Fitzsimons Memorial Fountain. "We pay a special tribute to this boy," declared Bishop Thomas F. Lillis, "because he was ours, because he reflected the spirit of the people of Kansas City." In 1955 another Kansan, President Dwight D. Eisenhower, received treatment in Denver, Colorado, at the Fitzsimons Army Hospital, named for the first American officer to die in the Great War.[20]

The Adjutant General's Office reports that just 157 men died out of the approximately 10,000 Kansans who served in the U.S. Navy during the Great War. Nine men died by accident or "other" causes, and the remainder succumbed to disease or unknown causes. Edgar Rayburn, a twenty-two-year-old from Kansas City, Kansas, drowned on October 30, 1917, while the USS *Alamance* was patrolling the Atlantic coast. The mayor of Kansas City, the city commissioners, and one hundred firemen and policemen helped escort his body to the Elmwood Cemetery. Less than a month later, the USS *Chauncey* was accidently rammed by a British freighter near Gibraltar. Chief Machinist Mate Algen Guttridge of Cullison (Pratt County) was one of the twenty-one members of the American crew who went down with the warship. He enlisted in November 1914 and was thirty-seven at his death. Private Cecil Rowan of Chanute, who was twenty-two when he died on November 1, 1917, was in the Headquarters Company, Sixteenth Regiment, First Division. Although a letter sent to his mother stated that his death was "caused by the accidental discharge of his rifle," the city of Chanute announced plans to honor its "first soldier killed in battle."[21]

On August 1, 1918, Donald Hudson became the fifth ace of the American Air Corps—the first from Kansas—when he shot down three planes in five minutes, bringing his total at that time to six kills, one more than required for such recognition. Hudson, who was born in Topeka, attended the University of Kansas in 1914 and 1915 but dropped out due to "an abrupt interest in the flying machine." As described in his Distinguished Service Cross citation, after being chased by four German planes, the twenty-two-year-old aviator "shot down one, drove off the other three, and started to our lines with a damaged machine, but was attacked by two planes. He shot down both of these planes and, by great perseverance and determination, succeeded in reaching our lines." Lieutenant Colonel Hudson retired after thirty-nine years of military service and was buried in 1967 at Arlington National Cemetery. He is credited as being the first pilot to fly over the Andes Mountains in South America, as an instructor in 1919 for the Bolivian Air Force.[22]

According to the records of the state adjutant general, eight Kansas soldiers were murdered while in service during World War I. Yet in the case of some of the men, available public documents suggest the deaths were accidental. It does appear that Private Delphis E. Chaquette of Clyde, Kansas, who died on November 8, 1917, was the first Kansan soldier to be killed by a civilian. Chaquette was stationed at Fort Douglas, Arizona. The *Bisbee Daily Review* reported that he was shot by a chauffeur hired to drive him and two other soldiers around the border town. An "authoritative source" stated that when the car reached the Mexican border, the men wanted the chauffeur to turn out the lights but he refused because he believed they desired to load the automobile with contraband. The soldiers then allegedly threatened to beat the driver, who supposedly fired several shots to attract attention, inadvertently killing Chaquette. In contrast, there was little doubt that Private Ira Addy of Galena was murdered on February 12, 1918. He was found with a bullet in his back in Chickamauga Park near Chattanooga, Tennessee, where he was stationed with the Sixth Infantry Division. The last recorded murder victim was Private First Class Frank Burdick of Burlington, who died on April 6, 1919, and is buried at Arlington National Cemetery. Although another soldier told Burdick's mother that a "serious accident" caused her son's death, a military chaplain said Burdick was stabbed by a Frenchman in the village of Odival, north of Dijon. The remains of the twenty-three-year-old soldier included a picture of his namesake son, who was born in September 1917.[23]

Rudolph "Rudy" Negrete of Topeka, a recipient of the Silver Star, Bronze Star, French Croix-de-Guerre, Purple Heart, and Gold War Service medals, was apparently the first Mexican to enlist in Kansas in World War I. It was reported in 1920 that Negrete "had an opportunity to leave the service because he was not a citizen of the United States, but believing he would be a slacker if he did, he refused to accept a discharge." When the war in Europe ended, the Mexican immigrant volunteered to join American forces sent to Siberia during the Russian Civil War (1918–1921). In 1921 he became a U.S. citizen pursuant to a law that accelerated the naturalization process for alien veterans. Negrete lived the rest of his life in Kansas and died in 1983 at the age of eighty-seven. According to his *Kansas City Times* obituary ("Topekan Lived His Belief in American Dream"), the local Veterans of Foreign Wars post fired a twenty-one-gun salute with World War I Springfield rifles as Negrete was laid to rest in Mount Calvary Cemetery.[24]

Lottie Ruth Hollenback was born in Paola, Kansas, on January 31, 1881, and moved with her family in 1885 to Comanche County and thereafter to Rooks County. After working as a school teacher, she graduated in 1907 from a nursing school at the Kansas City (Missouri) General Hospital. In 1917 she joined the Red Cross and was sworn in to military service by Major J. F. Binnie, the same medical officer who had enlisted Dr. Fitzsimons. Hollenback became a member of Base Hospital Unit 28 but was sent on temporary assignment to Fort Riley, where she served for two months and was appointed head of her ward. The thirty-six-year-old was stricken with influenza on January 2, 1918, and died the next day. The *Olathe Mirror* declared that Hollenback was the first Red Cross nurse to die in the service since the beginning of the war, whereas the *Paola Western Spirit* said she was the first Red Cross nurse to die at Fort Riley. In any event, she is the only woman whose name is inscribed (as "Loretto Hollenback") on the bronze tablets at the Liberty Memorial Tower that honor the 441 Kansas City citizens who died in World War I. Her body, which by coincidence was removed from Fort Riley by one of her former students, was laid to rest in a soldier's casket at Bethel Cemetery in Bethel, Kansas.[25]

1918

Photo 11.1: Soldiers from the 137th Infantry, 1918. Courtesy of the Kansas State Historical Society.

CHAPTER ELEVEN

Victory at Cantigny

Charles Avery, Harry Martin, and Clarence Huebner of the First Division

"I tell you, you can't tell when you are going to get yours and it is one mean sensation, too, men falling dead or wounded on all sides of you." Harry Martin's letter to his parents, which mixes pride with relief, was written on May 31, 1918, shortly after he and other soldiers from the First Division had captured and held the village of Cantigny. "I am awfully glad I was in it and wouldn't have missed it for anything," the twenty-five-year-old lieutenant from Emporia reported, "but I'm not overly enthusiastic about 'over the tops.' They all sound fine on paper but actually it is a mean thing." As it turned out, Martin survived the war, as did two other officers from Kansas who fought at Cantigny: Charles Avery, also from Emporia, and Clarence Huebner of Bushton. The three men, who were all in the Second Battalion, Twenty-Eighth Infantry, played important roles in the initial American offensive of World War I. The Battle of Cantigny was the first time an American infantry regiment would attack with the support of the modern armaments of war: machine guns, grenades, flamethrowers, poisonous gas, tanks, and airplanes. The planning and execution of what General Pershing called "the affair at Cantigny" has been extensively documented. In his memoir he describes three consequences of this victory: it displaced the Germans from advantageous high ground, it boosted Allied morale, and it undercut the argument that American troops should be "amalgamated" into the French and British armies.[1]

Charles Avery, Harry "Buzz" Martin, and Clarence Huebner each narrowly escaped death on the battlefields in France. Avery was the sole survivor of fifteen men who were buried when their trench was obliterated by artillery shells. Martin was seriously wounded on three occasions: twice by artillery and once by a machine gun. Huebner received multiple wounds as he rose in the ranks, including a bullet that hit him directly between the eyes. Lieutenant Martin would become a colonel in the U.S. Army Reserve and serve in the Pacific theater during World War II. Captain Huebner, who was a company

CHARLES AVERY
"Even crumbs are bread."

Photo 11.2: Charles Avery, 1912 Emporia High School yearbook. Courtesy of the Lyon County History Center, Emporia.

commander at the outset of the Battle of Cantigny, ended the Great War as a lieutenant colonel in charge of the Twenty-Eighth Regiment. In 1944 and a major general, he would assume command of the entire First Division and later direct the American Fifth Corps during its advance through Germany. Whereas another Kansan, James Harbord, was one of the most important army officers in the First World War, Huebner was one of the most important army officers in the Second World War. Both men enlisted as privates and ended their military careers as generals.[2]

Charles Dillison Avery was born in 1893 in Emporia. He graduated from high school in 1912, married in 1913, and became a father in 1914. By November 1915, he was employed by the *Manhattan Mercury*, having previously worked for the *Emporia Gazette* and in the advertising department of the *Kansas City Star*. In July 1917 Avery went to Rockford, Illinois, to attend an officer training camp at Fort Sheridan. After arriving in France in February 1918, Second Lieutenant Avery was assigned to Company E, Twenty-Eighth Infantry Regiment, First Division. In a letter to his wife before the Battle of Cantigny, he employed his journalistic skills to describe the aftermath of a German trench raid: "Three of our dead were laid out by accident on a bed of violets, and their yet warm blood turned the purple of the violets to crimson."

Harry Hood Martin graduated from Emporia High School in 1912, one year before Avery. His paternal grandfather was a U.S. senator, and his father once served as mayor of Emporia. Martin attended college at Purdue University, where he studied electrical engineering. While in Indiana, he enlisted and was commissioned a second lieutenant after completing his

Photo 11.3: Harry Martin, 1917 *Purdue University Yearbook*. Courtesy of Purdue University Archives and Special Collections.

training at Fort Benjamin Harrison near Indianapolis. "Buzz," as he was called, joined Company H, Twenty-Eighth Infantry and—like Avery—would lead a platoon at Cantigny.[3]

Clarence Ralph Huebner was born in 1888 near Bushton, a town located in the middle of Kansas with a population of 222 people in 1910 and 279 people in 2010. He was the oldest of six children, the son of a farmer and the grandson of German immigrants. After finishing the tenth (and highest) grade, Huebner attended a business school in Nebraska and worked as a stenographer and typist for a railroad company. In 1910, at the age of twenty-two, he enlisted as a private in the U.S. Army. Between January 1910 and July 1916, he was promoted to corporal, sergeant, mess sergeant, and regimental supply sergeant. Huebner experienced his first—but not last—brush with death during the Mexican conflict. "I was handing a canteen of water to a friend," he recalled, "when a .37 millimeter cannon round hit him right in the armpit.

If the cannon had been an inch or so to the right, it would have blown me to bits."

The Kansan was an excellent soldier, and one of his officers made the following prediction: "Young Huebner is destined to go far. I don't see anything to stop him—except possibly a bullet." Prompted by General Pershing and others, the sergeant earned an officer's commission and joined the Twenty-Eighth Infantry Regiment. When war was declared, the Twenty-Eighth became part of the First Division; consequently, Lieutenant Huebner was among the first American soldiers to arrive in France.[4]

Avery, Martin, and Huebner arrived in France in June 1917. At some point during the war, the men of the First Division began to wear a red numeral 1 on their shoulders, causing their division to be forever known as the "Big Red One." American infantry divisions, larger than their British, French, and German counterparts, consisted of approximately twenty-eight thousand soldiers and typically organized as follows: four squads in a platoon, four platoons in a company, four companies in a battalion, three battalions (or twelve companies) in a regiment, two regiments in a brigade, and two brigades in a division. Avery, Martin, and Huebner were in Companies E, H, and G of the Twenty-Eighth Infantry, which together with Company F formed the regiment's Second Battalion. All four regiments of the Big Red One bore the brunt of different battles, but it was the Twenty-Eighth that first attacked German forces at Cantigny, with the First and Third Battalions providing flanking support for the Second Battalion's direct assault on the village.

The Battle of Cantigny took place in the final days of May 1918, eleven months after the First Division arrived in France. For most of the summer and fall of 1917, the Big Red One was assigned to the French Fifth Army for training in trench warfare and infantry tactics. The Allied forces suffered several setbacks during the last half of 1917, including the tremendous loss of life that defined the British offensive at Passchendaele, the crushing defeat of the Italians at Caporetto, and the disintegration of the eastern front. In the days that preceded the Bolshevik Revolution in Russia, the four regiments of the First Division were assigned a "quiet" sector of the front lines between Lunéville and Nancy in eastern France. On November 2 the men in Companies E, F, G, and H—the second battalion of each regiment—took their turn in the trenches. At least five Kansans were at their stations—Charles Orr, Clyde Grimsley (both with the Sixteenth Infantry), Avery, Martin, and Huebner—when the Germans successfully carried out their first trench raid against the Americans, killing three members of the Sixteenth Infantry and capturing eleven men (including Grimsley).

By this time, Huebner had been promoted to captain and placed in command of Company G, Twenty-Eighth Infantry. The First Division was still on the front lines in eastern France when the Germans launched the first of five offensives that aimed to bring the war to a conclusion before the United States could effectively mobilize its forces in Europe. The Treaty of Brest-Litovsk, signed on March 3, 1918, ended Russia's participation in the war and enabled Germany to move troops to the western front. Three weeks later, on March 21, the Germans attacked the British Third and Fifth Armies in northern France, taking over twenty thousand prisoners and advancing as much as forty miles. The onslaught created a panic: it threatened to drive a wedge between the British and French forces, placed in peril the critical transportation hub of Amiens, and brought the enemy as close to Paris as Washington, DC, is to Baltimore. By the first week of April, the Somme offensive had created a bulge, or salient, that extended at its farthest point from Saint-Quentin to the villages of Mondidier and Cantigny. The Allies responded by authorizing General Ferdinand Foch to coordinate actions of the French and British armies. At the same time, both President Wilson and General Pershing were pressured to drop their opposition to the amalgamation of American troops into larger European formations. On March 28 Pershing placed American soldiers at the disposal of General Foch, and soon thereafter the First Division was sent to assist French forces.[5]

During this time, Huebner once again escaped death. While leading his men on a night reconnaissance mission, he was hit by a bullet that pierced the rim of his helmet before striking him between the eyes. When asked about the incident later in life, Huebner simply said, "my helmet saved me—slowed the bullet down a bit." As noted by biographer Steven Flaig, the bullet "cracked his skull, crushed his sinuses, and left him in such critical condition that an overzealous doctor . . . listed Huebner as Killed in Action." The veteran soldier survived and rejoined the rest of the First Division when it marched on April 17 to Cantigny. "The future is hanging upon your action in this conflict," General Pershing told the officers of the Big Red One. "The people at home," he added, were confident "that you are going to make a record of which your country will be proud." By the time the First Division arrived at Cantigny, the pressure to succeed had grown even stronger. On April 20 the Germans cast doubt on the fighting ability of the American doughboys by successfully raiding the village of Seicheprey, defended by the inexperienced Twenty-Sixth "Yankee" Division. Consequently, Pershing heartily approved the decision to retaliate at Cantigny, hoping to remove the "stain of Seicheprey."[6]

By the end of April, the First Division was in place near Cantigny, a small village in northern France on elevated ground three miles west of Montdidier. The American soldiers were now part of the French Tenth Corps in the First Army. For most of May, the opposing forces fortified their positions and exchanged a deadly mix of high-explosive and mustard-gas shells. French colonial troops had entered the village twice but were forced to retreat in the face of artillery barrages and infantry counterattacks. It was now the Americans' turn, and Major General Robert Lee Bullard, the division's commander, selected the Twenty-Eighth Regiment to lead the assault. The regiment's three infantry battalions, each accompanied by a machine-gun company, would secure Cantigny and establish a defensive perimeter to withstand the inevitable German response. The French would provide artillery cover, air support, tanks, and flamethrower teams. For two days, the Twenty-Eighth and its supporting personnel rehearsed the attack on similar terrain, complete with a mockup of the village. It was now up to the officers—twenty-five-year-old Lieutenant Avery among them—to prepare the men for the attack scheduled to begin on May 28.[7]

As fate would have it, Avery did not participate in the capture of Cantigny, but he did earn the Distinguished Service Cross for his actions the day before the assault:

> After a two-hour barrage, which caused many casualties in our forces, the enemy raided a sector occupied by our troops. During the attack, Lieut. Avery exhibited unusual courage in holding together his handful of men, after one-third had become casualties, and distributing ammunition to [the] remaining men, which finally stopped the attack. Two prisoners were taken during the battle. He was severely wounded about the head, and later buried in a trench, where he remained for three and one-half hours, before being dug out.

Thanks to the prompting of a newspaper editor, the veteran shared his incredible story of survival when he returned—"fit as a fiddle"—to Kansas in June 1919. According to Avery, he was as busy "as a hen with a flock of chickens," getting ammunition distributed and his men properly posted, when he was suddenly buried in a trench under four feet of earth. To make matters worse, one of the three exploding shells creating the collapse drove a piece of steel through his helmet and into the back of his head, causing a skull fracture and paralyzing him. The situation was dire:

> [Avery] had figured out that the thing to do was not to holler, because that would use up the small supply of air a man so buried could secure, but to get busy digging out. When he tried to start to do that, however, he found he could not move, except to wiggle his fingers a little and with these he scraped a little place before his face. The shell which paralyzed him made digging out impossible.

To make matters worse, a corporal was buried directly above him. He was alive, as were some of the other entombed men, but more of them died slowly over time: "As Lieut. Avery lay there for three and a half hours, fully believing that he would 'go out,' he heard these men, gurgle and 'go out,' one after the other, as the blood, which burst finally from their noses and mouths as they suffocated, ran into their throats and choked them." According to a nurse who cared for him, Avery was in a half-sitting posture and remained silent as "the boche line surged over him." Long after hope of rescue had faded, and with his own blood collecting in his nose, mouth, and throat, Avery heard familiar voices from above. He called out for help and also tried to calm the buried corporal: "He talked to the boy above him, telling him not to scream, as the chances for escape would be better if they saved their breath, but the boy could not stand it and lost his mind, apparently going crazy, screaming himself into unconsciousness and into another world."

Working under machine-gun fire, the soldiers used a steel pickaxe to dig out their comrade but stopped when they reached the dead corporal, thinking their efforts were in vain. When someone said, "Why, that isn't Lieut. Avery," the buried Kansan "yelled like a good fellow," and the digging resumed. "Pretty soon he felt the pick strike him in the back of the head, and he told his rescuers that that was his head, and to dig about a foot north of where they had been digging. In a few seconds, he was pulled out, and was on the way to five long weeks in the hospital."[8]

In a letter written on June 1 and published a month later in the *Emporia Gazette*, Harry Martin reported: "Charley Avery is in pretty bad condition in the hospital. . . . Not only is he shell shocked but his right side is partially paralyzed." After this partial paralysis went away, Avery suffered boils, scabies, and blood poisoning in his legs, but he eventually recovered and returned to Company E. According to his attending nurse, the young Kansan viewed his escape from death as “a miracle—a painful but wonderful experience.”[9]

* * *

Less than twenty-four hours after Avery was buried in a trench, his friend Buzz Martin was assembling with other members of Company H in the center of the attack formation. Lieutenant Martin and his platoon waited two hours, then moved out at 6:45 A.M. across an open field, which the young Kansan described in a letter to his parents:

> I honestly was nervous and rather excited, but when zero hour came and the rocket was shot up by our first division airplane I took my men, for the first time, over the top, all smiling and with the determination that all Heaven and hell couldn’t beat us. It was . . . really the most wonderful sight I have ever seen. All the men were walking with a firm step, rifles and bayonets fixed and at a high part, walking over No Man’s Land with worlds of artillery fire [passing] over our heads.

Although Cantigny was taken by the Americans in less than an hour, the Germans defending the village were not easily subdued. This was a different type of warfare—up close and personal. At one point a German waved his left hand and yelled “Kamerad” but then reached for his gun. “I was a trifle too quick for him,” recalled Martin, “and I gave him two bullets. Upon examining him and his pistol I found he had it cocked [and] ready for action.”[10]

Whereas the initial attack was preceded and supported by French artillery, tanks, and airplanes, the Twenty-Eighth Infantry defended Cantigny under different circumstances. On May 27, the day before the attack, the Germans unexpectedly began their third spring offensive, smashing the French lines between Soissons and Rheims. This new crisis compelled the French high command to withdraw a large portion of their forces at Cantigny. Nevertheless, the Americans were able to dig defensive trenches on the outskirts of the village and withstand five German counterattacks. Snipers killed four men in Martin’s platoon, while overall seventeen of the thirty officers in the Second Battalion were either killed or wounded. “I am alive, safe and sound, although awfully tired,” the lieutenant wrote shortly after being relieved. “We all did our share, and the American soldiers deserve a world of credit. They are surely some fighters.”[11]

* * *

Huebner also survived the Battle of Cantigny. The captain's immediate superior officer on May 28, 1918, was Lieutenant Colonel Robert Maxey, who commanded the four infantry companies (E, F, G, and H) comprising the Second Battalion, Twenty-Eighth Regiment. Next in the chain of authority was regimental commander Colonel Hanson Ely, followed by Brigadier General Beaumont Bonaparte Buck, who was in charge of the Second Brigade. At the head of the First Division was Major General Bullard, who was assisted by Lieutenant Colonel George C. Marshall, the future army chief of staff, secretary of state, and secretary of defense. By the end of that day, Huebner would command the Second Battalion; by the end of the Great War, he would be at the head of the Twenty-Eighth Regiment; and during the next world war, he would lead the First Division across western Europe.

Captain Huebner, age thirty, led Company H into Cantigny. Although the village fell quickly, there was, as he recalled, "hard fighting house to house." As vividly described by historian Laurence Stallings, "Germans were killed in cellars, in trenches, in the village square, [and] in farmhouse parlors musty with the smell of old velvet draperies." At one point, Huebner recounted, a French soldier used a flamethrower in the town, and a singed German soldier ran out of a home "just as I had seen rabbits in Kansas come out of burning strawstacks." Soon thereafter he was taken to Lieutenant Colonel Maxey, who had received a mortal wound from a shell fragment. "When I reached the colonel I found him upon the litter and helpless," Huebner later described, "but he could speak and gave me full and complete instructions as to how to carry on." At 9:08 A.M. the captain updated Colonel Ely by field telephone: "Maxey seriously wounded. I have assumed command." It was now up to the former private to organize and rally the Second Battalion in the face of imminent German counterattacks. To complicate the situation, the flanking First and Third Battalions had been unable to achieve all of their objectives, while the unexpected departure of French planes and long-range artillery made it easier for the Germans to seize air superiority and target American fortifications.

Huebner proved to be the right man for the moment, and his leadership over the next several days earned him his first Distinguished Service Cross: "For three days [Captain] Huebner withstood German assaults under intense bombardment, heroically exposing himself to fire constantly in order to command his battalion effectively, and although his command lost half its officers and 30 per cent of its men, he held his position and prevented a break in the line at that point." Huebner used the cover of the darkness to remove his wounded and to resupply the remaining troops with food, water, and ammunition. According to one account of the unrelenting German response, "the terrain in and around Cantigny was so blasted by shellfire that it began to resemble the cratered moonscape more typically associated with the battlefields at Verdun and the Somme." The enemy, however, could not breach the American lines, and their soldiers were forced to return to the surrounding woods. "We held Cantigny," Lieutenant Colonel Marshall later noted. "The Germans never afterwards reoccupied the village." Over 300 Americans died, and approximately 1,300 men were wounded in order to capture and hold the position. As for Huebner, he earned yet another promotion, exchanging his captain's bars for a major's oak leaf, and was officially given command of the Second Battalion.[12]

But the war did not end for the three Kansans at Cantigny. Avery rejoined Company E after five weeks in the hospital. He participated in additional fighting, went back to the hospital due to pneumonia, recovered, returned to the front, and served with the First Division until the armistice. He thereafter transferred to the Eighty-Ninth Division and was discharged in June 1919. Avery secured employment with the *Junction City Daily Union* and was an honored guest in January 1920 when General Pershing gave a speech during a visit to Camp Funston. At some point Avery left the newspaper business and Kansas, eventually settling in Omaha, Nebraska, where he died in 1953. "It was men like Charles Avery," declared the *Emporia Weekly Gazette* in 1919, "who restored the spirit of the Allies last summer and in so doing saved the world."[13]

Lieutenant Martin left Cantigny without injury but was wounded in June 1918 by a bursting shell, a fragment of which struck him in the back of the head, causing a severe gash. According to his Distinguished Service Cross citation, on July 18 he received a second shell wound—this time to his right side—but "refused to be evacuated and continued to direct his company in the attack through heavy artillery and machine-gun fire to the second and third objective." After being promoted to captain and placed in command of his company, Martin managed to avoid being shelled during the Meuse-Argonne offensive but was wounded on October 5 by a machine-gun bullet. After the war he settled in Indianapolis, married, raised a family, and worked for an insurance company. He also served as a colonel in the U.S. Army Reserve and was stationed during World War II at antiaircraft installations at Hawaii and Okinawa. Martin died in 1966 in Indianapolis at the age of seventy-three.[14]

Major Huebner led the Second Battalion, Twenty-Eighth Regiment during the Battle of Soissons and earned his second Distinguished Service

Photo 11.4: Clarence Ralph Huebner, portrait by Boris Chaliapan, n.d. Courtesy of the National Portrait Gallery.

Cross in July 1918 when, after all the subordinate officers had become casualties, "he reorganized his battalion while advancing, captured his objective and again reorganized his own and another battalion, carrying the line forward." On July 20 he was once again struck in the forehead, this time by a shell fragment that hit him with enough force to give him a concussion. By war's end, Huebner was one of the youngest regimental commanders in the American Expeditionary Forces, with a chest full of decorations that included a Distinguished Service Cross with Oak Leaf Cluster, a Silver Star, two Purple Hearts, the French Legion of Honor and Croix de Guerre, and the Italian War Cross.

A career soldier, Huebner spent part of the interwar years at the Command and General Staff School at Fort Leavenworth. In August 1943 he replaced Major General Terry de la Mesa Allen as commander of the First Division. The Big Red One, which by then had fought in North Africa and Sicily, was sent to England to prepare for the invasion of continental Europe. After going ashore at Omaha Beach on June 6, 1944, the division fought in France, Belgium, and Germany. In January 1945 Huebner was elevated yet again, taking command of the Fifth Corps as it advanced from the Rhine to the Elbe River, where it made contact with the Soviet Red Army. General Huebner was appointed in 1946 as chief of staff of U.S. forces in Europe and in 1949 as acting commander in chief of European Command. In connection with the latter promotion, the *Kansas City Times* published a laudatory article containing the following remarks:

> No West Pointer, Huebner's rise in the army since he enlisted in 1910 is singular proof that a man can advance militarily without benefit of social and financial influence. . . . No one begrudges him his position today. He earned it. He has at times been slowed up by enemy fire. The huskiness in his voice is the result of mustard gas. There is a scar just above and between his eyes, caused by shell fragments that crushed his helmet and broke his neck in World War I, and it reddens when his anger mounts.

Huebner retired in 1950, with the rank of lieutenant general, and served as the civil-defense director for the state of New York until 1960. He died in 1972 at age eighty-three and is buried at Arlington National Cemetery. The Kansan from Bushton shared with Theodore Roosevelt Jr. the distinction of having fought "in America's first victory in Europe, at Cantigny; its largest, the Meuse-Argonne; and its greatest, at Normandy."[15]

CHAPTER TWELVE

Belleau Wood

The Holton Marine Band and James Harbord of the Second Division

On the night of July 11, 1918, Brigadier General James Harbord was working in his quarters next to the Marne River when he was asked to step outside. His irritation disappeared when he looked upon his regimental commanders, their staffs, several hundred marines, and the Sixth Marine Regimental Band. The soldiers had gathered to congratulate him on his elevation from brigade command to leader of the Second Infantry Division. As he recalled in his diary: "It was a complete surprise and touched me very deeply. The band struck up the Marine hymn, '*From the Halls of Montezuma to the Shores of Tripoli.*' The men cheered and the band kept on playing."[1]

Harbord was one of the most important army officers in World War I, providing leadership in three distinct parts of the war effort: organization, supply, and command. The citation for his Distinguished Service Cross notes that he served "as Chief of the Staff of the American Expeditionary Forces, and later as Commanding General, Services of Supply," and also "commanded the Marine Brigade of the 2d Division, Belleau Wood, and later ably commanded the 2d Division during the attack on Soissons, France, on 18 July 1918." Born in Illinois in 1866, Harbord came to Kansas in 1879, graduated from Kansas State Agricultural College in 1886, and was employed by the college until his enlistment in 1889. When he returned to Manhattan in December 1919, he was hailed as "the greatest soldier of Kansas."[2]

The band that serenaded Harbord along the banks of the Marne River was also from Kansas. The Sixth Marine Regimental Band was known as the "Holton Marine Band," although it also included men from surrounding towns such as Corning, Denison, Fairview, Hiawatha, Horton, Sabetha, and Whiting. On August 13, 1918, its members were commended for services performed as stretcher-bearers "during the fighting before Lucy, Bouresches and the Bois de Belleau, June 1st to June 18th, inclusive." Lieutenant Joel Thompson Boone, regimental surgeon and a recipient of the Medal of Honor, praised the musicians from northeastern Kansas for their "distinguished services": "These men labored incessantly during and after the attacks, evacuating the many wounded over a most difficult terrain. . . . On several occasions they continued their difficult task for forty-eight hours without sleep, with very little food, and frequently under heavy machine gun and high explosive fire and during gas bombardment."[3]

Throughout June 1918, the Second Division fought relentlessly and famously in Belleau Wood. The U.S. Army's Ninth and Twenty-Third Regiments formed one of the division's two brigades. In an unusual arrangement, the other brigade consisted of the Fifth and Sixth Marine Regiments and was known as the Fourth Marine Brigade. General Harbord, a career army soldier, was an "honorary" marine, whereas musicians Martin Bender of Holton and Ralph Sinclair of Sabetha *were* marines. The two men trained with their Kansan comrades at Quantico, Virginia; learned first aid in France; and were shelled and gassed at Belleau Wood. They also played, respectively, alto saxophone and clarinet.[4]

* * *

"Wishing to assist our country in this time of strife, we the members of the Holton Municipal Band offer our services to the President of the United States." This resolution was published in the *Holton Signal* on April 26, 1917, and was likely written by Martin A. "Dad" Bender, the head of the organization. Bender was born in 1871 in Powhattan, northwest of Holton, and graduated in 1897 from the Cincinnati Law School. He obtained a master's degree in law in Washington, DC, and worked at the War Department before returning to Kansas at the end of 1899. Bender settled in Holton, a town of about 2,800 residents some thirty miles north of Topeka, and became a prominent citizen. After the Kansas State College Cadet Band joined the marines in the spring of 1917, it is possible that Bender used his connections to convince the War Department to accept a second band from the Sunflower State. Two marine officers came to Holton, listened to the musicians, and gave their approval—subject to the band's ability to recruit men who could meet the requirements for service in the Corps. As it turned out, some could not: Howard Rowe, who played the flute, was rejected due to bad teeth, while Pete Harnack, a drummer, could not obtain his mother's consent.[5]

Mark Hayward was the Holton band's director, but he did not go to France and was replaced by an outsider, Frederick "Fritz" Wilkins Jr. The assistant band director was twenty-seven-year-old Ralph Sinclair, who grew up in Sabetha and worked at a clothing store in Hiawatha. "Ralph Sinclair has started to raise a mustache," reported the *Sabetha Herald*, "and is learning to smoke cigarettes in order to be prepared." The oldest band member was "Dad" Bender, the attorney who would turn forty-seven in January 1918. In the July 15, 1917, edition of the *Topeka Daily Capital*, twenty-seven members of the band appear in a photograph wearing suits and posing with a marine in uniform. Upon arrival at Quantico, Virginia, the musicians marched and drilled but did not practice due to a lack of instruments. By August, most of the men had instruments, and on September 4 the band marched down Pennsylvania Avenue in a parade led by President Wilson. The band set sail in October and played concerts on the troopship three times a day, although most of the Kansas musicians suffered from sea sickness.[6]

"In case our regiment goes to the trenches," Coral Deaver of Fairview informed his parents, "the band boys will be used as hospital apprentices and stretcher bearers and administer first aid treatment." In February 1918 the band practiced wearing gas masks, received instruction in first-aid work, and drilled in "the art of carrying wounded." The following month the Second Division was stationed near Verdun, and the musicians went into the trenches. "The flashes from the big gun," wrote Bender, "look like lightning we have seen when a severe storm was about to break at night in Kansas." He also described when "Sinclair and myself carried our first wounded man, and before we could get him away, the shells began to drop near us." Sinclair recalled the same event in a letter that also mentioned the "rodent army":

> It is a hard proposition to keep from being a rabbit from the waist down and either running away from your patient to find shelter or else give him a h— of a fast ride, which wouldn't be the best for a man who is in much misery. . . . Am now living in a dugout. . . . [T]he rats do not travel in companies or in regiments, but in divisions of full war strength.

At this point the band stopped playing music and only performed ambulance duties. The Second Division was sent west at the end of May to the Marne River region, where the Germans were creating panic by advancing toward Paris. On June 2 the Sixth Regimental Band followed their fellow marines to the front, and by six o'clock, Private Bender recalled, "we were carrying wounded." The Battle of Belleau Wood was underway, with the American forces commanded by a Kansan, Brigadier General Harbord.[7]

* * *

When James Harbord was a child, his family moved from Illinois to Missouri and then—by covered wagon—to Kansas, where they settled near Bushong in Lyon County. In order to provide a better education for their son and two daughters, George and Effie Harbord rented out their farm and moved to Manhattan, the women traveling by rail and the father and son walking the seventy-six miles with their cow. In 1886 James was one of twenty-one graduates of the Kansas State Agricultural College, where he had served as a captain in a cadet company. He took the West Point entrance exam, tied for the top score, but was not selected, instead going to work as an assistant school principal, a librarian, and an instructor of telegraphy. He began his army career in 1899 in the same fashion as Bushton native Clarence Huebner would in 1910: he enlisted as a private. Harbord soon earned a commission as a second lieutenant and continued to rise in the ranks while stationed in Cuba and the Philippines. In what turned out to be a pivotal moment in his career, the fifty-year-old Major Harbord served with Brigadier General Pershing in 1916 during the Pancho Villa expedition.[8]

In the fall of 1916, Harbord went to the Army War College in Washington, where he remained until Pershing, now a major general, named him chief of staff for the AEF. Pershing and his officers sailed in May for Europe, and by August, Harbord was promoted to brigadier general. As noted by biographer Brian Fisher Neuman, General Harbord was instrumental in "creating the AEF General Staff as well as the development and implementation of policies covering, but not limited to, the organization of American forces, training, coordination, administration, and supply." Maintaining good relations with Great Britain and France was a monumental task, and the leaders of the AEF had to amalgamate doughboys into Allied units while also creating an independent army. When the Germans began a series of attacks along the western front in March 1918, General Pershing agreed to allow the four divisions currently in France to fight under Allied command. The First Division, attached to the French Tenth Corps, thereafter launched a successful attack on May 25 against the Germans at Cantigny.[9]

By this time, Harbord had left AEF Headquarters and commanded the Fourth (Marine) Brigade, Second Division. After leaving the Verdun sector and establishing a base northwest of Paris, Harbord described in his diary how a concert by "a good band"—the Sixth Marine Regimental Band—helped establish "friendly relations" with the French family compelled to host American officers. The Second Division was supposed to relieve the First Division at Cantigny, but plans were changed in light of the German offensive that began on May 27. The unexpected success of the attack along on the Rheims-Soissons front caused German general Erich Ludendorff to deemphasize operations in Flanders and focus on capitalizing on the advances made in the direction of the Marne River and Paris. Panic broke out in the French capital as the enemy smashed through the lines and, for the first time since 1914, was in position to cross the Marne and capture the critical east–west highway to Metz. Given the gravity of the situation, Pershing agreed to provide assistance and ordered the Second Division to take up a position near the town of Château-Thierry. The Third Division, which was also called forward, held up the Germans and provided time for French soldiers to withdraw and the Second Division to arrive. To the west of Château-Thierry is the Bois de Belleau, or Belleau Wood, a square mile of trees, dense undergrowth, ravines, and boulders. Next to the woodland are the villages of Bouresches (to the east), Lucy-le-Bocage (to the southwest), and Belleau (to the north). On June 3 the Germans occupied Bouresches and pushed the French beyond Belleau Wood. By nightfall, as the French hastily retreated through the newly established American lines, one of their officers passed along an order to withdraw. When Captain Lloyd Williams saw the note, his reply became part of U.S. Marine Corps lore: "Retreat, hell! We just got here!" The fight was on.[10]

* * *

The bloody month of June 1918 ended with American control of Belleau Wood, the battle for which has been extensively chronicled. Among those Americans who fought there were General Harbord and the Kansans of the Sixth Marine Regimental Band. Personal accounts of the conflict were published in several Kansas newspapers, including the *Holton Recorder*, which throughout 1920 shared Bender's war diary with its readers. As evident from his daily entries, the musicians were in the thick of the fighting:

> June 2: We saw a man die shortly after we got to the dressing station, and just then the Germans began to shell us, one shell (shrapnel) exploded just over us, and broken twigs from the trees were showered on us, but no one was hit. We started to the headquarters with the wounded in the midst of the shelling, and I was completely fagged when I got there, as two of us were carrying a man larger than either of us.
>
> June 3: After we got our wounded in last night, we went to the front line and lay in a wheat field all night, not allowed to go to sleep, but we took a dose [*sic*]. . . . The fighting is still fierce, but thank God we have stopped the Germans and are holding them.
>
> June 4: Left Belleau Wood last night. . . . I am sore and stiff from over-strain in carrying wounded the second and third.[11]

The French commander, General Jean-Marie Degoutte, ordered an attack for June 6. The marines would advance at dawn, establish positions, and then at 5:00 P.M. cross fields of wheat into Belleau Wood, supported by the Twenty-Third Infantry. When the appointed hour arrived, Gunnery Sergeant Dan Daly turned to his platoon and shouted, "C'mon you sons-of-bitches, do you want to live forever?" By the end of the day, the Fourth Marine Brigade had suffered more casualties—over one thousand officers and men—than had been suffered by the Marine Corps in its prior history. One of the wounded men was twenty-eight-year-old Sergeant Robert McGiffert, who returned to Topeka without his left leg to become a city park commissioner and an active member of the American Legion and the Republican Party.

The next morning Bender and Preston "Press" Heidrich of Holton carried a stretcher for about two hundred yards in plain view of the Germans. "They did not shoot at us," wrote Bender, "we thought it was because they saw our red crosses on our arms." John Carter of Denison was not as lucky: he suffered shell shock and was hospitalized until September. The battle affected men differently, as Bender noted in his diary: "Some fellows nearly shot to pieces make no fuss and joke about it, while others slightly wounded fuss as though they expected to die the next minute, if they were not taken care of."[12]

General Harbord, in his first action as brigade commander, appeared to misunderstand the strength of the German position in the woods and underestimate the terrible toll that was being exacted on his marines. Based on incomplete information, he ordered an unsupported attack on the morning of June 8 that resulted in many of his men being cut down by German machine guns. On the twelfth Harbord incorrectly informed the commander of the Second Division, Major General Omar Bundy, that the northern end of the woods "belongs to the 5th Marines." Meanwhile, the Kansas musicians continued to perform their ambulatory duties:

> June 10: We were relieved last night and we are resting today just outside of the range of the German's guns (except the very largest).
>
> June 11: Still in the woods. The first battalion is carrying on the fighting and gaining. Went hunting for cooties and found six. Left at 9 P.M. in support of the front line. Couldn't find any holes to crawl in, it being so dark, so lay down in timber and slept well under shell fire for the rest of the night.
>
> June 12: Remained in hiding during the day, but moved in the evening, and were shelled just as we were leaving, wounding a number of our men.

> We went to Chappelon and set up our dressing station, about a mile from the front. We went back to the front and slept in timber.

"We have been in action now up here for 12 days," Coral Deaver wrote on the twelfth. "My, but things were lively as our skirmish line moved across the wheat field."[13]

The shelling on June 13 was the heaviest enemy barrage of the battle, but the marines and the soldiers of the Twenty-Third Regiment held on in the village of Bouresches. This was followed by three separate gas attacks, which Richard Faulkner describes as both diabolical and deadly:

> [Soldiers looked for] the telltale smell of poison gas: new-mown hay for phosgene and garlic for mustard gas. . . . Men exposed to a lethal concentration of phosgene died a painful death; their last minutes filled with futile and labored gasping for air like a fish floundering after being removed from water. . . . Mustard [gas] killed by inhibiting the soldier's ability to breathe or by drowning as the blisters erupted and filled his lungs with fluid.

About half of the Kansan musicians on the field were gassed to some degree. Deaver asserted that he "wasn't worth a dime from that time on" and spent two months in a French hospital. Harlan Wolverton of Holton, who had his "eyes glued shut," said the gas "was thick enough to cut it with a knife." His stretcher partner, Orville Tomlinson, avoided being shot—"I could feel myself stepping over the machine gun bullets"—but inhaled a large quantity of gas and "was practically one big blister." At this point the first phase of the battle ended, and the battered Fourth Marine Brigade was relieved by men from the Third Division. By order of General Pershing, musicians would no longer be sent into battle, as Bender duly noted:

> June 16: We took a much needed bath from a spring, and made a raid on the cooties.
>
> June 18: Still resting and hiding in woods. Learned at noon that General Pershing issued an order that bandsmen were not to be used for stretcher bearers, but perform other duties back of the front lines. Our captain all worked up over it, and said he didn't want to let us go, but at 4 P.M. he said he guessed he would have to, and told us to report at headquarters, and we were soon on our way.
>
> June 21: We tried to practice, thirteen of us, with Sin [Ralph Sinclair] directing.

> June 22: [W]e went out to the woods . . . and played a short program, but my, what music; yet the boys enthusiastically cheered every piece. Hungry for music. We had to cover our instruments, so the reflection of the sun would not attract the Germans.[14]

On June 21 General Harbord ordered the Third Battalion, Fifth Marine Regiment (the "3/5") to resume the offensive. In over two weeks of fighting, four of his six battalions had lost at least 40 percent of their strength. Harbord "wanted Belleau Wood very badly and began pressing those below him to secure the victory that had been [prematurely] reported just days before." In his diary the fifty-two-year-old general expressed frustration with the fog of war: "You wish more than anything else in the world to know the exact position of your troops, and exactly where the enemy is with reference to them. . . . This information sometimes takes a day and night to filter in, and it is difficult to be patient." Biographer Brian Neumann suggests that Harbord's strategy of open movement and envelopment caused thousands of marines to charge "directly into the face of German machine-guns with little or no artillery support," while Alan Axelrod declares, "the attack by the 3/5 on June 23 was a catastrophe." But three days later the marines cleared the northern portion of Belleau Wood, and Major Maurice Shearer reported to Harbord that "Belleau Woods now U.S. Marine Corps entirely." Almost ten thousand men in the Second Division had been killed or wounded, with over half of the casualties suffered by the Fourth Marine Brigade. "The woods out there look now like a cyclone had gone thru it," wrote Sinclair on July 1. "Leaves have nearly all been shot off and about two thirds of the trees shot down." Bender observed, "Paris is wild over the success of the Americans," adding with pride, "a Marine emblem is a free pass to everything."[15]

* * *

According to one report, only twelve members of the Sixth Marine Regimental Band "came out unscathed." Three of the men gassed in Belleau Wood—Deaver, Tomlinson, and Wolverton—remained a long time in hospitals but eventually recovered. Deaver, who was told he "should not toot a horn until his lungs improve," lived until 1961; Tomlinson passed away in 1969; and Wolverton died in 1972 in Topeka, where he had been a repairman and tuner of pianos. The Kansas musicians who were not sent home went with the Second Division into Germany, where they were eventually split up, some returning to the United States and others assigned to different bands. Seward Niebling of Hiawatha played on a pleasure boat on the Rhine River;

Clarence Lutz of Holton was stationed in Honnigen, Germany; and Ralph Sinclair played in a jazz orchestra in Coblenz at "the swellest hotel in the city." On August 12, 1919, a few of the remaining band members, including Harry Artman of Denison and Ray Woodworth and Jack Bullock of Holton, participated in a parade in Washington to honor the "Devil Dogs" of the Fourth Marine Brigade.

Sergeant Sinclair came home (with the Croix de Guerre), resumed his job at the Hiawatha clothing store, married, and had two daughters. He later became a salesman. Sinclair passed away in 1977 in Texas. Martin Bender, who was awarded a Silver Star, served as a district court judge for ten years, winning a primary contest in 1920 against Will Smith of Oskaloosa in what newspapers called the battle of "infantry against marine, 'doughboy' against 'devil dog.'" Judge Bender, who also served as a state senator for four years, died in 1946 at age seventy-four and is buried in the Holton City Cemetery.[16]

* * *

After stopping the German advance toward the Marne, the Allies counterattacked in July, the month that proved to be the turning point of World War I. General Harbord was given command of the Second Division and instructed to advance—as part of the French Tenth Army—toward the town of Soissons. The division suffered "tremendous casualties" on July 18 but "made incredible gains," shattering the German lines. On the second day of battle, the Sixth Marine Regiment suffered the most casualties, and during its two days of fighting, the Second Division lost over four thousand men. Shortly thereafter, the Allies took Soissons, and the Germans began a general withdrawal. "It appears I have to congratulate you every time I see you," General Pershing remarked when he greeted his former chief of staff. Harbord had reached a high point in his career and hoped to command a corps or an army before the war ended.

Pershing instead surprised his trusted friend by removing him from the Second Division and placing him in charge of the AEF's logistical service as commanding general, Services of Supply. While displeased with the sudden change, Harbord worked hard in his new role, received favorable reviews, and became the choice of Secretary of War Baker to command the AEF should General Pershing die or become incapacitated. Harbord remained in France after the armistice, witnessed the signing of the Treaty of Versailles, and was sent on a fact-finding mission to the Middle East, where he collected information regarding the massacres of Armenians. Upon his return to the States, he was promoted to major general in the Regular Army and assigned (again)

Photo 12.1: James Harbord. Courtesy of the Library of Congress.

to command the Second Infantry Division, now at Camp Travis, Texas. In 1921 he was honored by his alma mater as "the Big Gun" and appointed (again) to work with General Pershing, who was now U.S. Army chief of staff. Although Harbord was considered the logical choice to succeed Pershing, he left the army to accept a position with the Radio Corporation of America (RCA), where he served as president from 1922 to 1930 and thereafter as chairman until 1947. Major General James Guthrie Harbord died on August 20, 1947. The *Wichita Eagle* described him as "a modest hero" whose service in World War I "placed second only to that of General Pershing."[17]

CHAPTER THIRTEEN

Rocks of the Marne

Ulysses Grant McAlexander and Thomas Reid of the Third Division

The American doughboys of the First Division captured and held the village of Cantigny in May 1918, providing a boost to Allied morale. This battle took place at the same time as Germany's third spring offensive, aimed at French lines between Soissons and Rheims. The Second Division responded by attacking German troops in and around Belleau Wood, suffering (and inflicting) tremendous casualties throughout the month of June. As noted by David John Ulbrich, "Belleau Wood occupies a hallowed place in U.S. Marine Corps lore and history," and the acts of heroism and sacrifice "are ingrained in the Marines' collective consciousness from the first days of boot camp, during ceremonies at birthday balls, on walls in museums, and on pages of publications."[1]

The Third Division—now based at Fort Stewart, Georgia—also continues to draw inspiration from the first role it played in the Great War. In the early hours of July 15, 1918, the German army, as part of a larger attack, crossed the Marne River east of the town of Château-Thierry. The defense of this portion of the winding Marne was assigned to the four regiments of the Third Division: the Fourth and Seventh Regiments, between Château-Thierry and the village of Fossoy, and the Thirtieth and Thirty-Eighth Regiments farther east and upstream. The Thirty-Eighth Infantry, commanded by Colonel Ulysses Grant McAlexander, defended the strategically important Surmelin Creek valley, which if taken could serve as a gateway to Paris. The higher ground east of the valley was assigned to the 125th Division of the French army, but as McAlexander had predicted, the French troops immediately fell back in the face of the German onslaught. The Thirty-Eighth Infantry faced the possibility of being flanked from high ground, and to make matters worse, the Germans had dislodged the Thirtieth Infantry from its defensive positions along the Marne. Consequently, the colonel and his men were compelled to reposition in a "horseshoe" formation in order to turn back a three-sided attack by numerically superior forces. The Germans were turned back.

McAlexander, who was born in Minnesota but raised on a farm near McPherson, Kansas, was praised for the remainder of his life as the "Rock of the Marne," an honorific also bestowed on the Thirty-Eighth Regiment and the entire Third Division. The combative "Old Mac," who had anticipated the possibility of encirclement, earned his famous nickname by expertly deploying and courageously rallying his troops. He was not, however, the only such "Rock." Another member of the Thirty-Eighth Infantry with Kansas connections, Captain Thomas Reid, also stood firm and rallied his men at perhaps the most critical juncture of the fighting.[2]

* * *

Ulysses Grant McAlexander was born on August 30, 1864, in Dundas, Minnesota. His father, Commodore Perry McAlexander, was a Civil War veteran who was also named after a famous military figure, the War of 1812 naval hero Matthew Perry. The family moved in 1872 to a farm near McPherson, Kansas, where Grant excelled in school. When his parents died in 1879 and 1880, the fifteen-year-old became the ward of a local citizen, John D. Milliken. After briefly attending the University of Kansas, McAlexander received an appointment to West Point and passed the examination for admittance. During his time in New York, the young cadet saw his namesake, former president Ulysses S. Grant, as well as two other Union army generals, William Tecumseh Sherman and Philip H. Sheridan. At his graduation in 1887, McAlexander received his diploma from Sheridan, who remarked, "Ulysses Grant! Young man, I hope that you may add an additional luster to that glorious name!"[3]

While serving in Montana and the Dakota Territory during the Indian Wars, McAlexander married Minnesota May Skinner (from Minnesota) and became a father when Perry McAlexander was born in 1888. Captain McAlexander fought in the Spanish-American War, earning a citation for "gallantry in action," and in the Philippines. He was thereafter appointed commandant of cadets and professor of military science and tactics at Oregon Agricultural College (now Oregon State University). While there, he was promoted to major and lieutenant colonel, oversaw the construction of the college armory (now called McAlexander Fieldhouse), and helped train National Guard and ROTC soldiers. Military training was an integral part of the college curriculum, and the popular commandant was said to have "cut quite a figure on campus."[4]

Photo 13.1: Ulysses Grant McAlexander. Courtesy of the Oregon State University Military Photographs Collection, 1875-1975, OSU Libraries Special Collections & Archives Research Center.

Lieutenant Colonel McAlexander became Colonel McAlexander in May 1917 and was sent to France the following month to command Clyde Grimsley of Kansas and the other men of the Sixteenth Infantry Regiment. He was reassigned to the Eighteenth Infantry (also part of the First Division) until December 31, 1917, when he was relieved of command and given a "desk job" at the Port of Saint-Nazaire. Historians disagree as to the reason for this reassignment. According to Laurence Stallings, the pugnacious colonel was sacked "because of his profane refusal to believe that the French could teach him anything about war." Stephen Harris states that McAlexander was declared unfit for command after supposedly sleeping at his post in a combat zone, a charge that Michael Neiberg believes was mistakenly asserted after the colonel spent the night at the front lines. In yet another version of the story, the decision to reassign McAlexander was made when he insisted that his officers should not be sent to staff school because they were needed to train the regiment.[5]

Two facts about Old Mac are not in dispute: he preferred to be in the middle of combat, and he was considered by many of his fellow soldiers to be, in the words of a West Point classmate, "the stubbornest creature that ever drew the breath of life." His fighting spirit was undeniable, and General Pershing gave the wiry fifty-three-year-old colonel a new command in May 1918: the Thirty-Eighth Infantry, Third Division. Given this reprieve, McAlexander intended to show everyone "what asses they made of themselves by sending me to the rear." Within two weeks of his appointment, the Thirty-Eighth Infantry was positioned on the Marne River, and in less than two months, McAlexander and his regiment would earn their cherished nickname, the Rock of the Marne.[6]

* * *

Thomas Campbell Reid was born in Missouri in December 1887, the oldest of three boys. His father, while in his forties, attended the American School of Osteopathy at Kirksville, Missouri, and in 1906 moved his family to southeastern Kansas. Tom graduated from Columbus High School in 1909 at age twenty-one, then went to the same medical school as his father, where he became the "honor man" of the class of 1912. Rather than return to Columbus, Kansas, the young doctor accepted an invitation to establish a practice in Demopolis, Alabama, a slightly smaller town of fewer than three thousand residents. During the next four years, Dr. T. C. Reid married his high school sweetheart, became a father, sang duets at social events, and became a leader in the Elks Lodge, the local brass band, and the business community.

Life changed drastically in 1917 for Tom and his wife, Vale, a graduate of the University of Kansas. In January the couple came home to bury their only child, a daughter who died suddenly just a few days prior to her second birthday. In April the United States declared war on Germany, and Reid reported in August to the officer training camp at Fort Oglethorpe, Georgia. He received his commission in November and was given command of Company F, Thirty-Eighth Infantry, Third Division. When Captain Reid left in March 1918 for France, his wife returned to Columbus, secured employment at the local drug store, and waited with family and friends to learn the fate of her husband. As it turned out, his fate would be intertwined with that of his commanding officer, Colonel McAlexander.[7]

* * *

The third German offensive of the spring of 1918, which began on May 27, caused the Allies to retreat to the Marne River. At Château-Thierry, where the river turns toward Paris, a machine-gun battalion of the Third Division slowed the German advance and diverted the enemy farther west toward the village of Vaux and Belleau Wood. In June, as the Second Division stopped the German momentum at great cost, the Third Division was assigned to defend the southern bank of the Marne east of Château-Thierry to the river's perpendicular confluence with the north-flowing Surmelin Creek, a distance of approximately seven miles. An untried outfit, the Third was commanded by Major General Joseph Dickman, a graduate of the University of Dayton (1871) and the U.S. Military Academy (1881). The Fourth and Seventh Infantry Regiments were part of the division's Fifth Brigade, whereas the Thirtieth Regiment and McAlexander's Thirty-Eighth Regiment were part of the Sixth Brigade, led by Brigadier General Charles Crawford of Paola, Kansas. In contrast to the Second Division, which was rushed into battle, the Third Division had over a month to establish its defensive positions and plot its response to the next German attack.[8]

McAlexander used this time wisely. He surveyed the sector himself, which included four successive lines of resistance—the Marne River, a railway embankment, an aqueduct roughly paralleling the railroad tracks, and a wooded area straddling Surmelin Creek. According to one story, a sergeant in a forward area who did not recognize his commander shouted, "Get down, you crazy idiot," to which Old Mac supposedly replied, "When you get to be a colonel, son, you can go where you please." Based on his personal observations, the colonel insisted that his regiment's area of responsibility be extended to include some of the hills on the eastern side of the Surmelin, roughly perpendicular to the Marne. McAlexander pointed out that if the French 125th Division retreated from there, "it would be like shooting fish in a bathtub for the Germans to be high above us and on my right flank." To protect the Thirty-Eighth Regiment, Captain Reid and the men of Company F were ordered to dig trenches on the hills facing this elevated area. McAlexander doubted the resolve of the French troops in part because their officers favored the principles of an "elastic" defense in depth. Having suffered tremendous losses in the past by concentrating forces near the front lines, some French generals now elected to oppose German advances with a token force, keeping the bulk of their defenders out of harm's way until the moment came to direct a counterattack against the exhausted enemy. McAlexander, on the other hand, insisted that his regiment would defend "with one foot in the water" and prevent the Germans from crossing the river. In contrast, the Thirtieth Infantry to his left deployed fewer men along the banks of the Marne and instead formed a stronger secondary defensive line.[9]

Due to a successful interrogation of prisoners, the Allied forces knew that the Germans would begin their offensive with an artillery bombardment ten minutes into the first hour of July 15. As a countermeasure, the American and French artillery initiated the fighting by shelling areas where the attacking forces had assembled. Despite the disruption of their plans, the Germans began sending soldiers across the Marne, which at points was fifty feet wide with a current and depth that prevented wading. The first line of defense for the Thirty-Eighth Regiment belonged to the Second Battalion, with Companies G and H positioned along the river west of Surmelin Creek, Company E between the railroad embankment and the aqueduct east of the creek, and Captain Reid's Company F on the other side of the aqueduct protecting the right flank. McAlexander had assured his wife that he "was never born to be ended by a shell" but was nearly proven wrong when one of the first German rounds landed near his command post and blew out the windows. "They may kill us," the colonel often told his troops, "but they cannot whip us."[10]

* * *

Not all Kansans in the Third Division were in the Thirty-Eighth Regiment. First Lieutenant C. William Ryan, a lawyer from Wathena, was in charge of a platoon in Company A, Thirtieth Infantry and was positioned on the morning of July 15 behind the railroad embankment running along the Marne. Lieutenant Ryan, whose first name, Colonel, undoubtedly generated a great deal of confusion, became alarmed when retreating doughboys reported that Germans were crossing in great numbers on a pontoon bridge. "I could see German infantrymen, wearing overcoats," Ryan recalled, "coming straight toward us in approach formation." He and his men stood firm and were able to utilize the high ground to their advantage, preventing the enemy from setting up machine guns and stopping their advance. "Our battalion saw the hardest fighting of our regiment," Ryan wrote to his sister, "and my platoon, the hardest of my company." Because their initial line of defense had been overrun, however, the commander of the Thirtieth Regiment ordered a withdrawal in order to shell the advancing Germans. This plan, Michael Neiberg notes, "made good tactical sense and it kept the Germans from breaking the 30th Regiment's second line, but it dangerously exposed the flank of the neighboring 38th Regiment." As for Ryan, he survived the Second Battle of the Marne, earned a Distinguished Service Cross during the Meuse-Argonne offensive, and returned to Kansas, where he served twenty years as a state judge for Nemaha, Brown, and Doniphan Counties.[11]

* * *

The threat to Reid and McAlexander also came from their right flank. Four companies from the Twenty-Eighth "Keystone" Division were assigned to the sector held by the French 125th Division. The men, mostly from Pennsylvania, were positioned next to the river and remained in place when the French forces withdrew after the onset of the German artillery bombardment. According to one account, the shelling was so intense that doughboys "had to be restrained forcibly by their comrades from rushing out into the open in their temporary madness." When the enemy troops crossed over and infiltrated the sector, the Americans attempted to fight their way to safety, either to the rear lines or west to the Thirty-Eighth Infantry. A few were successful, but most were not, particularly in Company C, 110th Infantry. Of the 158 Pennsylvanians from Somerset County in Company C, only 21 avoided capture, injury, or death. The Thirty-Eighth Infantry had stood firm on the banks of the Marne, but as Colonel McAlexander had predicted, the Germans were able to cross over upstream and would soon turn their attention to the Surmelin valley.[12]

When the German bombardment commenced, Captain Reid was in Moulins, a village east of Surmelin Creek. He immediately ordered two platoons "to move to the trenches and follow Col. McAlexander's instructions in case the French fell back on our right." When it became apparent that the Germans were in the adjacent sector, Reid understood that "if F Co. broke; E and H and possibly G Companies would have all been killed or captured from behind." Soon thereafter, the men of Company F saw soldiers approaching in the dim light from the east, men they first thought were French but soon realized were the enemy:

> [The Germans] were met by automatic and rifle fire and the few who were left were reinforced and tried to storm the trenches. They were again met with heavy fire and when they faltered Lt. [Ralph Eberlin] gave the command for a charge with bayonets fixed and this charge carried them back toward Varennes and across the Varennes–Crezancy road. The two platoons with me were deployed at the base of the hill, took care of the advance along the road and *not one* of the Germans ever passed along the road to Moulins, nor after the charge did they cross the road between Co. E and Varennes.

The trenches were targeted by German airplanes, machine guns, and artillery, causing Reid's men to withdraw and regroup atop a hill with a commanding view of the valley. Soon thereafter, they were under fire, both from the air and from a machine gun and mortar on their left flank. The situation was both untenable and critical:

> We had to move but we could not afford to abandon that position, for by so doing we abandoned the companies on the railroad and the Surmelin Valley. . . . Our decision was to go forward, clean out the German mortar and a machine gun, and get around the hill under cover. This was done. The men carried the attack forward with vigor and after a few bursts the machine gun was abandoned and we used same until the ammunition was exhausted. The mortar did not give us any more trouble, most of the crew being killed, but the remainder made away with the piece.

Reid's men were "pretty well torn up," but they held firm. With the Germans in complete control of the air, the Americans were once again forced from the high ground. The captain assembled his soldiers in a ravine east of Moulins, where they were joined by some men from other units. He gave a new order to attack: "It was at this time that I used my cooks, mechanics, Supply Sergeant, some stokes mortar men and my remaining 125 men, with very few N.C.O.'s. . . . We retook the position on the brow of the hill." As described by Stephen Harris, Reid's men "had no cover whatsoever, not a tree or bush or rock, and enemy planes were circling overhead," but they nevertheless "stormed the ridge before the enemy knew what had hit them" and "saved the right flank of the Third Division."[13]

At this point the men were exhausted, in danger of being surrounded, and subjected to misdirected friendly fire. As Reid reported to McAlexander:

> There were times during that long day and night that the men came to the breaking point. With machine guns across the river, on our flanks, behind us and two aeroplanes over us with their machine guns wide open, the German artillery AND OUR OWN pounding us, the men were ready to quit and only by personally going along the line and talking to the men were they held there.

The doughboys held their position and were reinforced at four in the afternoon, when Company E withdrew from its position near the railroad embankment. Two hours later Major Guy Rowe, commander of the Second Battalion, ordered the men to move farther away from the river. The French at 7:30 P.M. counterattacked east of the Surmelin valley, and the Germans began to withdraw to their prior positions north of the Marne. At five o'clock the next morning, Reid received an order from McAlexander to leave the field of battle. "We came out under machine gun fire from across the ravine," Reid reported, "but by using cover we were able to withdraw successfully by leaving automatic rifles to cover us." By noon on July 16, Major General Dickman was able to report: "There are no Germans in the foreground of the 3d Division sector except the dead."[14]

* * *

On July 30 Captain Reid sent a letter to his parents that was published in the *Columbus Daily Modern Light*:

> I suppose you have already read of the lone battalion that remained at its post all day. Well, that was us, and believe me, I thought several times we were on our way to Germany. . . . I just couldn't keep the tears back when I saw my brave fellows dead on the field facing the enemy without fear in their faces, and fighting for liberty. . . . But from a soldier's standpoint the men were magnificent, and when called upon to charge they went forward with a mighty rush and fairly swept the Germans off their feet.

Ten days earlier, McAlexander wrote to his wife, "But for the Third Division, the Germans would now be on another drive for Paris, but the 8 miles of line assigned to us held like a rock." The chief of staff of the division, Robert Kelton, praised McAlexander as the "Rock of the Marne" in a meeting with Major General Dickman and similarly described the colonel in a subsequent message to Pershing's staff: "He was like the rock of the Surmelin Valley as George H. Thomas was of Chickamauga." Both Reid and McAlexander were also commended by the men who fought with them. Captain Jesse W. Wooldridge of Company G, who earned a Distinguished Service Cross on July 15 for leading a counterattack "against an enemy of five times his own numbers," later described Reid as "every inch a soldier." But he reserved his most effusive praise for "the military genius of his time, that deep chested, square shouldered, square jawed 'Old Rock,'" who "radiated dynamic energy, vibrated punch, aggression, [and] initiative" with "an intense affection for his men that was felt and understood by all." Wooldridge asserted it was McAlexander's deployment of Reid's company that "saved the 2nd Battalion from annihilation" and declared that "the limitless courage and intrepidity of our Colonel . . . made valorous deeds seem a natural thing to do."[15]

* * *

Nineteen Kansans in the Third Division were killed in action on July 15, 1918, including six from the Thirty-Eighth Regiment. One of the men, Private George Wingate of Ogden, served under Captain Reid. Fourteen months earlier, on May 15, 1917, Wingate married Marie Eckert at the St. Joseph's Catholic Church in Pottawatomie County. His wife received a total of twenty-two letters from him, including one that declared, "Dearest, I will do my duty to my country and our flag and what our forefathers did for us, and when the war is over I'll be back and what a happy family we will be with God's blessing on us." Private Wingate left behind a son, George Raphael Wingate, who was born on April 1, 1918, after his father had left home.[16]

* * *

The Second Battle of the Marne had two phases: the failed German offensive that ended on July 17 and the successful Allied counteroffensive that began on July 18. Crown Prince Wilhelm, commander of the German Fifth Army, stated after the war that the failed offensive convinced him that Germany was "drifting towards the final catastrophe." Chancellor Georg von Hertling agreed: "We expected grave events in Paris for the end of July. That was on the 15th. On the 18th even the most optimistic among us knew that all was lost. The history of the world was played out in three days." When it became clear that the Allies had repulsed the Germans all along the fifty-mile front, Supreme Allied Commander Foch ordered an immediate counteroffensive to take the city of Soissons and sever enemy supply routes. The Allies had finally taken the initiative, and the Germans would be on the defensive for the remainder of the war.[17]

McAlexander's wartime heroics continued. After repulsing the Germans, the Thirty-Eighth Infantry crossed the Marne in July and helped push the enemy back as part of this sustained counteroffensive that continued until the armistice. On July 22 the colonel literally crawled in front of his regiment and earned a Distinguished Service Cross:

> [McAlexander] displayed exceptional gallantry . . . by going ahead of the most advanced elements of his command, and in full view of the enemy, leading his men by force of his own example to the successful assault of Jaulgonne and the adjoining heights. Later in the day, when progress was again checked, he personally reconnoitered to within 50 yards of hostile machine-gun nests, and through information thus obtained, was enabled to hold an advanced position, with both flanks exposed, for more than 36 hours.

In August Old Mac was promoted to the rank of brigadier general and given command of the 180th "Texas" Brigade, Ninetieth Division, which fought in the Saint-Mihiel and Meuse-Argonne battles. He stayed with the occupation force in Germany until 1919, then served five additional years at home, retiring in 1924 with the rank of major general. After his first wife died in 1928, McAlexander remarried and—at the age of sixty-nine—unsuccessfully sought the 1934 nomination as governor of Oregon. His second wife, Pearl Palmer McAlexander, died in 1935, he soon followed, passing away at his home on September 18, 1936. The following day the *Wichita Eagle* reported the news under the headline "American Hero of the Marne Dies" but failed to note that McAlexander had spent his formative years in Kansas. One side of his headstone at Arlington National Cemetery sets forth details regarding his life, his first spouse, and his military medals. On the other side are two stars and five words: "McAlexander" and "Rock of the Marne."[18]

In contrast to McAlexander, Thomas Reid was not a career soldier, receiving his discharge from the army in September 1919. Reid suffered from arthritis and apparently did not practice medicine after the war: the 1920 census lists him as the assistant manager of a dry-goods store in Demopolis. That same year he was awarded the Distinguished Service Cross for "fearlessly expos[ing] himself to heavy fire" on July 15, 1918, and "personally [leading] two counterattacks upon the enemy, breaking up their attack and forcing them to retire." In 1943 the Reids moved to Montgomery, where Tom was employed by the Alabama Chamber of Commerce. His wife, Vale, passed away in 1951, and Tom died at age seventy-one in 1959 from injuries suffered after crossing a street into the path of an oncoming automobile. His obituary states that he had been a shoe salesman, a singer who once owned a minstrel troupe, the chamber-of-commerce manager of several cities, and the director of the Alabama State Coliseum. Thomas Campbell Reid, another "Rock of the Marne," is buried in the City Cemetery in Columbus, Kansas, alongside his wife and their infant daughter.[19]

* * *

McAlexander was not the only Kansan in the AEF who was named for a president. The 353rd (All Kansas) Infantry, Eighty-Ninth Division had at least seven soldiers with famous names. George Washington Gardner, the first draft registrant selected from Decatur County, served in Company F, whereas George Washington Lempenau of Westmoreland was a member of Company A, and George Washington Brown of Topeka was in Company E. All three men survived the war, Private Lempenau living another seven decades before his death in 1989 at the age of ninety-six. Another "president"

Photo 13.2: Thomas Reid (on right), circa 1911–1913. Courtesy of the Museum of Osteopathic Medicine, Kirksville, MO, item no. 2013.27.45.65.

who survived the war was Andrew Jackson Galbreth of Mankato, who served as a sergeant with Gardner in Company F.

Thomas Jefferson Buchan, Chester Arthur Bird, and Benjamin Harrison Black of the 353rd Infantry did not return home. Buchan, who was from Wilson, died in July from a gunshot accident. Bird of Stockton and Black of Aulne were killed on September 12 during the Saint-Mihiel offensive. Bird, age thirty-one, died instantly when three machine-gun bullets struck him in the head as he was repositioning his own machine gun. Twenty-three-year-old Black, who had reported to Camp Funston on the day of his father's funeral, was also killed in action.[20]

The Thirty-Fifth Division included five men named in honor of presidents. Private John Tyler Harris of Topeka was gassed when the 137th Infantry advanced during the Meuse-Argonne offensive in the final days of September. "I never ate anything for the five days we were fighting," Harris recalled, "I just lived on excitement." Private Ulysses Grant Cassel of Beverly and the 138th Infantry was killed near the Argonne Forest on the third day of that battle. In a letter sent by his captain to his mother, Cassell is described as "a splendid soldier, absolutely fearless and a soldier and a man thru and thru." His body was returned to the United States and laid to rest in Arlington National Cemetery.[21]

In addition to Sergeant Theodore Roosevelt Blevins of Oskaloosa, Company B, 139th Infantry included Corporal William McKinley Pratt of Emporia and Private Grover Cleveland Miller of Valley Falls. Pratt would become one of the first casualties in Company B. He was mortally wounded on August 21 when his grenade exploded prematurely, dying the following day. According to the *Nortonville News*, Grover Cleveland Miller lost both his foot and his brother (Eugene) in France. He died at age sixty-eight in 1950 and is buried in Jefferson County.[22]

CHAPTER FOURTEEN

Death in the Trenches

Company B and the Vosges Mountains

In the six weeks between April 8 and May 21, 1918, the men in Company B, 139th Infantry traveled from Oklahoma to New York, over the ocean to England, and then across the English Channel to Le Havre, France. This was the first transatlantic voyage for nearly everyone in the Thirty-Fifth Division, and many Kansans, including Ted Blevins, became seasick during the journey. "I felt O.K. the first two days," the young soldier told his family, "but was sick for the next four, couldn't eat and fed the fishes regularly for the first afternoon. I wasn't seriously ill but I was feeling like the last rose of summer." He noted in his letter that "the grub on board was fairly good" but remembered things differently later in life: "A lot of fellows got sick. I got sick and lost 12 pounds. I think we were fed a lot of stewed rabbit!" William Davis told his father, "we did not travel very fast" and "kept a close watch for subs." According to another member of Company B, Clair Fletcher of Dunavent, there was a "sub scare" along the Irish coast that "didn't turn out to be anything." Not everyone from Jefferson County, however, made it across the ocean without incident. Louie Horr was a sailor on the USS *President Lincoln* when it was hit by three German torpedoes on the evening of May 31. The ship sank in twenty minutes, and twenty-six men died. In a letter published in the *Oskaloosa Independent*, Horr said he was adrift for eighteen hours before being rescued, observing that "the most lonesome place on the face of the earth is the middle of the ocean on a raft."[1]

In contrast to the trip, the men of Company B spoke positively about the destination. England in May, declared Blevins, was "like Kansas after an April shower, beautiful scenery, green grass, trees just leafing out and everything lovely." Fletcher also characterized England as "a beautiful country," most likely based on his view from the train that transported Company B from Liverpool to Romsey, next to the port city of Southampton. During their brief stay, the doughboys were commanded by Scottish officers. According to Blevins, they "were a nice group, even though we called them 'Ladies from

Hell' because of their kilts." The Kansans teased their hosts when celebrating the Fourth of July but understood the gravity of the current situation. "The English people sure appreciate the American soldier," wrote Ralph Nichols. "They know what it is to be at war." At this time Blevins was ordered to return to the United States to serve as a grenade instructor. Intent on "staying with the gang," he avoided the reassignment by finding a soldier from Emporia who agreed to go in his place.[2]

William "Bill" Smith was twenty-nine years old when he arrived in France, a graduate of Washburn College, a lawyer, and a commissioned officer. In contrast, Melvin Dyson and Nichols were only eighteen; Blevins was nineteen; Sam Gutschenritter, Billy Kimmel, and Vic Seagraves were twenty, and Davis was twenty-two. The men were issued gas masks, steel helmets, and British firearms, including the bolt-action Enfield rifle. After crossing the channel and spending two days at Le Havre, the troops squeezed into railroad boxcars marked "40 Hommes/8 Chevaux" (forty men or eight horses) and traveled up the coast to the towns of Eu and Millebosc. The front lines were less than forty miles away, and the newly arrived Kansans could hear enemy planes "humming here and there" and "big guns barking all night long." This was supposed to be a time for training with their Scottish instructors, but the First Division was already preparing for its attack on Cantigny, and there was a distinct possibility that other Americans would be sent into combat imminently. In a letter dated May 27, Blevins predicted that he would soon be "up yonder where the noise and excitement is going on," but the Thirty-Fifth Division remained in camp. A large crowd assembled on Decoration Day to listen to a patriotic speech by Lieutenant Smith, and the soldiers otherwise spent their idle time complaining about long hikes, tea for breakfast, and French girls—"it's hard luck," Blevins wrote, "that they can't talk American." Other cultural adjustments included listening to Scottish bagpipes and watching a game called "soccer football." In his letter published in the *Winchester Star*, Private Roy Mott said the Scots "made very pretty music, but it sounded like the same tune over and over to me." As for soccer, he explained, "you do not touch the ball with your hands, but try to kick it through the goal."[3]

The brief association with the British Thirtieth Division ended in early June, when the infantry units of the Thirty-Fifth Division were sent to eastern France. The men traveled by train, passing south of Paris and a safe distance from Belleau Wood, where Kansans in the Sixth Marine Regimental Band were being gassed as they assisted wounded marines. The crowded boxcars had two axles and "minimal springing" while "ventilation was poor, sleeping difficult, and sanitation nearly impossible." As described by Fletcher, the trip was both an ordeal and an adventure:

> Three days we rode. Oh what a time. . . . One night I had my rain coat over me; woke up in the night train going like sixty—cold, coat gone, some sucker had stolen it. Well I froze till day then I stole another one. Gee, it was dog eat dog I am telling you. We were a dirty bunch, I tell you. Sitting on top of the cars, looking thru the cracks in the car, riding any place we could hold on, passed thru Rouen [and] Versailles near Paris. Finally unloaded at Arches, in the mountains just ten miles from Epinal. Here we had our barracks I wrote of—a nice little camp yet the guns still barked and the planes flew around. Then in about a week loaded on a truck and drove all day. Passed thru Remiremont, went thru a great tunnel and into Alsace.

The three-hundred-mile trip to Arches ended on June 11. "We are still in France," wrote Blevins on the thirteenth, "but a long long way from where we were." One of the men who stayed behind was Dyson, who was with the Supply Company, 139th Infantry. In a letter dated June 2, Dyson told his father that he was in a hospital "somewhere in France" with a case of the mumps. Tobacco and candy were scarce, he reported; German prisoners were plentiful; and the American patients had to make do with "weak tea" and British rations. Despite the absence of "good old black coffee," the eighteen-year-old recovered and rejoined his company.[4]

Arches, a small town situated on the Moselle River near the Vosges Mountains in eastern France, was where, on June 14, Blevins survived a close brush with death. "I was out showing a rookie how to throw bombs," the sergeant told his family; "he mis-threw one and it burst just a few feet away and a piece of it went thru my shirt collar and struck me in the neck." The grenade shrapnel left a permanent scar, but no "wound stripe" was awarded because the injury was not caused by the enemy. Blevins and the rest of Company B left Arches in the last week of June and headed into the Vosges Mountains, traveling by truck to Moosch and then hiking to Cornimont, where the men were billeted for a month. They were now very close to the front line. The French geographical term for a mountain with a rounded summit is *ballon*, and Company B was not far from the Grand Ballon—the highest mountain of the Vosges—just five miles west of the German-controlled town of Guebwiller. Consequently, Sam Gutschenritter was stationed close to where his father, Charley Gutschenritter, was born and raised. When the

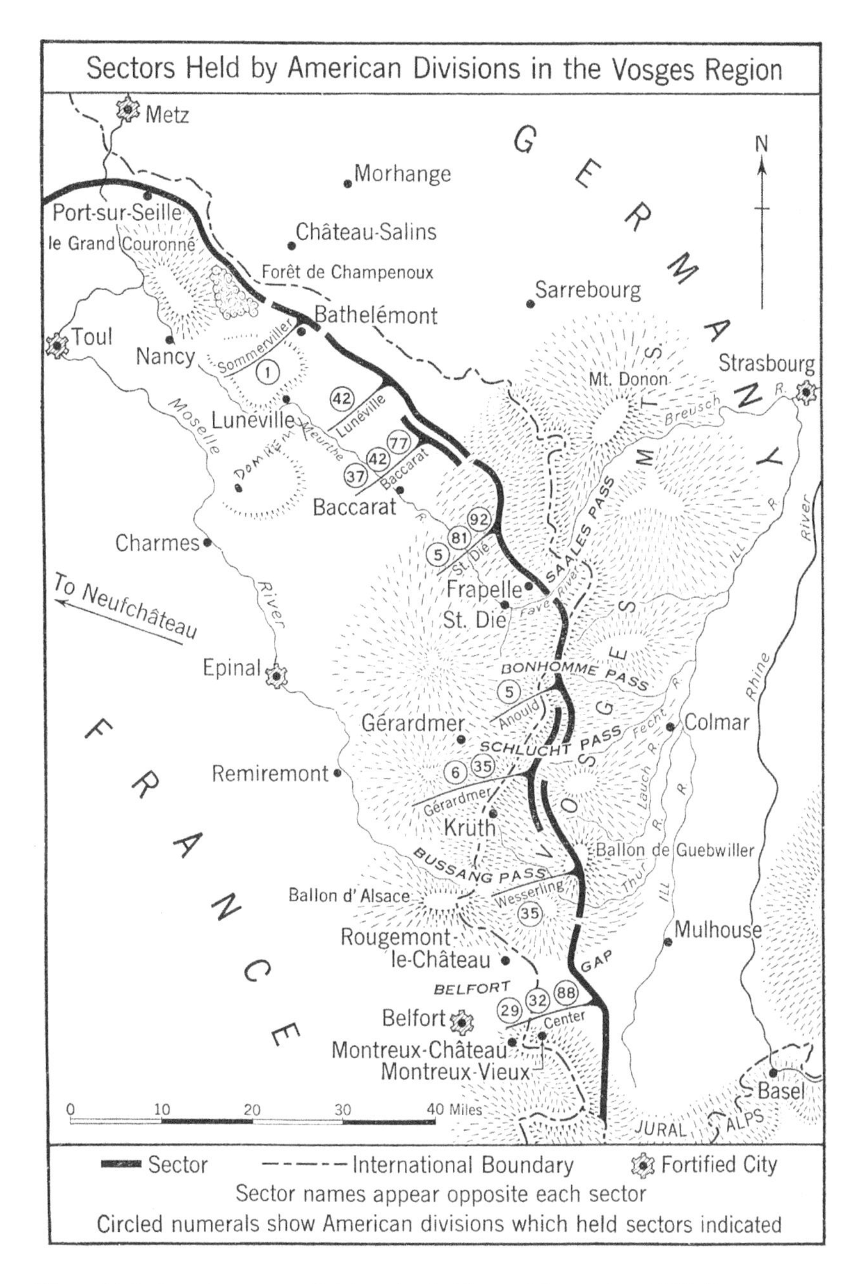

Photo 14.1: American army divisions in the Vosges Mountains, 1918. From American Battle Monuments Commission, *American Armies and Battlefields in Europe* (Washington, DC: Government Printing Office, 1938), 422.

elder Gutschenritter submitted his "alien enemy" affidavit in Oskaloosa in February 1918, he stated that his mother, if alive, resided in Guebwiller.[5]

The men of Company B were now at the front lines, but they were not yet battle tested. In some respects July 1918 may have been the most idyllic month of their combat tour. It began on a positive note: Captain Asbury Roberts of Missouri was relieved of command, and the popular Lieutenant Bill Smith was put in charge. "He will make good," predicted Sergeant Blevins to his parents, noting with pride that Company B had "all Kansas platoon sergeants, four Kansas lieutenants, and three-fourths [of] all the other non coms." The Independence Day celebrations in the mountains were dampened by cold weather and a heavy fog, but in the valleys there were festive parades, speeches, and band concerts among the American troops. Davis received a letter from his father, who relayed family news, commented on the corn crop, and joked about the fact that his son was now carrying a "musket" instead of "following an old walking cultivator in a weedy cornfield." Segraves spent two weeks at a school for rifle instructors, and Gutschenritter and Kimmel celebrated their twenty-first birthdays. Company B left their home base of Cornimont in the last week of July, traveling first to Kruth and then to Felleringen, a small village near the Bussang Pass. The heavily forested area was picturesque, but as Clyde Rogers of Nortonville explained, "climbing those mountains with a pack on our back took most of the beauty out of them." Joint responsibility for the Wesserling sector ended at this time, and the Americans were now in charge. According to the diary of Mess Sergeant Will Larkins, Company B was sent to the frontline trenches for the first time on July 31 at eleven o'clock in the evening.[6]

What happened next, in the darkness of night, is the subject of several different accounts. Corporal Fred Cole provided the following version, printed in his hometown newspaper, the *Ellsworth Messenger*:

> We didn't have charge of the trenches more than a half hour before the Germans came with some grenades and as we were all new at the game and the location of everything, it took us by surprise. I guess it was information that they wanted, for they threw a big grenade in one place where two of the boys were and just about put an end to them. . . . Well, after it went off, the Germans jumped in the hole and grabbed the smallest one and were going to take him back with them as a prisoner, but they didn't get far away with him for one of our boys threw a grenade at them and they dropped him and ran like sin.

According to Cole, the abducted soldier was found the next morning, tangled in barbed wire and severely injured: "He was shot up quite a bit and had a hole in the side of his head made by a piece of grenade, which was the worst wound he had. He is badly wounded but will pull through if blood poisoning doesn't set in." The wounded man was Davis, and the soldier who prevented his capture was Nichols. Another member of the company, Duane Dodge of Lyons, gave a slightly different account of the wounding of "Sox" Davis:

> When Sox Davis and another sentry were challenged by four big Boche, Sox opened fire on them. They threw a bomb into the trench, wounding both Davis and the other man. Well, the Boche jumped into the trench and dragged Sox out of the trench, kicking and beating him till Ralph Nichols saw them and opened fire on them. But he couldn't see Sox. Next morning Sox was missing, so they sent out a patrol to look for him and found him entangled in the barbed wire entanglement.

In yet another version, Nichols threw two grenades, and the Germans left a grenade under Davis that failed to explode. In a letter to his parents, Nichols did not elaborate on the incident other than to say that the Germans attacked shortly after the men took their positions but were "scared away." The *Oskaloosa Independent* noted that the sergeant modestly failed to mention his role in the affair.[7]

In his letter written on the third of August, Blevins said Davis had been severely wounded, but he "is getting along fine and [I] am sure he will come out O.K." He also added, to reassure his parents, that there was "no danger of them ever getting me." The *Winchester Star* reported that John Davis received the "sad news" on August 13 that William had been seriously wounded. What the elder Davis did not yet know was that his son had died six days earlier, on August 7. Official confirmation of Sox Davis's death was not sent until September 24, when his family received a Western Union telegram from the War Department reporting that "Private William L Davis Infantry died August Seventh from Wounds received in Action." The October 18, 1918, edition of the *Winchester Star* included a letter of condolence, sent from the office of the secretary of the interior, which ended: "I know that this brave soldier would not have you grieve for him but rather rejoice that he had so glorious an ending. For what can be finer than to die in an effort to save the lives and make happier the lot of others?" It is not known if John Davis rejoiced that his son met his death on the battlefield. The *Winchester Star* did

Form 1201

CLASS OF SERVICE	SYMBOL
Day Message	
Day Letter	Blue
Night Message	Nite
Night Letter	N L

If none of these three symbols appears after the check (number of words) this is a day message. Otherwise its character is indicated by the symbol appearing after the check.

WESTERN UNION TELEGRAM

WESTERN UNION

NEWCOMB CARLTON, PRESIDENT GEORGE W. E. ATKINS, FIRST VICE-PRESIDENT

CLASS OF SERVICE	SYMBOL
Day Message	
Day Letter	Blue
Night Message	Nite
Night Letter	N L

If none of these three symbols appears after the check (number of words) this is a day message. Otherwise its character is indicated by the symbol appearing after the check.

RECEIVED AT 3 KS CK 35 Gov't

Wa--Washington D C 508 PM Sept 24th 1918

Mr. John W. Davis

Winchester, Kans

Deeply regret to inform you that it is Officially reported that Private William L Davis Infantry died August Seventh from Wounds received in Action

Harris

Acting Adj. Gen'l

516 PM

Photo 14.2: Telegram, dated September 24, 1918, regarding the death of William Davis. Courtesy of the National WWI Museum and Memorial, Kansas City, Missouri, USA.

report on October 4 that "many persons wept" at the memorial service for William Davis, which was "one of the largest gatherings that ever assembled in Winchester."[8]

Davis was the first person from Jefferson County to die while fighting in France. On August 22 another member of Company B, Corporal William McKinley Pratt of Emporia, died from wounds received the previous day. The deaths of Davis and Pratt were the subject of an emotional talk given by Sergeant Lloyd Hair on September 27 at the Oskaloosa Methodist Church. Hair described how "Kinney" Pratt was mortally injured when a grenade blew off his hand and tore open his thigh. The sergeant from Iola also eulogized Davis and praised Sergeant Nichols, which was no doubt well received by the overflowing audience that included Reverend and Mrs. Nichols as well as many people from Winchester. According to historian Charles Hoyt, ninety-six soldiers from the Thirty-Fifth Division died in the Vosges Mountains, both on and off the battlefield.[9]

"We sleep in the day time and are on guard at night. If we hear Jerry coming across No Man's Land, we throw grenades and shoot automatics until he thinks hell has broke loose and he soon retires. But he seldom comes over." This summary of the daily routine of Company B in August 1918, provided by Private Will Hammond of Valley Falls, also serves as an apt description of life in the trenches: long periods of inactivity coupled with the constant threat of shelling, enemy attacks, and death. Ernest Hegendeffer of Oskaloosa provided a similar account:

> Our first line trench is about a half mile from the German trench and between the lines are old house, apple trees, English walnut trees and a tall grass something like our blue-steam at home. If a fellow gets out in no man's land old Jerry tries to wipe his name off the pay-roll. . . . I have nothing to do during the day—have to stand guard on the front line all night, so have to sleep through the day. The nights sure seem long.

Some of the men, including Blevins, Nichols, and Segraves, volunteered to venture into "no-man's" land. In order to gather intelligence on enemy movements, Blevins and Segraves "crawled up the mountain" on three separate occasions. On the first night they saw "sparks off a hot wire" but no Germans. The next evening the two Oskaloosa soldiers retraced their steps, cut the wires, and explored an empty trench. "We went back up [a third time]," Blevins recalled, "heard German voices, and found they were repairing the wires." In a letter to his parents, the sergeant described the experience with a mixture of pride and bravado: "It takes a good 'racoon' hunter to make a good scout so I'm about as good as they get. . . . I tell you 'Jerry' never wants to show up when I'm on patrol, because I'll sure give him all he wants." Nichols also scouted German positions, as he told his mother in a letter that included praise for Segraves, his high school friend:

> I have been on so-called no-man's land several times. I like it fine. I had rather be up there than back here going to school, altho I did have a German sniper shoot under and over me while lying out in the open in front of our lines. Vic Segraves sure is a dandy fellow. He has got nerve and common sense both together. When the light artillery opened up on us when we were on day patrol, he just laughed at it and told us to filter back to the trenches, which we did safely.

Blevins also acknowledged the nerve of Segraves but questioned his common sense: "He was a dare-devil sort of fellow, and hadn't worried about the Germans' shooting ability, and thought walking upright in the open paths was safe."[10]

The Thirty-Fifth Division left the trenches in the Vosges Mountains at the beginning of September. By the fourth, Company B was in the village of Neuves-Maison, southwest of Nancy. The Saint-Mihiel offensive was about to begin, and the division waited in reserve but did not see action. On September 18 it took part in the massive movement of men and equipment to the Meuse-Argonne region. Sergeant Blevins turned twenty on September 20 and five days later readied himself and his men for their defining moment: the initial four days of the largest and most costly battle in U.S. military history. The Thirty-Fifth Division in many respects was ill prepared for its next assignment. As historian Robert Ferrell points out, the signal battalion and artillery regiments trained elsewhere in France; the terrain of the Vosges precluded infantry field exercises; the experience of trench warfare "was not at all what the division was to meet with later on"; and many of the top officers, including the commander of the 139th Regiment and the head of the division, were replaced in the weeks and days prior to the offensive. Nevertheless, the men of the Thirty-Fifth Division would fight bravely and push forward through enfilading shelling and bullets without adequate air and artillery support. Led by Lieutenant Smith, the men of Company B would play their part, but several would not survive the battle.[11]

* * *

It is likely that the largest body of water William Davis had seen prior to becoming a soldier was either the Kansas River or the Missouri River. Shortly after his arrival in England, the young private described his trip in a letter to his father: "We sure had some ride on the water. There is sure lots of water. It don't look like there could be so much. We were fourteen days on the water. I got seasick about the second day but I soon got over it. I only want to ride over it once more and that's back across." The Jefferson County native did travel "once more" across the Atlantic Ocean. But it was to repatriate his remains from their resting place in the Vosges Mountains to his hometown in Kansas. The body of William Louis Davis arrived in Jefferson County on Saturday, June 4, 1921. The following day funeral services were held at the Christian church, followed by the burial at the Wise Cemetery southeast of Winchester.[12]

CHAPTER FIFTEEN

Saint-Mihiel and the Eighty-Ninth Division

September 12, 1918

The Saint-Mihiel salient—called "*L'Hernie*" (the hernia) by the French—was a triangular wedge of German-occupied territory southeast of Verdun. The Eighty-Ninth Division, formed at Camp Funston, was part of the American army tasked with removing this bulge. One of its four infantry units, the 353rd (All Kansas) Regiment, included a substantial number of Jayhawk draftees, but it never was an exclusively Kansas outfit. The division spent eleven months in France, Luxembourg, and Germany, returning to the United States in May 1919. Its soldiers trained with the French army, served in the trenches, fought alongside the Forty-Second Rainbow Division at Saint-Mihiel, and participated in the final phase of the Meuse-Argonne offensive.

Although Saint-Mihiel was an Allied success, the first day of battle was the deadliest single day in World War I for Kansans in the Eighty-Ninth Division. September 12 was also the fateful day that five of the men from Kansas in the 353rd Infantry earned the Distinguished Service Cross. Oscar May, a Kansas City lawyer who served in the 356th Infantry, likewise earned a Distinguished Service Cross that day, the first of his three medals for heroism. Saint-Mihiel involved the largest concentration of American military power since the Civil War, and the four days of fighting served as a baptism of fire prior to the decisive Meuse-Argonne offensive.[1]

The experiences of the Eighty-Ninth Division prior to Saint-Mihiel can be summed up in three words: transport, training, and trenches. The division sailed from New York harbor on June 4, 1918, having boarded three troop ships the day before. Major General Wood had been relieved of command a week earlier and replaced by Brigadier General Frank Winn, a West Point classmate of Brigadier General Ballou of the Ninety-Second Division. Kansans welcomed General Wood back to Camp Funston and condemned the "shelving" of "the best commander in the U.S. army to date," suggesting (with some cause) that he was removed because he was "guilty of being a

Republican." Colonel James Reeves of Alabama, a West Point graduate with prior postings at Fort Leavenworth and Fort Riley as well as Cuba, China, and the Philippines, remained in charge of the 353rd Regiment.[2]

After a short stay in England and quick crossing of the channel, the troops traveled by railroad boxcars to Reynal, France, a training area in eastern France near American Expeditionary Forces headquarters at Chaumont. Under the supervision of French officers, the men learned how to use grenades, raid trenches, and approach, flank, and attack machine-gun nests. At the beginning of August, the Eighty-Ninth Division moved to the front lines near the village of Limey on the south side of the Saint-Mihiel salient. It was at this location that Kansans in the 353rd Regiment first experienced aerial and artillery bombardment, gas attacks, rapid-fire machine guns, and life in the trenches. Company L helped repulse a morning raid on August 21, in part due to the alertness of Corporal Dean Billings of Maple Hill, who was not deceived when English-speaking Germans pretended to be Americans. On this day, too, Corporal Frank Rice, in the words of his hometown newspaper, the *Alma Enterprise*, became "the first man in the Division to get his boche."[3]

In September 1918 the Eighty-Ninth left the trenches and attacked the enemy. Throughout the spring and summer, the Americans fought with French and British forces to repel a series of German offensives. It had always been the intention of General Pershing and the Wilson administration, however, to put an independent American army into the field. During the summer, the Allies agreed that Pershing could form the U.S. First Army and use it to reduce the Saint-Mihiel salient. Although the French had not been able to dislodge the Germans, the protruding wedge-shaped position was vulnerable to a pincer movement. The battle plan positioned French troops at the apex of the salient, two American divisions to their north, and soldiers from seven American divisions along the southern edge. Supporting the infantry were aerial combat units led by Colonel William "Billy" Mitchell and tanks under the command of Lieutenant Colonel George S. Patton. The Fourth and Twenty-Sixth Divisions would attack from the north, the Eighty-Second would hold its position along the Moselle River, and the remaining divisions—the First, Forty-Second, Eighty-Ninth, Second, Fifth, and Ninetieth—would hit the Germans from the south. The Eighty-Ninth Division was part of the Fourth Corps and would fight between its other two battle-tested units, the Forty-Second (Rainbow) Division and the Second Division. For the 353rd Infantry, the chain of command was Colonel Reeves (regiment), Brigadier General Winn (brigade), Major General William Wright (division), Major General Joseph Dickman (corps), and General Pershing (army). The men of the Eighty-Ninth Division—who successively trained and fought under Wood, Winn, and Wright—would eventually adopt a "rolling W" shoulder insignia, which became the letter "M" if turned, signifying the "Middle West" origins of the draftees. Wright, who led the Thirty-Fifth National Guard Division from Camp Doniphan to France, assumed command of the Eighty-Ninth just six days before the scheduled assault.[4]

George C. Marshall and the other men who planned the attack designated September 12 as "D-day" and 5:00 A.M. as "H-hour"—the first time the terms were used in American military history. Nearly half a million soldiers waited in trenches as, at one o'clock in the morning, the artillery commenced four hours of continuous shelling of German positions. "Such a noise and confusion you can't imagine," recalled Corporal Benjamin Harrison Gilmore of El Dorado, "and the flash from so many guns made it almost as light as day." The 353rd Infantry was placed at the far right of the Eighty-Ninth Division's sector, adjacent to the Second Division. The terrain in front of the regiment, as described in Colonel Reeves's official report, was "heavily wooded, interspersed with open spaces . . . [and] largely a mass of barbed wire entanglements and entrenchments." When the appointed time arrived, the 355th and 356th Regiments advanced in the rain through a forest (Mort Mare), while the 353rd and 354th Infantry skirted its eastern edge. "Attacks of machine gun nests, strong points and centers of resistance," Reeves reported, "were made by a few riflemen or a machine gun or two bringing fire upon them from the front, and men, twos and threes, widely dispersed, turning the flanks and cleaning them out from the rear." By the end of the day, some soldiers reached Bouillonville and cleared it of Germans before moving back across the river next to the village.[5]

In his in-depth analysis of the Battle of Saint-Mihiel, Donald Carter writes that the Fourth Corps "provided the primary thrust of the opening attack" and "had the farthest to go and generally made good progress." He describes the Eighty-Ninth Division's "difficult assignment" as follows:

> German defenses included strongpoints with trenches, concrete machine gun nests, and deep dugouts. . . . [A]s they came within sight of the German positions, doughboys rushed forward individually and in small groups to take on the Germans. . . . Under such pressure, the German

line cracked, and soon hundreds of enemy prisoners were streaming to the rear. By 0800, the Mort-Mare woods were in American hands and the division was advancing toward the next defensive line.

The fighting continued for four more days, but the battle was won within thirty-six hours when the northern and southern forces came together and closed the salient. The limited objectives of the offensive were attained, in part due to the Germans being in the process of pulling back when attacked. The reduction of the salient diminished the possibility that the Germans would attack the rear of the American army in the upcoming Meuse-Argonne offensive. It also caused enemy leaders to move additional soldiers away from the front in order to protect Metz, an important railway center. Pleased with the results, Pershing met with General Wright and his officers on the evening of September 16 to congratulate the Eighty-Ninth Division on its conduct.[6]

Thirty-eight Kansans in the Eighty-Ninth were killed in action during the five-day period beginning on September 12, and sixteen others died of wounds. All but three of the men served in the 353rd Infantry. Thirty-one of the fifty-four deaths took place on the first day of the battle. Two of the men who died on September 12, Private Jesse Clark Reeves and Private First Class Willis Nixon, were from the small town of Medicine Lodge in south-central Kansas. The circumstances of Nixon's death are not known, but Reeves was shot in the right hip and died at a hospital in the afternoon. Their families did not learn of the deaths until a telegram arrived on the evening of October 10. In his last letter home, dated August 27, Reeves closed by saying, "I am still a child of God and will be until the end, so goodbye mother and father, and pray for us and we will be back in a few months." Jesse Reeves was buried at home, and Willis Nixon was laid to rest at Arlington National Cemetery.[7]

Of the five Kansans of the 353rd Infantry who were awarded the Distinguished Service Cross for heroism on September 12, three did not survive their wounds. Private William "Sonny" Hall of Winfield, acting as a runner, made several trips to battalion headquarters through severe artillery bombardment before he received a mortal wound, dying either the same day or three days later (records vary). Corporal Edward Kessler of Cheney, who died on September 24, was commended for singlehandedly silencing two machine guns with grenades. Private Dwight Lamson and a comrade went to the aid of their wounded lieutenant, placed him on a stretcher, and were returning to American lines when Lamson was shot in the right shoulder. The twenty-seven-year-old resident of Little River was operated on twice but died on October 30.

The two men who did live to receive their awards held very different jobs prior to the war. Captain Fred Albright of Garland, a graduate of Kansas City Medical College, left his practice to become a surgeon for the 353rd Infantry. When an adjacent regiment was forced to temporarily pull back, Dr. Albright went to the vacated area and cared for the wounded while under heavy artillery fire. Captain Moses Atkins, who had fought in the Spanish-American War, was employed as a prison guard at Leavenworth Federal Penitentiary. He received a leg wound early on at Saint-Mihiel but continued to lead his men forward: "He could hobble along fairly well on the level ground and . . . when he came to a trench he could send his runners down into it to boost him over. So he continued to fight until evening, when another wound forced him out." In addition to the Distinguished Service Cross, Atkins also received the Order of Leopold from Belgium.[8]

Oscar P. May was a thrice-decorated Kansan who was in the Eighty-Ninth Division but was not a member of the 353rd (All Kansas) Regiment. Born in 1893 on the family farm near Williamstown in Jefferson County, he was the ninth of twelve children. His father died in 1915 while Oscar was at the Kansas City School of Law, attending classes at night and working as a mail carrier during the day. May graduated in 1916, litigated a few cases (including one in Jefferson County with Will Smith), and then went to the Fort Riley Officer Training School. In August 1918 he found himself in France, a second lieutenant with Company M, 356th Regiment, Eighty-Ninth Division. In a letter to his brother written on September 3, May characterized himself as "a seasoned soldier" (after a month of trench duty) and described his experiences with an artistic flair: "I have slept with the rats and I have slept not at all. . . . I have seen men alive and I have seen men dead. I have heard the bullets sing and shrapnel whiz. I have heard grenades burst and shells explode. I have heard the machine guns purr and cannons roar."[9]

May earned the first of three medals—the Distinguished Service Cross—on September 12. The official citation describes his heroic actions in one sentence: "Without assistance, Lieutenant May very courageously attacked and captured a machine gun which threatened to wipe out his platoon." A more detailed description was provided by the hero himself in a letter to his brother, which was printed in several Kansas newspapers. While waiting for the assault to begin, May recounted, "I was blown down by a shell that made a direct hit in the trench" and implanted "a few rocks . . . in my hide on the left side and back of my head." After going over the top, the men of Company M met little resistance until a German soldier came out of a dugout and threw a grenade. It was at this time that Lieutenant May sprang into action:

> I closed in on the scoundrel and he ducked back into the dugout. I threw a couple of hot grenades in after him, and I saw about ten paces to my right, a machine gun staring my platoon in the face. I immediately threw two grenades into the emplacement and lunged forward, grasping the gun by the nozzle and slammed it back into the trench, and I saw another dugout about ten paces to my right, with a small square hole in the top, and I dropped a couple of grenades in that as we passed over.

"From then on," May told his brother, "I saw no Boche except those running or had their hands up, and we saw plenty." The lieutenant was commended by his government for his heroism at Saint-Mihiel, and his subsequent acts of bravery and leadership in the Meuse valley (described in chapter 18) would be honored by the Belgian and French governments.[10]

* * *

Not every Kansan who was wounded on September 12 won a Distinguished Service Cross, and not every Kansan who was killed on that day fought in the Eighty-Ninth Division. Sergeant William Burwell, a minor-league baseball player, was wounded but not decorated. Lieutenant Edward "Eddie" Wells, a collegiate football and basketball star, served in the Forty-Second (Rainbow) Division and died on the battlefield.

William Burwell was born in 1895 in Jarbalo and grew up on a farm in Leavenworth County. He pitched for Kansas State in 1913 but left to earn money in the minor leagues, playing for the Elgin (Illinois) Watch Makers and the Joplin (Missouri) Baseball Club. Burwell was drafted, assigned to the 353rd Infantry, and sent to France, where on September 12 he suffered an apparent career-ending injury: he was shot in his throwing hand while attacking a German machine gun. According to one newspaper account, the bullet "clipped the second finger" of his right hand and "shattered a joint, but Burwell refused to leave 'the game' until the last German was 'out.'" Prior to being drafted, he played three years in the minor leagues. "The only thing that I regret," he wrote his mother shortly after the battle, "is that I cannot play ball for a long while." Years later, Burwell recalled thinking, "the war was the end of me as a pitcher." He rejoined the Joplin (Missouri) Miners for the 1919 season and discovered that, with the loss of the tip of a finger and a permanently curled hand, he could throw an effective sinker and "a splendid curve ball." According to the Society for American Baseball Research, Burwell played two seasons for the St. Louis Browns and one season for the Pittsburgh Pirates. In 1920 he faced Babe Ruth at the end of a game with two

Photo 15.2: Eddie Wells. Courtesy of the Kansas State Historical Society.

men on base. "As soon as I heard Babe smack it I grabbed my glove and beat it for the dressing room," the Kansas hurler recalled. "I knew the ball was going out of the lot." Although he did not last long as a major-league pitcher, Burwell enjoyed a forty-eight-year career in baseball, including as the pitching coach for the Pirates when they won the 1960 World Series.[11]

Edward "Eddie" Wells was a star athlete, first at Wichita High School, then at Fairmount College (now Wichita State University), and finally in 1916 and 1917 at Kansas State Agricultural College. He was born in Greenleaf but moved with his mother to Wichita in 1909 after his father, a railroad brakeman, was crushed to death by the wheels of a freight train. In the fall of 1916, Wells was named to the All–Missouri Valley Team as a fullback, and in 1917 he was a guard and captain on the basketball team, again earning individual All–Missouri Valley honors as well as a conference championship. (The Aggies were 13-2, losing twice to Kansas University but also defeating the Jayhawks twice). The *Manhattan Morning Chronicle* reported in May

1917, "college football stock slumped with the announcement that 'Eddie' Wells, all-Missouri valley fullback, and star basketball guard, had been ordered to . . . camp." Although engaged to be married, when war was declared Wells applied for a position at the Fort Riley Officer Training Camp. Upon hearing the news, his coach, Zora Clevenger, said, "there goes nine-elevenths of my football team and four-fifths of my basketball team."

Wells joined the Forty-Second (Rainbow) Division as a second lieutenant and served in the Headquarters Company, 168th Infantry Regiment. In June and July he was hospitalized after being burned by mustard gas. He returned to the front at the beginning of August and was promoted to first lieutenant. On September 12, at the outset of the attack on the Saint-Mihiel salient, Wells was leading his platoon down a hill when a fragment of a high-explosive shell struck him in the abdomen and caused his death. His body was returned to Kansas in 1921 and laid to rest in the Downs Cemetery in Osborne County. In his last letter to his mother, written two days before his death, Eddie Wells warned, "hell is going to break loose very soon and I will be in the thickest of it as I go over in the first wave." Sadly, nine years after losing her husband, Odessa Wells lost her only child.[12]

CHAPTER SIXTEEN

Meuse-Argonne and the Thirty-Fifth Division

September 26–27, 1918

The Meuse-Argonne offensive was part of the last Allied campaign of World War I. On September 26, 1918, the First Army of the American Expeditionary Forces attacked German troops entrenched northwest of Verdun between the Meuse River and the Argonne Forest. As noted by Edward Lengel, the Meuse-Argonne region protected railway lines "that fed the Kaiser's armies along the entire Western Front," and consequently the Germans "fought tooth and nail for every inch of ground." At the same time, French and British troops attacked elsewhere in a coordinated effort to convince Germany that the war was lost. After forty-seven days of unrelenting combat, the fighting finally stopped on November 11.

Meuse-Argonne remains the largest and most costly military campaign in U.S. history. According to one estimate, over 1 million doughboys were involved, of whom 95,786 were wounded and 26,277 lost their lives—more than all of the men killed at Shiloh, Antietam, Gettysburg, and Cold Harbor during the American Civil War. The Thirty-Fifth Division took part in the initial attack and, according to one historian, "no Yank division anywhere ever had a rougher baptism or assignment" or "faced more pestiferous terrain" than the Thirty-Fifth. In the span of five days, beginning on September 26 and ending on September 30, its infantrymen crossed open fields without adequate artillery and air support, suffered grievously from enfilading shelling and machine-gun fire, and ultimately disintegrated as a cohesive fighting force.

Of the roles played by Kansans in the 137th and 139th Regiments, the focus here is on Company B, 139th Infantry, which according to a 1920 account lost a total of thirteen men killed or missing and suffered ninety-five additional casualties either gassed or wounded. On the first day of battle, the company and the rest of the regiment "leap-frogged" the 137th as both units encountered dense fog in the morning and strong resistance in the afternoon. On the second day of the battle, Company B bore the brunt of a murderous artillery barrage before participating in an evening attack that secured the villages of Charpentry and Baulny. The heroic achievements of the 137th and 139th came at a cost: both units suffered significant losses, each became badly disorganized, and both began to lose their ability to function as effective fighting forces.[1]

* * *

When the Saint-Mihiel offensive began on September 12, the Germans were already in the process of evacuating their positions in that salient along the Meuse River. The Forty-Second and Eighty-Ninth Divisions helped the AEF overwhelm a smaller force and removed a bothersome enemy bulge in the front lines. The Thirty-Fifth Division was designated as a reserve unit for this operation, and the men spent several days picking blackberries in the woods and sleeping in muddy tents. This period of inactivity soon came to an end, as recalled by William R. Carpenter of Marion, a first lieutenant in Company M, 139th Regiment:

> September 17th we left in trucks, which meant we were badly needed somewhere. The entire 1st Army was moving into position that night. The roads were blocked with big guns, supply trains, ambulances, trucks, wagons and troops. The whole country seemed alive and foretelling the gigantic events of the coming week. But we were soon located in the edge of the Argonne Forest, remaining until the night of September 25th, resting and preparing our equipment.

As the infantry moved into position, Sergeant Jesse Blevins of the 110th Ammunition Train was delivering shells to field-artillery batteries. The older brother of Ted Blevins kept two diaries—one personal and one for his company—which include the following entries:

> Reveille, Sunday, Sep. 22. [Company diary]—At 7 P.M. ordered to deliver the ammo . . . to the different Battery positions, some of which were only 500 yds. from our frontline trenches. The traffic along these roads was exceptionally heavy. . . . It was very dark and raining quite hard, causing driving to be very difficult without lights.
>
> Monday, Sep. 23. [Personal diary]—Visited Ted & the boys—muddy in the Forêt de Argonne—everything points to a big drive in this sector. Hauling ammunition. Shells flying overhead continually.
>
> Midnight, Monday, Sep. 23. [Company diary]—On road near Neuvilly

at a standstill. The road was hopelessly blocked with trucks, tractors, tanks, machine guns, horses, and infantry.

Midnight, Tuesday, Sep. 24, 1918. [Company diary]—We arrived at the Ammo Dump at 6:45 A.M. and by 10 A.M. were loaded and out on a side road waiting for orders to take the loads up. . . . By 1 P.M. we started for the positions of the 128th F.A., made good progress, passing thru Neuvilly, which was heavily shelled. . . . The return trip was even more hazardous as the roads in Neuvilly were under more intense shell-fire. Imagine our consternation at finding the road blocked—three shells would land on our left, and then three on our right, some hitting behind the column and several ahead—in fact, all around us with fragments of shells striking our trucks, and us at a standstill.

Supreme Allied Commander Marshal Foch had agreed to allow General Pershing to proceed with the Saint-Mihiel campaign on condition that the American First Army would participate in the Meuse-Argonne offensive. This compromise created two problems. First, because the most experienced troops (such as the First Division) were employed to ensure success at Saint-Mihiel, the next battle would begin with inexperienced divisions (including the Thirty-Fifth) in the front lines. Second, the decision to fight two consecutive major battles created the logistical challenge of "moving some 600,000 men, 2,700 guns, and all their equipment by three roads over a distance of sixty miles, all in the hours of darkness." The decision to fight at Saint-Mihiel, Richard Faulkner notes, "meant that the First Army would have to engage in one major battle while simultaneously planning for a much larger and more complicated operation." The mission was accomplished due in large part to the organizational genius of a future five-star general, George C. Marshall. The men of the Thirty-Fifth Division, however, were physically spent when they settled in the woods near the jump-off line, having traveled in trucks over poor roads by night and under threat of shell fire.[2]

A third problem peculiar to the Thirty-Fifth Division was self-inflicted: the widespread replacement of commanding officers. As noted by Robert Ferrell, Major General Peter E. Traub, the Thirty-Fifth's commanding officer, "ensured trouble by making drastic changes of the division's senior commanders just before the battle opened." One change in particular rankled Kansans: the removal on September 21 of Charles Martin as commander of the Seventieth Brigade (which included the 139th Regiment). After the conclusion of the war, the former Kansas adjutant general testified before Congress that he had interacted with Traub for only a few minutes, leading

Governor Henry Allen and other Kansas politicians to charge the army with prejudicial treatment of guardsmen. Colonel Kirby Walker of the 139th took over for General Martin, which in turn led to the last minute (and temporary) elevation of Lieutenant Colonel Carl Ristine of Missouri as the new regimental commander. In what Ferrell describes as "incompetence of a high order," Traub belatedly installed a new chief of staff, new commanders for two field-artillery regiments and a machine-gun battalion, and new officers at the head of each of the four infantry regiments. Most of the replacements were Regular Army, although the new commander of the 137th Regiment, Colonel Clad Hamilton of Topeka, was from the Kansas National Guard. The chain of command for Company B was now as follows: Lieutenant Bill Smith (company commander); Major Samuel Clarke (First Battalion); Lieutenant Colonel Ristine (139th Regiment); Colonel Walker (Seventieth Brigade, including the 139th and 140th Regiments); Major General Traub (Thirty-Fifth Division); Major General Hunter Liggett (First Corps); and General Pershing (First Army and the AEF). Ralph Nichols and Vic Segraves were battalion scouts, and Ted Blevins, Sam Gutschenritter, and Billy Kimmel were company sergeants. Private Melvin Dyson was a wagoner with the regiment's Supply Company.[3]

* * *

The First Army began the offensive with nine infantry divisions organized in three corps, situated along a front that extended less than twenty miles west from the Meuse River to and including a portion the Argonne Forest. The First Corps, on the left side of the American line, included the Seventy-Seventh Division, which was to advance through the Argonne; the Twenty-Eighth Division, which would proceed along the west bank of the Aire River; and the Thirty-Fifth Division, assigned to the open valley east of the Aire. On the right side of the Thirty-Fifth was the Ninety-First Division. The Fifth Corps (Ninety-First, Thirty-Seventh, and Seventy-Ninth Divisions) was given the task of taking Montfaucon, an elevated central area, while the Third Corps (Fourth, Eightieth, and Thirty-Third Divisions) was responsible for moving the right side of the line along the Meuse. Of the nine divisions, only three (the Fourth, Twenty-Eighth, and Seventy-Seventh) had significant combat experience.

Pershing wanted the nine divisions to move forward in unison and without delay in order to take key defensive positions before the Germans could respond. As noted by Meirion and Susie Harries, he gave his army "less than two days to advance over heavily fortified and difficult terrain for a distance

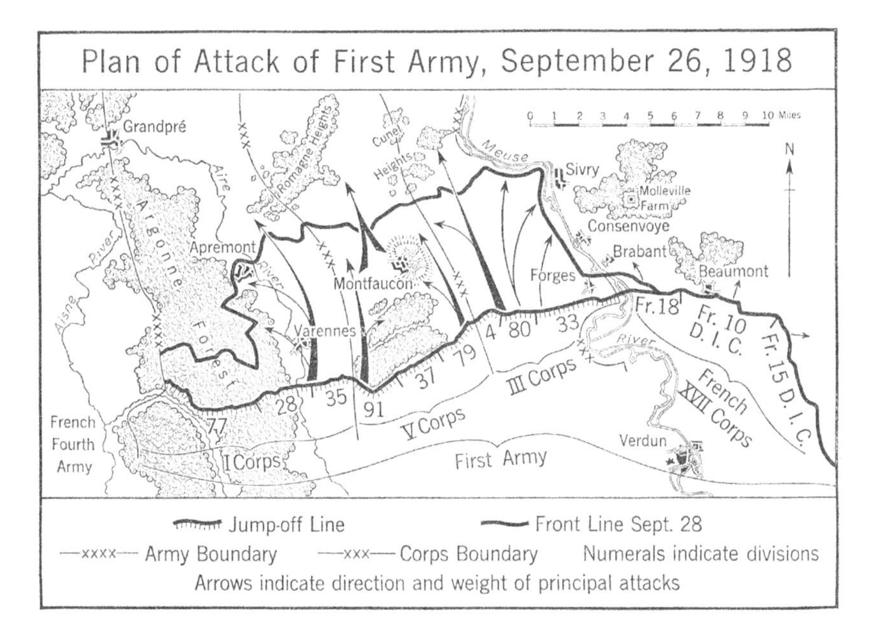

Photo 16.1: Meuse-Argonne offensive plan of attack, AEF, September 1918. From American Battle Monuments Commission, *American Armies and Battlefields in Europe* (Washington, DC: Government Printing Office, 1938), 172.

of ten miles—which would mean advancing at twice the speed achieved at Saint Mihiel, where the Germans had been in full retreat." As it turned out, the ambitious objectives were not met, and the enemy was able to concentrate fresh troops along three ridgelines that served as ideal defensive positions. The American advance was slower than hoped in part due to expertly placed enemy artillery: the Germans could shell the right flank of the First Army from the high ground east of the Meuse River and could direct long-range artillery fire against the Thirty-Fifth and other divisions in the left flank from hidden positions in the Argonne Forest. The Germans had also built a military rail line to transport troops and supplies, carefully positioned interlocking machine-gun nests, and constructed field fortifications from which to repel attacks and initiate counterthrusts.[4]

The Thirty-Fifth Division was ordered to take the villages of Cheppy, Véry, Charpentry, Baulny, Exermont, and Fléville. The Sixty-Ninth Brigade (137th and 138th) led the attack on the first day, with the Seventieth Brigade (139th and 140th) placed in reserve. As it turned out, however, the two regiments associated with Kansas—the 137th and 139th—quickly became mixed on the left flank. The first natural obstacle was Vauquois Hill, where the French and the Germans had created gigantic craters over four years by exploding hundreds of underground mines. On the east side of Vauquois Hill is Buanthe Creek, flowing north past Charpentry, and to the left is the Aire River, which runs past Boureuilles, Varennes, Apremont, and Fléville. The Aire was the line of demarcation between the Thirty-Fifth and Twenty-Eighth Divisions, and the village of Varennes was a shared responsibility. Located on the road running east from Apremont (present-day D242) is Chaudron Farm, north of which is an open area leading to Montrebeau Wood and Exermont.

Other than a few scattered thickets, the area was mostly cultivated fields interspersed with shallow creeks and deep ravines. Because the Aire valley was favorable terrain for tanks, the First Provisional Tank Brigade—commanded by thirty-two-year-old Lieutenant Colonel George S. Patton—was assigned to the sector. These open areas proved to be killing fields for the infantrymen who were, in the words of Laurence Stallings, "easily seen from the heights and speedily punished."[5]

Final preparations for the battle commenced on September 25. The men of the Thirty-Fifth Division spent several nights in the Forêt de Hesse, northwest of Aubréville, where the almost constant shell fire prevented restful sleep. Movement finally began in the afternoon. After eating a hot meal, each soldier gathered his equipment, including a rifle, steel helmet, gas mask, rounds of rifle ammunition, and grenades. Haversacks contained two days' rations—typically hard bread and corned beef, although Ted Blevins recalled starting the drive with "a small carton of hard tack and a can of goldfish [that is, salmon]." Everyone carried a canteen, and a few men also placed a loaf of bread on a fixed bayonet. Company B may have been one of the last units to depart, as Nichols said that "at 8:10 P.M. Sept. 25 we left the woods in which we were camping for the 'jumping off place' (that is, our front line)."

Robert Bryan Greene of Centralia, age twenty-one, took time on September 25 to write to his father:

> I suppose you can see by the papers what is going on over here. The biggest one ever known is starting. How is Earl? Tell him to be careful around horses. . . . Well I have wrote you all the news so guess I had better close so write often as you can. Will write as soon as I can. So good bye. From your son, Pvt. Robert Greene, Co. E, 139th U.S. Inf.

It was Greene's last letter, as he was killed in action two days later. Corporal Fred Cole of Ellsworth, who survived, provided his wife with a personal account of the battle, including this description of the evening hours of September 25 and the early hours of the following day:

> Well, Lily, . . . on the evening of the 25th, we packed up and left the woods, hiking until about two in the morning of the 26th up behind the big guns. There we waited until about four for daybreak, so we could see to go over after the Huns. The artillery sure sent over some heavy barrage before we went, and talk about noise, I never heard so much in my life and never expect to again. But, believe me, it was pretty to see the flash of the big guns in the dark and hear the whistle of the big shells going through the air.

According to Charles Hoyt, the "starry night" of September 25 "was unusually quiet and unusually dark," in sharp contrast to the next morning, when it "seemed that for a while the lid of hell had been pushed back a little space."[6]

The barrage on September 26 began at 2:30 in the morning. "We were lying next to an 18 in. naval gun that was on the railway track," recounted Nichols, who had turned nineteen in August. "Maybe you think that thing didn't roar. It sure did and also shook the surrounding country by its terrible recoil." In addition to the unforgettable noise, the twelve-inch shells cast a greenish-white light as they hurtled through the night sky. Batteries in advanced positions used the ammunition delivered by Jesse Blevins to obliterate barbed-wire barriers and machine-gun nests. Over 2,700 guns were employed in the American sector, temporarily rendering Captain Harry S. Truman "deaf as a post from the noise." In a letter to his father, Eugene Prall of the 139th dryly noted that "the American artillery was sure sending the Dutchmen their iron rations."[7]

When the Thirty-Fifth Division launched its infantry attack three hours later, the soldiers descended into a heavy fog. According to Clair Kenamore, "men would be observed marching ahead, but a moment later they would entirely disappear, and there would be nothing to see but the opaque gray bank of fog. It was impossible to tell friend from foe 25 yards away." The 137th Regiment led the way on the left, followed by the 139th, while the 138th advanced on the right, with the 140th in reserve. "This thing of going over the top isn't like you read about," Nichols told his father. "They don't go forth in a grand and glorious charge, but instead they steal forward at a slow pace." He and fellow scout Vic Segraves likely assisted in spacing the battalions as they moved forward behind the 137th. Ted Blevins decades later recalled how Company B advanced in formation during the first day of battle:

> We'd go forward, about 10 feet or so between us. If someone was killed, or wounded, we'd fill up the space and continue to advance. We'd go over or under the barbed wire strung to slow us down—some fellows used wire cutters. We kept low, crouching, then when it sounded safe, we'd get up and run a distance, guns in position all the time. At one time we got too far ahead of those on our right, and got shot at from the side, so we had to hold until our lines were intact again.

The fog proved to be a mixed blessing. The German machine guns remained silent at first, their crews unable to spot their targets, but the advancing doughboys quickly lost contact with other units and with headquarters. Signal flags were useless, and the telephone wires failed to work properly. According to historian John Eisenhower, "the plans for the officers to lead their troops by compass went awry because the steel fragments embedded in the ground from previous battles interfered with the accuracy of the compasses."[8]

The division's first objective was to secure the famed Vauquois Hill. General Traub ordered most of his troops to bypass the area, assigning the task to the Second Battalion, 139th Infantry and the 130th Machine Gun Battalion. As it turned out, the German garrison had been reduced to seventy-five men (commanded by a nineteen-year-old lieutenant), and the area was taken with minimal casualties. At the same time, the 138th and 140th Regiments proceeded past the east side of Vauquois Hill toward the village of Cheppy, where they faced stiff resistance. It was at this location where tank commander Patton earned his first Distinguished Service Cross:

> Colonel Patton displayed conspicuous courage, coolness, energy, and intelligence in directing the advance of his brigade down the valley of the Aire. Later he rallied a force of disorganized infantry and led it forward, behind the tanks, under heavy machine-gun and artillery fire until he was wounded. Unable to advance further, Colonel Patton continued to direct the operations of his unit until all arrangements for turning over the command were completed.

Cheppy fell just after midday. At this point the wounded 138th commander, Colonel Harry Howland, was taken from the field in a state of physical and psychological collapse. The regiment, now led by Lieutenant Colonel Henry W. Parker, ended the day on the southern slope of a hill located one-half mile north of the deserted village of Very. Because the Ninety-First Division of Fifth Corps had not kept pace, the men from Missouri were subjected to flanking shell fire from the east.[9]

The all-Kansas 137th Infantry on the left flank faced little opposition at first as it advanced through the fog. Led by Colonel Hamilton, the troops cut barbed wire, removed a road barricade, and entered Boureuilles. The German soldiers who remained in the village shouted "*Kamerad*" (comrade) and surrendered. At 7:40 the initial barrage ended, yet all but one of the field-artillery units were unable to reach their assigned positions. One reason for the delay was the failure of the French to inform the Thirty-Fifth Division that their engineers had previously rendered the Boureuilles–Varennes road impassable by using explosives to create a crater in it forty feet deep and ninety feet wide. To further slow the Americans, the Germans mined the fields adjacent to the crater, which was discovered only when an explosion killed several men. African American labor battalions worked constantly to repair the roads, but as Clair Kenamore reported in the *Kansas City Star*: "on every road for twenty miles there was the tangle of vehicles trying to get up with supplies, and the counter current of ambulances trying to get back with the wounded."[10]

Four years earlier, in September 1914, Clad Hamilton, then a captain with the Kansas National Guard, addressed the students of Oskaloosa High School—including Ted Blevins, Billy Kimmel, and Vic Segraves—about successful study habits. Now in September 1918, fifty-one-year-old Colonel Hamilton led the men of the 137th Regiment past Boureuilles to a field roughly equidistant between Cheppy and Varennes. The Twenty-Eighth Division had not yet reached Varennes, so when the fog suddenly lifted, the entrenched Germans there opened fire. The men in Company E found themselves in an exposed area, and nineteen-year-old Private Joe Sargeant of Neodesha was shot thirteen times before falling dead. At this point Colonel Hamilton collapsed in exhaustion and was found "lying on his back in a shell hole, arms and legs splayed, eyes closed, mumbling out orders but unable to move." The regiment, pinned down without artillery support and without a functioning leader, became disorganized, with some men remaining southeast of Varennes and others moving beyond the village to attack German machine gunners in the "Grotto," a wooded hill with a chapel and shrine. With the aid of French tanks, two battalions of the 137th were able to take possession of the part of Varennes east of the Aire River. Flanking fire from the Argonne heights and the remaining portion of the village, however, prevented any further advance.[11]

With at least part of the 137th at a standstill, Lieutenant Colonel Ristine ordered the 139th to take cover in an orchard against increasing artillery fire. At some point he realized that his men had unknowingly passed the reserve battalion of the 137th in the fog. After waiting for two hours, the former guardsman (and Mizzou star athlete) went ahead to inquire about the delay. When Hamilton said he could not proceed without artillery support, Ristine responded that the advance was to be continued at any cost. He then sent a runner to his brigade commander, Colonel Walker, requesting permission to bypass Hamilton's regiment. At this point the 139th was being heavily shelled, as Fred Cole of Company B described in a letter to his wife:

> We didn't catch up with the Huns until nearly noon, and when we did, believe me, things picked up right now and the shells, both high explosive and shrapnel, gas and machine gun bullets sure were thick. The shells, when they hit and bursted, would tear big holes in the ground and throw dirt all over us. . . . The ground was soft and the shells would bury themselves before going off and that is all that saved lots of us.

When attempts to communicate with brigade headquarters failed, Ristine decided on his own to change the formation order, pass through the 137th, and resume the forward push. In the words of Private Nichols, "we leap-frogged the 137th about noon of the first day." As scouts, he and Sergeant Segraves likely went ahead with their regimental commander, who formed a skirmish line and left Major William Stepp in charge of the remaining soldiers. Ristine's detachment went around a hill and threatened to outflank the Germans in front of the regiment, causing the enemy to yield its position. Further progress was impeded by enfilading fire, however, and the forward group stopped a mile south of Charpentry to wait for Major Stepp to bring up the other men. Once again Lieutenant Colonel Ristine became impatient and went back to investigate. He learned that, shortly after his departure, Stepp had been struck by a piece of shrapnel and killed. Ristine, whose "take charge" attitude was both admired and criticized, led the soldiers in the orchard up to the skirmish line, now just south of Charpentry. He then left in the evening to go to headquarters. The First Battalion—including Company B—posted as guards for the regiment during the night and repulsed a German patrol that attempted to penetrate the lines. "When night came," Nichols recalled, "the men 'dug themselves in.' I slept in a shell [hole] with three other battalion scouts."[12]

General Traub's men secured over four hundred prisoners and advanced a respectable three miles during the first day. On the other hand, leadership, liaison, and communication deficiencies plagued the Thirty-Fifth Division:

> On the right, the 138th Regiment had taken heavy casualties and undergone a change in command. On the left, the wretchedly led 137th no longer existed as a coherent force. Its unscheduled replacement, the 139th remained reasonably fresh but had become disorganized. Only the 140th, still in reserve, remained in full fighting trim. . . . The 35th Division had become a dangerously weak link in the American front.

Despite such problems, the Thirty-Fifth had advanced farther than the Twenty-Eighth Division to its west and the Ninety-First Division to its east. The failure of the adjacent units to keep pace was extremely problematic, exposing Traub's men to enfilading fire. The sector assigned to the Thirty-Fifth widened beyond Cheppy and Charpentry, making it more difficult for the left and right flanks to stay in contact. Perhaps most concerning, however, was the ability of the Germans to move four fresh divisions into the Meuse-Argonne region that night.[13]

Thirty-five Kansans were killed in action on September 26. Eighteen soldiers from the 137th Regiment fell that day. Nine men from the 139th were killed but none from Company B. One of the 139th's wounded on the first day of battle was Paul West of McCracken. Lieutenant William Ellenburg of Company K told West's mother that her son was a "runner" who was hit while relaying messages to the Twenty-Eighth Division. The lieutenant offered consoling words—"He was a soldier of the finest type"—but also spared no details—"He was in much pain, having one leg blown off and abdomen torn open by shrapnel." Private West, at the age of twenty-two, died on October 2.[14]

* * *

Logistical difficulties continued on the second day of battle. General Traub faced a difficult situation in the early hours of September 27. Because the field artillery was not yet in a position to provide support, he had initially told the Seventieth Infantry Brigade to wait until 8:30 A.M. before moving forward. The Germans had placed fresh troops in front of his division, and Traub knew his men would also be exposed to deadly flanking fire. His concerns, however, were not shared by his superiors, and as sunrise approached, Traub directed Colonel Walker to attack at 5:30 A.M., explaining, "It is General Pershing's order; it must be done." This last-minute change in plans created a great deal of confusion, which was exacerbated when Traub—at 5:00 A.M.—changed the "H-hour" yet again, pushing it back one hour.

Lieutenant Colonel Ristine of the 139th Regiment received the third order, but Lieutenant Colonel Channing Delaplane of the 140th did not, and consequently his regiment advanced at 5:30 on its own. The men were quickly pinned down, bringing the attack on the right side of the sector to a standstill. The 139th (with the 137th in reserve) was poised to advance on the left at 6:30 but instead waited over two hours for the promised artillery barrage. When Ristine requested further instructions, he once again received no answer and was forced to decide whether to proceed without support. He ordered the men forward at nine o'clock; Charles Hoyt describes what happened next:

> It was an advance of certain death. From the flank the Germans poured into the ranks a costly fire. From left and right, and ahead, the sputter of machine guns greeted every step. It was a test of morale. The damp gloom of the September day; the excitement and strain of the fighting the day before; the lack of food and sleep—all contributed against, and not for, the soldier. The German artillery bit into the ranks at every pace.

With less flourish, Private Nichols provided a similar account of the unsuccessful attack: "We resumed the drive, but hadn't gone far when our progress was checked by the Germans' many machine guns. We lay around in shell holes sniping and being sniped until 5:30 P.M." The 139th followed Buanthe Creek toward Charpentry, but the men were forced to stop short and dig in. According to Hoyt, the American airplanes "politely withdrew" at this time, and German pilots swooped low to strafe the doughboys. According to Clair Kenamore, "the entire brigade threw less than 1,200 shells, against more than 40,000 fired the preceding day." A cold rain began to fall on the men, wearing their summer uniforms. They were also thirsty and running out of rations.[15]

Just before noon the attacking battalions of the 139th were joined by several slow-moving tanks, which prompted Ristine to order an advance up a slope in front of Charpentry. The tanks, however, were quickly disabled by enemy fire, and the infantry dug in once again, waiting for the Twenty-Eighth Division to bring up its line west of the Aire River. It appeared to Lieutenant Bill Smith and the men of Company B that they were done for the day. What they did not know, however, was that Traub had been informed in the late afternoon that General Pershing wanted the division to move forward at all costs. The message conveying Pershing's displeasure—"He is not satisfied with the Division being stopped by machine gun nests here and there"—prompted a second assault. Lauren Finnell and Arthur Whitesell of Newton, however, did not advance. The two friends were killed while engaged in observation duty, positioned ahead of their comrades in Company K, 139th Regiment. Whitesell was wounded by a high-explosive shell, and as the two awaited the arrival of medical assistance, another shell landed with fatal results. Privates Whitesell and Finnell, both 1916 graduates of Newton High School, were returned to Kansas and laid to rest on September 18, 1921. The local Veterans of Foreign Wars Post 971 was renamed in 1922 in their honor.[16]

In the most detailed portion of his letter to his father, Private Nichols described the role played by Company B in the attack on Charpentry at 5:30 P.M.:

> Suddenly our artillery opened up on a town in front of us. Sergeant Segraves, Private [Fred] Wind and myself were starting back to battalion headquarters but when we saw old Co. B going toward the Germans with Lieut. Smith in their lead, we could not resist the impulse to fall in with them. Say! You ought to have seen the way those men followed Lieut. Smith—the formation was perfect. When we lay down the bullets would knock dirt in our faces, but when Lieut. Smith would say, "Let's go!" every man was on his feet following him. When we lay down on a side of the hill for the last time, I happened to be close to Lieut. Smith, and let me say right here that he has sure got nerve. He talked just as calmly when on the side of that hill as if it was a drill field.

Nichols also described an incident in which a German machine-gun nest in or near Charpentry was silenced:

> There was a small house about 50 yards in front of us that was concealing a German machine gun that sure was pouring the lead into our midst. But on looking close I saw that it would soon cease to bother us, for what I saw was three "Yanks" creeping up on the gunner's left flank. They went in the door and came out the window on the other side. The machine gun had ceased firing. The three Yanks brought out no prisoners. We had quit taking prisoners.

The other existing account of the heroics of Company B, "Tribute to 'Cap'n Bill,'" written by an unknown author, comes from a pamphlet printed in connection with the 1955 company reunion held in Oskaloosa:

> We well remember September 27, 1918, second day of battle in the Argonne, the going had been tough, all day long we lay pinned in our foxholes, covered with mud and water, enemy fire too hot to make the slightest advance. We had actually moved ahead perhaps fifty yards. An order came for the Company to be a part of an attack on the village of Charpentry, 5:30 P.M. Promptly at the time set, "Cap'n Bill," mud from head to foot, with one shirt sleeve torn off at the elbow, rose to his full stature and with a forward motion of his hand high above his head, yelled, "Come on men, we're gonna have a helluva fight." Down over the hill he went with Company B, those still able to go, right at his heels.

Contemporary accounts were equally laudatory. "You ought to see Lieutenant Smith lead Co. B," Private Albert Owen wrote to his mother. "The best commander there is, believe me." Sergeant Fred Kelley of Caruthersville, Missouri, praised both Smith and his company: "You should have seen him take old Company B over the top. They were up and at them like bulldogs." When Lieutenant Smith became Captain Smith in October, Sergeant Henry Williamson of Oskaloosa said, "all of the boys are 'for him.'"[17]

The 139th, along with elements of the 137th, attacked directly up the Charpentry ridge, using rifles and grenades, while the 140th advanced from the right with tanks. As Kenamore reported, the 139th "came out of its foxholes like war dogs off the leash" and "charged over the machine guns and stamped them out like nests of rats." Charpentry was taken at 6:00 P.M. as darkness descended. Lawrence Quaney of Company B was struck in the right thigh by shrapnel during this last attack. "It is pretty sore," he told his family, adding with bravado, "Every boy that goes down falls facing Berlin—SO DO MOST OF THE FRITZES!" According to the *Oskaloosa Independent*, another local boy, Sergeant Joe Vendel, was gassed after a shell burst near him and dislodged his protective mask. In a letter dated October 8, the sergeant simply wrote: "I hope peace will be declared and we will be on our way home by Christmas. Have plenty of fried chicken and banana pie when I get there." Joseph Vendel returned to Kansas, married in May 1919, and had a daughter. He died in 1944 of a heart attack at age forty-seven while working at the Boeing airplane factory in Wichita.[18]

Company B and the rest of the Thirty-Fifth Division did not stop at

Charpentry. The 139th Infantry went forward and helped capture Baulny, situated on the crest of a high hill, and then established a defensive line on a slope north of the village. When the regiment finally stopped on September 27, its Third Battalion was north of Baulny, the Second Battalion was in Montrebeau Wood, and Company B and the rest of the First Battalion was near Chaudron Farm. The day was not over, however, for Nichols, Segraves, and Wind. Company B ended its pursuit of the Germans at 11:00 P.M., but the battalion scouts "had to go on in front and find if there were any Yanks in front of us in a certain bunch of woods." The "certain bunch of woods" was Montrebeau Woods, and it was still held by the Germans, although the Americans had reached its southeastern edge. In order to capture Exermont and Fléville, the Thirty-Fifth Division would need to move the enemy from this fortified position.

September 27 was the high point for the Thirty-Fifth Division, rallying to take the villages of Charpentry and Baulny and advance to the southern edge of Montrebeau Wood. The division, however, was unable to solve its fundamental problems of logistical support. In his personal diary, Jesse Blevins recorded that he began the day at 2:30 A.M., took three hours to drive a short distance to an ammunition depot near the front line, and was then forced to wait many hours "for the roads to be repaired by the engineers." Finally, by two o'clock in the afternoon, a plank road was built around a mine crater, and he was able to move forward through a jumbled mixture of ambulances, artillery caissons, and infantrymen. The division's leadership problem also persisted:

> The 35th Division collapsed as a fighting division by the second day of its attack. Nonetheless, its regiments continued their individual, uncoordinated attacks for two more days until they disintegrated in the face of fresh German forces. Before the division entered battle, the frequent changing of key commanders . . . weakened the chain of command. Once the attack began, the command structure within the division failed to adequately function. Division lost contact with its brigades as soon as the attack began. Brigades lost control of their regiments the first afternoon. Regiments lost control of their battalions by the second day.

A prime example of the disintegrating chain of command was the 139th Regiment. Leading from the front, Lieutenant Colonel Ristine got lost on the evening of September 27 and found himself behind enemy lines. Although he was able to avoid capture, his regiment was without a commander throughout the next day. Brian Fowles states that each battalion of the 139th assumed Ristine was elsewhere and that the First Battalion "had a captain in charge with only one officer to a company." The other regiments were also disorganized. A gap had formed in the line between the Thirty-Fifth and the Ninety-First Division on its right, while the Twenty-Eighth Division on its left had not yet removed the threat of enfilading fire. Many of the men wanted to stop and regroup, but General Pershing continued to pressure the First Corps to advance.[19]

* * *

Twenty-four Kansans were killed in action on September 27, including nine from the 137th and eleven from the 139th. The First Battalion, 139th lost only one man, Company D's Sergeant Frank Coate of Plymouth. In addition to Lawrence Quaney and Joe Vendel, at least two other members of the 139th were wounded on the second day of battle. Meanwhile, Willis C. Miller of Valley Falls, a company cook with the 110th Engineers, earned a Distinguished Service Cross for extraordinary heroism:

> When his platoon had been fired upon at short range by a hostile machine gun, Cook Miller advanced alone, armed merely with a pistol, and although knocked down by an aerial bomb, went forward to the emplacement, killed the two gunners, captured the gun, and made prisoners of the reserve crew of two men who were in a neighboring emplacement.

Grover Cleveland Miller (also of Valley Falls but no relation) was struck in both legs and had his gas mask pierced by a bullet. After lying on the battlefield for several hours, he was taken to a hospital, where his left leg was amputated below the knee. Private Miller returned home and was furnished a "cork leg" by the government. He died in May 1930, eleven years after his younger brother, Eugene Miller, was killed in action on October 23, 1918.[20]

CHAPTER SEVENTEEN

Meuse-Argonne and the Thirty-Fifth Division

September 28–30, 1918

More men from Kansas were killed in action on September 28, 1918, than on any other day in World War I. Eighty-three Kansans in the Thirty-Fifth Division gave their lives in battle, including forty-seven men from the 137th Infantry. It was also the bloodiest day for Company B, 139th Infantry, which lost four men, more than any other company in the regiment. This toll of Kansans included one commissioned officer, Second Lieutenant Leslie Campbell of Iola, who was killed while in temporary command of his battalion. Seven sergeants, eighteen corporals, and fifty-four privates died. The remaining three men were Robert Asplund, a mechanic from Kansas City; Bugler Ernest Bagwell of Tonganoxie; and Paul Adamson of Kansas City, a musician third class who was attached to the headquarters of the 110th Engineers Regiment.

Most of these eighty-three men died in the successful effort to secure Montrebeau Wood. The disintegrating Thirty-Fifth Division thereafter pushed forward on September 29 and took the village of Exermont but then fell back and yielded the gains of the previous day. With the assistance of the 110th Engineers, a tenuous defensive line was established near Chaudron Farm, where the exhausted doughboys held off German counterattacks. The last day of September would be the last day of battle for the 139th Regiment and the rest of the Thirty-Fifth Division. According to Robert Ferrell, the final tally of casualties for the division in the Meuse-Argonne offensive "was nearly 7,300 [men] with 1,126 killed or died of wounds, 4,877 severely wounded, [and] the balance lightly wounded or suffering from combat fatigue and returned to duty." In his 1919 divisional history, Charles Hoyt includes a casualty report for the entire war that states that 1,480 men from the Thirty-Fifth died, another 6,001 were wounded, and 163 were taken prisoner.[1]

The third day of battle began with a drizzle that chilled the autumn air. The 140th Infantry attacked on the right at 5:30 A.M. but made little progress. On the left, the intermingled 137th and 139th fended off a counterattack from Montrebeau Wood, then prepared to advance over the same open field. Lieutenant Colonel Carl Ristine was still trapped behind enemy lines, and his scheduled replacement, Colonel Americus Mitchell, would not arrive until late in the day. Command of the regiment thus belonged to Major James Rieger of the Second Battalion, but he was under the impression that Ristine was with one of the other battalions. The Germans continued to harass the Thirty-Fifth Division with enfilading fire, the strongest barrages coming from Apremont and the Argonne Forest. The weather was rainy and cold, there was no sign of the rolling kitchens, and potable water was scarce.

As Edward Lengel has noted, the capture of Montrebeau Wood "was essential to I Corps' advance east of the Argonne," and consequently Pershing demanded an attack "without regard to artillery support, terrain, or the state of German defenses." The men from the 137th and 139th advanced at 7:30 A.M. but were soon slowed by unseen machine guns. "They were not the dashing lads who went over the top two days before," reported Clair Kenamore, "but they were veterans of battle, hardened soldiers who no longer had any delusion about a soldier's life." On the right the 140th and 138th fell in behind some tanks and moved slowly toward the forest. On the left the 137th and 139th crossed the large, open field north of Chaudron Farm. By the afternoon and after many casualties, most of the Germans were dislodged from their entrenched positions.[2]

Company B, 139th was in the thick of the fight. For battalion scout Ralph Nichols, September 28 would be his last day of battle:

> The Germans began to give us a barrage. Well, I was lucky enough to get through the barrage, but about 11 A.M. a machine gun bullet got me thro the face. Back at the field hospital I saw five of the Erie, Kansas, boys. They gave me chocolate and bread with jam on it, but my teeth were set and I could not pry them open enough to get even a crumb of bread in.

Nineteen-year-old Private Nichols likely would have died if the bullet had been an inch or so higher, but he instead "picked up a little souvenir about the size of a dime." His high school friend, Sergeant Billy Kimmel, also avoided serious injury, as his family learned when a letter from Corporal Clinton Davis was published in the *Valley Falls Vindicator*:

> We crossed the field under artillery and machine gun fire that was as thick as any hail storm I ever saw. . . . They made me dig one hole in the

Photo 17.1: Thirty-Fifth Division field hospital in a church in Neuvilly, France, September 1918. Courtesy of the National WWI Museum and Memorial, Kansas City, Missouri, USA.

> ground with my hands so that I could hide in [it]; and I dug it in no time at all. . . . And that wasn't the only hole I dug or helped dig. Ross Taylor and I dug one and Bill Kimmel dug another. Boy, tell the world Taylor and Kimmel couldn't dig fast enough for me. . . . This all took place in the rain and we had only our raincoats to keep us dry.

Other soldiers in Company B were not as lucky. Frank Vigus of Oskaloosa was killed by a shell, and Rafael Zidek of Irving was mortally wounded. Paul Gibson of Winchester was hit in the thigh by a machine-gun bullet, which he kept after it was extracted. Sergeant Henry Williamson of Oskaloosa was wounded by shrapnel and came close to death when a bullet tore off his gas mask. Bill Smith, Sam Gutschenritter and Melvin Dyson, on the other hand, made it through the day without mishap. It seemed to the men of Company B that there was no rhyme or reason as to who would become a casualty. "I had all the chances in the world to get killed," Private Clarence Winrick told his parents in Ozawkie. "I certainly thought Old Jerry had my address." Albert Owen of Valley Falls survived but watched helplessly when his older brother Wade received a fatal wound. Kimmel, reported the *Oskaloosa Independent*, "came through the scrap all right and doesn't care for any more of it." Virgil Barnes of Circleville, who turned in his bugle and became a runner during the battle, was gassed in Montrebeau Wood but survived. After the war he followed his brother Jesse and became a professional pitcher; in 1924 the brothers became the first siblings to face each other as starters in a major-league game.[3]

As company commander, Lieutenant Bill Smith had the task of leading his men into a steady enemy fire. One of his most trusted subordinates was Sergeant Ted Blevins, who had turned twenty the week before the battle. On October 10, after the Thirty-Fifth Division had been relieved, Smith urged his superiors to grant Blevins an officer's commission. The recommendation was based on the courage and leadership displayed by young Blevins on the morning of September 28:

> While his company was going through a heavy barrage of machine guns and artillery this sergeant even though he was not in command of any platoon got out in front of a line of skirmishers deployed at wide intervals and ran the whole length of the line cautioning the men to keep wide intervals and to keep a straight line and to keep going.
>
> Thus by his fearlessness under fire and his leadership ability and by his example [he] enabled the company commander of this company to bring his company through this barrage in a wide skirmish line thereby suffering comparatively few losses and made it possible for the company commander to have perfect control of the company when it reached the objective and this enabled it to assist in resisting a counter attack which was already under way when this company arrived at the edge of Montrebeau Woods.

Both battalion commander Williamson and regimental commander Ristine approved the recommendation, with the caveat that "no vacancy exists in this regiment." Blevins did attend an officer training school in France, but he decided after the armistice to forego a military career and go to college. His bravery on September 28 also earned him a nomination for a Distinguished Service Cross—a fact that his children did not learn until after his death.[4]

By the third day of battle, the regiments had become so mixed that commanders decided in the afternoon to reorganize the brigades. The 137th and 139th now formed the Sixty-Ninth Brigade, controlling the left side of the division's sector, while the 138th and 140th became the Seventieth Brigade on the right flank. During the day's fighting, Colonel Hamilton of the 137th was once again incapacitated, replaced by Major John O'Connor. Throughout the afternoon and evening, the doughboys attacked machine-gun nests in the woods. Enemy artillery fire remained a constant threat, and at about three o'clock, William "Ed" Blevins, a first cousin of Ted and Jesse Blevins, was killed instantly by a bursting shell. Ted wrote to his aunt and told her that her son was buried where he fell, about three hundred yards "south of Exermont in the edge of a woods."

That same afternoon Vic Segraves was wounded. The details of his battlefield injuries and subsequent treatment are muddled. Ted Blevins wrote to his parents and described how he came to the aid of his former football teammate: "I was with him and he was shot in the ankle and also through the stomach. I gave him first aid dressing and carried him to Field Hospital. He was in bad shape, the wound pained him awfully but he wouldn't let on. One of the sergeants saw him later or thought it was him, it was dark and he couldn't tell for sure." Ted's letter was written in December. Two months later the leader of the battalion scouts, Lieutenant Owen Ridlon of Council Grove, sent a letter to Patrick and Louise Segraves that gave a different date and a secondhand account:

> On the afternoon of the 29th day of September, 1918, while I was out with a patrol, Victor voluntarily formed a patrol and captured a machine gun which was causing loss to the battalion. While trying to capture another in the vicinity he was wounded. Later I saw him after he had been evacuated to a field dressing station, located at Chaudron Farm. At this time I saw that he had medical attention.

A third source, Private Fred Wind of Emporia, went into Montrebeau Wood with Nichols and Segraves on the night of September 27–28. Although he did not mention them by name in a letter to his family, Wind said that the Germans "wounded one of my best pals, and another was killed by my side." Ted Blevins and other members of Company B later searched the battlefield in vain for Segraves's grave, and for several months, his friends and family wondered whether he was dead or recuperating in an army hospital.[5]

The third day of battle ended with the Thirty-Fifth Division in control of most of Montrebeau Wood. A steady rain set in at 5:00 P.M., and darkness followed. The men were now about six miles from the jump-off point. According to James Heiman, the "three units of field artillery in the 60th Artillery Brigade had fired only 3,200 shells the third day, 2,000 rounds better than the 1,200 shells fired during the second day, but less than ten percent of the 40,000 shells hurled at the enemy on the first day of the battle." Jesse Blevins, who spent the day transporting ammunition to the front line and bringing back wounded soldiers, described one instance where a soldier "made a thrilling leap in his parachute" after "a Boche plane suddenly shot straight down from the clouds, attacking one of our observation balloons." While the men of the Thirty-Fifth had experienced their most deadly day, they were not defeated. When Otto Russell "Jack" Stites of Emporia, whose left arm was shattered by shrapnel, informed his aunt and uncle about his injury, he made sure they understood that he was moving forward:

> I didn't get shot in the back, so you see that I wasn't running when I was wounded. Shrapnel got me in the left arm and shoulder, and I almost lost my arm, but it is coming [along] fine and in time will be as good as ever, I think. My division tried to whip the whole German army by itself, and we didn't do too bad at that, only when we wound up the battle there weren't enough of us left to start a dog fight.

Although September 28 was the single most deadly day for Kansans in World War I, the Thirty-Fifth Division had moved forward for the third consecutive day. By midmorning on the twenty-ninth, however, it would find itself in full retreat.[6]

* * *

General Pershing visited Major General Traub on September 28 and ordered him to attack "tomorrow morning regardless of cost." The Thirty-Fifth Division was expected to take Exermont and advance toward Fléville that day. It had rained throughout the night, but as Ted Blevins recalled, the men "were usually so tired after a day of battle that we'd sleep in spite of ourselves. When it got dark, we'd fix ourselves for the night right where we were, probably in the mud." The situation for the most part had not changed: the men were cold, thirsty, hungry, and exhausted; there were insufficient officers to organize and lead the troops; the artillery struggled to provide support; the enemy held an elevated and fortified position; and the Twenty-Eighth and Ninety-First Divisions had not been able to remove the Germans from their flanking positions.

An uncultivated field and a large ravine lay between Montrebeau Wood and the village of Exermont. Men from the 137th, 139th, and 130th Machine Gun Battalion constituted the left side of the attacking force. At 5:30 A.M.

a mixed detachment of about 125 Americans emerged from the north edge of the woods and advanced as General Pershing had ordered. They reached the ravine west of Exermont but were forced to return at 8:00 A.M., when reinforcements were stopped by enemy machine guns and artillery. A second group, composed mostly of soldiers from the Second Battalion, 139th, did temporarily take control of the village, where they were joined by doughboys from the 140th Regiment. Casualties were high, with Company H, 139th losing four men on September 29, including Anthony Shook and Dewey Buchanan from Abilene. The Shook family sent three sons to France, and Anthony's brother Grover was killed on the same day as him near Baulny. Not to be outdone, Dewey served in Company H with two of his brothers (Ward and Paul) and two of his first cousins (Frank and Harry). Of the five Buchanan boys, only Dewey, age twenty, did not return to Abilene.[7]

It is not clear whether Company B, 139th took part in the morning attack, but at least two men from Oskaloosa were wounded on September 29 and another was killed. Private Fred Pottorf, who served with his younger brother Frank, was wounded when a piece of shrapnel struck the back of his left knee. Ted Blevins was also wounded and almost killed, as he recalled toward the end of his life:

> On about the fourth day of the battle, I was hit on the shin by shrapnel (I can't remember which leg!). At first it stung and bled profusely, and I went back to a first aid station. Here it was dressed and back to the front I went. . . . I carried a gun and . . . one German bullet went through the handle of the .45 while it was fastened to my waist, so the handle may have saved my life. The bullet lodged in the cartridge holder. It's a wonder it didn't explode one of the shells in the holder.

The unlucky Oskaloosa native was Sergeant Marlin Brey, age twenty-one. His parents, who were required to register as an alien enemies, brought Marlin's body home to be buried in the city cemetery under a headstone that describes him as a "Hero of the World's War."[8]

By midmorning, it was evident to General Traub that a defensive line must be established, given the increasing likelihood that the division would be forced to retreat. A noncombat unit, the 110th Engineers Regiment, was ordered to prepare a line south of Montrebeau Wood on a ridge parallel to the Chaudron Farm road. Private Joseph Rizzi recalled that when the acting battalion commander, Captain Orlin Hudson of Fredonia, received the order by telephone, he immediately turned to his men and, with "a roar of

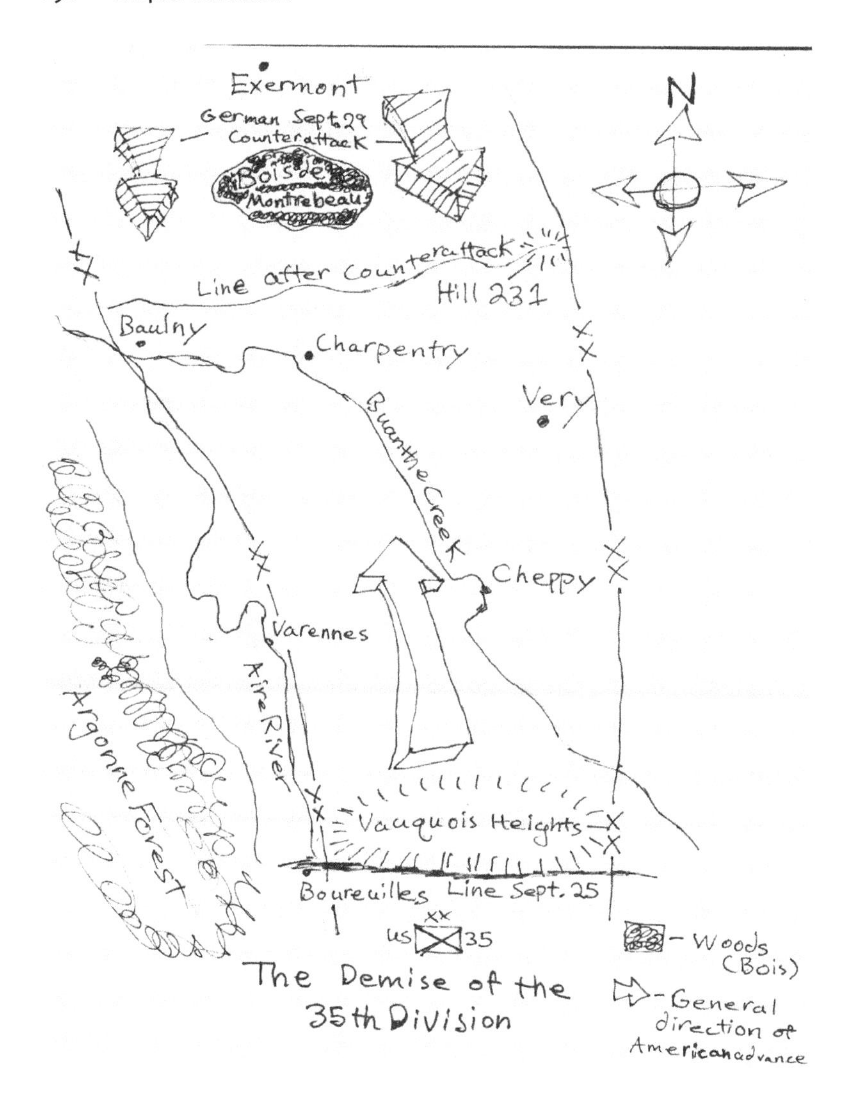

Photo 17.2: Map of movements of the Thirty-Fifth Division, September 1918. Courtesy of Benjamin H. Allen.

command, a wave of his hand," shouted, "Engineers—follow me! Come let's go! Doubletime!" As the engineers hastily constructed a makeshift defensive line, the Germans began to expel the small occupying force at Exermont. The men fought a rearguard action as they returned to Montrebeau Wood, only to find that the forest was also in imminent danger of falling to the enemy. Melvin Dyson and other Americans found themselves surrounded by Germans, and the situation quickly became chaotic: "By 3:00 P.M. the Germans had begun forming an infantry line on the woods' south edge. . . . Frightened Doughboys streamed across the open ground south of the woods and were shelled. The Thirty-Fifth Division was in a state of rout."

The previous day's hard-fought gains were lost as the infantrymen joined the engineers. German machine gunners took up positions on the south edge of the forest, and enemy artillery and airplanes took aim at doughboys as they dug foxholes or crouched in shell craters. As the Americans regrouped, it was unclear whether they would be able to repel the advancing enemy. The first attack came at dusk and was repulsed. The next day the Germans launched several more assaults, but all were unsuccessful.

The heroes of the day were the engineers, who used picks, shovels, and rifles to build and hold the line. Captain Hudson, soon promoted to major, earned a Distinguished Service Cross for his heroism:

> At a critical period in the attack when the assaulting troops were compelled to withdraw, he advanced his battalion of engineers from a support position in the face of heavy artillery and machine gun fire and established a line of resistance. Rallying to his support elements of retiring units, he repulsed three strong counter-attacks and held the line until reinforcements arrived. Although severely wounded early in the operations, Captain Hudson refused to be evacuated and remained with his command throughout the entire action.

Alfred Baker of Glade, Charles Jessop of Newton, and Fred Norris of Hutchinson were among the soldiers of the 110th Engineers killed by explosive shells. Harold Thurman of Altoona, who studied electrical engineering at the University of Kansas, was wounded by shrapnel, taken to a dressing station, and then killed by a second shell. John Vigor of Pomona was mortally wounded while directing men to safety. The corporal's last request was to have his pocketbook, watch, and ring sent home. "I did take the pocket book and the watch," noted Sergeant W. Ray Wilson, confessing, "but I didn't have the nerve to take his ring off and it was left on his body."[9]

The last day of September 1918 was also the last full day on the battlefield for the Thirty-Fifth Division. The engineers and assembled infantrymen worked all night to deepen and extend trenches. Once again, the weather was windy, rainy, and cold. Historian Robert Ferrell notes that "nothing much worthy of mention happened during the last day the Thirty-fifth Division was in line." Still, more Kansans in the Thirty-Fifth died on September 30 than on September 27 (twenty-nine to twenty-five men). One of the last to be killed was Private First Class Hugh Gibson of the 137th Infantry. Gibson was the first soldier from Jewell City to die; according to the local newspaper, he was "a steady, industrious boy, clean minded, reliable and well liked by everybody." Robert Austin of Oskaloosa left the battlefield without "receiving a scratch" only to be accidently shot in the foot by one of his friends in Company B. The young soldier, who would not turn seventeen until November 1, survived the war and passed away in 1956 in Los Angeles, California.[10]

Melvin Dyson of Oskaloosa was with a detachment of soldiers who remained in Montrebeau Wood on September 29. When daylight came the next day, he and his comrades discovered that the Germans now occupied the forest. "We knew we would be either captured or killed when we saw our position," Dyson later told a reporter. "But we determined to do some fighting even if it meant the end of us." Many of the men with him were killed, but at some point the nineteen-year-old Kansan found himself alone and facing six Germans already with two prisoners. "My first impulse was to fire into those Huns, but the thought flashed into my mind that if I did it would mean the end of the two Americans." Dyson instead sought to avoid detection but was soon spotted. "I threw myself on my stomach on the ground and the next minute two German bayonets were pressed against my back." Private Dyson was captured on September 30, becoming a prisoner of war in Germany (see chapter 22).[11]

When General Pershing learned that fresh German divisions were being brought into the American sector, he decided to relieve the Thirty-Fifth, Thirty-Seventh, and Seventy-Ninth Divisions. The First Division replaced the Thirty-Fifth in the early morning hours of October 1. Steve Trout has provided the following sober assessment of the Kansas-Missouri Division's performance: "The 35th Division . . . lost more men, in less time, than almost any other engaged in the Meuse-Argonne . . . [and] essentially went to pieces, hemorrhaging more casualties than any other division at that point (an estimated 1,126 killed and 4,877 wounded) and failing to meet its objectives." Brian Dexter Fowles is less critical: "The 35th Division did as well as could be expected considering the external factors of weather, terrain, enemy resistance, and limited technology. . . . The common soldiers . . . broke through the *Kriemhilde Stellung* and took Exermont by sheer grit and determination. The fault was not theirs if they could not hold it; high casualties and the limits of endurance forced a prudent withdrawal." On October 26, 1918, Colonel Robert G. Peck, inspector general of the First Army Corps, filed a report that was highly critical of the division's performance. He noted that "the fighting spirit and bravery of officers and men was excellent" but spared no details in describing deficiencies in leadership, liaison, training, and artillery support. His report also denigrated the division's "National Guard attitude," which provoked anger back home. Consequently, when Peck's promotion came before the Senate Military Affairs Committee in 1921, Kansas and Missouri senators delayed action for almost a year.[12]

The surviving guardsmen from Jefferson County recuperated and regrouped. Nichols, who had been shot through the cheek, lived on a liquid diet for four days at Base Hospital 46 and then spent four weeks convalescing as an assistant cook at an officers' mess. In November, when he wrote to his father about his experiences, he was in Sainte-Agnès, France, not far from Geneva, Switzerland. He eventually joined the rest of Company B in the village of Vignot, located south of Saint-Mihiel along the Meuse River opposite Commercy.

The doughboys of the Thirty-Fifth, preparing to attack the city of Metz, were ecstatic when the armistice was announced but were less thrilled to spend the winter in northern France, where daily life was monotonous, discipline was lax, influenza and pneumonia were constant concerns, and lodgings consisted of hay lofts and unheated buildings. "If we had some billets with stoves in them we could get along pretty well," wrote Horace Glock, "but when we are out and get all wet and then have no way of drying our clothes, it makes it pretty uncomfortable." In defense of his commanding officer, the Oskaloosa native noted, "It isn't Capt. Smith's fault, as he doesn't like to drill in the rain any better than I do, but he can only take orders from higher up." In addition to the rain, Glock most likely also disliked daily drills because five German bullets had hit him during the fighting in France, including one that went through his left foot.[13]

In a letter dated January 11, 1919, Ted Blevins enclosed "a couple of cooties" as requested by his youngest brother, Frank. The Kansas doughboys joked about their discomfort, such as Orville Tomlinson of the Holton Marine Band, who told his brother, "I can now understand why Napoleon always had his picture taken with his hand in his shirt." But the ubiquitous body lice spread disease and were a constant nuisance, as Ted recalled:

> We'd have to take off our clothes and put them through a de-louser, and we'd take a delouser bath. I have no idea what the 'delouser agent' was, but

Photo 17.3: Company B, 139th Infantry, Newport News, Virginia, April 1919. Courtesy of the Kansas State Historical Society.

> it sure killed the cooties. Cooties looked like bed bugs—about the same size. They'd get in the seams of our clothes, so they were also called seam rabbits. We'd often take off our shirts, turn them inside out, and shake them to get rid of a lot of cooties.

Jesse Blevins (who complained about both cooties and rats in his diary) saw his brother Ted on October 2 and learned that their cousin Ed had been killed. After a brief rest, Jesse was sent back into action, hauling ammunition to the reformed First Corps, which consisted of the Eighty-Second Division (in relief of the Twenty-Eighth), the First Division (in relief of the Thirty-Fifth), and the Seventy-Seventh Division. His company delivered ammunition to the Eighty-Second on October 8, the same day that one of its soldiers, Corporal Alvin York, earned a Medal of Honor. When the armistice was announced, Jesse was billeted in a village about five miles west of Commercy. An elderly Frenchman, he later recalled, "gathered three or four of us boys and took us down to the cellar and got out his auger and bored a hole in a keg and treated us all to a drink."[14]

Bill Smith was promoted to captain after the battle and briefly served in February 1919 as acting commander of the First Battalion. Dyson was transferred to Company A after he returned from captivity. Sam Gutschenritter, who had received a severe foot wound, was sent back to the United States in November. He would spend several months recuperating at a resort hotel in Indiana that had been converted to an army hospital. Ted Blevins, who spent time in an officer training school in southern France, returned to Company B after the armistice, serving as de facto company commander when Captain Smith led the battalion and Billy Kimmel was on leave. When the USS *Matsonia* sailed from France on April 13, 1919, Ted Blevins and Nichols were on board, joined by Kimmel, who decided at the last minute not to spend the next three months in France at an officer training school. Dyson departed two days later with Company A on the USS *Nansemond*. Smith remained a while longer in France and did not march with Company B in the homecoming parades in Virginia and Kansas. "We were mustered out May 8, 1919," Ted recalled, "and I was ready to forget the army and become a college man!"[15]

* * *

Paul Jeffords of Kansas City enlisted in the Kansas National Guard when he was sixteen and spent time at the Mexican border. His older brother, Frank, also became a guardsman, and the two brothers were sent to France as part of Company A, 137th Infantry. On September 28, 1918, Corporal Paul Jeffords was leading a section of the line when he was hit in several places by machine-gun bullets. Frank, who saw his brother drop, soon thereafter succumbed to mustard gas and was left on the battlefield. Ella and Frank Jeffords Sr. were informed by the War Department that both of their sons had been killed in action. Hope was briefly revived in January 1919 when the *Kansas City Star* reported that Frank had returned to action, but in March the *Kansas City Times* once again reported that he was dead.

Frank did not die in France. Red Cross workers found him near where he fell and sent him to a hospital in Nice, on the southern coast of France. He was badly burned except where his face had been covered by his gas mask. As soon as he recovered, Frank attempted to tell his family about his situation, but for some reason his efforts did not succeed. His mail was marked "deceased," and his parents were instructed to claim his life insurance. Consequently, when the phone rang at the family's home on April 24, 1919, and Ella Jeffords answered, she received a shock when a voice said, "Just landed at Hoboken, am well, and oh, mother, I am sure anxious to get home." When she said, "Who is this talking," her son replied, "Why, [it is] Frank, mother; didn't you get my letters?"

On August 1 the War Department announced that the Distinguished

Service Cross had been posthumously awarded to Paul Jeffords for extraordinary heroism. Seven years later Frank Jeffords traveled from Chicago to Arkansas to attend his mother's funeral. When asked about his war experiences, he said he had never fully recovered from the mustard gas and was obliged to work outdoors because inside work caused his skin "to burn like fire." Frank E. Jeffords Jr. died in 1986 at the age of eighty-eight.[16]

CHAPTER EIGHTEEN

Meuse-Argonne and the Eighty-Ninth Division

November 1–2, 1918

On the morning of November 1, 1918, the Eighty-Ninth Division was "at the very center of action on the western front." Although September 12 was the deadliest single day in World War I for Kansans in the division, the defining moment for the "Rolling W" came during the Meuse-Argonne offensive on November 1–2. During forty-eight hours of fierce fighting near Barricourt, thirty-two Kansans were killed and eight others died of combat wounds inflicted either during or before the battle. In large part due to the leadership of men such as Sergeant George Gardner of Traer, who survived, and Lieutenant Jared Jackson of Atchison, who did not, General Pershing ranked the Eighty-Ninth as one of the four best combat units in the American Expeditionary Forces. Sixteen Kansans received the Distinguished Service Cross (two posthumously) for "extraordinary heroism" during this action. Other Kansas soldiers in the division, such as Lieutenant Oscar May, were decorated for bravery before and after the two pivotal days of battle.[1]

May's first medal, the Distinguished Service Cross, was awarded for his leadership during the Saint-Mihiel offensive, when he attacked and captured a German machine gun position. Although the battle ended on September 16, the fighting did not cease, and the Germans sent a large quantity of gas and high-explosive shells from prepared positions. From September 17 until October 8, the day the Eighty-Ninth Division went to the Meuse-Argonne sector, fourteen Kansans in the 353rd Infantry were killed in action and another eleven died of wounds. It was during this time that Second Lieutenant May of the 356th Infantry earned his second medal, the French Legion of Honor (Ordre national de la Légion d'honneur). The lawyer from Jefferson County found himself on October 7 in a very different situation than during the battle. While on a night patrol, he and soldiers from Company M entered a valley filled with mustard gas. Although Lieutenant May had not seen the area in daylight, he was able to lead the men to safety, as he told his mother, "by a compass and my memory of the map." The situation was dire, but

May's leadership skills saved the day, according to Private William "Billy" Benvenuto:

> We got gassed mighty bad, and what do you think he did? He says "We're not going to stay here and be gassed and the fellows don't know what retire means, so we'll go ahead." He just advanced right there with the whole company, out of the gas and into No Man's Land almost to the Jerry wire. It was so dark we had to do the shoulder-to-shoulder stuff to keep from getting lost from the outfit. Then he got us back without losing a single man. Pretty good, hey?

Sergeant Albert Meyer of Hartsburg, Missouri, likewise praised the lieutenant in a letter dated October 20, 1918, sent to May's widowed mother in Williamstown, Kansas. "I never saw a braver man or a better leader of a platoon," he wrote, adding that "every man in the whole company would like to have him for their Captain for he has proven his ability on several occasions of handling a company."[2]

May and the rest of the Eighty-Ninth Division were still in the Saint-Mihiel sector when the final American battle of World War I began on September 26 in the region between the Meuse River and Argonne Forest. Richard Faulkner has identified six phases of fighting by American forces west of the Meuse River:

Initial Phase of the Battle:	26 September–1 October 1918
The Attack Resumes:	4–12 October 1918
Breaking the Hindenburg Line:	14–27 October 1918
Preparing for the Final Push:	27–31 October 1918
A Triumph of a Set-Piece Battle	1 November 1918
Exploitation and Pursuit	2–11 November

The prior employment of the most experienced divisions in the Saint-Mihiel offensive necessitated a greater reliance on inexperienced troops during the first phase of the Meuse-Argonne operations. The initial advance stalled due to exhaustion, stiff German resistance, lack of artillery support, and other logistical issues. To renew the attack, General Pershing replaced several frontline divisions at the beginning of October, including the Thirty-Fifth National Guard Division, and reorganized his forces. The Eighty-Ninth Division became part of the Second Army, commanded by Lieutenant General Robert Lee Bullard, and was placed in reserve. In the center of the

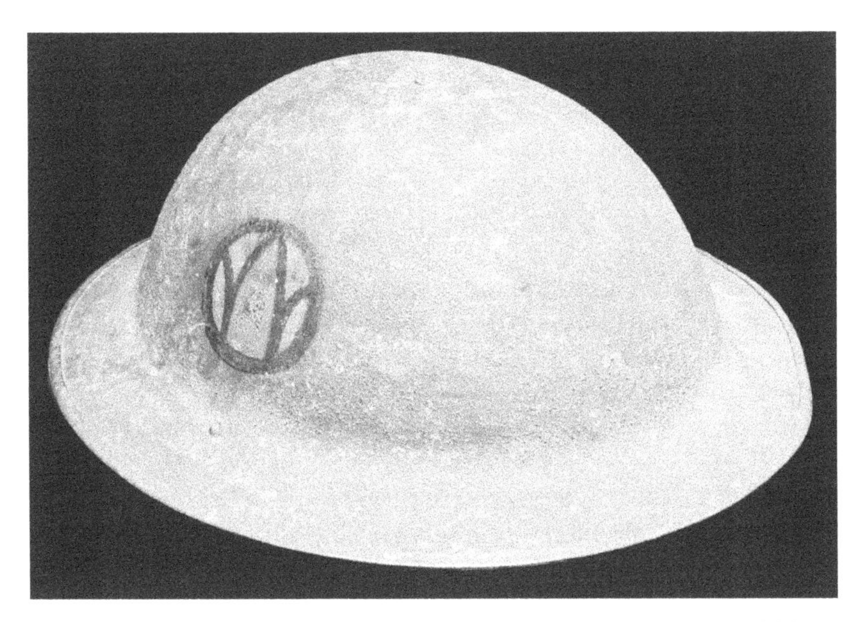

Photo 18.1: Helmet featuring the "Flying W" insignia of the Eighty-Ninth Division. Courtesy of the Dan Bartlett Collection, Washington University Libraries.

American front, the three divisions of the Fifth Corps were replaced by the Third and Thirty-Second Divisions. The latter command, formed from National Guard units from Wisconsin and Michigan, pushed north through the German Hindenburg Line and beyond the village of Romagne-sous-Montfaucon (later the site for the Meuse-Argonne American Cemetery). But the success of the Thirty-Second came at a high cost, as it suffered a significant number of casualties and was in dire need of relief. On October 19 the Eighty-Ninth Division, transported north by French trucks to the Meuse valley, took the place of the Thirty-Second on the front lines.[3]

The Eighty-Ninth was now part of the Fifth Corps, U.S. First Army, which also included the Forty-Second (Rainbow) Division. Directly in front of the Eighty-Ninth Division was the Bois de Bantheville, a large forest west of the village of Bantheville. The "mopping up" of the woodland was an essential precondition to another general assault along the American front and would also assist the Forty-Second Division in taking a German fortified position on the west side of the forest. The assignment of clearing the Bantheville Wood was initially given to the 178th Brigade, which included the 355th Regiment and May's regiment, the 356th Infantry. But on the morning of October 22, the 353rd (All Kansas) Infantry, 177th Brigade joined the fight, which George English called "the most desperate that any element of the Division had encountered up to this time." The mission was accomplished by the end of the day, and for the remainder of the month, the division dug in and held off German counterattacks.

It was during one of the counterthrusts that, on October 25, Private First Class LaRue Kingsbury of Company C was hit in the head by a piece of shrapnel while in a shell hole. The twenty-four-year-old Kansan died of his wounds while being carried to the rear on a litter. Kingsbury was born in Hutchinson but grew up in Smith Center, where his father was a lawyer. The oldest of three children and the only son, he went to Oberlin College in Ohio and studied law at the University of Kansas. Prior to joining the 353rd Infantry, the young man worked as a purchasing agent for a company in Hutchinson that produced soda ash. Private Kingsbury's body was laid to rest in the Meuse-Argonne Cemetery, to which his ailing mother, Grace Kingsbury, made the pilgrimage from Smith County in 1930 to view her son's grave.

Sergeant George Washington Gardner's unit, Company F, was particularly affected by gas shells on the night of October 26, with many casualties resulting from direct hits splashing their contents on the men. Major George Blackinton, commander of the Third Battalion (Companies I, K, L, and M), 353rd Regiment, recalled that in the last ten days of October, his men were subjected "to the most constant and severe shelling any organization ever experienced." Casualties were kept to a minimum by disciplined troops who "used their masks intelligently, kept their clothes carefully buttoned up, did not sit down or linger in low places, and reported for treatment at the first sign of injury from the effects of the gas." Nevertheless, during this period of intense bombardment, thirty-seven Kansans in the 353rd died, including Private First Class Chester Hagerman of Medicine Lodge, who was killed instantly on October 27 by an artillery shell. In a letter to his mother written on September 21, Hagerman had happily reported receiving "some clean clothes for the first time in six weeks." He was apparently unaware of the September 12 death of Jesse Clark Reeves and had only heard rumors of the death of Willis Nixon:

> I guess poor shorty Nixon got killed, from all we can hear about him. I suppose Medicine Lodge looks dreary and lonesome now, doesn't it? Wait 'till we all come marching home. Whew! Won't that be grand. . . . Well, Mother, I must close now and write again when I can. I will be a good

soldier, as I have been, and trust to God to return me to those I love. . . . Tell Sybil many thanks for the little card.

On December 4, 1918, the *Barber County Index* published a poem written by Sybil Hagerman in memory of her brother, which included the following lines: "No sweetheart's kiss; no mother's tear. No sister's love his heart to cheer. Alone he fell—alone he died. His dear one's faces—all denied." Chester Hagerman, who in 1917 had worked with a construction company that built the barracks at Camp Funston, was twenty-two years old.[4]

November 1, 1918, was a pivotal date in the history of the Eighty-Ninth Division. Clearing the Bantheville Wood enabled the Fifth Corps to assault the heights of Barricourt. Richard Faulkner describes the attack planned for November 1 as a "set-piece" battle in which the Fifth Corps would "spearhead the American effort" by "capturing the Barricourt Heights and breaking through the Freya Stellung, the last prepared German defensive belt south of the Meuse." Robert Ferrell (in his notes accompanying the diary of General William Wright) asserts that the mission of the Eighty-Ninth Division was critical to the overall success of the operation insofar as the occupation of the heights "would break the German hold in the entire sector of the First Army" and "force the Germans back to the line of the Meuse, inflicting not merely a major but probably a decisive defeat." It was clear to both sides that, with artillery on the high ground near Barricourt, the First Army would control the Meuse valley.[5]

The guns of the Eighty-Ninth Division began to fire during the third hour of November 1, with the 353rd Regiment posed on the right side of the division's sector. Colonel James Reeves described the Bois de Barricourt as "thick, tangled woods with quite rough ground," and the terrain between the forest and the village of Tailly as "sharply rolling with occasionally patches of trees." At H-hour, 5:30 A.M., it was barely light, and a heavy fog obscured the field, aided by a barrage of smoke shells. The attackers "swept on down the slope, through the valley and attained the intermediate objective on the heights beyond by 6:15." Success, however, came at a high cost: within minutes after the fighting began, Lieutenant Jared Jackson and several of his men in Company M were dead.[6]

* * *

Jackson, a Kansas University law student, was the twenty-two-year-old acting commander of Company M when he died on November 1, 1918. The

Photo 18.2: Jared Jackson. Courtesy of the Kenneth Spencer Research Library, University of Kansas.

circumstances of his death were provided to the residents of Atchison by Major Blackinton, who commanded the Third Battalion, 353rd Regiment. The battalion was selected to lead the assault, and Company I and Company M were the frontline units. "We had a rather wide front to cover," Blackinton recalled, "and we were at the point of the big wedge to be driven into the German lines." The major was about three hundred yards from Company M and therefore must have been told of the circumstances of Lieutenant Jackson's death: "Unfortunately right in front of Jared's two platoons the enemy had five machine gun nests and succeeded in getting them in operation in spite of our heavy barrage, and it was there that Jared fell with five or six of his men within a few minutes after 5:30 November 1. His death was instantaneous from machine gun fire."

According to the *Daily Globe,* word of Jackson's death did not reach Atchison until a telegram arrived on November 25, a few hours after his mother, Edith Fox Jackson, received a letter from him and one hour after his father, Judge William Jackson, posted a letter to France. The news not only devastated his parents and his fiancée but also "depressed and saddened the entire community." Blackinton's letter of consolation was not published until February 21, 1919. The Michigan major (who, incidentally, would help develop the "bazooka" antitank weapon), praised "the wonderful men of Kansas who . . . never looked back, never faltered and never failed to do the task that was laid down from them. . . . I love them, every man, and am proud of them and Kansas should be proud of them."

Jackson's death is erroneously reported in state records to have occurred on November 6. Six of his comrades from Company M were killed on the first: Joseph Block (of Pollard), Arvid Hansen (of McPherson), Charles Harvey (of Quinter), Earl Lyon (of Lincoln), and Peter Trapp (of Herington). This corresponds with Blackinton's statement that "Jared fell with five or six of his men."[7]

* * *

By four in the afternoon, soldiers of the Eighty-Ninth Division stood on terrain that sloped down to the Meuse River. When Marshal Foch was told that the Germans no longer controlled the Barricourt Heights, he supposedly sprang to his feet, overturned a table, and exclaimed, "Then the war is over!" Major General Wright wrote in his diary that he was "delighted with what has been accomplished," noting that his division captured "over one thousand prisoners, over three hundred machine guns, a battery of 88s, known as whiz-bangs, and one 77 field piece." For such heroic acts as the elimination of machine-gun nests, the capture of enemy soldiers, and the maintenance of liaison under fire, five Kansans in the 353rd Infantry were awarded the Distinguished Service Cross: Sergeant Elmer Guthrie (of Hutchinson), Sergeant John Clayton Malone (of Liberal), Corporal John W. McKay (of Independence), and Private (and Bugler) Frank T. Tomanek (of Quinter). Sergeant "Dutch" Malone killed two Germans in hand-to-hand encounters and helped his platoon capture fifteen machine guns and seventy prisoners. His first child, Patric Griffith "Pat" Malone, who was born a month later in December 1918, served in World War II as a pilot and died at age ninety-six in 2015.[8]

After taking the heights, the men of the Eighty-Ninth Division spent the next day, November 2, pushing the Germans across the Meuse River. The enemy put up a determined resistance on the north edge of the Bois de Barricourt. Due to the dense woods and logistical issues, American artillery barrages were repeated throughout the morning, delaying the attack until early afternoon. What followed, according to George English, was "one of the most heroic achievements in the history of the Division—the successful advance of the troops against bitter resistance of the enemy in strong and well-prepared positions across the open and with the use of practically nothing but the infantry's own weapons." The 353rd (All Kansas) Regiment was once again part of the attack, and Companies E, F, G, and H of the Second Battalion were in the thick of the fight. Major James Peatross ordered a simultaneous advance along the whole line, understanding that losses would be great. When someone shouted "Give 'em hell," there were yells that "reverberated down the valley" as the men moved forward. By evening, the village of Tailly was taken and the village of Barricourt was surrounded. Around midnight Colonel Reeves received a congratulatory message—"Bully work"—from the division's chief of staff, Colonel John C. H. Lee, a West Point graduate and Junction City native.[9]

Of the twelve Kansans who received the Distinguished Service Cross for their actions on November 2, three were from Company F, the unit that suffered the most casualties on that day. Private Quincy Seymour of Rantoul was a posthumous recipient, whose self-sacrificing act of advancing into open space enabled his comrades to flank and destroy several machine-gun nests. Sergeant Otis Dozer of Cedar Vale also "fearlessly exposed himself in the face of machine-gun fire" but survived his wounds, becoming a mail carrier in Wichita after the war. The third medal recipient from Company F was Sergeant Gardner of Traer, who "led his platoon through shell and machine-gun fire in an attack on strong enemy positions, capturing two machine-guns and assisting in the destruction of several others that were holding up our advance." Gardner was the first person selected in the draft from Decatur County and the only Kansas member of the "Number 258" club to be decorated for heroism, earning the French Croix de Guerre in addition to the Distinguished Service Cross. As sheriff of Decatur County, he "waded right into action" and quelled "a near riot" during a baseball game in 1921 between Oberlin and Traer. He returned to farming after his tenure as sheriff ended and died in 1965, survived by his wife and two children.[10]

The Eighty-Ninth Division pursued the retreating enemy and on November 5 reached the west bank of the Meuse River, which had been transformed into an even more imposing barrier as German engineers flooded the surrounding area. Two potential crossing points—Pouilly and Inor—were considered, but more information about each was needed. According to historian George English, the former site was selected because "reconnaissances had been more successfully pushed at Pouilly, [providing] better knowledge

Photo 18.3: George Gardner. Courtesy of the Decatur County (Kansas) Museum.

of the terrain and indicating that the place was not so strongly held as Inor." One of the reconnaissance missions was led by Lieutenant May, who would be decorated for a third time as a result. On November 7 the twenty-five-year-old led a daylight patrol across the river valley to the assigned objective and back, through artillery shells, sniper bullets, and machine-gun fire. Private Billy Benvenuto, who described May as a "fighting bearcat," once again praised his leadership: "Did we follow him? I'll say we did, we would follow that bird anywhere. He sure had nerve."[11]

In light of his bravery, May received the Belgian Croix de Guerre. He survived the Meuse-Argonne offensive (although a bullet dented his helmet) and returned to Jefferson County in 1919, having decided to relocate his law practice from Kansas City. During the next three years, May helped organize the Oskaloosa post of the newly formed American Legion and became the Jefferson County attorney. In 1922 he moved to Atchison, where he served two terms in the state legislature and practiced law. His life was cut short in 1947 at age fifty-four by anemia and uremic poisoning, ailments that also affected his son.[12]

The Eighty-Ninth Division on November 10 crossed the Meuse in force south of Stenay, an important railway center and one of the chief objectives of the American forces. On the following day a platoon from Company A, 353rd Infantry entered the town prior to the start of the armistice. Although the Ninetieth Division also claimed credit as the first to reach Stenay, Colonel Lee, the Eighty-Ninth's chief of staff, asserted that the men of the All Kansas Regiment entered the town "while the 90th Division apparently sat still and waited for the cessation of hostilities."[13]

The Eighty-Ninth Division lost 479 men in its advance to and across the Meuse River, with 168 additional soldiers gassed and 1,662 wounded. After the armistice the division became part of the American Army of Occupation, crossing Luxembourg into southwest Germany. On March 29, 1919, the Eighty-Ninth's football team defeated the Thirty-Sixth Division's team in front of General Pershing and fifteen thousand spectators. The game featured two former Jayhawk players, Adrian "Ad" Lindsey and Howard "Scrubby" Laslett, and a future Kansas coach, George "Potsy" Clark. Two months later the All Kansas Regiment crossed the Atlantic on the USS *Leviathan*, its men discharged in June 1919 at Camp Funston.[14]

* * *

One of the professional baseball players in the 342nd Field Artillery, shortstop Charles "Chuck" Ward, described his postwar experiences and hopes for the future in a letter written in December 1918:

> We are well on our way into Germany and are now resting in a German village called Spang for a few days. . . . Alexander, Noyes and Lambeth and myself sat down in one of the towns of Luxembourg for over two hours relating some of the great times we had while playing ball and wishing that we were again in the real country, the good old U.S.A. getting ready for the spring training trip to the southern climate instead of trying to make these people understand us.

Grover Cleveland Alexander played baseball until 1930 and won 225 games after the war. He did not return home unscathed, however, and suffered for the rest of life from partial hearing loss and residual shell shock, which may have exacerbated his epileptic seizures and drinking problem.

Otis Lambeth of Kansas escaped injury in September 1918 when several men in his artillery battery were killed by an incoming shell. The war, he told a newspaper reporter that December, "takes all a fellow's nervousness away.

I don't care how the Red Sox and Tigers try to ride me any more." Lambeth, who may have sustained an injury to his knee while in France, returned to the Cleveland Indians in 1919 but was sent to the Columbus Senators in the American Association and never again pitched in the major leagues. On October 24, 1919, he faced the Hall of Famer Walter Johnson in an exhibition game on Walter Johnson Day in Humboldt, Kansas. Johnson, who grew up near that town, pitched for the home team, which defeated Lambeth's team from Moran by a score of 11–5 before a large crowd. Otis Lambeth worked after his baseball career ended in the sheriff's department and as a mail carrier. The "Kansas Cyclone," who was once "known to virtually every person who has lived in Allen County for any length of time," died at age eighty-six in 1976.[15]

CHAPTER NINETEEN

Black Kansas Soldiers

Fighting Germans and Segregation

"The war is going to put the black man on a different footing. It will do this by drawing all races closer together." George Archibald Gregg, a professor at Western University in Quindaro, Kansas, made this statement in June 1917. In some ways he was correct. Looking back a century later, Black historian Chad Williams noted that World War I "was in many ways the beginning of the 20th-century civil rights movement." But improvement in race relations was a slow and contested process. Gregg, who was born in Eureka only eight years after slavery was abolished, graduated from the University of Kansas and later became the president of two colleges. He was residing in Tulsa, Oklahoma, when a white mob in 1921 attacked Black residents and destroyed their homes and businesses in one of the worst incidents of racial violence in American history. Gregg supported the war against Germany until its conclusion in 1918 and fought the war against segregation until his death in 1940.[1]

During World War I, Black Kansans in the Ninety-Second and Ninety-Third Infantry Divisions served with French forces, whereas the soldiers in various pioneer regiments provided essential services for the American Expeditionary Forces both during combat and after the armistice.

The 369th Infantry, commonly referred to as the "Harlem Hellfighters," was the first regiment of the Ninety-Third Division to reach France. After arriving in December 1917, the former New York National Guard soldiers were put to work in the Service of Supply, unloading ships and transporting supplies from ports to railroad depots and military bases. By May 1918, however, they had joined the French army at the front lines, and the other regiments of the Ninety-Third Division were also in France. The African American soldiers who trained at Camp Funston arrived in July, as did the other units of the Ninety-Second Division. Consequently, Black soldiers from Kansas and elsewhere were in position in the summer of 1918 to serve their country, defeat Germany, and make the world safe for democracy.

On August 7, 1918, a member of General Pershing's staff issued a directive to the French Military Mission—"Secret Information Concerning Black American Troops"—that provided explicit instructions regarding interactions with African Americans:

> It is important for French officers who have been called upon to exercise command over black American troops, or to live in close contact with them, to have an exact idea of the position occupied by Negroes in the United States. . . . Although a citizen of the United States, the black man is regarded by the white American as an inferior being with whom relations of business or service only are possible. The black is constantly being censured for his want of intelligence and discretion, his lack of civic and professional conscience, and for his tendency toward undue familiarity. . . . We must prevent the rise of any pronounced degree of intimacy between French officers and black officers. . . . We must not eat with them, must not shake hands or seek to talk or meet with them outside of the requirements of military service. We must not commend too highly the black American troops, particularly in the presence of Americans.

Although race relations in France were by no means perfect, it does not appear that the French adopted the American attitude toward Black soldiers. Private William Harrison of Abilene, who served in the 317th Supply Train, said the French people "treated him fine." Fred Carson of Lawrence, a member of the African American 806th Pioneer Regiment, which repaired bridges and roads, said Black soldiers "had a real square deal" and "were given every chance to show what we could do, just like the white boys." When asked in 1919 about his experience, Carson said, "From the time I left Camp Funston until I returned there for discharge, I would not have known that I was colored." He then added, "Only when I got to Funston was there any distinction made."[2]

The Ninety-Second Division held a sector in the Vosges Mountains near Saint-Dié from the end of August to the end of September. During this time, the 365th Infantry was commended for repelling an attack. On the morning of September 12, a part of the 367th Regiment was shelled, not by gas or explosives, but by propaganda leaflets:

> TO THE COLORED SOLDIERS OF THE AMERICAN ARMY: "Hello, boys, what are you doing over here? Fighting the Germans? Why? . . . Do you enjoy the same rights as the white people do in America, the land of Freedom and

> Democracy, or are you rather not treated over there as second-class citizens? Can you go into a restaurant where white people dine? Can you get a seat in the theater where white people sit? . . . Don't allow them to use you as cannon fodder. To carry a gun in this war is not an honor, but a shame. Throw it away and come over into the German lines. You will find friends who will help you along.

"The Germans invited the men of the 92nd to join them," recalled Lester Clark, a Black chaplain with the YMCA, "but the colored soldiers were too loyal to do that." Robert Sweeney, who was born in Highland, Kansas, and lived in Kansas City, said he was "very proud" to serve with the 317th Sanitary Train. When interviewed in 1980 about his World War I experience, he said he felt like "a full-fledged American citizen" because the French "treated the black soldiers just like they treated the white soldiers." After the war Sweeney maintained a friendship with Harry Truman and was the first Black supervisor appointed in the Kansas City postal system. Looking back over six decades, he recalled standing in review with all of the units of the Ninety-Second Division: "That's one of the most impressive things that I remember, and it makes you proud that you are an American citizen. It makes you proud that you serve, notwithstanding the fact of all the injustices."[3]

The Ninety-Second Division was split up during the Meuse-Argonne offensive, with most of its soldiers placed in reserve. Two of the three battalions of the 368th Infantry were positioned between the French and American forces in the Argonne Forest south of Binarville. The 368th (like the Thirty-Fifth Division) was relieved after several days of fighting without having achieved its objective. As described in a 1944 pamphlet by the American Battle Monuments Commission, the mission was to fill the gap between the American Seventy-Seventh Division and the French Thirty-Seventh Division, but "due to their lack of training with the French, shortages of equipment, and unfamiliarity with the terrain, the regiment did not successfully complete this important assignment." Thirty Black junior officers were court-martialed, whereas "white regiments and officers who conducted retreats as disorderly as that of the 368th were not punished." On October 5 the entire Ninety-Second Division was withdrawn from the Meuse-Argonne sector and sent to the Marbache sector, which bisected the Moselle River about six to eight miles south of Metz, an important railway junction for the Germans.[4]

October and November proved to be memorable for Wesley Jamison, William Bly, and Lee Hicks, three of the twelve Black Kansans who completed the officer training school in Des Moines, Iowa. Wesley Herbert Jamison was a graduate of Topeka High School, Washburn College, and Northwestern Law School in Chicago. Prior to the war, he practiced law with his father in Topeka, continuing his legal career in Chicago after the war. In a letter dated October 27, 1918, Second Lieutenant Jamison described life with Company D, 351st Machine Gun Battalion:

> This is one continuous affair—day, night, and Sunday, no rest for the weary, and you have to hustle to keep in the land of the living. . . . Night before last I just reached the edge of [a] dug-out entrance as a big bomb exploded near-by and threw a plank across my nose, knocked my helmet off and otherwise stirred me up. Ordinarily I would have dodged down into the dugout but I had a bunch of men to look after, so I took care of them. . . . [F]ound my helmet safe and sound except for a little dent on the rim. Also examined my nose and found only a little skin knocked off, and a little sore.[5]

William David Bly was selected to become an officer based on his exemplary military record since 1896 as an enlisted man. He had just turned thirty-seven when his men, Company E, 365th Infantry, were ordered to participate in an attack on the heights east of Champney-sur-Moselle. The November 10 assault was successful, though at the cost of over five hundred casualties. As Private Leslie Locke of Delphos recalled, "the battle ended with the 92nd holding their positions and dead Germans so thick you couldn't walk anywhere without getting blood on your shoes." Although he was officially reported as severely wounded, Lieutenant Bly told his wife he was "slightly" gassed and anxious to get home: "You don't know what a God's sent blessing it was for the war to end before winter. The Germans were whipped all right, but we have paid dear for it." Bly returned home, lived until 1957, and is buried in the Fort Leavenworth National Cemetery. His former residence is now the Richard Allen Cultural Center and Museum, which preserves the stories of the Buffalo Soldiers and other African Americans in the military, particularly those from Missouri and Kansas.[6]

Lee J. Hicks of Ottawa was the only Kansan at Fort Des Moines to receive a captain's commission. Prior to the war he had graduated from Western University in Quindaro, Kansas, and had worked with John Washington, brother of Booker T. Washington, at the Tuskegee Institute. He was the commanding officer of a truck company in the 317th Ammunition Train. On November 11, 1918, he shared his feelings of relief with his mother:

Photo 19.1: Wesley Jamison. Courtesy of the Library of Congress.

> Dear Mamma: Well, it's all over. . . . I got word this morning as I was conducting a convoy of munitions to our big guns. . . . I have gone thus far unhurt, though I have had many narrow escapes from death, so it looks as if I shall return home whole in body if not in mind. The bursting of big shells is terrible. I cannot describe it to you.

Captain Hicks taught at a Black vocational school in Topeka after the war; moved to California, where he worked for the U.S. Postal Service; and died in 1972 at the age of seventy-eight.[7]

The Ninety-Third Division, comprising the 369th, 370th, 371st, and 372nd Regiments, also served in France. There were few Kansans in the division as it was primarily based on Black National Guard units from other states, including New York, Illinois, Ohio, and Connecticut. There were some draftees (particularly in the 371st Infantry), some enlisted men, and some Black Kansans who became regimental officers. Most of the officers, however, were white, including Lieutenant George Robb of Salina, who won the Medal of Honor while serving with the Harlem Hellfighters (369th Infantry Regiment). The men of the division fought with the French, were issued French weapons and rations (and the poilu's blue helmet), and received a multitude of French medals and decorations. The Black soldiers fought tenaciously and effectively, in the Meuse-Argonne offensive and elsewhere along the western front. Included in their ranks were Isaac Valley of Girard, Clemmie Parks of Fort Scott, Aldon Logan of Lawrence, and Sherman Scruggs of Kansas City.[8]

Corporal Isaac Valley, who had served for three years in the Philippines, was assigned to Company M, 370th Infantry. He was awarded the Distinguished Service Cross for extraordinary heroism in action on July 22, 1918. When a grenade landed in his trench, Valley quickly covered it with his foot to protect his comrades. "I saved the others," he said as he was carried away, "even if it did get me." While recuperating from his severe wounds, he wrote to his widowed mother in Girard. "I am coming back," he said, "all of me but one foot."[9]

First Lieutenant Clemmie C. Parks was born in 1894 and was one of the older siblings in a family of at least fifteen children. His father, Andrew Jackson Parks, was a manual laborer who moved his family to Kansas from Tennessee. Clemmie enlisted with 24th Infantry at the age of nineteen and served in the Philippines. He was discharged in 1915 but selected in 1917 for officer training school at Fort Des Moines. Assigned to the 372nd Regiment, Parks was gassed while in France. On Mother's Day, 1918, he wrote a letter that was poetic in tone: "My heart and mind today are as pure as the dew that glistens in the rising sun and the fond and cherished thoughts of home are as the sweet chimes of music in my ear. We love our family, home, and friends, but not until we are absent from one another does it strike us so strongly." In a letter written in June 1918, Parks observed, "this is a red-blooded man's job and I am doing my bit," and he advised that "any pessimistic person that tells you our government is asleep slap him on the head." After the war Parks worked as a postman, raised a family, and died in Wichita in 1983 at the age of eighty-nine. One of his younger brothers, Gordon Parks, was the author of *The Learning Tree* (about being a Black teenager in Kansas), director of the movie *Shaft* (about a Black private eye who "won't cop out"), and inductee in the International Photography Hall of Fame.[10]

Aldon Leslie Logan graduated from Lawrence High School in the spring of 1915 and entered the University of Kansas that fall. He left his job with the Griffin Ice Company of Lawrence to attend officer training school in Iowa. The *Lawrence Daily Gazette* reported that Lieutenant Logan was initially assigned to Company G, 372nd Infantry, but after "his company was almost annihilated he was made lieutenant of Company I of the 370th Infantry." He was gassed three times while in France and awarded the Croix de Guerre. After the war Logan attended Northwestern University, where in 1926 he earned his doctor of dental surgery degree. He was a dentist in Chicago for many years but was living in Michigan when he died in 1950.[11]

Sherman Dana Scruggs Jr. was the subject of a front-page feature in the *Kansas City Advocate* on August 23, 1918, entitled "Kansas City's First Patriotic Testimonial to Sgt. Scruggs—Particularly Distinguished and Decorated in France under Heavy Shell Fire June 23 and 24." As described in the article, he attended Washburn College in Topeka before becoming an instructor at Tougaloo College in Mississippi. When war was declared, he joined the "Army YMCA" and was sent to Houston, Texas, to assist the Illinois guardsmen of the 370th Infantry. In December 1917 Scruggs enlisted and joined the 370th and, by April 1918, was serving in France as a corporal in Company A. While overseas, he became a sergeant major and was commended by the French army for his bravery: "Sergeant-Major Sherman D. Scruggs, an American Negro of Co. A, 370th, attached to the 34th Division . . . [has] particularly distinguished himself during the days of the 23rd and 24th of June, 1918, in securing under heavy shell fire the liaison with contiguous units." Scruggs was the subject of two additional articles praising his war record. The *Kansas City Kansan* noted that he had completed an officer training program in France and had been commissioned as a first lieutenant. The *Kansas City Advocate*, a Black-focused newspaper, published a letter from Scruggs in which he praised his comrades and described his career:

> I have only done my part as a soldier in this war for democracy. . . . But I must say that at present my former regiment (370th Infantry) has had about 400 men and officers decorated with the Distinguished Service Cross and the French Legion of Honor medal and Croix de Guerre. . . . As you know I voluntarily enlisted in the ranks as a private and by hard work and soldierly effort I was promoted from grade to grade until now I am a commissioned officer. I was selected as one of seven from a possible 2,900 men to become a candidate at the Army Candidates' School in France. There were about 300 men in the school. Only 61 were colored. Fifty-five of these were commissioned. . . . I am [now] with the 92nd Division in the 365th Regiment. We are preparing to return to America.

As an introduction to its story on Scruggs, the *Advocate* expressed its own views regarding the treatment of Black soldiers: "The survivors of America's greatest fighters begin to return to the land they love—a land that calls them [n——s] . . . and gives them the worst of every bargain—yet these valiant sons return with a smile stained with mud and blood with many vacancies in their ranks."[12]

Scruggs returned to Washburn College and obtained his degree in 1920. He became a teacher, principal, and supervisor in the Kansas City, Kansas, school system. After earning a master's degree and a doctorate from the University of Kansas, Scruggs was named president of Lincoln University in 1938. At the request of the U.S. Department of Education, he went to India in 1954 to make a study of their education system. Scruggs moved to Los Angeles in 1970 and passed away in 1976. Lincoln University, located in Jefferson City, Missouri, has honored him with the Sherman D. Scruggs Hall. His son, Dr. Frank Scruggs, earned degrees at Cornell, Princeton, and Harvard Universities and was an officer in the "Black Frogs," a segregated unit of the U.S. Navy SEALs. "To father, education was paramount," he remarked in 2014. "He said to me 'no matter what you major in, get your education. It will be valuable and you will not have to be a field hand or do labor work.'"[13]

In addition to the Ninety-Second and Ninety-Third Divisions, African Americans served in pioneer regiments. The Black combat units of the U.S. Army during the First World War totaled 42,000 men, or 11 percent of all

Photo 19.2: Dr. Sherman Scruggs. Courtesy of the Lincoln University Picture Collection, Inman E. Page Library, Jefferson City, MO.

African Americans who served in the army. The rest (approximately 340,000) were assigned to noncombat units. Some worked in labor units, such as the 325th Labor Battalion at Fort Riley. Other African Americans were part of pioneer regiments that supported the fighting soldiers. Members of these units were trained as infantry and could take part in battles if required, but typically they worked with engineers and built and repaired structures such as bridges and roads. The work often took place in active sectors and within range of enemy artillery. There were thirty-seven "nondivisional" pioneer regiments (attached to corps or armies on an ad-hoc basis), and fourteen of the seventeen African American pioneer units served in France.

James "Henry" Irwin was a member of Company A, 803rd Pioneer Regiment, organized at Camp Grant, Illinois. He was born in 1893 and in 1915 became the first African American male to graduate from Oskaloosa High School (in the same class as Ross Taylor of Company B and two years ahead of Ted Blevins). Irwin attended Western University in Quindaro,

Kansas, which was one of fourteen educational institutions selected by the War Department to provide vocational training for Black soldiers. Corporal Irwin—his name is misspelled "Irvin" in some military records—went to France in September 1918 and died of meningitis on November 8. His body was returned to Kansas in 1921 and laid to rest in the Oskaloosa Pleasant View Cemetery.[14]

The Sixty-Fifth (Black) Pioneer Regiment was organized in October 1918 at Camp Funston but remained stateside. The 805th, 806th, 815th, and 816th Regiments—organized at Camp Funston in June and September 1918—served in France both before and after the armistice. According to one roster list, of the 2,810 men in the 805th Pioneer Regiment, over 70 percent came from three states: Missouri (918), Louisiana (620), and Kansas (459). One of the white officers, Major Paul Bliss, authored a regimental history in 1919. In it he states that many of the soldiers were transferred from depot brigades at Camp Funston and that the commander, Colonel Chauncey Humphreys, came up with the nickname "Bearcats" for the regiment. When the men entered the Meuse-Argonne sector in October 1918 to build ammunition dumps, fix railways, and repair roads, they "took the attitude that every stone pounded into a hole to smooth the way meant as much as the discharge of a shell or a clip of cartridges." Their work continued after the armistice but shifted to salvage operations, filling in trenches and shell craters, and reinterring bodies. The 805th Bearcats were known for their musical and vaudeville talent, as described by Peter Lefferts:

> The 805th had enrolled a large number of skilled musicians and minstrel/vaudeville actors, and they now went to work immediately to put together some concert repertoire and a vaudeville show. . . . The regiment "became famous overnight" for the Bear Cat Entertainers show and for a section of the band that was spun off as a Jazz Orchestra. . . . From February to May 1919 they . . . went on the road to many French villages around the Argonne-Meuse area, with famous Kansas City professional comedian, actor and singer Billy Higgins . . . as their principal soloist.[15]

The 815th and 816th Pioneer Regiments, along with the 813th and several labor battalions, were given a special but unenviable assignment: they constructed cemeteries and reburied bodies at Romagne, Beaumont, Tehiencourt, Belleau Wood, Fere-en-Tardenois, and Soissons. Some 6,000 Black soldiers built the Meuse-Argonne American Cemetery and Memorial 150 miles northeast of Paris at Romagne-sous-Montfaucon. The cemetery contains the largest number of American military dead (14,426) in Europe. One of the men who dug up dead soldiers, checked their identities, and then reburied them was a talented and remarkable African American: George Sweatt of Humboldt, Kansas.[16]

George Alexander Sweatt was born in Allen County on December 7, 1893, not far from the birthplace of Hall of Fame pitcher Walter Johnson. He graduated from Humboldt High School in 1912 and played in the summer for a local Black baseball team, the Iola Go-Devils. In the fall he attended the Kansas State Normal School at Emporia (now Emporia State University) and earned a county teaching certificate. There were more teachers in Allen County than positions, however, and Sweatt worked for a short time at a cement plant and then—as stated on his 1917 draft-registration card—as an automobile repairman. He was living in Peoria, Illinois, when he was drafted and returned to Kansas, where he was assigned at Camp Funston to the 816th Pioneer Regiment. While in France, Sweatt was promoted from private to sergeant major. He joined other Black soldiers who "built cemeteries and reinterred dead soldiers in varying states of decomposition for several months after the war."[17]

After his discharge from the army on November 11, 1919, Sweatt attended the State Manual Training Normal School at Pittsburg, Kansas (now Pittsburg State University). In 1921 and 1922 the recently married veteran was the first Black student athlete to letter in basketball, football and track and field (but not baseball). He obtained a teaching degree, which allowed him to work anywhere in the state and still play baseball in the summer, and secured a job at an African American public school in Coffeyville. In 1922 the twenty-eight-year-old signed a baseball contract with the Kansas City Monarchs, for whom he would play for two seasons before being traded to the Chicago American Giants. Sweatt's departure from Kansas came at about the same time as his testimony in *Thurman-Watts v. Board of Education of the City of Coffeyville*, a 1924 case challenging school segregation.[18]

Known as "Never" Sweatt or "The Teacher," he was one of only two players to have played in the first four Negro World Series—1924 and 1925 with Kansas City and 1926 and 1927 with Chicago. On October 4, 1924, at Griffith Stadium in Washington, DC, Walter Johnson struck out twelve New York Giants but lost the opening game of the Major League World Series. That same day at the Baker Bowl in Philadelphia, Sweatt watched from the bench as the Kansas City Monarchs were shut out 11–0 by the Hilldale Athletic Club. The "Big Train" would get the win on October 10 in the deciding seventh game, four days before Sweatt's triple in the twelfth

Photo 19.3: Frank Duncan, George Sweatt, and Howard Bartlett, Kansas City Monarchs, 1924. Courtesy of the T. Y. Baird Collection, Kenneth Spencer Research Library, University of Kansas.

inning helped Kansas City draw even in its series. The Monarchs would go on to win the inaugural Colored League World Series (referred to simply as the "World Series" in Black newspapers). After his baseball career was over, Sweatt worked for the U.S. Postal Service until 1957, when he and his wife (also a teacher) moved to California to be with their son. George Sweatt died in Los Angeles on July 19, 1983. His wife, Evelyn Groomer Sweatt, passed away in 1995 at age ninety-seven.

In 1974 Humboldt named its baseball and softball fields the George Sweatt Park. The town's baseball museum now features photographs, articles, and memorabilia associated with both Walter Johnson and George Sweatt. Pittsburg State University in 2005 elected Sweatt to its athletic hall of fame, and he was similarly recognized in 2012 by the Kansas Baseball Hall of Fame and in 2016 by the Kansas Sports Hall of Fame.[19]

* * *

When the 805th and 806th Pioneer Regiments returned to the United States in June 1919, they were welcomed in New York by a Kansas delegation that included Adjutant General Martin; Elisha Scott, a prominent Black attorney from Topeka; and S. E. J. Watson, pastor of the African American Topeka Shiloh Baptist Church. The soldiers were thankful and in a good mood, as described by Paul Bliss:

> When Colonel Humphrey arose he was cheered with an enthusiasm which was touching. "Who was it got there in time to help put it over?" he began. "The Bearcats," came the answering roar. "Who was it took $13,000,000 worth of war material out of the Argonne when it was all over?" "The Bearcats." . . . "Who had a baseball team that . . . was never beaten?" "The Bearcats." . . . It is doubtful if any regiment in the American Expeditionary Forces, white or black, ever had an assembly in which regimental feeling ran so high.

Shortly thereafter, fifteen officers and 448 men were sent to Camp Funston to be discharged. A white officer, Captain Arthur Harvey of Salina, was put in charge of the men of the 805th and 806th on their journey from Camp Upton to Camp Funston. According to the *Kansas City Advocate*, the captain did not intend to stop as the train passed through Kansas on the evening of July 3 and only agreed to stop in Kansas City after Mayor Mendenhall intervened. The soldiers were welcomed by more than six thousand people at eight o'clock and enjoyed food and conversation in Huron Park before marching back to the train. Captain Harvey at this point spoke by telephone to an assistant to Governor Henry Allen and promised that the train would briefly stop in Topeka. But it did not make that stop. According to the train conductor, immediately after making his promise, Harvey boarded the train, said he was going to bed, and informed the crew that he was not to be disturbed until they arrived at Camp Funston.

One month earlier the city of Topeka welcomed home the white soldiers of the Thirty-Fifth Infantry Division with a parade. No parade was planned for the men of the 805th and 806th Pioneer Regiments, but five thousand citizens had assembled to meet and feed the soldiers. The disappointed crowd watched as the train passed by, and the food prepared for the veterans was donated to local charities. Mayor Herbert Corwine and Governor Allen demanded an investigation, and Harvey's decision was condemned by the Black community. "It doesn't seem like white men would treat dogs that way," said attorney Scott. "Every one of my race feels that we have been grossly mistreated," declared Reverend Watson. "The Negro soldier, who has a right to be honored for what he has done, has never had the chance to march down our streets as other soldiers have done."

Kansas officials pressed for an investigation, but the U.S. Army's chief of staff, General Peyton C. March, said that Harvey's honorable discharge stripped the War Department of any authority to examine his conduct. "The War Department is merely 'passing the buck,'" observed an ex-soldier in Salina. "It is the easiest way out of the matter."[20]

CHAPTER TWENTY

Medals of Honor

John Balch, Erwin Bleckley, George Mallon, and George Robb

The Medal of Honor is the highest award for valor in action against an enemy force that can be bestowed upon an individual serving in the armed forces of the United States. Just over 3,500 individuals have been awarded the medal since 1863 (19 having been twice decorated). In World War I there were 121 recipients of the medal, 2 of whom are credited to Kansas: Erwin Bleckley and George Robb. John Balch is apparently considered to be from Missouri because he volunteered in Kansas City, and George Mallon is listed as being from Minnesota, where he located as a young man after marriage. Balch and Mallon, however, had backgrounds similar to Bleckley and Robb: they all were born and raised in Kansas and went to high school in the Sunflower State.[1]

John Henry Balch was born on January 2, 1896, in Edgerton but attended high school at Syracuse, where he excelled in track (winning a state meet in 1915 with a four minute, forty-six second mile). In September 1915 Balch enrolled at the University of Kansas but left school in September 1917 to enlist in a navy officer training program at Kansas City. He became a pharmacist's mate first class, a petty officer who administers medical assistance to naval personnel or, as in the case of Balch, members of the U.S. Marine Corps.[2]

As a medical corpsman, Balch was assigned to the Sixth Marine Regiment, Second Infantry Division. He would earn three Silver Stars, a Distinguished Service Cross, and the Medal of Honor for courageous actions on three separate occasions. One Silver Star and the Distinguished Service Cross were awarded for heroism at Belleau Wood in June 1918. During a night attack on the enemy, Balch evacuated wounded men at the risk of his life and displayed conspicuous coolness under shell fire. In a letter to his mother on June 17, 1918, the twenty-two-year-old shared his experience: "I was right out with the men advancing through open wheat fields and woods, taking care of the wounded as fast as I could get to them. They were calling for help on all

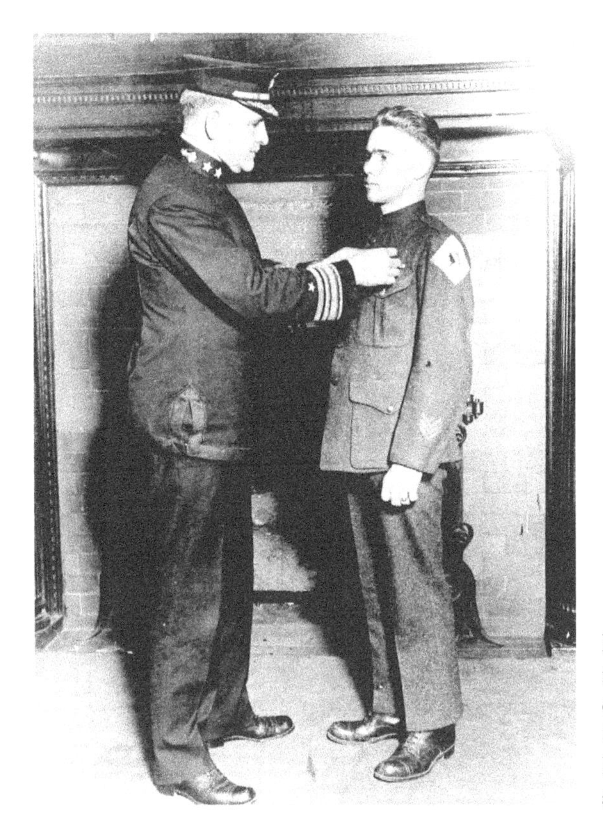

Photo 20.1: John Balch receiving the Medal of Honor. Courtesy of Collection, Archives Branch, Naval History and Heritage Command.

sides." Balch may have worked at this time with Kansans in the Sixth Marine Regimental Band, who were temporarily detailed as stretcher bearers.[3]

Balch's bravery on July 19 at Vierzy, a village a few miles south of Soissons, was mentioned in his Distinguished Service Cross and Medal of Honor citations. He "worked unceasingly for sixteen hours, giving assistance to the wounded on a field torn by high explosive shells and covered by direct machine-gun fire," as he "unhesitatingly and fearlessly exposed himself to terrific machine gun and high-explosive fire to succor the wounded as they fell in the attack, leaving his dressing station voluntarily and keeping up the work all day and late into the night." Of the 2,400 marines who participated in the July 19 attack, nearly half were killed or wounded.[4]

The third act of recognized heroism took place on October 5 near Saint-Étienne-à-Arnes and Sommepy (east of Rheims). Balch "gave proof of excellent judgment and courage in establishing an advance dressing station under violent shell and machine-gun fire, thereby saving many lives which would otherwise have been lost." His "exceptional bravery" on the fifth was the basis for two Silver Stars and was cited in connection with the award of his Distinguished Service Cross and Medal of Honor. Years later, when asked about his medals, Balch told a reporter: "I just followed those Marines around for two years. . . . I watched them walk into that machine gun fire, and they deserved honor more than I did. I was just lucky."[5]

An Indiana newspaper in 1942 noted that Balch, then a forty-five-year-old manager of an insurance agency in Mishawaka, Indiana, volunteered with the U.S. Navy—without consulting his wife. "If MacArthur can fight at his age," Balch declared, "I sure can." He served in New Guinea and Australia and was promoted in 1944 to lieutenant commander. After his death in 1980, the veteran of two world wars received one more honor: on July 21, 2005, the naval health clinic at Quantico, Virginia, was renamed the John H. Balch Clinic.[6]

Whereas Balch participated in several battles, Erwin Bleckley is remembered in connection with a singular event: the valiant efforts to come to the aid of the Lost Battalion. Margaret and Elmer Bleckley were presented their son's Medal of Honor on March 4, 1923, four and a half years after his death. The ceremony took place on a Sunday at the Wichita Forum, a municipal auditorium located at site of the current Century II Performing Arts and Convention Center. At eight o'clock in the evening, the blare of trumpets called the audience to attention, followed by the National Anthem. Episcopal bishop James Wise gave an invocation, and the Lyric Club sang two songs, "The Crusader" and "The Supreme Sacrifice." Governor Jonathan Davis served as master of ceremonies, and former governor Henry Allen provided brief remarks. "I sometimes wonder," said Allen, "if we realize what these boys did for us." Several thousand people attended, including Bleckley's fiancée, Enid Jackson, and the Gold Star mothers of other deceased soldiers. Major General G. B. Duncan presented the medal, awarded posthumously to Bleckley "for extraordinary heroism in action as an observer in the 50th Aero Squadron, 130th Field Artillery, Air Service, A.E.F., at Binarville, France, 6 October 1918." The citation goes on to describe the events of that day:

> Second Lieutenant Bleckley, with his pilot, First Lieutenant Harold E. Goettler, Air Service, left the airdrome late in the afternoon on their second trip to drop supplies to a battalion of the 77th Division, which had been cut off by the enemy in the Argonne Forest. Having been subjected on the first trip to violent fire from the enemy, they attempted on the second trip to come still lower in order to get the packages even more

Photo 20.2: Erwin Bleckley. Courtesy of the Kansas State Historical Society.

precisely on the designated spot. In the course of his mission the plane was brought down by enemy rifle and machine gun fire from the ground, resulting in fatal wounds to Second Lieutenant Bleckley, who died before he could be taken to a hospital. In attempting and performing this mission Second Lieutenant Bleckley showed the highest possible contempt of personal danger, devotion to duty, courage, and valor.

"A young life given to his country," remarked Bleckley's father after accepting the medal, "makes my heart strings vibrate with the memory of his service." A cannon provided a twenty-one-gun salute, the American Legion band played "Taps," and the ceremony was concluded.[7]

Erwin Russell Bleckley was born on December 30, 1894, the oldest son of a prominent Wichita family. He graduated from Wichita High School in 1913 and worked with his father at the Fourth National Bank. When war was declared, young Bleckley expressed a desire to become an aviator, but his family objected, so he joined an artillery unit of the Kansas National Guard, which in August 1917 became the 130th Field Artillery Regiment of the 35th Infantry Division. Promoted to lieutenant, Bleckley left Camp Doniphan and went to France in April 1918 as part of an advance detail. Soon thereafter the young Kansan volunteered to be an aerial observer and was attached to the Fiftieth Aero Squadron of the Army Air Service (the forerunner of the Army Air Corps, which later became the U.S. Air Force). Known as "Bleck" in his squadron, Bleckley flew his first combat mission with pilot Harold E. Goettler on September 12, the opening day of the Saint-Mihiel offensive.[8]

The squadron relocated on September 24 at Remicourt, south of the Argonne Forest. In the first week of October, nine companies of the Seventy-Seventh Division were surrounded by German forces in the dense woods, which prompted the divisional commander, Major General Robert Alexander, to request that the Fiftieth Aero Squadron locate and resupply this "Lost Battalion" with ammunition, rations, and medical supplies. On October 6 pilot Goettler and observer Bleckley flew two missions in their biplane at low altitude and within range of German guns (whose fire provided clues as to their location). In the morning Bleckley dropped bundles of chocolate, cigarettes, bandages, and ammunition, hoping they would not fall into enemy hands. When told by their squadron leader that a second mission would be exceedingly hazardous, Bleckley reportedly replied, "We'll make the delivery or die in the attempt." He also went to his quarters and wrote his will. During this second flight, German bullets riddled the plane and killed Goettler. Bleckley attempted to land the plane, but it crashed in a field behind Allied lines. The Wichita native was still alive when he was found unconscious near the damaged aircraft but died during the journey to the hospital.[9]

Goettler and Bleckley were posthumously awarded the Distinguished Service Cross in November 1918. The awards were changed to the Medal of Honor in 1922. Margaret Bleckley traveled twice to France, in 1920 and 1931, to visit her son's grave at the Meuse-Argonne American Cemetery and Memorial. In 1932 Wichita officials renamed Harding Boulevard as Bleckley Drive. The Bleckley family later donated the Medal of Honor to the U.S. Air Force, which displays the decoration at the National Museum in Dayton, Ohio. In October 2009 Goettler and Bleckley were honored with a monument at Remicourt, France, in a ceremony commemorating the American aviators based there during the Meuse-Argonne offensive. On October 6, 2018, the centennial of his death, Bleckley was again honored when Wichita

Photo 20.3: George Mallon. Courtesy of the Hennepin County Library, Minneapolis Newspaper Photograph Collection.

celebrated "Bleckley Day" with speeches and flyovers from vintage and replica World War I aircraft. "I never dreamed, "said Nancy Erwin, a niece of Bleckley, "that people would be remembering him, 100 years later."[10]

Another Medal of Honor recipient with Kansas connections is George Henry Mallon, the son of an Irish immigrant. His father, Robert Mallon, came to the United States in 1850 as a young man and settled in Riley County on a farm north of Ogden and adjacent to Fort Riley. George was born in 1877, the second of ten children. He enlisted in 1898 with the Twenty-Second Kansas Volunteer Infantry but was not sent to Cuba. After being discharged, the twenty-one-year-old signed up in January 1899 with the Regular Army and was sent to the Philippines, where he received a bullet in his chest that he would carry the rest of his life. A cousin described him as "unusually strong and brawny," and at some point prior to 1901, Mallon earned a belt as the army boxing champion of the Philippine Islands.[11]

The Kansan left the army in 1902 and moved to St. Louis, where in 1905 he knocked out two opponents in the first round of an amateur boxing tournament. According to the *St. Louis Globe-Democrat*, both fights ended when

Mallon's right fist connected with the jaw of his opponent. The *St. Louis Post-Dispatch* praised his "short half-hooked blow," stating that it "reminds one of nothing so much as a piston rod." What appeared to be a promising career, however, came to end in 1906 when "Spike" Kennedy knocked out a battered and bloody Mallon in the third round in a fight at Kansas City. A few months later Mallon married Effie Campbell in Kansas City, Kansas. By 1909, the couple was living in Minneapolis, Minnesota, where George found work as a pipe fitter. Because his family stayed in their adopted state, both Minnesota and Kansas can claim the World War I hero as one of their own.[12]

Just prior to his fortieth birthday, Mallon enlisted for the third time in May 1917. He went to an officer training camp, was commissioned as a captain, and was assigned to the 132nd Regiment of the Thirty-Third Division, an Illinois National Guard unit. The division arrived in France on May 26, 1918, and four companies, including Mallon's unit, fought alongside Australian troops on July 4 at Le Hamel in northern France. When the Germans counterattacked in the evening, the Allies repulsed the charge with guns, artillery, and—in three instances—their fists. As biographer Stephen D. Chicoine describes one of such encounter: "They came to a German officer and Mallon, still disdaining his automatic, brought up a sharp left against the enemy jaw and knocked the German out. . . . Mallon [then] leaped into the trench and felled the two Germans with the same fist that had done for their officer."[13]

The captain would use his boxing skills again on September 26, 1918, the first day of the Meuse-Argonne offensive. The Thirty-Third Division was assigned the easternmost position on the American front, along the Meuse River. Its mission was to advance across marshland and small tributaries and then break through entrenched enemy positions in a forest on higher ground, the Bois de Forges. Dense morning fog caused Mallon and nine of his men to become separated from the rest of the company. According to the citation accompanying his medal, the captain and his men "pushed forward and attacked nine active hostile machine guns, capturing all of them without the loss of a man." Mallon then led the soldiers in an attack on an active battery of four 155-mm howitzers, "rushing the position and capturing the battery and its crew." In this encounter, the official citation reads, "Captain Mallon personally attacked one of the enemy with his fists." As Mallon himself later recounted: "A Prussian officer about my size, and I'm over six feet tall, met me halfway to the bottom with half-drawn pistol. There was no chance to argue and I let him have one full on the chin. . . . I always will contend that a good solid fist inspired more fear and obedience in the Germans than did anything else unless it was naked steel." But the day was not over. When the

He fought for you in the regular American way—two-fisted and hard-hitting.
Lend here as Mallon fought there. Fight with your dollars in the Victory Liberty Loan.

The war is won, but the bills must be paid. The success of the Victory Liberty Loan is our job. We are only lending, not giving, our money and our Government guarantees its return with interest. Buy today.

Photo 20.4: Liberty Loan advertisement featuring George Mallon. Courtesy of the National WWI Museum and Memorial, Kansas City, Missouri, USA.

ten Americans came upon two more machine guns, Mallon "sent men to the flanks while he rushed forward directly in the face of the fire and silenced the guns, being the first one of the party to reach the nest." At the end of the day, the ten men were alive; one hundred Germans were prisoners; eleven machine guns, four 155-mm howitzers, and one antiaircraft gun were silenced; and George Mallon had earned the Medal of Honor.[14]

The fighting days for the pugilistic captain ended on October 1 due to a wound in the right thigh caused by a high-explosive shell. Mallon was still recuperating in February 1919 when he received his Medal of Honor from General Pershing at the AEF headquarters. At about the same time, the War Department asked Pershing to select one hundred of the best stories of American heroism to be used in a promotional campaign for the postwar "Victory" Liberty Loan drive. Both Mallon and George Robb of Kansas made the list of the commanding general's "100 Heroes." As described in the *Advertising and Selling* trade magazine, the exploits of some of "America's Immortals" would be depicted in newspapers with words and drawings that would serve "as the foundation for an appeal to American pocketbooks." Captain Mallon was chosen, and the drawing accompanying his story shows a soldier using his right fist to strike the chin of a German, who helplessly drops his gun and loses his helmet as he is knocked off his feet. Next to the illustration are the words: "He fought for you in regular American way—two-fisted and hard-hitting. Lend here as Mallon fought there. Fight with your dollars in the Victory Liberty Loan."[15]

George Robb of Salina was the fourth Kansan to win the Medal of Honor in World War I. The 369th Infantry Regiment—known as the Harlem Hellfighters—was an African American National Guard unit from New York commanded by white officers. The Black soldiers experienced significant racism during their training in South Carolina and were relegated to labor and service duties upon arrival in France. In March 1918 Robb, a thirty-year-old white Kansan with a master's degree from New York's Columbia University, was assigned to the unit. Soon thereafter Lieutenant Robb and the 369th Infantry were issued French weapons, helmets, belts, and pouches and sent to the front in their American uniforms to fight with the poilu (French infantry). For the remainder of the war, the Harlem Hellfighters fought hard and fought well. Lieutenant Robb greatly admired the bravery of the soldiers he commanded, and his men likewise thought highly of his courage and fortitude, particularly during the fighting on September 29–30 at the village of Séchault.

Robb, like Mallon, was the son of an Irish immigrant who settled in Kansas. Thomas Robb put down roots in Saline County, where George was born in 1887. The family moved several times during George's youth but settled in Salina, the county seat of Saline County, by 1907. After graduating in 1912 from Park College in Parkville, Missouri, Robb went east, taught school, and earned a master's degree in American history from Columbia University. He then returned to Kansas and taught at the Iola High School in 1916 and 1917. He became a principal in Great Bend, Kansas, but resigned in August 1917 when he was accepted to attend officer training school at

Camp Sheridan, Illinois. He joined the 369th Regiment in France in March 1918 as a replacement officer. The Harlem Hellfighters were, on paper, part of the Ninety-Third Division, but the four regiments (which included the 370th Black Devils from Illinois) never fought as a cohesive unit. The 369th Infantry was instead attached to the French army and fought in the Champagne-Marne and Aisne-Marne sectors prior to the Meuse-Argonne offensive. During the summer, the regiment lost all of its African American officers (except for two chaplains) when General Pershing ordered that Black regiments were to be commanded either by all white officers or—as in the case of the Ninety-Second Division—all Black officers.[16]

The Harlem Hellfighters and the French army fought on the left flank of American forces during the Meuse-Argonne offensive. The First Battalion, 369th Regiment was assigned the task of taking Séchault, located north and west of the Argonne Forest. Company D engaged German machine guns at the edge of the village, and during the fight, Lieutenant Robb was wounded, as he described in a letter to his parents:

> On September 29 I was grooved in the left side and back by machine gun bullets. Luckily they did not get anything on the inside so I went on with it. They were surely coming along thick that day. One hit my pistol and put it out of commission, another went through the bottom of my trench canteen, one went through the top of my helmet and a fourth went through one of my side pockets. That happened about two o'clock in the afternoon.

Robb, who briefly passed out, refused evacuation and continued to lead his men. The battalion fought Germans in hand-to-hand combat in the village, capturing machine guns, 77-mm cannons, and an ammunition and grenade dump. By 5:30 P.M., the village was taken, but the Germans threatened to counterattack. Lieutenant Robb had been hit again—a shrapnel wound in his arm. Major Arthur Little, commander of the First Battalion, later wrote about the evening of September 29: "We sat on the floor in darkness. . . . Over in the corner, by himself and very quiet, sat 1st Lieutenant Robb. He was suffering from his wounds and quite weak; but he persistently refused to quit."[17]

With the village of Séchault secured, the 369th Regiment had to advance another mile or so to take a railroad junction at Challerange. The heavily defended ground consisted of both open spaces and a forest known as Les Petits Rosier. As he calmly related in his letter to his parents, Lieutenant Robb was hit for a third time:

Photo 20.5: George Robb. Courtesy of the Kansas State Historical Society.

> The next day about dark I got hit by pieces of a shell. One piece went through the palm of my right hand and broke a couple of bones there. Another piece hit the bone which runs across from the neck to the right shoulder, broke that and damaged me farther in. After I was in this hospital a week they took the piece out. It was about half an inch square. I was lucky for one piece went up beside my ear and knocked a hole in my helmet. The same shell killed the lieutenant commandant [lieutenant in command] and another lieutenant.

With the other officers dead, the twenty-one-year-old assumed command of Company D and led the men forward to their objective. While recovering the next day in a hospital at Séchault, Robb was visited by Major Little, who declared, "Lieutenant, you are a man after my own heart, and you have enough guts for ten men."[18]

On February 4, 1919, the War Department released a list of forty-one recipients of the Medal of Honor, which included George Mallon and George Robb of Kansas. Robb's citation describes the three wounds that he received on September 29–30, 1918, and states that his "example of bravery and fortitude and his eagerness to continue with his mission despite severe wounds set before the enlisted men of his command a most wonderful standard of morale and self-sacrifice." His medal and his bullet-damaged helmet are on display at the Kansas Museum of History in Topeka.[19]

* * *

Robb and Mallon grew up in Kansas towns that are about sixty miles apart. They both are among Pershing's "100 Heroes" and both were modest about their wartime exploits—Robb initially suggested that the War Department send his medal to him in the mail rather than hold a presentation ceremony. Both men also supported veterans organizations and participated in the dedication of the Tomb of the Unknown Soldier on November 11, 1921. Yet in terms of politics, the two men were quite different. Shortly after the Unknown Soldier was laid to rest in Arlington National Cemetery, Mallon urged President Warren Harding (with success) to release socialist Eugene Debs and others similarly imprisoned for their opposition to the war. Whereas Robb belonged to the American Legion, Mallon was an active spokesperson for the World War Veterans, a service organization with strong ties to organized labor. Robb held two government positions—postmaster of Salina and auditor of the State of Kansas—by virtue of Republican appointments and Republican voters. Mallon ran unsuccessfully in 1920 for the office of lieutenant governor as the candidate of the Minnesota Non-Partisan League, a profarmer group that sought to wrest power from grain merchants, railroads, and eastern banks. When Mallon returned to Kansas in 1921 in an attempt to persuade farmers to support the Non-Partisan League, he encountered strong opposition, although the *Manhattan Tribune* noted, "after his record in France . . . he can talk all the economic heresies in the calendar, if he wants to, and we shall not interfere."

George Mallon was elected to the Hennepin County Board of Commissioners in 1922 and served for eight years. He died in 1934 and is buried at the Fort Snelling National Cemetery in Minneapolis. George Robb lived much longer, passing away in 1972 at age eighty-four. His remains are in the Gypsum Hill Cemetery in Salina. The two men held divergent political views but shared common traits, including courage, modesty, interest in public affairs, and love of country.[20]

CHAPTER TWENTY-ONE

The Kansas Home Front, 1918

Distrust, Coercion, and Influenza

Floyd Quiett of Ozawkie did not remain quiet on April 1, 1918, about his upsetting discovery: glass-like particles in bread purchased from a local restaurant. Quiett immediately contacted the proprietor, Ross Swing, who said the Butter Krust bread was made at the Royal Bakery on West Tenth Street in Topeka. According to the *Topeka Daily Capital*, the two Jefferson County men did not view the matter as an April Fool's Day prank:

> Mr. Quiett and Mr. Swing both carefully examined the loaves, which had remained untouched, and could plainly discern glistening particles of unknown substances on the outside crust. A more minute examination disclosed that the same bodies were plentifully distributed thru the interior of the loaves examined, and it was decided to lay the situation before the federal officials in Topeka without delay.

Beginning in the fall of 1917, newspaper stories had regularly appeared across the United States about ground glass being inserted in bread and other edibles by German spies and disloyal individuals. Consequently, the suspicious Butter Krust bread was carefully examined by the U.S. marshal, O. T. Wood, who also detected the small particles. Wood responded in two ways: he announced that he would send the bread to Kansas City for chemical tests, and he summoned the owners of the Royal Bakery, Samuel and Moses Alexander, for questioning. "We called the Alexander brothers to our office," reported the deputy marshal, C. C. Jackson. "They could give no explanation for the presence of the shining particles. Now, everything depends upon the finding in the analyses at Kansas City."[1]

* * *

This incident is an example of how Kansans in 1918 were becoming distrustful of others and easily influenced by rumors and propaganda. The United

States had entered the Great War one year earlier, and the European conflict was now affecting the lives of people in Kansas. Captain Tom Reid's hometown newspaper, the *Columbus Weekly Advocate*, published an editorial a few weeks later entitled "Using Yellow Paint." The article acknowledged—and justified—the increasing harassment and coercion of individuals suspected of disloyalty or insufficient patriotism: "The war has reached the stage now where feelings are getting pretty hot. Our soldiers' blood is being spilled over there. The public is not in a temper nowadays to stand for any traitorous talk, nor even for any slight expression of sympathy for Germany." Kansans in the final year of World War I were both saddened and angered by the mounting number of deaths caused by war and influenza. They distrusted "alien enemies," who were registered, fingerprinted, and in some instances placed in confinement. With the approval of Governor Capper, "slackers" were coerced into contributing to the war effort, and the so-called Night Riders and other vigilantes applied tar and feathers and yellow paint to ethnic Germans and others deemed lacking in pro-American sentiment. Kansans turned against Kansans, even during the celebrations of the armistice.[2]

* * *

The "ground glass" scare had its beginnings in the fall of 1917. The September 15 edition of the *Junction City Daily Union* contains one of the first stories published in Kansas suggesting that agents of Germany were placing glass in the food of patriotic Americans:

> A GROUND GLASS PLOT. Federal Agents at St. Louis Suspect Teuton Sympathizers. St. Louis, Sept. 15.—Federal agents are seeking persons responsible for ground glass which has been found in a certain brand of breakfast food. The investigation began after Alfred Myer, 14 years old, had been made ill by the food. Federal authorities are working on the theory that the ground glass may have been placed in the food by German plotters.

This story was printed in dozens of Kansas newspapers. The plot thickened when, in the following month, the *Wichita Beacon* reported that two boys in Texas, ages seven and nine, were hospitalized due also to glass found in breakfast food. Concern gave way to mild panic when, in a span of five days in December, three similar incidents received widespread coverage: breakfast food samples containing ground glass were distributed in Los Angeles; restaurant owner Enos Moon of Wellsville, Ohio, discovered glass in his cracker meal while frying oysters; and Major General William Carter issued a warning to army training camps that ground glass had been found in canned tomatoes and breakfast food. In connection with General Carter's announcement, the *Leavenworth Chronicle* offered the following commentary: "The ways of the modern Hun are devious. It seems a German cannot be trusted anywhere in our civil life and the Government may be compelled to intern all foreigners belonging to the Central Empires in its efforts to protect the life and health of its civilian population and soldiers." Not to be outdone, the *Topeka State Journal* stated, "what was good for the goose, was good for the gander," and published a soldier's poem that advocated retaliation: "In 'No Man's' Land where the Irish fell, I'd start the Kaiser a private hell. I'd jam him, stab him, give him gas. In every wound I'd pour ground glass."[3]

Kansas newspapers reported in March that glass was found in bread at an orphanage in Fort Smith, Arkansas; in a shipment of candy in Albuquerque, New Mexico; and in chocolate bars sold to the Thirty-Fifth Infantry Division at Camp Doniphan, Oklahoma. Rumors also abounded that glass was found in the food at Fort Leavenworth despite the statement in the *Leavenworth Times* that "not a pinch of ground glass has been discovered in any food product prepared for soldiers." Nevertheless, reasoned the *Salina Daily Union*, the numerous stories of embedded glass "indicates that it happens too often to be an accident." In view of past events, it was not unreasonable for Quiett to suspect foul play when he discovered glass in his Butter Krust bread. The U.S. Department of Justice, after all, was in the process of investigating reports of glass in bread, candies, and other edibles in Brooklyn, New York, and had arrested a German-born confectioner and his clerk. To underscore further the gravity of the threat, the federal food board ordered all alien enemies employed in Brooklyn bakeries to be discharged. Closer to home, the *Coats Courant* in Pratt County declared that the dire turn of events could only be attributed to the depraved enemies of America: "One reason we are sure it is the Huns putting ground glass in candy is because candy is eaten mostly by women and children."[4]

One Kansas official who was not convinced was Walter P. Innes, the state food administrator, who declared that he had quit making analyses of bread sent to his office. "In many of these cases," he explained, "we find that the cause of the glass scare is due to good old Kansas sand getting into the food thru carelessness." As it turned out, it was glass—not sand—in Quiett's Butter Krust bread, but the perpetrator was a careless packer instead of a German agent. When Moses Alexander went to Ozawkie to examine the carton used to transport his bread, he discovered that it had formerly been used to ship electric lightbulbs. In view of this information, Marshal Wood announced that he would not send the loaves to Kansas City for further analysis. The Alexander brothers paid for a prominent advertisement in the *Daily Capital* that assured their customers that they need not fear German treachery, but most likely it did not otherwise allay their concerns:

> The thrilling story of "German spy work" and "ground glass" in "BUTTER-KRUST BREAD" blows up and the truth leaves nothing but a very commonplace tale of one man's carelessness. . . . [O]ut of some 12,000 loaves of bread, baked by the ROYAL BAKERY Monday, 35 loaves were packed in a cardboard carton in which electric light globes were originally shipped; one of the globes broke in transit and a few particles of broken glass remained in the box. One of our packers very carelessly neglected to thoroughly clean out the box before expressing it to Ozawkie, and several slivers of glass penetrated the wax paper of several of the loaves and became partially embedded in the outer crust.

A few days later the *Daily Capital* reported the results of an investigation by the federal Committee on Public Information regarding "thousands of stories of ground glass in food." The committee found only one case in which glass was found by inspectors—a disgruntled bakery employee in Arkansas who put glass in bread sent to orphans that caused his employer to close his business after being accused of being a German agent. Ironically, the *Daily Capital* article, entitled "Only One Real Case," appeared on page six of the newspaper, directly following a story continued from page one entitled "Ground Glass Is Found in Food at Camp Travis."

Despite repeated assurances to the contrary from government officials, fears of a German "ground glass plot" continued for the remainder of the war. The *Atchison Daily Globe* reported on April 24 that a boy on a train found glass in his salted peanuts, only to inform its readers three days later "that one or two of the peanuts were petrified, and that the boy mistook them for ground glass as he crushed them with his molars." By the summer of 1918, it was not just peanuts that were petrified: the *Winfield Daily Courier* ran a story in June about a woman from Erie, Kansas, who "purchased a high power microscope and carefully investigates everything she cooks." On November 8, armed with the knowledge that the war would soon end, the *Burden Times* of Cowley County smugly observed that "the man who found a bit of ground glass in his breakfast food and blamed it on the Kaiser was going a little too far with his imagination."[5]

* * *

Whereas the "ground glass" hysteria had limited ramifications, the registration and treatment of alien enemies was widespread and more harmful. When war was declared on Germany on April 6, 1917, President Wilson proclaimed that certain "unnaturalized" Germans were "alien enemies" and thus subject to arrest and confinement if they engaged in specified activities, including possession of firearms, entry into prohibited areas, publication of attacks or threats against the government, and the commission of "hostile" acts. Prior to February 1918, alien enemies were not required to register, but they were subject to internment for saying the wrong thing or being in the wrong place. For example, two men from Kansas City, Kansas, were jailed in December 1917 because they had praised Germany and Austria. According to the *Topeka Daily Capital*, Charles Johnson and Joseph Fisckale were reported to the government authorities by their wives and "sent to a place of safe keeping until after the war." On January 3, 1918, a well-known Topeka photographer, Charles J. Boeger, was charged with being an alien enemy who had not obtained a required permit. It was never explained in the newspapers why Boeger needed a permit, but the matter was dropped when it was determined that he was in fact a U.S. citizen.[6]

On November 16, 1917, President Wilson by proclamation further regulated the movement and activities of alien enemies. Such individuals were no longer allowed to "ascend into the air in any airplane, balloon, airship, or flying machine" or "enter or be found within the District of Columbia." In addition, all alien enemies were required "to register at such times and places and in such manner as may be fixed by the Attorney General." Registration for male German alien enemies who were fourteen or older commenced at six in the morning on Monday, February 4, 1918; the term "alien enemy" was extended to women in April. Individuals in towns and communities with fewer than five thousand residents were instructed to present themselves at their local post office, whereas registrants in more populated areas were required to go to local police stations. Aliens who failed to register were subject to imprisonment. Those who registered returned within two weeks to obtain their identity cards, which they signed and marked with thumbprints in the presence of the registration officer. One congressman, J. Walter Kehoe of Pensacola, Florida, wanted to require all registered alien enemies to wear an identifying button "conspicuously upon his or her person at all times when in a public place." His bill, H.R. 12056, was introduced during

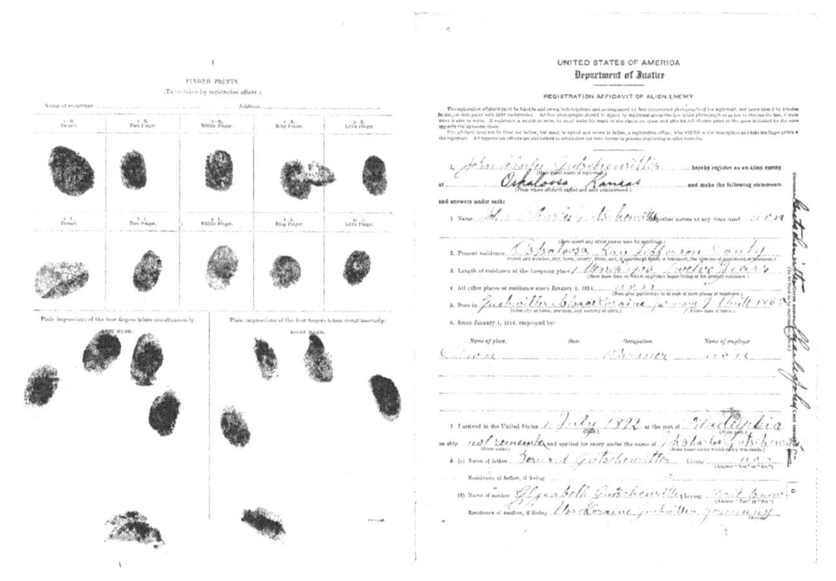

FINGER PRINTS

UNITED STATES OF AMERICA

Department of Justice

REGISTRATION AFFIDAVIT OF ALIEN ENEMY

I, John Charley Gutschenritter hereby register as an alien enemy at Oskaloosa Kansas and make the following statements and answers under oath:

1. Name

2. Present residence

3. Length of residence at the foregoing place

4. All other places of residence since January 1, 1914

5. Born in

6. Since January 1, 1914, employed by:

Name of place.	Date.	Occupation.	Name of employer

7. I arrived in the United States at the port of on ship and applied for entry under the name of

8. (a) Name of father Living

Residence of father, if living

(b) Name of mother Living

Residence of mother, if living

Photo 21.1: John Charles Gutschenritter's alien-enemy registration, pages 1 and 4. Courtesy of the National Archives, Record Group 118, Identifier 288493.

the second session of the Sixty-Fifth Congress but was not passed in part due to concerns that the button mandate might incite lynching and other violence.[7]

The affidavit submitted by John Charles "Charley" Gutschenritter is a representative example. The first page contains his fingerprints. On the second page Gutschenritter registered "as an alien enemy at Oskaloosa, Kansas," and then answered questions under oath regarding his residency status (twelve years at current home), place and date of birth (Guebwiller, in the Alsace-Lorraine, on January 9, 1855), occupation and employment since January 1, 1914 (farmer), and date of arrival in the United States (July 1, 1892). As for his parents, Charley stated that his father was deceased and that his mother, if alive, was residing in Guebwiller. On the third page, in response to the question of whether the registrant has or had "male relatives in arms for or against the United States and its allies during the present war," he stated that three relatives were fighting for the United States: his brother-in-law Birt Blockwicz and two of his sons, Samuel B. and Charles T. Gutschenritter. With regard to his own prior military record, Charley noted that he served as a private for three years in the German army and had taken an oath of allegiance in 1885 as part of his service. The final page includes statements that the registrant had not served any foreign country since January 1, 1914, had never been arrested or detained on any charge, and did not possess a permit to enter forbidden areas. His photograph is included, with his signature written across the front of the picture, along with identifying information such as his age (fifty-three), his height (five feet five inches), and his weight (145 pounds).[8]

Just under six thousand Kansans submitted alien-enemy affidavits in connection with World War I. Seventeen of the fifty-seven registrants in Jefferson County listed family members fighting for the United States, four listed family members fighting against the United States, and one registrant (Catherine Hopf of Valley Falls) had one son in the German army, two sons in the American army, and a fourth son in the French army. Five members of Company B, 139th Infantry—Birt Blockwicz, Bert Boehme, Marlin Brey, Charles Thomas Gutschenritter, and Sam Gutschenritter—were training at Camp Doniphan at the same time that their fathers, uncles, and grandfathers were being fingerprinted and issued identity cards. By June, when women in Jefferson County registered as alien enemies, Tommy Gutschenritter was dead, having succumbed to pneumonia three days after his father submitted his affidavit. Sergeant Brey, who was killed in September on the Meuse-Argonne battlefield, was survived by six alien enemies: his parents, one uncle, and three grandparents.[9]

The *Jefferson County Tribune*, in its February 1, 1918, edition, attempted to downplay the enrollment of alien enemies by stating that registration "is simply an indication that the man is a loyal citizen of this country regardless of the fact that he is legally a subject of the German Kaiser." But as noted by Helen Divjak and Lee Ann Potter, fingerprinting was associated with criminals, and for many ethnic Germans, "signing one's name to a piece of paper that acknowledged him as an 'enemy' was offensive and humiliating." The U.S. attorney for the District of Kansas, Fred S. Robertson, had twenty-six cases pending against alien enemies in November 1918, and he reported after the war that thirty persons from Kansas had been confined. One of the internees was John Sattler from Reading, who did not register, did not contribute money or purchase bonds "in proportion to his means," fed scarce wheat to his chickens and hogs, and stated, "Germans are better Christians than are Americans." He was interned in July 1918 at Fort Oglethorpe, Georgia. His brother, Gottlieb Sattler, was also confined for not registering but only after he complained about his brother's imprisonment and after he had withdrawn his pledge for the purchase of Liberty Loan bonds.[10]

* * *

The plight of the Kansas Mennonites who opposed military service intensified in 1918, particularly in smaller communities. Harper is a town of fewer than eighteen hundred residents (both in 1918 and today) located fifty miles southwest of Wichita. On April 18, 1918, the *Harper Advocate* published an open letter from Reuben M. Weaver, a farmer and pastor of the local Mennonite church. Weaver acknowledged that "unpleasant feelings" existed in the community but expressed confidence that "when our attitude is fully understood we will not be charged with disloyalty to the government, or Pro-German tendencies." He then argued that Mennonites could be both pacifists and patriots:

> Many of our fore fathers left Germany because of the military spirit and demand of that country, and came to America by invitation of this noble government, where we were promised recognition for our religious and conscientious convictions. My fore fathers came from Switzerland before the Revolutionary war and truly, we love our government, we pray for our rulers, we willingly pay our taxes, and loyally support every department of the government.

Jacob Gerhard Evert of Hillsboro wrote a similar letter in June that was published in the *Topeka Daily Capital.* The Mennonites, he stated, "believe that the inviolate sacredness of all human life is one of the foremost ideals that Christ has brought into this world." The Tabor College professor asked for tolerance and understanding: "Should a body of Christians not be permitted to live out what they are convinced is their Christian duty?"

Both letters were quickly answered. "Christian loyalty means a patriotic willingness to fight if the nation's honor or preservation is at stake," Pastor Frederick Weltge of Wells Creek wrote in response to Evert, adding, "no other interpretation of loyalty is possible or biblical." Charles Andrews of Harper, who had served in the Philippines, was more disdainful in his reply to Weaver:

> Your church won't let you go to war, but Sam Jones can go and give his life to make this a safe world to live in, for he doesn't belong to your church, and if he gets killed it's all right. . . . You and your bolshevik whiskered followers cannot make a Liberty loving American people believe that you have a right to fold your arms and enjoy peace and happiness, while we

> give our lives and money to keep our fair land from under Prussianism brutality and bestiality.

In case his point was not clear enough, Andrews penned a second statement, also published on the front page of the *Harper Advocate*, declaring, "the pro-Germans, pacifists or Socialists" ought to "move somewhere else" and should be given "a necktie party if they ever came back."[11]

Criticism of Mennonites in 1917 focused mostly on conscientious objectors and the desire of congregants to avoid any involvement in the war. Criticism turned into condemnation in 1918, and the harassment of church members, both in the military and in Kansas communities, accelerated dramatically. One Mennonite man who experienced both types of mistreatment was Henry F. Cooprider of McPherson County. Cooprider was born on November 11, 1896. His great-great-great grandfather had emigrated from Germany in 1762. His paternal grandfather, a widower, settled in Kansas, remarried in 1878, accepted the Mennonite faith of his new wife, and was ordained as a minister in 1885. Cooprider grew up on a prosperous farm with his paternal grandparents; his parents, Walter and Minnie; an older brother, George; and a younger brother, Glen. As Sara J. Keckeisen describes of the Cooprider family, "George, Henry, and Glen learned . . . the basic precepts of their faith, among which was that participating in war and taking revenge or taking a life was entirely wrong."[12]

James C. Juhnke contends that the third Liberty Loan drive in April was the impetus for vigilante actions against Mennonites in McPherson and surrounding counties. The bond campaign began early that month. On the eighteenth residents in several Kansas towns discovered that handbills had been distributed during the night that urged other "True Blue Americans" to join "the Night Riders" and take action against "German spies, German sympathizers and Dirty Slackers." Pacifists and other targeted groups were forewarned: "We are now among you and know all of these who are secretly traitors to their country and these parties may expect a visit from us. There is No Neutral Ground. You Are Either For or Against the Government. LINE UP AND GET RIGHT." The *Pratt Daily Tribune* commended the "loyal Americans" who distributed the handbills in Barton County: "There are a number of disloyalists in that county, it is said, and the Night Riders have a large and important work to perform. Luck to them."[13]

Such encouragement may have emboldened members of the secret organization to visit the Cooprider farm on the evening of April 22. A group of men arrived in vehicles, cut the telephone wires, called Walter Cooprider out of the house, and demanded that he purchase Liberty bonds or be tarred and feathered. At this point George Cooprider, the eldest son, volunteered to be the target of punishment. The men applied a coat of warm roofing paint to his head and upper torso and rolled him in a sheet of feathers. Although some men wore masks, the Coopriders recognized many participants, including neighbors. According to the *Williamstown News*, Walter's bedridden father "was made to kiss the flag." Two days later Walter went to McPherson and purchased some war bonds.[14]

Later the same night the vigilantes tarred and feathered the Spring Valley Mennonite Church in McPherson County as well as its pastor, Daniel A. Diener, and his son Charles, also an ordained minister. In its coverage of the two incidents, the *McPherson Freeman* noted that "the man with means who has enjoyed the protection of Uncle Sam had better come across with a little when asked to, or move out, because the peace and quiet they have been enjoying will not last if they don't." When D. A. Diener refused to invest in Liberty bonds, the Night Riders returned and whipped the pastor, applied tar and feathers, and used yellow paint to write the word "slacker" on his house and on two automobiles. Once again, reaction was mixed. The *McPherson Daily Republican* noted, "opinion as to the advisability of treatment of this kind for 'slackers' seems to be divided." A letter submitted to the same paper from "An American" suggested that yellow paint was preferable to tar and feathers: "A man can cover up his coat of tar and feathers with his clothing, but in order to hide the 'streak of yellow' he must repaint the building so marked."[15]

Similar attacks took place throughout 1918. Conrad Gastrock, the pastor of the Worden German Lutheran Church, was taken from his home in May and tarred for making pro-German statements and refusing to contribute to the Red Cross, allegations that were denied in a statement issued by members of his church. Another notable incident involved Gustav Harder, a member of a Mennonite church near Whitewater in Butler County. When Whitewater citizens threatened violence for his alleged refusal to display a U.S. flag, Harder insisted that he would be happy to comply, then turned the tables on the mob by proposing that they join him in singing "America the Beautiful." By the time he ended the second verse—"America! America! God mend thine every flaw. Confirm thy soul in self-control, Thy liberty in law!"—the mood had changed from self-righteous anger to muted awkwardness, as explained by James Juhnke: "The abashed mob joined in on the first verse, but their voices trailed away and their feet shuffled as they didn't know the words of the other verses. The embarrassed Whitewater patriots had been out-Americanized by a Mennonite German-American."[16]

At the same time that Kansas Mennonites were being harassed and attacked in their homes, churches, and communities, the War Department was revisiting its policies regarding conscientious objectors. On March 16, 1918, Congress authorized it to grant furloughs to enlisted men to help farmers during peak harvest periods, a highly popular decision in Kansas. The Farm Furlough Act "opened the door" to alternative forms of service for conscientious objectors. Four days later, on March 20, 1918, President Wilson issued an executive order allowing conscientious objectors to serve in noncombatant positions, including the Medical Corps, Quartermaster Corps, and Engineer Service. The executive order also declared that men who refused to accept such service were to remain segregated but not subjected to "punitive hardship of any kind." Yet by direction of Secretary of War Baker, instructions were issued on April 27 to court-martial men who declined noncombatant service "whose attitude in camp is defiant; . . . whose sincerity is questioned; [and] who are active in propaganda." In June the "defiant" segregated men were transferred to Fort Leavenworth, where a board of inquiry—future Supreme Court justice Harlan F. Stone was one of its members—determined whether the men should be furloughed for agricultural service. Conscientious objectors who were not recommended for furloughs or who refused to accept this option were court-martialed, totaling 503 men, including 138 Mennonites of whom approximately 20 were from Kansas. Prison sentences ranged from less than five years to life, averaging about twenty years in length. The men were required to work, and those who refused were placed in solitary confinement. Although most were released in January 1919, some conscientious objectors did not return to their homes until November 1920.[17]

Henry Cooprider was drafted and sent to Camp Funston in September. According to George English, the historian of the Eighty-Ninth Division, conscientious objectors at Camp Funston "were put to the performance of tasks of a necessary but non-military nature, collecting garbage, removing manure, working on the roads, serving as kitchen police and the like." Shortly after Cooprider's arrival, five Mennonites who refused to haul trash on a Sunday were struck repeatedly by soldiers, and two majors who were in charge were censured for neglect of duty (but granted honorable discharges). Because Cooprider refused to wear a uniform, he was issued some old coveralls, interrogated, and then assigned to a detention area connected to the training battalion of the 164th Depot Brigade. He initially agreed to manual labor but eventually refused to cooperate because his activities aided the war effort. Consequently, his food rations were restricted, and he was no longer permitted to receive visitors. As described in Sara Keckeisen's vivid account, "Henry's family was not permitted any closer than about 240 feet; they could just peer at him through binoculars and wave to him through the fence."[18]

In one respect conscientious objectors such as Cooprider were treated equally: they received the same medical care during the Spanish flu outbreak as other soldiers. Cooprider was in the camp hospital on his twenty-second birthday, which happened to be when the armistice went into effect. He recovered and was discharged on December 29, 1918. Prior to returning to McPherson County, Cooprider joined with other pacifists in presenting a Bible to an abusive sergeant and donating their government pay to a relief fund. Henry Friedley Cooprider married in 1930, raised twins, and passed away in McPherson County in 1975 at the age of seventy-eight.[19]

* * *

Kansans were not immune from a practice that was commonplace in 1918: the bullying of German Americans and other individuals who were deemed to be insufficiently patriotic. In light of the dehumanization of the enemy as barbaric "Huns" and beastly villains, it is not surprising that 1918 was not a good year for ethnic Germans in the United States. German measles was renamed as "Liberty" measles, high schools stopped teaching the German language, and in Aulne—an unincorporated community in Marion County—the telephone company instructed switchboard operators to "cut off" anyone who could converse in English but chose to speak German. Some actions were humorous, such as the distribution of toilet paper with the phrase "do your bit" printed above a picture of Kaiser Wilhelm. Other actions were not, such as the decision of vigilantes to burn the Lutheran church and adjoining school in Herington because services and instruction were not conducted in English. But not everything associated with German culture was banned or destroyed. The University of Kansas continued to teach German, reasoning that "a listening post out in No Man's Land that does not know the German tongue is no better than a fence post." States without prohibition laws kept brewing and selling beer, despite arguments that hops, barley, and other grains were better utilized as food ingredients. In support of a nationwide moratorium, Methodist bishop William A. Quayle of Kansas argued that beer consumption was " a very significant form of pro-German friendship" and suggested that "the unthinkable barbarism of the German armies in this present war is, in all reasonableness to be accounted for largely by their centuries of beer drinking." President Wilson and Congress were not persuaded.[20]

The 1917 Espionage Act was strengthened by the 1918 Sedition Act, which criminalized "disloyal, profane, scurrilous, or abusive language" directed at the government or the military as well as speech that incited insubordination or disloyalty. According to Herbert Pankratz, the Sedition Act was never implemented in Kansas "since the Espionage act proved adequate and the entire staff of the United States attorney was tied up in the investigative and secretarial work necessary for enforcing it." Kansans, nevertheless, were fined and arrested for speaking out. Reverend Manasse Bontrager of Dodge City was fined five hundred dollars for writing an article that criticized the Liberty Loan campaign. Franz "Frank" Nienke of Ellsworth paid a one-hundred-dollar fine and agreed to "contribute" three hundred dollars to the Red Cross after pleading guilty to a charge of casting contempt upon the American flag. The incautious Nienke remarked, while attending a flag-raising ceremony at a local school, that the outhouse behind the school was a more appropriate location. The Committee on Public Information, in an article entitled "Spies and Lies" that was published in numerous Kansas newspapers, suggested that "German agents are everywhere" and urged citizens to report "the man who spreads pessimistic stories . . . or belittles our efforts to win the war." Many Kansans told state and federal officials about individuals suspected of disloyalty, and some went even further, such as Grant Walter of Utica, who sent a letter to the Governor Capper to inform him of two neighbors who are "a lazy worthless set" and in the past year "haven't done a half man's work."[21]

In February 1918 the Home Guard was replaced by the State Guard, which was controlled by the adjutant general and subject to deployment throughout Kansas. Over time, 281 companies were organized, including seven segregated units of Black men in Independence, Kansas City, Lawrence, Coffeyville, and Topeka. The companies took part in parades; performed escort, guard, and funeral duties; and assisted in Red Cross fund drives and Liberty Loan campaigns. In a speech to some of the State Guard companies in April, Governor Capper echoed the words of the Night Riders with regard to slackers and German sympathizers: "There can be no half-way loyalty at this time. You are either for the United States or for the Kaiser. You have got to line up with Uncle Sam or leave Kansas." The governor also personally pressured individuals who were suspected of tepid patriotism. A resident of

Enterprise in April received a letter from Capper written, not in his official capacity, but rather "as a citizen of Kansas who earnestly desires to see not a single slacker within the boundaries of our state." The letter concluded with this warning: "You cannot afford to be known in your community as a disloyal, undesirable citizen." Presumably, to avoid any suggestion of disloyalty, the German Catholic citizens of Germantown petitioned to change the name of their community. Their request was granted in July, and the Brown County village was renamed Mercier in honor of Désiré-Joseph Mercier, the Belgian cardinal noted for his staunch resistance to the German occupation.[22]

Slackers and German sympathizers were often the target of "yellow paint" squads. The people of Goreham painted yellow stripes on the front of a store owned by M. K. Getts, who was said to have made "pro-Enemy" remarks, and H. B. Hewitt's building in Stafford was likewise decorated after he refused to buy war bonds. Neighbors of J. E. Stone, who was described in the *Coffeyville Daily Journal* as "Caney's chief slacker," painted "I am a friend of the Kaiser, judging by my patriotism" on the side of his house. When William E. Johnson of Kansas City was painted yellow by his fellow workers after refusing to buy a Liberty Loan bond, he demanded that the police arrest his attackers. No arrests were made, and Johnson was referred to federal authorities, then sent to the Wyandotte County jail. "He is one of the religious objectors that have caused trouble before," noted Arthur Mollett, an assistant U.S. attorney. "We will watch him until we can find what is best to do for his own protection." The notoriety of yellow paint was so well known that when it was seen at the Cherryvale Royal Theater, the local newspaper explained that it "was not because of any signs of disloyalty on the part of S. A. Davidson, the owner of the place," but was instead the result of carelessness on the part of Lloyd Davidson, age nineteen, who spilled a bottle of yellow paint in the lobby.[23]

The efficacy and morality of painting automobiles, buildings, and individuals became the subject of public commentary in May and June. When three houses in Natoma were painted yellow while the occupants were at church, the local paper simply noted, "sentiment against enemy sympathizers and slackers is bound to grow stronger, and parties who are not actively assisting our government must expect little sympathy from loyal citizens." The *Jamestown Optimist* was even more direct, stating, "it may be that yellow paint will yet win the war." The *Russell Record*, in response to statements made by the *Russell Informer*, took the contrary view, pointing out, "You can't always determine the patriotism of a man by the amount of yellow paint he is able to use." The editor of the *Norton Real Westerner* made the same point: "It's not always a proof of patriotism to paint a bank, an individual or a business yellow just because it fails to be in full accord with all the agitators in the community. . . . [W]e are overwrought and we are overestimating our dangers in many sections." The *Chetopa Clipper* also counseled against combining vandalism with patriotism: "Mature consideration shows that yellow paint is a poor remedy, and generally goes with poor judgment, and casts a shadow which often is undeserved and leaves a bad taste in the mouth of the entire community." Nevertheless, the yellow-paint offensive continued. Frank Kelsh of Leavenworth was painted yellow by the employees of the Schalker Packing Company for refusing to subscribe to the Red Cross and because he supposedly blamed the United States for the war. As reported in the June 27, 1918, edition of the *Atwood Square Deal*, after Howard Savage parked his car at the corner of Main and State Streets, citizens painted it with the German insignia in yellow and the skull and crossbones in black. "This is war," stated the *Square Deal*, "and the man that don't help in every way he can is as guilty as the one who fights with poisoned candy against our little ones or uses ground glass in flour." Savage was arrested and a trial was scheduled, but there is no report of further proceedings, suggesting that the matter was not prosecuted. In September, after a crowd in Independence gathered at the German Lutheran church and painted "Yellow dogs" on the side of the adjacent school building, the county attorney announced that he would require the persons responsible to remove the paint—but only if the school promised to eliminate the teaching of German and its use in church services.[24]

The cessation of hostilities in Europe did not end the harassment of ethnic Germans in America. On November 7 the pastor of the German Lutheran church near Kensington was forced to ring the church bell to celebrate the end of the war, and when reports of an armistice proved premature, a mob set fire to the church. When the armistice was officially declared, the celebrants in Nortonville drove to the homes of suspected slackers and German sympathizers, brought them to town, and forced them to lead the parade procession and kiss a U.S. flag. Some of the citizens of Burrton, in Harvey County, drove on November 11 to the farm of John Schrag and ransacked several buildings before bringing the "slacker" back to town. John Juhnke describes what happened next:

> When they thrust a flag into his hand, it fell to the ground and someone shouted, "He stepped on the American flag." The crowd turned into an angry mob. They kicked and hit their victim, poured yellow paint on his

> hair and beard, and went for a rope to hang him. Tom Roberts, the head of the Burrton Anti-Horse Thief Association, intervened with drawn pistol to get Schrag into the Burrton jail where he was protected from the mob until the Harvey County sheriff could come from Newton and take him to the county jail. The mob satisfied its remaining lust for violence by burning some "buggies and things" belonging to the slackers.

Schrag was prosecuted in December for violation of the Espionage Act but was acquitted.[25]

* * *

In addition to the aforementioned issues, Kansas and the rest of the world were subjected in 1918 to a major health crisis: the onset of the Spanish influenza pandemic. John Barry postulates that the 1918 Spanish flu pandemic started in Haskell County, Kansas; gained traction at Camp Funston; and was then carried by soldiers to Europe: "Epidemiologists today estimate that influenza likely caused at least fifty million deaths worldwide, and possibly as many as one hundred million." While some historians and medical experts dispute Kansas as the point of origin, there was a notable increase in influenza-related illness and death at Camp Funston. On March 4 a cook reported ill with influenza, and on the eighteenth a WaKeeny resident, Private Ira Hobbs, returned home and reported that "several" soldiers were in the camp hospital with mumps, measles, scarlet fever, and influenza. The *Trench and Camp*, published at Fort Riley, on March 23 suggested that a recent dust storm was the likely cause of "a lot of sickness in the form of severe influenza." By the end of the month, more than 1,100 soldiers were sick enough to be admitted to the camp hospital. According to one historical account, of the nearly 17,000 men treated for influenza at Camp Funston, some 900 passed away. "In many ways," observed camp commandant Major General Wood, "it was worse than battle."[26]

The Spanish flu received its name because Spain was not directly involved in the war and consequently was more open to reporting on the spread of the disease. Some Americans, however, believed there was a sinister connection between "germ" and "Germany," with the *University Daily Kansan* stating that the virus "should be called the Hun influenza because it is a slick, sly, tricky and heartless ailment." At some point a new nursery rhyme became popular in Kansas and elsewhere: "I had a little bird, its name was Enza. I opened the window, and in flew Enza." A darker poem, entitled "The Flu," concludes: "It thins your blood and brays your bones, and fills your craw with

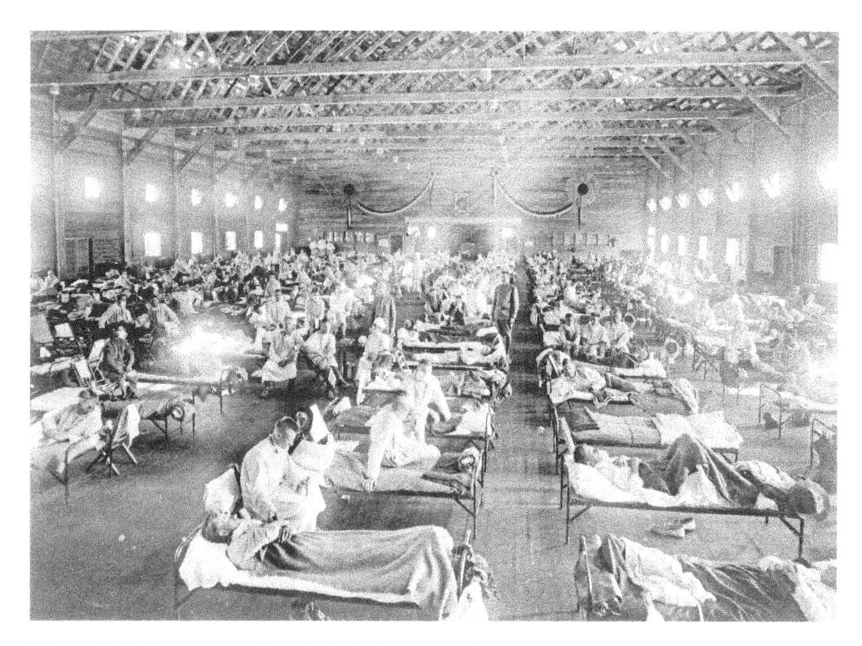

Photo 21.2: Emergency hospital during the influenza pandemic, Camp Funston, 1918–1919. Courtesy of the New Contributed Photograph Collection, Otis Historical Archives, National Museum of Health and Medicine, item OHA 250.

moans and groans. And sometimes, maybe, you get well. Some call it Flu, but I call it HELL." The epidemic quickly became a global catastrophe due to the rapid transmission of the flu strain and its unusually lethal effect on young adults. It is estimated that approximately twenty-five million Americans (one-quarter of the population) suffered from influenza, resulting in some 675,000 deaths. Included in that total were 12,000 Kansans who died from the flu or pneumonia, primarily during the "second wave" in the fall and winter of 1918. Judith Johnson describes the connections in the Sunflower State between the epidemic and the ongoing war:

> The scarcity of doctors and nurses in the state, because of the war, hampered efforts to treat those already sick and to confine the spread of the disease. By the fall of 1918, more than six hundred doctors or almost half of those licensed in Kansas left their practices to serve in the military. During the height of the fall wave of influenza, numerous counties in the western part of the state reported a total absence of physicians, while eight of ten others had only one or two doctors.

At Camp Funston over 1,200 soldiers reported sick on a single day—October 4—and a soldier with a temperature of 102 degrees Fahrenheit remained in his barracks because hospital beds were limited to patients with fevers of 103 degrees or higher.[27]

In the weeks prior to the second onslaught of influenza and pneumonia, several Kansas colleges and universities established units of the newly authorized Student Army Training Corps (SATC). The schools, which included the University of Kansas, Kansas State Agricultural College, Emporia Normal, Fairmount College, Kansas Wesleyan, Ottawa University, and Washburn College, intended to train soldiers at the government's expense to become officers or proficient electricians, engineers, and mechanics—all needed to win the war. At Lawrence, Green Hall was converted into an army training headquarters, and university students were paid thirty-five cents an hour to build barracks. At Manhattan over a thousand Kansas State students swore an oath of allegiance and became soldiers, entitled to rations and required to complete eleven hours of military training each week. The SATC program, however, proved to be short lived for two reasons: the resurgence of the Spanish flu in October and the cessation of hostilities in November.[28]

The University of Kansas was closed for much of October, and the new barracks were converted into sick wards. Public gatherings were either prohibited or highly discouraged, and the Kansas-Missouri football game was canceled. On November 9 a second-year student, Lucy Catherine McLinden of Marion, contracted pneumonia and "died a soldier's death" after volunteering to provide medical assistance. By the time the university reopened on November 11, thirty-two students (including ten from the SATC) had become victims of the pandemic. In December the barracks were removed, and the Jayhawk community struggled to return to normalcy. At Kansas State the Sigma Alpha Epsilon and Beta Theta Phi fraternity houses became hospitals. The plaque that commemorates the "Fallen 48" from World War I includes nineteen Aggies who died from either influenza or pneumonia.[29]

Kansas civilians, too, were plagued by the Spanish flu, which was also called the "grip" or "grippe," as in the final verses of a popular poem published in the *Wichita Catholic Advance*:

A marvelous weakness, come on in a day—
That's the grippe!
A petulant wonder: "How long will it stay?"—
That's the grippe!
A season of fever, a season of freeze,

A quivering weakness, that's felt at the knees—
Say, if ever there was a cuss-ed disease,
That's the grippe!

By the middle of October, a rising panic caught hold in many communities. Governor Capper issued a proclamation temporarily prohibiting public gatherings and closing schools, churches, and theaters. Topeka issued its own closure order, restricting the hours of downtown stores (but allowing cigar stores to remain open if occupancy was limited to no more than ten persons). The incidence of flu decreased at the end of October before rising again, likely in connection with Election Day and armistice celebrations. Fortunately, Kansans were able to turn to Samuel J. Crumbine, a physician from Dodge City and a remarkable pioneer in public health. Dr. Crumbine had previously waged successful campaigns against spitting in public, the common cloth towel, and the common drinking cup. He also invented the "Fly Bat," a screen attached to a yardstick, which was the forerunner of the modern flyswatter. After the state board of health was put under federal jurisdiction for the duration of the war, steps were taken to improve sanitation and reduce disease at Fort Leavenworth, Fort Riley, and Camp Funston. As part of the effort to prevent the spread of venereal disease, Crumbine disclosed in June 1918 that 50 percent of all venereal infections in eastern Kansas were traced to Kansas City women, prompting the *Wichita Beacon* headline "DR. CRUMBINE SAYS K.C. IS NAUGHTY!"

With regard to the Spanish Flu, the state board of health educated citizens about the disease and how to minimize its effects. "The influenza travels as fast as the people travel," Dr. Crumbine advised the readers of the *Topeka Daily Capital*, explaining how infected individuals "spread the germs thru the air." Thanks in no small part to his relentless efforts, Kansas in 1918 and 1919 experienced a lower death rate than the neighboring states of Missouri and Colorado. Nevertheless, over 12,000 citizens succumbed to influenza and pneumonia—more than double the number of Kansans who died in battle—and it is likely that 250,000 people in the state were afflicted. (In comparison, there were 10,214 deaths in Kansas attributed to COVID-19 as of May 10, 2023.)[30]

* * *

Charley Gutschenritter, father of Sam Gutschenritter, survived the Spanish flu epidemic and eventually became a U.S. citizen. When he lived in Alsace-Lorraine, he considered himself to be a Frenchman even after he

Photo 21.3: Dr. Samuel Crumbine. Courtesy of the Kansas State Historical Society.

became a German subject, and when he settled in Kansas, he viewed himself as an American. According to the *Oskaloosa Times*, Gutschenritter was "a good, practical farmer," but his original petition for citizenship was denied in 1916 due to the war. His status as an alien enemy ceased as of Christmas Day, 1918, when President Wilson ended the enforcement of federal regulations (but continued the detention of all Germans then under arrest or interned). When Gutschenritter refiled his petition, it was supported by J. C. Blevins, father of Ted Blevins, and presented to Judge Martin Bender, the marine musician from Holton. On June 7, 1920, John Charles Gutschenritter became a citizen of the United States. He died in Oskaloosa on November 10, 1937, and is buried near his son Tommy at the Mount Cavalry Cemetery in Perry.[31]

CHAPTER TWENTY-TWO

Prisoners of War and the YMCA

Clyde Grimsley, Melvin Dyson, and Conrad Hoffman

Over 6 million soldiers and civilians were imprisoned during the Great War. Russians were the most numerous prisoners of war among the Allies, followed by the French, the British, "other" Allies, and finally the Americans. According to a contemporary list produced by the Red Cross, 3,602 American prisoners (3,446 army, 12 navy, and 144 civilians) spent time in seventy German camps. An official U.S. estimate provided in 2005 is higher: 4,120 Americans were interned, with 147 dying as prisoners and 3,973 returning from captivity. It appears that at least forty-eight Kansans were prisoners of war, including three men from Coffeyville—Clyde Crocker, Edgar Jones, and Earl Van Winkle—and two men from Cawker City—Lawrence Deal and Aubrey Ladow. Roland Beaver, who lived in several towns in central Kansas, died of spinal meningitis in a prison hospital. Clarence Brodie of Wichita and Alson Viles of Muscotah also died while in captivity.[1]

Two prisoners from Kansas who came home, Clyde Grimsley of Stockton and Salina and Melvin Dyson of Oskaloosa, were assisted by another man with Kansas connections: Conrad Hoffman of the Young Men's Christian Association. Hoffman resided in Berlin during the war and served as the YMCA senior secretary of the War Prisoners' Aid. Without his assistance, it is possible that Grimsley and many other Americans would not have survived their captivity.

* * *

Clyde Grimsley, one of the eleven Americans captured on November 3, 1917, did not expect to go to prison. "Just knew I'd be killed," he recounted in 1919 after returning to Salina. A fellow prisoner, Private Hoyt Decker, had been seriously injured when an explosion caused one eye to be dislodged from its socket. What happened next seemed to confirm Grimsley's worst fears:

> I saw one of our captors after we had reached their trenches grab that eye and jerk it out of its socket. . . . Their trenches had cement walls, and as

> we walked along they would jam our heads against the sides. . . . One of our men, Enright, was wounded so he couldn't walk, and as they didn't want to carry him further, they cut his throat from ear to ear. I saw him out in No-Man's Land quite a distance, and I recognized him as he lay on the ground. Two other men, Hay and Gresham, were cut all to pieces, and chunks of meat hung on the barbed wire. . . . Their leaders probably considered this sort of frightfulness would scare the Americans. It did show what we were up against and that we were really into the war.

The Germans interrogated the Americans and "made ominous threats" when information was not provided. "Of course we did not know much," Grimsley recalled, "it was so early in the game that we had not even been assigned to a [French] division—which the Germans would not believe." During his first day of captivity, Grimsley was photographed with his left fist clenched standing between Sergeant Edgar Halyburton of South Carolina and another doughboy. That evening the prisoners were taken to Saint-Avold, about thirty miles east of Metz. They were separated, questioned again, called "vile names," and "spit on and abused." At one point the Germans made the men believe their execution was imminent by taking them on a midnight walk while accompanied by "a priest with a long black cloak." The prisoners did receive medical treatment, and Decker was taken to a hospital for an operation. "I apparently received the same professional attention as did the German soldiers," recalled Decker, who died in 1983 at the age of eighty-five in his hometown of Vincennes, Indiana.[2]

Grimsley and the other Americans spent a month in a damp dungeon cell "infested with rats, mice, lice and vermin of every character." With the exception of Thanksgiving, when "they gave us boiled cat," the men dined on bread, watery soup, and raw apple and potato peelings. Conditions improved during the short stay at Giessen, where the men were bathed, shaved, and deloused, and at Darmstadt, where they had a bed, blanket, and a daily bucket of coal. It was at Darmstadt, south of Frankfurt, where Grimsley wrote his first letter to his father. "I will come back some time," he assured him, "I hope in the near future." The letter, which was published in the Stockton newspaper, was written on December 29, 1917, but not received until mid-February 1918. At that point the Red Cross had already informed Grimsley's parents that their son had been moved to the Tuchel prison camp in West Prussia (modern-day Tuchola, Poland). Because he had lost his helmet, the intrepid Kansan tore off the top of his sock and fashioned a hat for the six-hundred-mile journey. On January 13, 1918, the American prisoners were jeered as they were paraded through the streets of Berlin. "I looked straight ahead all the while," remembered Grimsley. "A man walked up beside me and said in English, 'don't look so downhearted. It will soon be all over.' I think he was an American."[3]

In March a rumor circulated in Kansas that Grimsley had sent his watch to a friend with a concealed message that said the Germans had cut off his ears, nose, and tongue. After investigating the matter, however, the *Salina Daily Union* reported there was "no credence placed to the story of torture." In June a letter arrived, dated April 5, in which Grimsley assured his family that his "health is very good and I am not in need of anything." Although he did retain all his body parts while in captivity, such declarations of well-being and fair treatment were not truthful. When safely home, Grimsley explained that he always wrote "cheerful" accounts because otherwise "his letters would never have been sent." The actual conditions at Tuchel were unquestionably wretched, especially for prisoners from eastern Europe. Grimsley saw "Roumanian prisoners so starved that they would watch for men to die and grab their food and clothes as soon as they fell." Some 50,000 Russians died from disease, malnutrition, and exposure. "They were buried ten or a dozen in a hole, dumped in like refuse. If on some days there were not enough corpses for one of these big graves, they would stack the naked bodies against the side of a building until the required number had accumulated." The camp was, in short, "a first class hell hole."[4]

The harsh winter months were the most challenging. In February 1918 a neutral inspector reported ten Americans, 3,700 Romanians, and 22,200 Russians assigned to the camp. Prisoners were hitched to wagons and forced to walk long distances in wooden shoes to haul wood or to plow fields. It was extremely cold, and the Americans lived in a wet, sunken dugout that "combined all the stenches living men could possible generate with unwashed bodies, breaths, and excretions." Disease was rampant and food was scarce, consisting primarily of black bread and watery soup with desiccated turnips and carrots. "We subsisted for a while on Jerry soup, or barbed-wire soup," said Grimsley, "so called because it was always received and eaten behind barbed wire." After three months the twenty-nine-year-old Kansan and his comrades were so weak that it was difficult to walk, but they did not give up hope. "I always knew I could live, somehow, and beat those Germans," Grimsley recalled, "and every day I bet my life against their old bowl of soup that I'd get back home safe." It appears that Grimsley survived for three reasons: he avoided work, he received food from the Red Cross, and he was transferred to another camp.[5]

Grimsley managed to miss most of the backbreaking work at the Tuchel prison camp. "I schemed in every possible way to shirk it, and most of the time managed to stay in the hospital, being really sick much of the time." When Decker was taken to the prison hospital, Grimsley took extreme measures to join his friend:

> I poured a kettle full of boiling water over my left foot, scalding it so that I could get into the hospital with him—the only way to get into the hospital was to have a temperature. Some of the fellows accomplished this by eating soup or putting tobacco under their arms—but I just scalded my foot. So I was in the hospital five months. As my foot improved I had to have another excuse to remain so I exaggerated a little sore throat and whenever a German doctor came along was unable to speak . . . , so I got to stay in 10 weeks longer because of that.

The Germans were sensitive to criticism and sometimes responded when news of abject prison conditions reached the outside world. On February 9, 1918, the neutral representative from the Spanish embassy inspected Tuchel and questioned why Decker had not been released due to his wounds. (Germany had agreements with France and Russia to repatriate severely injured men.) A list of the Americans was compiled and forwarded to the Red Cross at Bern, Switzerland, after which packages soon arrived containing food, cigarettes, and clothing. Although some of the supplies were stolen, Grimsley claimed the Americans "never ate another bite of German food" and "turned our prison rations over to the Russians." The YMCA also began to provide assistance, first in the form of "comfort kits" filled with sewing supplies, toiletries, and other items. More important, however, was the role that the YMCA played in convincing the Germans to transfer Americans from Tuchel to Rastatt, a prison camp located in Baden-Württemberg near the Rhine River. The person most responsible for this lifesaving action was Conrad Hoffman, who prior to the war had been the head of the campus "Y" organization at the University of Kansas.[6]

* * *

Conrad and Katie Hoffman both grew up in Germany before immigrating to the United States. Their oldest child, Conrad Hoffman Jr., was born in Chicago in 1884. After receiving an undergraduate degree in 1906 from the University of Wisconsin, he studied in Germany for two years afterward, and then returned to Wisconsin and earned his doctorate in 1910.

Remaining in Madison, Hoffman accepted a position as an assistant professor of bacteriology, married, became a father, and taught a Bible class at a local Lutheran church. Hoffman resigned his position in 1913 and moved his family to Lawrence, Kansas, where he became the secretary of the YMCA at the University of Kansas. In his new position Hoffman helped organize social events, assisted students in need of employment, and spoke on religious topics, in many instances with his Jayhawk colleague Dr. James Naismith. In the spring of 1915, however, a new opportunity arose: to serve in Germany as the YMCA secretary of the War Prisoners' Aid.[7]

It may seem odd today that an American associated with the YMCA was granted permission by the German War Ministry to "visit all prisoner-of-war camps and hospitals for the purpose of securing information relative to the condition of the prisoners of war interned herein and of inspecting camp equipment and organization." The YMCA and the Red Cross were the two most prominent private organizations that provided services to military forces during the First World War. When fighting began in 1914, the International Committee of the Red Cross in Switzerland became an accepted intermediary for compiling information about prisoners of war, connecting prisoners with their families, and supervising conditions at internment camps. Like the Red Cross, the YMCA also had experience—dating back to the Civil War—with helping prisoners and assisting soldiers. Consequently, when the United States sent troops to Europe in 1917, the association provided educational, social, recreational, postal, and religious services by sending individuals such as Laird Archer of Wichita and Naismith (who went to France at age fifty-five). As noted by Jennings Bryan Tatman, a private from Hartford, Kansas, and a prisoner of war, "if it hadn't been for the Red Cross we would have starved, and if it hadn't been for the [YMCA] Red Triangle we would have wished we were dead, anyway."[8]

Hoffman arrived in Berlin in the summer of 1915 and soon thereafter obtained permission to visit Allied prisoners. In contrast to the Red Cross, which supplied food and other material needs, the YMCA focused on providing social, recreational, and religious programs. Hoffman remained in Germany after the United States entered the war, and in June 1918 was allowed to observe American prisoners at several prison camps, including Brandenburg (where Walter Perkins of Wichita was confined) and Tuchel. Sergeant Halyburton later wrote that he suspected that Hoffman was a German sympathizer because he was living in Berlin. What Halyburton did not know was that, based on his tour of Tuchel, Hoffman strenuously objected to a plan to move all enlisted Americans to that prison camp, pointing out that the men lived in

Photo 22.1: Conrad Hoffman. Courtesy of the Kenneth Spencer Research Library, University of Kansas.

"underground hovels" that "were bitterly cold and damp, resulting in much sickness." The turning point came in July when Hoffman returned to Tuchel with an officer from the War Ministry, who viewed the conditions with dismay and agreed to support an alternative proposal to concentrate American enlisted men elsewhere. Camp Rastatt was chosen in part for its location in the Rhine valley in close proximity to both France and the International Red Cross in Switzerland. Thanks largely to the efforts of Hoffman, Grimsley left Tuchel at the end of July and spent his remaining time in captivity at Rastatt. In the final months of the war, many other Americans were sent to that camp, including Melvin Dyson of Oskaloosa.[9]

* * *

Melvin Dyson was one of several soldiers from the 139th Regiment who found themselves surrounded on the morning of September 29, 1918. After some of his comrades were killed or wounded, the nineteen-year-old private was captured in Montrebeau Wood. He and about thirty other captives were taken to Sedan, France, where they received "a small piece of black bread and soup once a day" and worked in a gun-repair shop. When interrogated, Dyson told a German captain that he was just a "buck private" and could provide no information about the ongoing battle. "I said why ask me questions, you know more about the war than I know," he recalled. "I didn't know anything . . . , after all I was just a kid." One thing that he did understand, however, was that Germany was in a desperate situation. "The supplies that the Germans had was all used up and they were spread out all too thin." In response to the advances made by Allied forces during the last part of October, the city of Sedan was evacuated with the assistance of American prisoners: "There were about 182 American POWs engaged in this effort. . . . Of the details one was responsible for loading large artillery guns on railroad flat cars; another collected and loaded brass shell casings for return to factories for reuses; the third group was a burial party and . . . the fourth group worked in the bakery." Dyson recalled, "The Germans managed to move most of their stuff as they withdrew," adding, "believe me, I know, because they kept us busy moving it."[10]

The prisoners at Sedan were moved about 175 miles to Friedberg, north of Frankfurt, Germany, were they worked in a sawmill. According to Dyson, they received fair treatment from their guards, with the exception of one teenage boy who refused to provide water until the work was finished. Food was in short supply, and Red Cross packages were intercepted by the Germans, leaving the prisoners with a daily ration of soup and black bread. Conditions apparently improved when Dyson was sent to Camp Rastatt, where the Red Cross was able to provide supplies, clothes, and a weekly food allotment.[11]

The Rastatt prison camp was also called the "Ukrainerlager" ("Ukrainian Camp") because it had originally held Ukrainian prisoners. With some exceptions, German prison officials began to send American officers to Villingen, enlisted navy sailors and civilian merchant marines to Brandenburg, and enlisted soldiers to Rastatt. During Clyde Grimsley's four-month stay, the American prisoner population at Rastatt increased almost fivefold, from 550 to 2,600 men. On September 3, 1918, Hoffman traveled down from Berlin and spent, as he put it, "two most splendid days in the camp with the 800 or more of my fellow-countrymen there." The secretary would return on several occasions and was able to improve camp conditions. Sergeant Halyburton continued to doubt "the mysterious Mr. Hoffman, of the International Y.M.C.A.," who would conclude a prayer service by "in one breath asking

God to allow America to win the war and in the next to have mercy on the Germans." Yet suspicions of Hoffman began to fade when, in addition to Red Cross food parcels, prisoners began receiving clothing, shoes, underwear, uniforms, razors, cigarettes, athletic equipment, board games, and sixty sets of pajamas. The Germans agreed to construct a YMCA hut and an athletic field, and Hoffman arranged for a listing of major-league baseball scores. A library was established—nearly one thousand books were shipped from Switzerland—and prisoners were offered educational and language instruction. By November, even the dubious Halyburton conceded that Hoffman had been "a real friend in time of need." According to YMCA historian Kenneth Steuer, American prisoners interacted freely, exercised a degree of self-government, and "enjoyed a far better lifestyle than other Allied prisoners—not to mention the German guards—due to the efforts of U.S. organizations." Grimsley recalled: "It was a model camp, the men acknowledging only the authority of their chosen officers, and never gave the Germans any trouble. They paid no attention to them."[12]

The prisoners also amused and entertained themselves. On September 14, 1918, the first edition of a handwritten prison newspaper, the *Barbed Wireless*, included the following tongue-in-cheek mission statement:

> The BARBED WIRELESS . . . is published solely in the interests of the American soldiers who find themselves temporarily the guests of the enemy in the delightful community of Rastatt, formerly a summer resort, but now open to Americans throughout the entire year. The purpose of this embryonic journal is to keep alive the spirit of Americanism, to drive away any gloom and depression that might take root from time to time, and to set down in durable form a record of all events and happenings among us which may prove of interest later on when our life at Rastatt is but a dim memory—a passing flash in the kaleidoscope of life. Incidentally, it may prove of sanitary value if used with discretion in the bungalow adjoining Barrack 1.

Music was a primary form of entertainment. Hoffman and the YMCA provided the men a piano and sent enough musical instruments for a twenty-piece jazz band, an eight-piece orchestra, and a bugle corps. He also obtained supplies for a musical show, and on one occasion the prisoners rented a theater in Rastatt for a production. Not surprisingly, bandleader Grimsley was instrumental (so to speak) in organizing and leading musical events. "I had to write all the music," he recalled, "and arrange it for the different instruments—some I remembered and the rest I made up." Music was performed at sporting events and at night in the barracks. In his memoir Hoffman describes his final visit to Camp Rastatt on Thanksgiving Day, 1918: "For the evening we had a vaudeville show scheduled . . . [and the] band did its part in furnishing plenty of stirring music. The evening was concluded by the singing of 'My Country, 'Tis of Thee.' . . . This was my last evening with the American boys."

Music also played a part in two memorable events at Camp Rastatt prior to the armistice. The first occurred during an outdoor Sunday afternoon concert. As Sergeant Halyburton later related, the band unexpectedly departed from its scheduled performance and "electrified" the men by playing "The Star-Spangled Banner":

> I jumped to my feet . . . [and] I saw that every prisoner in the camp was standing like a statue. . . . The German guards along the barriers and officers inside the field had not realized the significance of the tune at first. When they grasped it, the band was half through the song. . . . "Go!" they shouted to us in German, and to the musicians, "Stop!" Not an American stirred from his tracks. The band went on playing.[13]

The second event was the funeral of Roland Beaver of Kansas. Beaver's family moved frequently, living in Jetmore, Kirwin, and Stockton, among other places. While in Stockton he went to the same school that Clyde Grimsley had attended ten years earlier. As it so happened, when Beaver was transferred to Camp Rastatt, he occupied the bunk next to Grimsley, who spoke to him daily but never asked him where he was from. Beaver died in the prison hospital on September 29, 1918, apparently from spinal meningitis. He was buried in his uniform and given a full military funeral, with a procession of thirty mourners led by the camp chaplain. Grimsley wrote the music for the ceremony, and when the white cross was placed on the grave, he learned for the first time that Beaver was from Kansas. "We gave the boy a military funeral as far as possible," reported Grimsley when he returned home. "I'd like to get in touch with his family, so I could tell them about him."[14]

According to one source, the news of the armistice reached Camp Rastatt in less than two hours after the signatures were affixed to the document. "We sure raised the devil the night the armistice was signed," Grimsley recalled, "and the Germans were glad too." The tenth clause of the ceasefire agreement mandated "the immediate repatriation without reciprocity . . . of all allied and United States prisoners of war." Not all prisoners at Camp Rastatt, however, were immediately released, as revealed in a postcard that Marion Dyson received in December from his son: "I am well and out of Germany and am eating breakfast in Switzerland furnished by the Red Cross. I was in the last lot that left Germany, two trains being on before us. I will be in France tonight, I think. Will be in good old U.S.A. before long. There are 500 on this train." When interviewed in 1995, Melvin Dyson revealed why he waited patiently for a train: "I had walked most of the way in [so] I was looking for a ride out." He arrived in France on December 11, was taken to a hospital, and given his first bath since September. Dyson returned to the United States on April 15, 1919.[15]

Grimsley also had to wait to be released from his long captivity. In fact, he considered the worst part of his imprisonment to be the first month, "because the punishment was so severe," and the last month, "because we were waiting every day to get out of there and every day stretched out interminably, as though it would never end." Finally, on December 18, 1918, he sent his parents a note: "I am in France again and alive. Will write a long letter later." After recovering in a French hospital from influenza, Grimsley returned to Kansas and was discharged from military service at Camp Funston. On the same day, March 5, 1919, he took the evening train to Salina to be with friends and Mary Crandall, his future wife. When asked the next day to reflect on his ordeal, Grimsley smiled and said: "I can't understand now why they didn't kill me—I pulled so many tricks on them. It seems so funny to get back—I can scarcely realize it."[16]

People wanted to hear Grimsley's story, and soon after he arrived home he was asked to speak in several Kansas towns. On March 28, 1919, adults and children over ten years of age paid twenty-five cents each to hear of his prisoner-of-war experience. The invitation was extended by E. J. Beaver, the father of Roland Beaver, with eight hundred people (in a town with less than six hundred residents) attending the event at the Kirwin Opera House. This speech was followed by talks in other towns, including Leavenworth, where he urged a crowd of five thousand to purchase Liberty Loans, and Kansas City, where he addressed the prestigious City Club. On April 16 Grimsley was an honored guest when Lieutenant George Robb was awarded his Medal of Honor in Salina. This appears to have been one of his last public events, and with his marriage to Mary Crandall at the end of April, Private Grimsley returned to private life. According to the January 24, 1922, edition of the *Salina Evening Journal*, the couple temporarily relocated to Chicago in order for him to study "drapery and other phases of the ready to wear business" as part of a government vocational-training program. After a brief stay in

Photo 22.2: Carved sculpture of a Jayhawk by a Russian prisoner of war, circa 1918. Courtesy of the Kenneth Spencer Research Library, University of Kansas.

Nebraska, the couple settled in Denver, Colorado, where Clyde died in 1967 and Mary died in 1969.[17]

* * *

In 2010 Professor Marc Greenberg, the chair of the Department of Slavic Languages and Literatures at the University of Kansas, wrote an article about a sculpture of a Jayhawk that includes the inscription "Sent by Conrad Hoffman, YMCA at a German Internment Camp in 1917." The wooden bird, which was originally displayed in 1921, was found stored in a box in

2009. Although the sculpture was called the "Bolshevik Jayhawk" in a 1921 article in the *Kansas City Star*, it is unlikely that a Russian Bolshevik would have been in a German prison in 1917. Whatever may have been his political views, the sculpture's creator was likely the master carver at the prison camp in Worms, Germany, described in Hoffman's memoir:

> In this same camp we discovered a young Russian who was most expert with wood-carving tools. . . . Our secretary was able . . . to secure permission to take this Russian artisan to the near-by city and there to permit him to pick out such additional tools as he required, as well as to go to one of the large lumber yards where he was told he could choose the kinds of wood he needed for his carving and that we would pay the bills. A happier individual would have been hard to find than this Russian, coming thus into a veritable paradise of material from which he was told to choose freely.

Greenberg believes, with good reason, that the prisoner "applied his skill to manufacture a token of appreciation to Conrad Hoffman of the University of Kansas, a heartfelt sign of esteem for the good works that Mr. Hoffman did for his fellow man on another continent." Hoffman did briefly return to his old position after the war ended, but he left Kansas for Europe in 1920 to work for the World's Student Christian Federation. In 1936, as a secretary of the International Missionary Council, he gave a speech in New Jersey on "Fascism and War as Threats to Religion." During World War II, he worked with German prisoners of war and the YMCA's War Prisoners' Aid of Canada. Afterward he helped relocate hundreds of European refugees to the United States. Conrad "Con" Hoffman died in New York in 1958 at the age of seventy-three.[18]

1919–2024

Photo 23.1: Parade on November 11, 2015, in Emporia, Kansas, the town credited for having Armistice Day renamed Veterans Day. Courtesy of Mark Reinstein, Alamy Live News.

CHAPTER TWENTY-THREE

The Kansas Home Front after the War

Joy, Uncertainty, Anger, and Remembrance

The year 1919 began with the death of Theodore Roosevelt, reached the halfway point with Kansan Jess Willard (the "Pottawatomie Giant") losing his heavyweight boxing crown to Jack Dempsey, and ended with the sale of Babe Ruth from the Boston Red Sox to the New York Yankees. The Eighteenth Amendment went into effect in January, and national prohibition was enforced in October by the passage of the Volstead Act. Americans yearned for normalcy, but the Great War had changed lives, and the song "How Ya Gonna Keep 'em Down on the Farm (after They've Seen Paree?)" became a national sensation. For African Americans, the hope that the service of Black men in the military would lead to fair treatment was quickly dashed: violence erupted all across the country, including in Chicago, where a race riot left thirty-eight people dead. Congress sent the Nineteenth Amendment, guaranteeing suffrage to women, to the states for ratification, but the Senate refused to ratify the Treaty of Versailles. President Wilson suffered a stroke, members of the Chicago White Sox "fixed" the World Series, and the federal government responded to the "Red Scare" by arresting thousands of suspected anarchists, communists, and socialists.

For the men, women, and children of the Sunflower State, the twelve months of 1919 were an intense mixture of celebration among the living and mourning for persons lost to warfare and disease. There were a multitude of medal ceremonies and parades. Many families, however, still did not know the fates of their loved ones, and some expressed anger over the high death rate of Kansas soldiers, particularly in the Thirty-Fifth Infantry Division. In 1919 and the decade that followed, people processed their grief with the help of private organizations—among them the newly formed American Legion—as well as the federal government, which paid for the repatriation of fallen soldiers and for Gold Star pilgrimages. While it was a time of joy and celebration, it was also a time of uncertainty and sadness.

The sense of relief and joy that followed the armistice turned into a feeling of anticipation in subsequent months. Many individual Jayhawk soldiers were sent home during this period, but the first groups of men to be discharged from military service in Kansas were units of the Ninety-Second (Buffalo Soldiers) Division. The March 7, 1919, edition of the *Kansas City Advocate* announced that arrangements had been made to honor the returning soldiers in two weekend parades. When the men were instead sent directly to Camp Funston, another Black newspaper, the *Kansas City Sun*, said the decision "was a grievous disappointment to us and will rankle for a long time in the breast of our people." As it turned out, a second detachment from the Ninety-Second was permitted to stop in Kansas City, Missouri. Thousands of people lined the streets on March 21 as the men marched with the Negro Kansas State Guard, local high school cadets, and other Black organizations. The parade procession ended at Twenty-Fifth and Grand, where a luncheon was held in the Overland Building (the future home of Hallmark Cards). Two days later half a dozen white men and women and two thousand African Americans gathered at the Topeka city auditorium for a celebratory program. According to the local Black newspaper, the *Plaindealer*, four members of the Ninety-Second Division spoke to the crowd, including the twice-wounded Lieutenant Wesley Jamison, who described the battlefront from "our side" and "proved that German shells and gas had not robbed him of any of his eloquence, forcc and logic." Governor Henry Allen was not present, but he and the City of Topeka officially honored the Kansas soldiers of the Ninety-Second on July 29, 1919, with a downtown parade and a picnic dinner at Garfield Park. In contrast, the Black soldiers of the 805th and 806th Pioneer Regiments were not honored in Topeka because their white commanding officer ordered their train to bypass the crowd and travel directly to Camp Funston.[1]

Topeka hosted several parades in May, including major celebrations for the 139th Infantry, the 137th Infantry, and the 353rd Infantry. On May 5 there were four parades in a single day, beginning with the employees of the Santa Fe Railway, who marched in their working clothes, followed in succession by the "big" parade of the 139th Infantry and the 110th Field Signal Battalion, a Shriners' parade, and then a final parade for the late-arriving 110th Sanitary Train. The soldiers went to the statehouse grounds, mingled with family and friends, and then returned to the train station for the trip to Camp Funston. Both the *State Journal* and the *Daily Capital* provided their readers with humorous and bittersweet vignettes about the homecoming:

> Said one soldier: "Atlantic Ocean and France—bah! Give me the Kaw river and Kansas!"
>
> "Back to God and Kansas" was printed in chalk on one of the coaches of the 110th Sanitary Train.
>
> A girl asked a soldier from her hometown, "Where is Bill? I want to kiss him and I can't find him and now they are all going away." The soldier replied, "I don't know where Bill went. Kiss me instead." She did.
>
> One mother waited in vain to greet her son. When members of his company told her that he had been left in France in a hospital, she did not say anything, just smiled, and an instant later sank unconscious to the platform.
>
> A signal corps man laughed and said, "I saw dad this morning. All he could do was stand there and jump up and down like a six year old kid without saying a word."

As reported in the *State Journal*, Sergeant Safford Thacher of the 110th Field Signal Battalion was met at the train station by his wife, Anne, and their baby daughter, Betty Jean, who was born on October 11, 1918. The birth had been difficult, but both mother and child survived. Betty Jean Thacher Smith, who met her father for the first time on May 5, 1919, would live for another century, passing away in Topeka on August 24, 2019.[2]

On the following Thursday, May 8, 1919, the residents of Topeka re-grouped to provide a rousing welcome to the men of the 130th Field Artillery and several companies of the 137th (All Kansas) Infantry. The men earned their accolades, declared the *State Journal*, because they "helped make the Argonne Forest the Slough of Despondency for the Hun hordes." The parade was the "climax of days of celebration," observed the *Daily Capital*, noting that the crowd was "a little wilder" because "there are no other two regiments that contain as many Topeka boys as the 130th field artillery and the 137th infantry." Other cities—Hutchinson, Independence, Kansas City, Lawrence, Wichita, and others—also paid tribute to the soldiers as they made their way to Camp Funston to be discharged.[3]

Patriotic celebrations in Kansas were also held in small towns. In Chanute citizens watched a hearse drag the "Kaiser's coffin" through the streets. The five thousand residents of Pratt hosted a "Big Victory Home-Coming Jubilee" on May 22 in honor of local soldiers. A flag pole, donated by the Eggleston Plumbing Shop, was erected in the middle of Main and Third Streets, with a large light bulb on top and colored pennants and electric

Photo 23.2: Chanute, Kansas, after announcement of the armistice, November 11, 1918. Courtesy of the Kansas State Historical Society.

globes extending to the four corners of the intersecting streets. The business area was likewise decorated with pennants, flags, and streamers. The parade began with a band, immediately followed by "old soldiers" and returning soldiers and sailors. Among the other participants were Red Cross canteen squads, Grace Heaton (as Joan of Arc), Boy Scout troops, Camp Fire girls, Odd Fellows, Colored Knights of Phythias, the fire department, the U.S. Army Nursing Corps, and most of the local businesses. A replica of a train, in honor of the 117th Ammunition Train, was built with a Ford tractor and several automobiles. One of the county officials dressed up as Uncle Sam, and Pratt Ice and Coal Company created three massive ice sculptures depicting the flags of France, the United Kingdom, and the United States. Women representing the Salvation Army distributed doughnuts, and the Eggleston Plumbing Shop float—for unknown reasons it consisted of a "colored lad" in a tub under a functioning shower—caused "much merriment." One of the other floats was "drawn by a team of patriotic mules" that were "painted with the national colors." In the opinion of the local newspaper, the parade "was a fine pageant and one which delighted the thousands of people who assembled in town early in order to see it."[4]

The final large-scale celebration for returning soldiers took place over the Memorial Day weekend. Members of the 353rd Infantry arrived on the morning of May 30 in Kansas City, Kansas, and were honored and entertained for three hours, then departed for Topeka, Atchison, Emporia, and finally Camp Funston. The mood in Kansas City was festive, and the incoming trains were lined with signs prepared by the soldiers:

The Fighting Farmers
No Cooties Now
From the Rhine to Funston
No Beer, No Parade

Over three thousand people were present. After being served dinner in Huron Square, the men danced with "a host of Kansas girls" to music provided by bands placed at both ends of Seventh Street between Minnesota and Ann Avenues (the present site of the Wyandotte Indian Nation's Seventh Street Casino). The next stop for most of the men was Topeka, where they took part in what the *State Journal* described as the "Greatest of All Memorial Days":

> America at peace with the world; huge guns that a few short months ago belched forth flame and iron and steel into living ranks of men now standing all mute and silent; . . . swords beaten into plowshares and bayonets sheathed to drip no more with human blood; honor to those who fought so valiantly to protect mankind from the blight of autocracy; and hearts too full for utterance—that's Memorial Day, 1919, in Topeka.

The first group of the 353rd, which included Corporal Dean Billings of Company L and comrades of Lieutenant Jared Jackson of Company M, arrived shortly after one o'clock and paraded before a large crowd before returning to the station for the trip to Emporia. When the second group of infantrymen pulled into Topeka in the afternoon, a boy scout recognized his brother, "gave a sharp howl of delight," and leapt into the train window, where "brawny arms caught him in midair." After some delay the men fell in to formation and marched to the statehouse grounds, "with fixed bayonets throwing back the rays of the sun." The *Daily Capital* "conservatively estimated" that ten thousand out-of-town cars came to Topeka for the reception.

In Emporia residents waited patiently to greet some of the exhausted soldiers, who marched to Fremont Park, stacked their arms, and were dismissed. "They wouldn't have gotten us out of this train if they had told us [we had] to carry our equipment," said one doughboy. "It's only our third parade in one day since 4 o'clock this morning." The men were fed roasted chicken, sandwiches, deviled eggs, dill pickles, bananas, pie, and cake, then told to march back to the train station, where they departed at 11:30 P.M. for Camp Funston. At about the same time, residents in Atchison paid tribute to the Third Battalion, 353rd Regiment, which included forty-five men from Atchison and Doniphan Counties. "We're through, we've had enough," Sergeant Jack Woodhouse told a reporter for the *Weekly Globe*, who observed that other doughboys "agreed with him in characteristic and somewhat profane language."[5]

* * *

Whereas some Kansans were overjoyed by the knowledge that their loved ones had survived the war, others had to endure a period of painful uncertainty. James and Ida Ellison, who lived in Cloud County, were notified by telegram on August 6, 1918, that their son, Clarence Cleveland Ellison of the Fifty-Ninth Infantry, was killed in action on July 19. But on September 9 the couple received a letter from Clarence dated three days after his reported death. The twenty-five-year-old had been reported missing, and no one knew that he was in a hospital recovering from a gas attack. The *Jamestown Optimist* suggested that he would "probably enjoy the distinction of being the first and only Jamestown man to read his own obituary." Although reports of his death were exaggerated, they unfortunately were not greatly exaggerated: Private Ellison was killed on October 2 during the Meuse-Argonne offensive. His parents were not officially informed this time until May 1919. In its second report of Ellison's death, the *Optimist* took a more cautious approach, suggesting that the message from the War Department "may be merely a continuation of the first report, which was proven to be an error." This was not the case, however, and the young man's body was returned home and laid to rest in October 1921. Despite repeated efforts, the Ellisons were never able to obtain an account of the manner in which their son was killed and presumably were never told why the official notification was delayed for seven months.[6]

In at least three more instances, Kansas privates were erroneously declared to have died in action. Albert Sartain of Denton, a member of the 140th Infantry, claimed in a letter to his parents that the report of his death was "a far-fetched falsehood." Milton Marzolf of Mitchell County, who served with Company M, 139th Infantry, was not killed as reported but was instead taken prisoner. In the case of Leonard Williams of Perry, it was the War Risk Insurance Bureau that listed him as deceased, whereas the War Department advised his family that he was still with the 353rd Infantry. Williams, who insisted in a letter that he was the liveliest dead man that the world ever knew, was not laid to rest until 1973. Marzolf survived his captivity and lived another fifty years, while Sartain passed away at the age of eighty-eight in 1984.[7]

In the cases of Sartain, Marzolf, and Williams, the erroneous reports were soon proven to be incorrect. In contrast, the families of three members of Company B, 139th Infantry were not provided closure until several months after their sons were killed. Mary and William Rogers of Nortonville feared the worst when they heard nothing about their son Clyde, who had been wounded on the second day of the Meuse-Argonne offensive. On February 1, 1919, the War Department said Private Rogers was alive when in fact he had died on October 10, 1918, which was not communicated for another three weeks. In light of the circulation of false reports, the parents of Rafael Zidek of Irving initially refused to accept that their son had died, and the *Irving Leader* noted in January 1919 that "inasmuch as other errors have been made by the War Department, we sincerely hope that Pvt. Zidek may yet be found in some hospital or prison and may return to the United States alive." In March, however, the family received a letter from another soldier in Company B who stated that Sergeant Blevins had recently marked the location where Zidek was buried. The news—and closure—came more than six months after a shell had killed Rafael between Baulny and Exermont.[8]

The third example of uncertainty and false hope concerns Victor Segraves and his family. On October 7, 1918, just over a week after Company B left the battlefield, Ted Blevins wrote that Segraves had been shot in his presence and "was wounded dangerously." Two months later, on December 10, Blevins said that when he had last seen his high school friend, he was alive. "I gave him first aid dressing," Ted told his parents, "and carried him to Field Hospital." What happened thereafter is shrouded in mystery. Blevins said another sergeant told him that he had seen Segraves lying dead in the hospital, but the unnamed sergeant said, "it was dark and he couldn't tell for sure." Ted was certain that Vic did not survive but could "find no one who really knows."

Several months passed after the Segraves family was notified on October 24 that Vic had been seriously wounded. The unofficial reports were contradictory. On November 4, 1918, the *Topeka Daily Capital* reported that the sergeant had been killed based on a letter from Corporal Ross Taylor that mentioned Segraves and described the men of Company B falling "like grain before a reaper." In contrast, the *Oskaloosa Independent* on the eighth included the following story:

> SGT. VICTOR SEGRAVES NOT KILLED. While in one or two letters from France it was stated that Victor Segraves was killed, it has been learned since that he was wounded in two places, and although the wounds were dangerous it is hoped the skill of the surgeons and nurses will save his life.

The *Independent* on November 29 also reported "the welcome word, long waited for, that Victor Segraves was getting along all right." This statement was based on a letter, dated October 27, from Sergeant Sherman "Henry" Williamson of Oskaloosa, who told his parents that Segraves had a narrow escape, being very seriously wounded in the stomach or abdomen.[9]

There was a simple reason for the confusion. "Vic never wore his tags," Ted Blevins told his parents, referring to the identification tags issued to Company B at Camp Doniphan in February 1918. The need for bodily identification became apparent during the Civil War, as evidenced by the fact that over three-fourths of the seventeen thousand men in the Vicksburg National Cemetery are buried under "Unknown Soldier" markers. The army experimented with different types of identification badges and in February 1918 began to issue tags with service (or serial) numbers. "My number is 1,455,896," Ted told his family, "just like a convict." (Vic Segraves's service number was 1,455,903.) Soldiers immediately referred to the circular aluminum discs as "dog tags," most likely because they resembled canine identification tags but possibly due to claims that soldiers were treated like dogs. The men each received two tags. "One is to be cut off and sent to the War Department if I get killed," Jesse Blevins explained to his family, "and the other one is to be buried with me so that after the war they can dig my body up and ship it back to the United States." Frank Sterns of the 117th Ammunition Train, while stationed "somewhere in France," provided the same information, although in more succinct and colorful language. "They say when you 'check in' they cut one off and the other they leave on the body," wrote the twenty-five-year-old from Hiawatha. "I think that I will see that they don't get a chance to cut any off me." Sergeant Major Sterns succeeded in surviving the war and returned to Hiawatha and his position as clerk of the district court of Brown County.[10]

Frank Roberts, in the January 24, 1919, edition of the *Oskaloosa Independent*, blamed unnecessary censorship and "the stupidity and utter incapacity of the soldiers' mail service" for the mishandling of the matter:

> Sergeant Victor Segraves . . . was reported wounded by the officials weeks after the news had filtered in a guarded way thro letters written by

Photo 23.3: Identification "dog tag" for Theodore Blevins. Courtesy of Kathleen Blevins Pattee.

> comrades who evidently feared the stupid censorship. Then vague intimations came that the boy had died in the hospital, but no certain information, and his parents and other relatives have been held in cruel suspense. A Y.M.C.A. man wrote a long letter to his wife and in it said "I will tell about Victor Segraves in a separate letter, as I do not want this one to be cut up by the censor, and will send it at once but it will have to go thro the central office." That letter telling the facts about Victor has never arrived, altho it was written long after the armistice was signed. Now, what under heavens is the reason that such word should be withheld from suffering parents?

A week later Patrick and Louise Segraves received a letter, dated January 12, 1919, that was written by Lieutenant Owen Ridlon of Council Grove. "It is with the deepest feeling of sorrow and sympathy that I write you this letter, which will tell you of the death of your son, Victor." Lieutenant Ridlon saw Segraves at the field hospital near Chaudron Farm. "After that no one, it seems, saw or heard anything of him until I came across the information that a Lieutenant Davidson of our regiment had found him dead, later, at this Chaudron Farm." According to Ridlon, there was "no doubt" in the mind of the lieutenant, who pinned a tag on the unidentified body. When the

Thirty-Fifth Division came to Topeka in May, Louise Segraves spoke with Sergeant Virgil Miller of Howard and Lieutenant "Davidson," who most likely was Burr Davison of Montana. The men told her that Vic said, "this was a good time to go to sleep," then quietly passed away.

Owen Ridlon searched for the grave of his comrade, as he promised to do in his letter, but was unsuccessful. Battle conditions caused temporary graves to be marked by rifles or sticks in the ground, and explosives often obliterated markers and even bodies. Victor Segraves is one of 4,452 unaccounted American soldiers from World War I.[11]

* * *

Another prevalent postwar emotion was anger, best exemplified in Kansas by its governor, Henry J. Allen. The newspaper owner and editor of the *Wichita Beacon* was inspecting hospitals in France for the American Red Cross when it became apparent in 1918 that he would receive the Republican nomination to become the state's next governor. Because candidates for political office could not work for the Red Cross, Allen switched to the YMCA and spent his remaining time in France working with the Thirty-Fifth Infantry Division, both in the Vosges Mountains and during and after the Meuse-Argonne offensive. He won with two-thirds of the vote in the gubernatorial election, returned home in December, and was sworn into office on January 13, 1919. A capacity crowd assembled later that day at the Topeka city auditorium, and the new governor proceeded to tell the story "that Kansas had been waiting for": the experiences of the 117th Ammunition Train, Eighty-Ninth Division, and Thirty-Fifth Division. "I did not come here to complain," he said at one point, "but to tell the truth, I may show my feelings; if I do I can't help it." What particularly rankled Allen was the lack of support provided to the Thirty-Fifth Division as it fought its way toward Exermont. There were insufficient horses and machines to transport the artillery, he said, which led to an abundance of casualties due to German shelling and machine-gun fire. "Where were the airplanes?," he rhetorically asked the families of the soldiers. "There was domination of the air on the English and French fronts, but on the American front the Germans had domination of the front." Allen also said it was "unfortunate" that Charles Martin—the former Kansas adjutant general—had been relieved of his command of the Seventieth Infantry Brigade on the eve of battle. Without saying so directly, Allen strongly suggested to his audience that the "regular" army officers had deliberately mistreated and ineptly directed the "magnificent" national guardsmen of Missouri and Kansas. In the words of historian

Robert Ferrell, the Kansas governor was "angered to the core by what had happened."[12]

Allen turned up the heat two days later in Kansas City. "Let the War Department open its records," he demanded, "and give full facts on the actions of the American war machine in France." The commandant of Camp Funston, Major General Wood, lent his support, telling a joint session of Congress, "everything that Governor Allen said relative to the terrific losses of the Thirty-fifth division is true." Soon thereafter, with the help of Senator Charles Curtis and Representative Philip Campbell of Pittsburg, the army's handling of the Thirty-Fifth Division became an issue of national debate. Congress held three sets of hearings, in which the army was ably defended by Secretary of War Baker and General Peyton March. In response, Governor Allen made a strong case for his position but was undermined by the testimony of Major General Traub, the division's commander. Based on "a careful reading of his remarks," Robert Ferrell has concluded that "Traub knew he had failed personally and was seeking to defend the War Department with the hope it would forgive his own transgressions." The hearings did not lead to reforms, and in a year or two, Governor Allen moved on. Nevertheless, argues Ferrell, it was a worthy effort:

> It was an unsuccessful, if praiseworthy, effort to change an institution that in many ways needed it. . . . The cost of the learning experience in France was borne by such divisions as the Thirty-fifth with its inept leadership and heavy casualties. The battle of the Meuse-Argonne not merely involved the most troops ever brought into a battle in all of American history (1.2 million men), but the highest number of casualties, twenty-six thousand men killed and tens of thousands wounded.

By directing his anger at the Regular Army, Allen also shielded the guardsmen of Kansas from blame. The editor of the *Oskaloosa Independent*, Frank Roberts, joined ranks with his Republican governor and criticized the Regular Army and the Wilson administration:

> So many of our own boys suffered in this battle—more than would have been necessary if they had been given the artillery and air support which they should have had; but the Administration and all its thick and thin supporters are so afraid that something may reflect upon the acts of the War Department that they deny or belittle all criticisms and suppress reports which would throw light upon the facts.

Roberts also heaped praise on Company B and the rest of the Kansas guardsmen who were, in his words, "not machine-made and life-long soldiers—just farm boys and town boys jumped hastily into uniforms and drilled into shape in a hurry—and they surprised the world with their efficiency." Ted Blevins agreed, telling his parents in February 1919, "Gov. Allen should know about the 35th and I think he told the truth myself." The soldiers of the division and their families were represented by a governor who was on their side, and it made them feel better as they transitioned from war to peace.[13]

* * *

When the immediate emotional responses to the end of the Great War waned, many Americans sought ways to remember the dead and process their grief. Politicians often chose to honor citizens who gave their lives in service by funding the creation of structures, such as statues, buildings, and football stadiums (as discussed in chapter 26). Individuals and communities likewise created physical reminders of the Great War (on a smaller scale) and also formed and joined organizations in which they could come together to grieve, remember, and support each other.

Three community-based organizations emerging from these efforts were the American Legion, the Veterans of Foreign Wars, and the Gold Star Mothers. The American Legion was first conceived in France at the conclusion of World War I. In 1937 Colonel Theodore Roosevelt Jr. recalled that he got the idea for the new veterans group when a convalescing sergeant told him, "we have stuck together in the bad times; let's stick together in the good ones." In March 1919 a group of soldiers met in Paris and adopted the name "American Legion"; the "American Legion of the Great War" was also considered because the initials matched those for Abraham Lincoln and George Washington. In contrast to the Veterans of Foreign Wars (VFW), which was formed before World War I, membership in the legion was extended to veterans who had not served in an overseas theater of conflict. By the first week in May, a total of thirty-five counties in Kansas had established legion posts, and in most instances the local organization was named in honor of the first man from the locality who gave his life in the Great War. Congress officially chartered the American Legion that September. Historian Steven Trout counted 332 American Legion halls operating in Kansas in 2006, describing them as "the most widespread, but perhaps least noticed, form of World War I commemoration in the state."[14]

To honor three men of the 117th Ammunition Train who were killed by a single airplane bomb, the Ford County American Legion post is named after Charles Ernest Scott, the Ford County VFW post carries the name of Howard Gotschall, and an American Legion post in Kansas City honors Hewitt Swearingen. The legion post in Winchester is named for William Davis, and the Oskaloosa post bears the name of Victor Segraves and Leland Larner, a teacher who was killed on August 12, 1918. The VFW post in Atchison honors Jared Jackson of the 353rd Infantry, who died on the heights of Barricourt, and one of the VFW posts in Wichita is named for Erwin Bleckley, who earned a Medal of Honor for his efforts to assist the Lost Battalion. There are at least two American Legion organizations in Kansas that honor U.S. Marines who died at Belleau Wood: the Wayne Austin Post of Newton and the Joseph Lysle Rishel Post of Hutchinson. The Overland Park American Legion post is named for Dwight Cowles, who helped the Thirty-Eighth Infantry become the "Rock of the Marne" when he lost his life on July 15, 1918. Several VFW and American Legion posts pay tribute to Kansans who died during the Meuse-Argonne offensive, including the Isadore Hoehn VFW Post in Lenexa. On September 26, the first day of battle, Private Hoehn advanced three miles with Company H, 137th Infantry to a small hill near Varennes. According to a letter of condolence sent to his mother, his squad received a direct hit from a shell. Hoehn was taken to a dressing station, where he said, "Tell mother I was not afraid to die," and then passed away.[15]

The American Legion Moore Post 197 in WaKeeney is named for two brothers. Edmond "Eddie" and Dalton "Day" Moore were raised by their mother, Nettie, after their father died of tuberculosis in 1898. Eddie enlisted in the Kansas National Guard and ended up in the 137th Infantry. When Day was rejected in Kansas as too young, he managed to enlist in the Missouri National Guard and became a member of the 140th Infantry. Both took part in the Meuse-Argonne battle and were killed in action. Nettie Moore and her daughter Georgia learned the fate of Eddie in November but were told in January 1919 that the previously missing Day had recently reported for duty. "Isn't it strange how we cry when we are sad and cry when we are glad," Nettie wrote to a friend. "Georgia just lost the use of her knees for about half an hour . . . and I had my first good night's sleep." The consoling news that her youngest son survived was tempered, however, by the absence of letters from France. The information proved to be incorrect: at the end of March, the War Department reported that Day Moore had been killed in action sometime between September 26 and 29, 1918. On August 21, 1921, hundreds of mourners attended a joint funeral service held on the east side of the WaKeeney courthouse. Georgia died in 1958, and a year later Nettie passed away at the age of ninety-five.[16]

By the end of the war, a new term, "Gold Star Mother," had been added to the American lexicon, and the American Gold Star Mothers group became a formidable political organization. The *Oswego Democrat* on January 4, 1918, reported that an effort was being made in Chicago "to substitute for the present mourning garb some simple designation as a gold star, in memory of the American soldier who falls on the battle field, the thought being to turn the mind from sadness to the brighter phase of the death." At the same time, gold stars were being sewn on service flags that paid tribute to residents or students and alumni in the military. At Ottawa University, for example, the first of many gold stars was added to honor Harold Boice of Spring Hill, a member of Company K, 137th Infantry, who died in October 1917 of pneumonia at Camp Doniphan. In anticipation of Mother's Day in 1919, newspapers across the country featured a heartfelt plea from the "First Gold Star War Mother," Alice Gresham Dodd of Evansville, Indiana. "I would like to have them bring back my boy," said the mother of Jimmy Gresham, one of the first three Americans killed in combat. "I hope they bring him back before I die." James B. Gresham, who served alongside Clyde Grimsley in the Sixteenth Infantry, was returned to the United States and reburied in 1921, six years before his mother was laid to rest in the same cemetery.

After the war the Office of the Quartermaster General asked each family who had lost a servicemember whether they wanted the body to be returned to them. The War Department's Grave Registration Service was responsible for finding, identifying, and reburying fallen doughboys. Some men, such as Corporal William "Kinney" Pratt of Emporia and Private Zidek of Irving, were laid to rest at American military gravesites in France, the most prominent being the Meuse-Argonne Cemetery. Others were repatriated, and by the end of 1922, a total of 45,588 soldiers were returned at a cost of over eighteen million dollars. Many of the dead were buried in their home states, such as William Davis of Winchester and Clarence Ellison of Cloud County, but some were laid to rest at Arlington National Cemetery, including Ulysses Grant Cassel of Beverly and Willis Nixon of Medicine Lodge. In the decade following the Great War, many families of the soldiers left behind pressured Congress to authorize—and pay for—organized pilgrimages to Europe. In March 1929 President Calvin Coolidge signed legislation authorizing pilgrimages to European cemeteries "by mothers and widows of members of military and naval forces of the United States who died in the service at any

Photo 23.4: Gold Star Mothers at the Tomb of the Unknown Soldier, November 11, 1925. Courtesy of the Library of Congress.

time between April 5, 1917, and July 1, 1921, and whose remains are now interred in such cemeteries." Of the 17,389 eligible women, 6,693 made the journey between 1930 and 1933. One who traveled in 1930 was Catherine Fitzsimons of Kansas City, Missouri, the mother of William Fitzsimons, the University of Kansas graduate who was the first American officer killed in the war. African American women who made the pilgrimage were segregated from the white pilgrims. In March 1930 Senator Henry Allen of Kansas proposed legislation extending to fathers the same pilgrimage privileges; Senate bill 3589 did not pass.[17]

According to records kept for Kansas, 95 of the 222 eligible women (43 percent) took part in the program, including 11 from Sedgwick County, 13 from Shawnee County, and 18 from Wyandotte County. The women traveled in groups escorted by military personnel; some carried Kansas dirt in boxes to sprinkle on graves. Six mothers from Hutchinson—Flora Irwin, Anna Norris, Martina Oberg, Ida Raymond, Lillie Rishel, and Delia Walker—made the trip in 1931. One of those who did not go to France was Margaret Shook of Abilene. Before the war, her oldest son, Frank, had spent time in prison, and two of her other sons, Grover and Anthony, had been jailed as youths for stealing chickens, bootlegging, and illegal fishing. In May 1917 the youngest son, Wilbur, enlisted in the Kansas National Guard, and Grover and Anthony joined him in July. The three brothers served together in Company H, 139th Infantry, with Anthony promoted to private first class. On September 29, 1918, Anthony was killed near Exermont and Grover was killed near Baulny. Another member of the company, Private First Class Mark Curran of Abilene, had died on the first day of the Meuse-Argonne offensive. His widowed mother, Mary Curran, was able to visit the resting place of her son and may have also visited the graves of the Shook brothers.[18]

* * *

Some of the Gold Star Mothers were elderly or infirm, including Laura Keller of Manhattan. Her son, Clede Keller, joined the National Guard after earning a degree in animal husbandry from Kansas State Agricultural College. He did not return with the rest of Company I, 137th Infantry, but his death was not officially reported until April 1919. The local American Legion shortly thereafter voted to name its post after Keller and Captain Willis Pearce, another Kansas State student killed in September 1918. Laura Keller signed up to be a member of the first Gold Star Mothers group to go to France. She suffered a stroke, however, and died on July 26, one month prior to her scheduled departure.

Grace Kingsbury of Smith Center was also unwell, but she was able to make the trip despite uremic poisoning and a prior stroke. Her son, Private LaRue Kingsbury of the 353rd Infantry, died on October 25, 1918, after being struck in the head by shrapnel. He was later moved to Plot B, Row 40, Grave 24 of the Meuse-Argonne American Cemetery. On September 6, 1930, Grace Kingsbury visited her son's final resting place and suddenly collapsed into an unconscious state. She died six days later in the neighboring city of Verdun. "Is it such a tragedy," asked the editor of the *Pittsburg Booster*, "if one closes her tired eyes forever in the land that claimed her boy?"[19]

CHAPTER TWENTY-FOUR

The Boys of Company B

William Davis, Victor Segraves, Ralph Nichols, and Samuel Gutschenritter

The life stories of William Davis and Vic Segraves have largely been told. Private First Class Davis, a farm boy from Winchester, was wounded shortly after entering the trenches on July 31, 1918, and died a week later on August 7. His body was buried in the Vosges Mountains but later brought home. Sergeant Segraves, whose family lived at different times in Perry and Oskaloosa, was shot on September 28, 1918, during the third day of the Meuse-Argonne offensive. His death was not confirmed until February 1919, and his body was never recovered.

The life stories of Ralph Nichols and Sam Gutschenritter continued after the war, although not as long as one would expect. Nichols met an accidental death at age twenty-nine, having lived in Kansas, Venezuela, Connecticut, and Texas. Gutschenritter passed away at age fifty-seven in Jefferson County, where he grew up, married, raised a family, and was known as a man who was "always thoughtful of others" and who "could be fully trusted in anything."[1]

* * *

"My dear Mr. Davis," began the letter from the American Red Cross, dated April 5, 1919, "We have just received a report which gives the location of the last resting place of your son and we hasten to forward it to you." When John Davis learned his son was buried near the village of Moosch in the Alsace region of France, William had been dead for eight months, and Jefferson County residents had attended several memorial services on his behalf. Davis wanted his son's remains to be buried in Winchester, so the body was returned to Kansas on June 4, 1921. The following day funeral services were held at the Christian Church, followed by the interment at the Wise Cemetery southeast of town. Participants in the burial ceremony included a firing squad from Leavenworth, members of the local William Davis American Legion Post, and a delegation from Company B, who laid roses, carnations, and sweet-scented jessamine on the casket.[2]

Photo 24.1: William Davis. Courtesy of the National WWI Museum and Memorial, Kansas City, Missouri, USA.

William Davis, while at Camp Doniphan, had purchased a $10,000 insurance policy. The original 1914 War Risk Insurance Act, which promoted insurance for shipping vessels, was amended in 1917 to create the Bureau of War Risk Insurance within the Treasury Department and to make available, among other forms of assistance, government-backed life-insurance policies for soldiers and sailors. In a letter dated November 26, 1918, the Insurance Bureau informed John Davis that, as the beneficiary of William Davis, he would be paid $10,000 in monthly installments of $57.50 per month from August 8, 1918, to August 8, 1938. The State of Kansas also sent money. Pursuant to legislation creating the Soldiers' Compensation Fund, John Davis was notified in November 1923 that the Compensation Board had ordered a one-time payment of $368.[3]

The 1921 burial of William Davis in Winchester is the subject of a painting by John Steuart Curry, *The Return of Private Davis from the Argonne*. Curry, who grew up in Winchester and was two years younger than Davis, is often grouped with Thomas Hart Benton and Grant Wood as the masters of American Regionalism. Many of his paintings are set in Kansas, including *Baptism in Kansas*, which Gertrude Vanderbilt Whitney purchased in 1930 for the Whitney Museum in New York. Curry is best known for *The Tragic*

Photo 24.2: *The Return of Private Davis from the Argonne*, by John Steuart Curry, 1940. Courtesy of the Museum of Fine Arts, Houston. Museum purchase funded by the Caroline Wiess Law Accessions Endowment Fund.

Prelude mural, located on the second-floor rotunda in the Kansas State Capitol, in which a colossal version of abolitionist John Brown stands—arms outstretched, a rifle in one hand and a Bible in the other—in front of Civil War soldiers, settlers in covered wagons, a prairie fire, and a tornado.[4]

Steven Trout provides a contextual understanding and a critique of *The Return of Private Davis from the Argonne.* He says it is not clear whether Curry attended the 1921 burial and suggests that the artist's personal connection to Davis "may have been exaggerated." Curry began the painting in 1928, a year after he visited an American war cemetery in France, and finished it in 1940. The rectangular canvas was purchased by an American Legion post in Milwaukee and is currently owned by the Houston Museum of Fine Arts. It depicts mourners forming a semicircle around a flag-covered casket, with friends and family on one side, heads bowed, facing uniformed soldiers, standing at attention and holding rifles, flags, and a bugle. One man—presumably John Davis—kneels beside the casket as the minister looks upward, clutching a Bible in his left hand and raising his right arm in the air. A line of gray automobiles behind the crowd divides the painting into two parts, and the eye is drawn to a distant flat landscape, with the suggestion of a town off to one side and open prairie elsewhere.[5]

William Davis, the subject of *The Return of Private Davis from the Argonne*, died in the Vosges Mountains in eastern France without having seen the Argonne Forest. The title was not the only artistic liberty taken by Curry. Whereas the painting depicts a seemingly limitless horizon, the actual gravesite sits below the summit of a hillside, preventing such panoramic views. Trout argues that, by "tying Private Davis to the Argonne," Curry made him "a more representative symbol of the nation's war dead." Having written extensively on how Americans in the interwar years interpreted and remembered World War I, Trout gives Curry's painting high praise: "To view this canvas is to feel simultaneously the force and the failure of war remembrance when confronted with a conflict fought far away—somewhere far over the Kansas rainbow—for a questionable cause and with dubious outcomes."[6]

Although *The Return of Private Davis from the Argonne* was not finished until 1940, the work-in-progress was displayed in 1938 in Emporia. It is not known whether John Davis, who died in 1959, was aware of this viewing opportunity and, if so, made the one-hundred-mile trip from Winchester to Emporia to see this depiction of his son's second burial. It is also unknown whether he attended the burial of John Steuart Curry, who was laid to rest in 1946 in the Reformed Presbyterian Church Cemetery on the north side of Winchester.[7]

* * *

As mentioned, the body of Vic Segraves was never found, and his parents received conflicting information about their son until Lieutenant Owen Ridlon of the Seventieth Brigade headquarters finally confirmed his death in February 1919. Ridlon praised Segraves's bravery: "he was never foolish or [took] unnecessary chances but when his duty called he utterly disregarded himself." In the same letter he noted that "in the Vosges or Alsace Sector he was out on patrol nearly every night—penetrating the German lines and doing much good." Ralph Nichols characterized his high school friend in a similar fashion, stating on one hand that he "has got nerve and common sense both together," and then on the other describing a man who took risks: "When the light artillery opened up on us when we were on day patrol, he just laughed at it and told us to filter back to the trenches, which we did safely." Ted Blevins, who carried Segraves from the battlefield to the first aid station, did not provide a similarly balanced assessment: "He was a dare-devil sort of fellow, and hadn't worried about the Germans' shooting ability, and thought walking upright in the open paths was safe."[8]

Newspapers reported in the spring of 1919 that Segraves was a posthumous recipient of the Distinguished Service Cross. Once again, however, the family had to endure a lengthy wait for an official confirmation. Meanwhile, on June 15 Reverend Townsend Nichols "preached a feeling service" at the Methodist church in memory of two Oskaloosa boys: Segraves and Leslie Hudson. With regard to Sergeant Segraves, Nichols read the laudatory letter from Lieutenant Ridlon, described Segraves's military record, and concluded by saying, "his life here and in the public schools and the athletic circles of the high school, as well as his home life, all attested to his sunny, cheerful disposition which made him a favorite with all." There were many uniformed soldiers in attendance, including Merle Trapp, who concluded the service by playing "Taps" on his bugle. Another honor was bestowed in the fall when the Oskaloosa American Legion post was named Larner-Segraves Post 36.[9]

It was not until October 1923 that Patrick and Louise Segraves were officially notified by the War Department that a Distinguished Service Medal had been awarded to their son. The award was presented by Brigadier General Harry A. Smith on December 26 at the Oskaloosa Methodist Church. After an American Legion quartet sang a patriotic song and the invocation was given by Reverend Thorp (Reverend Nichols having left in 1921), Lieutenant Ridlon spoke of Segraves's fine character and described the cause and manner of his death. General Smith then rose and read the citation given to "a country boy, known to all of you, Victor L. Segraves," sergeant, First Battalion Scout Platoon, 139th Infantry:

> For extraordinary heroism in action near Baulny, France, September 28, 1918. Sergeant Seagraves voluntarily formed and led a patrol against an enemy machine-gun nest which was causing many casualties in his battalion, and captured one of the guns. With utter disregard for his personal safety, he advanced alone on another gun of the nest, but was severely wounded by the intense fire in the performance of this heroic act.

The newspaper account of the ceremony included a poem composed in France by Trapp, which concluded with the following lines: "I shall always remember this kind fearless lad; the best old pal I ever had."[10]

The Meuse-Argonne American Cemetery, which contains the largest number of American military dead in Europe (14,246), does not contain the

Photo 24.3: Larner-Segraves American Legion Post 36, Oskaloosa, Kansas. Courtesy of Jane Hoskinson.

body of Victor L. Segraves. His name, however, is one of the 954 names etched on the Walls of the Missing, which are located on either side of the chapel in the memorial situated on a ridge overlooking the rows of Carrara marble headstones.

* * *

On May 15, 1919, Ralph Nichols and Allan Austin were the last Oskaloosa boys in Company B to be discharged at Camp Funston. Lieutenant Charles Nichols, who remained stateside, left the aviation service in January but was not at home to greet his brother, having gone to Texas to work in the oil fields. Ralph's oldest brother, Corporal Arvil Nichols, who served in France as a military policeman, came home unannounced in June, shortly after Ralph went to Emporia State Normal for the summer to prepare for his senior year in high school. In the fall of 1919, twenty-year-old Ralph Nichols, veteran of the Meuse-Argonne offensive, was elected senior-class president and starred on the Oskaloosa football team. There were ninety-two students enrolled at the high school, including the ubiquitous Merle Trapp, the bugler who spent time in the Oskaloosa jail for taking unauthorized leave from Camp

Doniphan. On Armistice Day, the seventh and eighth grades were brought to the high school to listen to Nichols and Trapp, who presented a dialogue entitled "Over There, and Home Again."[11]

After listening to his father preach at the baccalaureate, Ralph Nichols graduated from high school in May 1920. He enrolled that fall in the Civil Engineering Department of Kansas State Agricultural College, which at the time was considering shortening its name to avoid misleading people "who regard it as a purely agricultural school." The *Oskaloosa Independent* applauded Ralph's choice, declaring Kansas State to be "a great school" and predicting "sometime they may beat K.U. at football." While in college, Ralph joined the Phi Kappa Alpha fraternity and continued his gridiron career. As a junior in the fall of 1922, he was an All–Missouri Valley Conference offensive tackle, and as a senior he was all-conference again as well as the team captain. Described in the *Royal Purple*, the college's yearbook, as "an able aggressive leader, a student of the game," Ralph did not lose to the University of Kansas in either year—both games ended with a tie score.[12]

Ralph Nichols left school in February 1924 to take a job with the Standard Oil Company, which sent him to Venezuela in April to work with his brother Charles as an engineer and surveyor. Upon his return to the United States in 1926, Ralph played one season in the National Football League for the Hartford (Connecticut) Blues. Although lacking a colorful nickname like some of his teammates (such as "Dilly" Dally, "Dimp" Halloran, and "Mule" Werwaiss), he did earn some mention in the newspapers. The *Hartford Courant*, in describing a 7–2 loss to the Kansas City Cowboys, noted that the players "were compelled to wade with water above their ankles" and praised Nichols as a "powerful performer in the Hartford line." An even more memorable game took place on November 7, a 16–7 victory over the Canton Bulldogs, who struggled as their injured star, Jim Thorpe, watched from the sidelines. In a delightful article sports reporter Leslie Young describes how the Bulldogs, "showing all the characteristics of the animals for which they are named," lost a "bitter fight" in which the players not only "hurled every ounce of strength into the struggle" but also in one instance went too far in the view of the referee:

> Ralph Nichols of Hartford and Stan Robb of Canton were dismissed for shooting punches at each other. Robb had made a tackle of a Hartford player, and Nichols, endeavoring to protect his teammate, grasped Robb's shoulders and pulled him away rather roughly. Robb resented the act and

Photo 24.4: Ralph Nichols. *From The Royal Purple 1924* (yearbook of Kansas State Agricultural College), courtesy of the Morse Department of Special Collections, Kansas State University Libraries,.

> drove a right at Nichols' chin. Ralph responded with a swirl of blows to all parts of the body before Halloran [the referee] told them both to quit the performance.

As darkness descended on the poorly lit field, Hartford kicked off to the Canton team, which executed the "hidden ball" trick by having a player run with his headgear under his arm down the sideline opposite of where the football was being carried. After a touchdown was narrowly averted, one offensive end, who "sought to hide himself near the sidelines, apparently waiting for a forward pass," instead became embroiled in an argument with the Hartford fans, "and soon the crowd was chasing him across the gridiron with arms flailing threateningly." The referee announced the game was over, but when a policeman attempted to send the fans home, someone "launched a tackle at him . . . while the crowd gathered about the combatants." As reported by Young, "the policeman won, scoring six knockdowns, but he lost his hat."[13]

Nichols retired from professional football after one season and went to San Angelo, Texas, where he was the head of the Geophysical Department of the Sun Oil Company. On the afternoon of January 22, 1929, while driving on the outskirts of town, he crashed his automobile into a telephone pole. A companion escaped injury, but Nichols suffered a crushed spine and died two hours after an operation. Michael Ahearn, the head of the Department of Physical Education and Athletics at Kansas State (and the namesake for Ahearn Field House), described the former Aggie football captain—he called him "Nick"—as "a matchless leader." Ralph Nichols died at age twenty-nine and is buried at the Pleasant View Cemetery in Oskaloosa, Kansas.[14]

* * *

Sergeant Samuel Gutschenritter was described by one of his men as "a mighty cool soldier under fire" who made sure "the boys were all safely stowed before he ducked." He was shot in the foot—a "severe wound"—during the Meuse-Argonne offensive and left France on November 11, 1918. After arriving at Newport News, Virginia, he was sent to a most unusual convalescent hospital: the West Baden Springs Hotel near French Lick, Indiana. The resort hotel—still in operation in the 2020s—is a circular domed building with six floors and a large interior atrium that spans two hundred feet. It was leased to the United States during the war and became Army General Hospital No. 35. In addition to enjoying such elegant surroundings, Gutschenritter and the other patients were treated to an unforgettable Christmas celebration. The atrium was decorated with a large decorated tree as streamers hung from the highest balconies. In the afternoon the Hagenbeck-Wallace Circus gave a performance, which included five lions, five elephants, a clown and his two boxing dogs, and "a graceful exhibition of equestrianism with a beautiful big white horse, assisted by a small black pony." This was only the opening act: "Salvation army girls then donated doughnuts and boxes of fruit and nuts to the boys, all of which they gladly accepted. The men ate supper at 5 o'clock. At 7:15 the evening performance began. The Christmas tree and big star were lighted with multi-colored bulbs. . . . Entertainment was furnished by the hospital orchestra, a playlet by French Lick people, and professional talent from Indianapolis."[15]

Gutschenritter returned home—less one toe—in April 1919. The following January he married Edna Brown in a ceremony conducted by Reverend Nichols at the Oskaloosa Methodist Church. A month later the Gutschenritter family attended a memorial service at the Presbyterian church in honor of seventeen fallen soldiers from Jefferson County, including

Photo 24.5: Samuel Gutschenritter marker, Pleasant View Cemetery, Oskaloosa, Kansas. Courtesy of Jane Hoskinson.

Thomas Gutschenritter, Ed Blevins, Davis, and Segraves. Ted Blevins's father served as a witness in June 1920 when Charles Gutschenritter was finally granted U.S. citizenship. Sam and his family escaped injury in 1939 when their farmhouse burned to the ground but lost all of their possessions except two featherbeds, some quilts, and a radio. Sam continued to farm until February 1954, when he was employed by a construction company. He passed away in Oskaloosa on October 24, 1954, at age fifty-seven, less than a year prior to the 1955 reunion of Company B. His obituary describes him as a "kind and loving husband and father" who was "a good neighbor . . . always willing to give a helping hand in time of need" and "always a hard worker."

Samuel B. Gutschenritter was survived by his wife and five children, eight grandchildren, two brothers (John and Francis), and his sister Helen. He is buried at the Pleasant View Cemetery in Oskaloosa.[16]

CHAPTER TWENTY-FIVE

The Boys of Company B

William Smith, William Kimmel, Theodore Blevins, and Melvin Dyson

William Smith died in 1968 at age seventy-nine, while William Kimmel, Theodore Blevins, and Melvin Dyson lived into their nineties. Dyson and Kimmel overcame humble origins to enjoy long rewarding lives, although the latter was touched by the tragedy of war. Smith and Blevins excelled in their respective fields, law and education; were greatly respected by their peers; and left positive legacies.

In 1921 organizers for the Ku Klux Klan appeared in southern Kansas in Wichita and smaller towns such as Arkansas City, Caney, Fort Scott, Independence, Pittsburg, and Winfield. The state attorney general, Richard Hopkins, responded the following year by requesting the Kansas Supreme Court to enjoin the KKK "from acting or doing business as a corporation within the state." In 1923 Charles Griffith succeeded Hopkins as state attorney general and appointed Bill Smith as his assistant. Captain Smith, upon his return from France, practiced law briefly in Jefferson County before taking the position of assistant attorney for the Kansas Utilities Commission. In his new position with the state, he was part of a determined effort to counter the growing influence of the Klan and pro-Klan politicians in Kansas. The KKK infiltrated the Republican Party, which so angered William Allen White that the Emporia newspaper editor ran for governor as an independent in 1922 in order to shame the Republican candidate, Ben Paulen, for accepting the Klan's endorsement. Paulen was elected, and KKK supporters won control of the state senate, but some anti-Klan politicians, such as Attorney General Griffith, were returned to office. The stage was set for a series of legal battles, instituted by Griffith with the support of Smith, that turned the tide against the Kansas Klan.[1]

One of the lawsuits was filed in Jefferson County. In September 1924 the KKK was enjoined from holding a parade in Valley Falls. The next year the Kansas Supreme Court held that the KKK needed to obtain a charter to conduct business in the state, which led to two unsuccessful charter applications. In January 1926 Smith announced that he was a candidate to replace Attorney General Griffith, who was retiring. When asked in June about a proposed Klan gathering in Emporia, he referred to the Valley Falls ruling that prohibited masks in a parade and noted that "the wearing of Ku Klux Klan regalia is also illegal" because it would create a disturbance. Rejecting Smith's argument that the parade would "excite the ignorant," the Lyon County District Court judge permitted the event to take place, and thousands of people marched through the streets of Emporia to the city park, where an electric cross had been installed. The KKK charter became a key issue in Smith's campaign: William White praised his "courageous stand," while the pro-Klan *Mulberry Independent* denounced him as "Wild Bill" and "Stupid Bill." On November 2, 1926, Smith was elected state attorney general, and on February 28, 1927, the U.S. Supreme Court denied the Klan's petition for review of the Kansas Supreme Court's charter ruling.[2]

As a state's top lawyer, Smith helped expose Richard Brinkley—the "goat gland doctor"—as a hoax, debunking his claim that transplanted goat testicles could cure male impotence and other ailments, including dementia, emphysema, and flatulence. In 1930 Attorney General Smith became Justice Smith, serving in that capacity until 1956, when he was elevated to Chief Justice of the Kansas Supreme Court. While serving on the high court, Smith authored over one thousand opinions, including *Webb v. School District No. 90*, which has been called a "prelude" to *Brown v. Board of Education*, in which the U.S. Supreme Court held that racial segregation in public schools is unconstitutional. The Johnson County School District, Smith wrote in the 1949 *Webb* case, "unlawfully organized and established a separate grade school for the attendance of Negro children and forced them to attend that school." The allocation of students must be "without any regard at all as to color or race of the pupils within any particular territory," and the "standards and facilities of each school must be comparable." In 2016 Don C. Smith, a law professor at the University of Denver College of Law, wrote an opinion piece in the *Topeka Capital-Journal* in which he praised the "Kansas Republican Party of the mid-20th century, of which my grandfather was a proud member his entire life." After describing William Smith's authorship of the *Webb* decision and his opposition to the Ku Klux Klan, Professor Smith urged Kansans to continue to act in a manner consistent with "the state's long history of dealing with racial bigotry."[3]

Chief Justice William Smith retired in 1957 and died in 1968. He was survived by his wife, three sons, a sister, and seven grandchildren. In 1961 he was honored by his former colleagues as a man whose "practicality and unusual

Photo 25.1: William Smith. Courtesy of Sarah Barr.

grasp of the meaning of the common affairs of man resulted in his making a substantial contribution over the years to this Court." Six years earlier, in the pamphlet distributed at a reunion in Oskaloosa, the men of Company B not only recalled the heroics of their leader on September 27, 1918, but also included the following tribute: "There can be no question of his thorough understanding of his soldiers and the men whose lives depended on his leadership. He was most capable of exercising authority sternly when it was required, yet he was able to do it with kindness and a display of confidence, that assured his men he knew where he was going." In his own remarks Smith described his time with Company B as "the high point of my life," declaring that, in his biased opinion, Company B was "the grandest company in the AEF."[4]

* * *

William Kimmel, who was abandoned by his impoverished parents as a child, returned home as a noncommissioned officer of Company B. The leading headline of the May 6, 1919, edition of the *Topeka Daily Capital* proclaimed "Thousands of Yank Heroes Given Royal Welcome Here; Troops Parade Thru Out Day." The newspaper also included the following story: "A few years ago some New York orphans came out to Kansas. One boy was given a home in a family of a well-to-do farmer near Oskaloosa. Yesterday when the 139th infantry was forming for the march back to the train from the state house grounds 100 people from Oskaloosa cheered the boy—Sergt. Billy Kimmel—as he whirled his platoon into line and marched away." Editor Frank Roberts of the *Oskaloosa Independent* brought the story to the attention of his readers, adding: "Billy is one example of 'young America' which shows the possibilities and opportunities in this land for young men without regard to ancestry, station or social position. . . . And the Oskaloosa people . . . were mighty proud of Sergeant Kimmel as he sang out 'By fours right—march!' Billy had 'made good.'"[5]

Louis Kimmel had relocated his family to Topeka during the war to start a meatpacking company, and William worked there briefly before taking a job with the Santa Fe Railroad. William married Emma Kragon in 1921, with whom he had two sons, one dying in infancy. First Sergeant Kimmel stayed with Kansas National Guard, became a captain, and served during World War II, ending up with the Army Air Corps in the Pacific theater. After the war Major Kimmel returned to Kansas and attended the 1955 Company B reunion in Oskaloosa, where he was chosen to say a prayer in memory of "our departed comrades." That same year he received a job promotion and was transferred to Colorado Springs, Colorado. He retired in 1966. In 1967 his son, Lieutenant Colonel Robert G. Kimmel, died in a helicopter crash in Vietnam. Colonel Kimmel, who left behind a wife and three children, was a former Kansas State student, West Point graduate, and recipient of a Bronze Star in the Korean War. He was posthumously awarded the Silver Star for "extraordinary heroism and exemplary devotion to duty," having survived a helicopter crash earlier in the day only to return to the air to direct the battalion he commanded.[6]

William and his wife made several trips to New York, where they met his biological mother and saw where he and his sister Anna grew up. He visited Anna in Topeka from time to time and developed a close relationship with her children after she died. He also stayed in touch with his second family, describing Margaret Kimmel as "a fine mother." William James (Potthoff) Kimmel died in 1987 at age ninety in Colorado; his wife, Emma, passed away in 1991. "He was a good man," says Geoffrey Kimmel, "and he and his wife raised a great son, my father."[7]

Photo 25.2: Robert, Emma, and William Kimmel (left to right), 1952. Courtesy of Geoffrey Kimmel.

* * *

Theodore "Ted" Blevins narrowly escaped death on the battlefield, but his twenty-year-old cousin, William "Ed" Blevins, was not as fortunate, dying instantly on September 28, 1918, after being struck by shrapnel. Ed's younger brother, Fred Blevins (1899–1971), left high school to enlist and served in France in an antiaircraft battalion. Their older brother, Beeler Blevins, served stateside as an instructor in an army flying school. Beeler moved in 1921 to Atlanta, Georgia, and was the first pilot to land an airplane on Candler Field, a converted raceway that would become Hartsfield-Jackson Atlanta International Airport. The Blevins airplane hangar was only slighter smaller than the airport terminal at the time. When Beeler died in an automobile accident in 1934, the *Atlanta Constitution* called him the "dean of aviation in Atlanta and guiding spirit in the development of Candler field."[8]

On October 10, 1918, Captain Smith of Company B recommended that First Sergeant Theodore R. Blevins be promoted to a commissioned grade.

Lieutenant Colonel Carl Ristine approved the recommendation but noted that the 139th Regiment had no room for another officer. Ted left Company B to attend officer training school at La Valbonne (near Lyon) but decided after the armistice to turn down a commission: he needed to work in the summer to attend college and "didn't want to be tied up to summer army camps." He returned to Company B at Vignot, France, and was recommended in March for the Distinguished Service Cross. "I don't think I will ever get the D.S.C.," he informed his parents, "as the recommendation went astray and didn't get to Hdqrs. in time." The prediction proved to be correct, although Blevins was eventually honored for his heroism.[9]

In the fall of 1919, Ted Blevins enrolled at Washburn College in Topeka and played football, where the "husky Oskaloosa lad with aggressive actions" earned honors as an offensive guard and captained the 1923 football team (but lost games in 1922 and 1923 to Ralph Nichols and Kansas State). After graduating with a degree as well as athletic letters in football, basketball, and track, Blevins became the athletic director at Atchison High School. He married Margaret Seaton, who was also a teacher and a Washburn graduate, and in 1925 the couple moved to Fort Collins, Colorado, where they would remain for the rest of their lives. In 1926, when asked by a student reporter from the high school newspaper about his most thrilling experience in France, Blevins provided a surprising answer:

> I was resting with three others in a sea of mud, thinking what a fool I had been to become a "fighting man," when I heard my name called. It was my captain and the substance of his message was for me to collect as many of the boys as possible, as he had heard a rumor that some rations had been unloaded a few miles back and that we might be able to keep some of them from spoiling. We started out, supposedly in the right direction. The night was as dark as, yes even darker than, the blackest ink. We had traveled probably two miles when we were commanded to "halt." We halted all right but not until a good half mile was between us and that voice, as the language was German.
>
> This time we got our bearings and arrived at the ration dump without further mishap. Needless to say, pork and beans and bread disappeared as if by magic. But the thrilling part was yet to come. As we were loading ourselves with bread for our buddies, imagine my surprise when rummaging through cans of pork and beans, I found one quite a bit smaller than the others. A hurried examination showed my find to be a can of good, old-fashioned strawberry jam made in U.S.A. The next five minutes

Photo 25.3: Theodore and Jesse Blevins, 1958. Courtesy of Scott Pattee.

I count not only as one of the most thrilling but most pleasant experiences of my career.

When the Blevins's youngest child was ten, Martha agreed to "help out" the Mathematics Department at Colorado State University, retiring twenty-three years later in 1965 as an assistant professor. Ted—he went by "T. R." and "Coach Blevins" after college—taught in public schools in Fort Collins for fifty years. While coaching and teaching at Fort Collins High School from 1925 to 1940, he compiled an outstanding 319-44 record and led the Lambkins to eight conference titles, advancing four times to the state tournament semifinals and four times to the championship game. Blevins also served as an assistant track coach when the Lambkins won three national track championships.[10]

T. R. Blevins moved to a junior-high-school position in 1940, where he taught math classes until 1965. He also was active in summer recreational sports in Fort Collins, served as the head judge at Colorado State track meets, earned a master's degree in administration and counseling, and was a church elder, a Little League commissioner, and an assistant Boy Scout leader. In 1968, three years after his retirement, his family gathered for the dedication of the Blevins Junior High School in Fort Collins. The following year Blevins was named to the hall of fame of the Colorado High School Coaches Association, and in 1973 he received a distinguished service award from the Washburn Alumni Association. Margaret and T. R. also celebrated their fiftieth wedding anniversary that year with their three children—all graduates of Colorado State University—and their families.[11]

Ted's older brother Jesse passed away in 1969, and Margaret tragically died six years later when Ted's car went off the road and crashed. T. R. continued to serve as a substitute teacher until he was eighty years old, passing away in 1989 at age ninety-one. "He was always so friendly," recalled a colleague, "and did so much for the kids." Ted was survived by his brother, Frank Blevins; his three children, Lois Austin, Ted Blevins Jr., and Kathleen Pattee; and eleven grandchildren. "I don't know of any teacher," remarked a former school superintendent, "that had more compliments over the years than Ted, from students, from parents, from teachers." Frank Faucett, a former coach at Fort Collins High School, said simply but profoundly, "He'll be missed." Theodore Roosevelt Blevins is buried next to his wife, Margaret, at Grandview Cemetery in Fort Collins, Colorado.[12]

* * *

The youngest of these Jefferson County guardsmen—Melvin Dyson—also lived the longest. Dyson's parents divorced soon after their Oskaloosa home was destroyed by fire in 1906, and his father's second marriage ended at some point after 1910, when eleven-year-old—called "Frosty"—went missing in Texas. He and his father, Marion Dyson, reunited and returned to Jefferson County, where they lived with Marion's sister and her family. When Melvin came home from the war, he once again stayed with his aunt's family. His father, who lived nearby, married a third time in February 1921 but was sued for divorce in July and left for California. Melvin followed him to Los Angeles and remained there after Marion died. By 1926, Dyson was in northern California working as a rigging employee. According to the *Siskiyou County Daily News*, he escaped serious injury when he was caught in a cable and thrown a distance of fifty feet. The former prisoner of war "landed on his feet" (once again); although badly bruised, he suffered no broken bones.[13]

Dyson moved to Grants Pass, Oregon, and married Flora Gillott in 1930. He was employed in 1940 as a gas-station manager but in 1942 moved to

Photo 25.4: Melvin Dyson, 1995. Courtesy of the National Park Service, Andersonville National Historical Site, ANDE OH 642.

Portland, where he worked for a company that dismantled ships to produce scrap steel. Dyson retired in 1970 but worked at a golf course, attending the Sunnyside Centenary United Methodist Church. Melvin and Flora Dyson in 1979 received the sad news that their only child, Shirley Dyson Willis, died from injuries suffered in an automobile accident. She had served during the Korean War as a corporal in the Women's Army Corps.[14]

Throughout his life, Dyson was a member of the Veterans of Foreign Wars and an active participant in organizations and gatherings for war prisoners. In 1984, when asked at a Seattle convention to comment on his experience, he said he was not treated as badly as some prisoners: "There wasn't anything to eat, but I didn't suffer mentally and physically like some." In 1986 he attended a meeting of the American Ex-Prisoners of War Association in Arlington, Texas, and in 1990 he was honored, along with eleven younger ex–prisoners of war from Oregon, at the American Legion post in Salem. In November 1995, seventy-seven years after the armistice, Dyson was interviewed by staff members of the National Prisoner of War Museum in Andersonville, Georgia. In the twenty-minute interview—C-Span television network broadcast it on May 14, 2003—Dyson recalled his capture: "I had a sneaking hunch," he said, "that we were going too fast, that we were getting . . . behind the German lines which turned out to be that way. But there was nothing you could do. I was a buck private, I was following orders and so forth and so on." After describing his subsequent imprisonment,

Photo 25.5: Albert "Jud" Wagner. Courtesy of Joel and Robert Wagner.

Dyson recounted how he "came out through Switzerland" to freedom and food: "We got fed a big meal in a depot put on by the American Red Cross. That was really something because . . . we didn't have that much to eat, the Germans didn't have it either. But that was the tops, yep."[15]

Melvin "Frosty" Dyson passed away two months after the interview. The ninety-six-year-old veteran is described in his obituary as "Oregon's last known surviving prisoner of World War I." He is buried at Willamette National Cemetery with his daughter, Shirley, and his wife, Flora, who passed away in 2001 at the age of ninety-four.

* * *

The last surviving American soldier of World War I was Frank Buckles, who was born in Missouri and died in West Virginia in 2011 at the age of 110. The last Kansas doughboy was Corporal Albert "Jud" Wagner, who was born two months after Melvin Dyson—September 5, 1899—and died on January 20, 2007, at the age of 107. Wagner's father was born in Berlin, and three uncles fought for Germany, which prompted the following headline in the *Topeka Daily Capital*: "His Relatives Are Huns—So Young Kansan Is Out After Them with a Gun." After seeing action at Belleau Wood with the Sixth Marine Regiment, Wagner lived many years in Smith Center, Kansas. By the end of his life, he was an annual guest of honor in the Veterans Day Parade in nearby Kensington, riding in a 1966 Mustang owned by Wanda Gibson, an employee at his long-term-care center. "In his late 90s, he'd throw candy from the Mustang," said Gibson. "As he got older, he'd like to eat it instead."[16]

Conclusion

Kansans came together after November 1918 to rejoice, to grieve, and to pay tribute to the men and women who served in the Great War. People cheered at homecoming parades, and veterans joined organizations such as the Veterans of Foreign Wars and the newly formed American Legion. Family members requested the return of loved ones for reburial, and Gold Star Mothers traveled to France to visit cemeteries. At the same time, communities across the state began to raise funds to create permanent tributes. Steven Trout has written about "the more than fifty World War I monuments (statues, victory arches, obelisks, and so forth) that survive in Kansas communities." James J. Heiman has documented the doughboy monuments and memorials of Kansas City (in both Kansas and Missouri). Robbie Jane Thomas created the American Memorials Directory website, which endeavors to list all of the monuments and memorials "that honor the Fallen" in the United States. The site catalogues over seven hundred entries for Kansas, including World War I memorials, monuments, statues, markers, plaques, buildings, arches, cemeteries, pavilions, armories, benches, flag poles, two bridges (in Independence and Neodosha), and a clock tower (in Columbus). Millions of motorists have traveled on the portion of Interstate 35 that crosses Kansas, which in 1963 was designated the 35th Infantry Division Memorial Highway. The most unusual location for a memorial may be the Ol' Glory Car Wash in Frontenac, which includes a large American flag displayed in front of a red, white, and blue building. Near the flag is a plaque donated by the John F. Derby Post of the American Legion, named for a local resident who was killed during the Meuse-Argonne offensive.[1]

According to official records, 589 communities in Kansas experienced a death of a resident in military service during the First World War. Seven of them lost thirty or more soldiers: Wichita (69), Kansas City (68), Topeka (58), Hutchinson (32), Leavenworth (31), Pittsburg (31), and Lawrence (30). Of the 40 communities that lost ten or more men, 3 of them lost more than

1 percent of their 1910 population: Lyndon (10 of 763, or 1.311 percent), Oskaloosa (11 of 851, or 1.293 percent), and Augusta (13 of 1,235, or 1.053 percent). Statues, arches, monuments, memorial halls, school buildings, stadiums, and museums stand today as tributes to the role played by Kansas and Kansans in World War I. In addition to these reminders of the Great War, recent commemorative activities include the creation of the Kansas World War I Centennial Committee, the induction of Dr. James Naismith and Captain William Smith into the Kansas National Guard Hall of Fame, ceremonies at Kansas State University and the University of Kansas, and statewide events celebrating the centennial of the armistice.[2]

According to Steven Trout, there are seven "stone or bronze doughboys that still brave Kansas weather each year." In addition to a limestone infantryman in Wilson created by an unknown sculptor, statues by Ernest M. Viquesney are displayed in Axtell, Oakley, and Parsons, while statues by John Paulding are located in Leavenworth, Olathe, and Onaga. The *American Doughboy* statues by Paulding and the statue in Wilson show a vigilant soldier standing with his rifle at his side and his eyes fixed on the horizon. Viquesney's *The Spirit of the American Doughboy* and Paulding's *Over the Top* sculptures depict a soldier moving forward, with his left arm holding a rifle and his right arm raised in the air.[3]

On May 4, 1923, the Oakley Marble and Granite Company installed the *Spirit of the American Doughboy* in the city park on Second Street. The *Oakley Graphic* described the statute, purchased at a cost of $1,500, as "surely worth the money" and "a wonderful piece of work" that "certainly teaches a lesson in Americanism." Two years later a similar dedication in Axtell took place on Memorial Day, 1925. That town, located near the Nebraska border in Marshall County, had fewer than eight hundred residents during the war, but approximately 150 men and two women served in 1917–1918. Nineteen families contributed more than one member, and four residents—Ray Creevan, Ray Hendricks, Arthur Nelson, and Arthur Ross—did not return. The local American Legion post is named for Corporal Hendricks, who helped the Thirty-Eighth Regiment become the "Rock of the Marne." Writing about the famous battle, Hendricks told his family that "a shell dropped about two feet from my right, exploded and knocked the cigar out of my mouth; my right foot slipped in the hole, but I never got a scratch." His luck, however, ran out on October 9, when he was killed in action. The doughboy statue and accompanying plaque were purchased at a cost of $1,850, with one $150 coming from the town treasury and the rest raised by public subscriptions.

Photo 26.1: World War I statue, *Over the Top*, in Oakley, Kansas. Courtesy of Oakley Area Tourism.

Each year the Axtell American Legion begins its Memorial Day services at the statue, located at the intersection of Fifth and Maple Streets.[4]

The statue in Parsons, a town in southeastern Kansas, was dedicated five years later, on November 11, 1930. As described in the local newspaper, the event was both solemn and festive:

> Close to 1,000 persons gathered on the Municipal lawn. Church bells began tolling at 10:55 o'clock and at 11 o'clock they ceased. . . . Then U. S. Wells, bugler, sounded taps and men stood with bowed heads and traffic and other activities all over the city were stopped by Boy Scouts for a moment of silent tribute to the war dead. A short concert then was given. . . . The Rev. B. J. McKernan of St. Patrick's church offered invocation and then

Photo 26.2: Wichita Victory Arch, 1919. Courtesy of the Wichita–Sedgwick County Historical Museum.

> Mr. Armstrong gave the address. That was followed by benediction said by the Rev. T. W. Perks of the United Brethren church, a volley salute by the firing squad, taps and the raising of the flag from half to full mast. An aerial bomb was shot into the air and an American flag floated down on a tiny parachute.[5]

In addition to statues, there are several memorial arches and monuments in Kansas. On May 16, 1919, the city of Wichita dedicated its Victory Arch, which spanned Douglas Street at North Broadway. "Joy reigned supreme," reported the *Beacon*, and residents "jazzed over town, up one avenue and down another." The elation, however, was short lived. The arch was built in such a manner that people had to step into the busy street to walk under it, and in January 1920 a petition was presented to the city to remove the structure because "it is a peril to life and obstructs traffic." Plans to relocate the arch to Riverside Park proved impractical. Wichita officials admitted defeat in August 1920 and dismantled the Victory Arch.

A more enduring World War I arch is found on the campus of St. Mary's College in the town of St. Marys, about twenty-five miles northwest of Topeka. The freestanding structure was dedicated during the diamond-jubilee celebration of the college in 1923, attended by Kansas governor

Photo 26.3: Memorial Arch, St. Mary's Academy and College. Courtesy of St. Mary's Academy and College.

Jonathan M. Davis. The memorial honors nineteen alumni who gave their lives during the war, including Lieutenant William T. Fitzsimons, the first American officer to die in France. The college, which was founded along the Oregon Trail in order to serve as a mission, was one of the schools of higher education in Kansas that instructed soldiers in the Student Army Training Corps. The *Catholic Advance*, a Wichita newspaper, lauded the school as a bulwark against bigotry and "Ku Klux Klanism," declaring that its Memorial Arch "will be, in a sense, a protest against this un-American spirit." To mark the centennial of the arch's dedication, St. Mary's College in 2023 launched a fundraising project—Bringing the Honor of Sacrifice Back to Life—to rebuild the deteriorating structure according to its original design. The project intends to make the Memorial Arch more accessible in order to reconnect visitors and the community to the story of sacrifice by its alumni.[6]

In October 1926 the Haskell Institute's football stadium and adjacent memorial arch were dedicated during a weekend celebration that included a kicking exhibition by Olympian Jim Thorpe and speeches by Hubert Work, the secretary of the interior, and Kansas senator Charles Curtis, a member of the Kaw Tribe. The stadium was rededicated in 2001 with a plaque "in honor of the 415 'Haskell Warriors' that served in World War I and in

Photo 26.4: 1926 dedication of the Haskell Institute Stadium Arch, Lawrence, Kansas. Courtesy of the Duke D'Ambra Photograph Collection, Kenneth Spencer Research Library, University of Kansas.

memory of those 'Warriors' who made the supreme sacrifice for their country." In connection with the 2018 armistice centennial, the Haskell Cultural Center and Museum and the City of Lawrence hosted an event—Keeping Legends Alive—to "commemorate the WWI Memorial and honor all those who served in the military as well as the history, legends, and stories the community has of enjoying the Haskell Stadium throughout the decades."

Numerous volunteers from Rosedale served in the 117th Ammunition Train of the Forty-Second (Rainbow) Division. The Rosedale World War I Memorial Arch is located in Mount Marty Park, now part of Kansas City, Kansas. It was designed by a local resident, John Marshall, who had studied architecture at the University of Kansas in 1912. While in Paris during the war, Private Marshall sketched the Arc de Triomphe and used it as a model. After years of neglect, a new access road was built in 1962, and the Memorial Arch was rededicated to veterans of all wars. Additional changes were made in 1972, when a plaza with benches, lighting, and walkways was constructed to provide a place to reflect and view the Kansas City skyline.

Photo 26.5: Rosedale World War I Memorial Arch, Kansas City, Kansas. Courtesy of the Library of Congress.

Mount Marty Park is approximately six miles southwest of the Liberty Memorial Tower, located in Penn Valley Park in Kansas City, Missouri. Suzanne Hogan notes that there were many memorials in the planning stage after the war, but "what made Kansas City's monument unique was the quick, community-driven financing and the scope of the design." Civic leaders raised $2.5 million in ten days for the monument, and a local haberdasher—thirty-seven-year-old Harry S. Truman of the Thirty-Fifth Division—presented flags to General John Pershing, Marshal Ferdinand Foch, and other Allied commanders at the 1921 groundbreaking ceremony. "When Kansas City does anything," said a visiting legionnaire, "you can bet on its being done right."[7]

On November 11, 1926, President Coolidge told the assembled crowd, "the magnitude of this Memorial, and the broad base of popular support on which it rests, can scarcely fail to excite national wonder and admiration." The 217-foot-tall tower is situated between two stone sphinxes, one facing east and hiding its face from the horrors of the past, the other facing west, with its eyes shielded from an unknown and uncertain future. The tower is also flanked by Exhibition Hall, which originally served as a museum, and Memory Hall, which houses bronze tablets listing the 440 men and one woman from Kansas City who died in the Great War. That lone woman was

Photo 26.6: Liberty Memorial Tower, Kansas City, Missouri. Courtesy of the Library of Congress.

Lottie Ruth Hollenback (not "Loretto" Hollenback as inscribed), who grew up in Kansas, became a nurse, and was stricken with influenza at Fort Riley.[8]

* * *

Another form of war remembrance is the construction of memorial buildings. In addition to the more than three hundred American Legion halls in Kansas, there are dozens of halls, auditoriums, and schools in the Sunflower State that also provide functional forms of commemoration. Steven Trout has described six memorial buildings that continue to serve the communities of Atchison, Independence, Kansas City, Ottawa, Salina, and Wellington. The largest is the Soldiers and Sailors Memorial Auditorium in Kansas City, Kansas, located on North Seventh Street—just south of where members of the 353rd Infantry danced with "a host of Kansas girls" during their homecoming celebration. The building, which opened in 1925, briefly served as the national headquarters for the Veterans of Foreign Wars. According to the nomination form for its inclusion in the National Register of Historic Places, the Memorial Hall space within the building functions as a memorial and a lobby. In the arches that adorn the hall are "two large bronze plaques enframed with Carthage marble, giving the names of the honored dead." The building has retained most of its original features, but its use has evolved over time. In addition to commemorative events, the site has hosted professional wrestling, roller derbies, and music concerts, including Patsy Cline's final performance on March 3, 1963, two days before her death in an airplane crash.[9]

Liberty Memorial High School in Lawrence was dedicated in 1923 after students convinced voters in April 1919 to approve construction bonds. Students held a "whiz bang" (circus) to defray the expenses of their campaign and emulated the Four Minute Men by giving short speeches between the acts of the senior-class play. The public was invited to view the crowded conditions of the existing high school, where posters were displayed that read "Give Us Room to Breathe and Room to Grow" and "Things Go Wrong When We're All in a Throng." The climax of their fundraising efforts came on March 27, when 2,200 children paraded down Massachusetts Street. The procession featured an eight-year-old "Uncle Sam" riding a Shetland pony and a living American flag formed by grade-school children. The parade marshal was nineteen-year-old Mahlon Weed, who managed to fight in France and return in time to graduate with his class. Sergeant Weed of the 137th (All Kansas) Regiment was struck on September 29, 1918, by shell fragments that penetrated his left leg and damaged his right hand, taking off the tips of two fingers and part of the thumb. He came home in January 1919 and resumed his schooling. After he graduated, Sergeant Weed returned to the military and became Brigadier General Weed, serving in World War II and in Korea. His namesake son, Colonel Mahlon Weed, served in Korea and Vietnam. They are both buried at the Fort Leavenworth National Cemetery.

Of the 300 or so young men from Lawrence who fought in the war, 144 had not yet graduated from high school. Six high school girls became nurses, and two of them did not return. The Liberty Memorial High School was dedicated on August 27, 1923. Above the auditorium stage are words from a poem by Rudyard Kipling describing King George V's 1922 visit to British cemeteries in France. One of the graduating classes donated eighteen stained-glass windows made in Belgium. Over time the building became a junior high school and is presently Liberty Memorial Central Middle School, home of the Mustangs.[10]

One immediate consequence of the war was that the Washburn graduating class of 1919 consisted of fifty-five women and just eleven men. As part of the commencement activities, Verna Womer, wife of college president Parly Womer, placed a spade in the ground to begin the construction of a building to honor "the deeds of the sons of Ichabod in 1917 and 1918." Although initially referred to as Memorial Dormitory, the residence hall was called Benton Hall when it was formally opened in 1923. The building was originally a women's dormitory. It survived the 1996 Topeka tornado and now houses the School of Applied Studies and Academic Outreach. Veterans of the Great War are also commemorated at the Washburn University Memorial Union, dedicated in February 1952 to honor "all Shawnee County residents, including Washburn students, who lost their lives in World War I, World War II and the Korean War." A bronze plaque in the McVicar Room lists the Shawnee County residents who died in World War I (144 names), World War II (469 names), and the Korean War (21 names). A functional memorial—a bench near Benton Hall—honors Louis Lloyd Larrick, a 1916 Washburn graduate from Lenora who succumbed to influenza and pneumonia at the Great Lakes Naval Training Station. Larrick was a three-sport athlete, a member of Phi Delta Theta fraternity, and the class president his senior year in the School of Law.[11]

The 1923 Kansas State yearbook is dedicated to forty-eight Aggies who died in service during the World War. To honor their memory, the university paid tribute to "those who . . . died in our stead, pouring the blood of Kansas on the fields of France." Acknowledgement of "the Fallen 48" was not limited to the 1923 *Royal Purple*. School officials decided that a stadium would be a fitting tribute, and the campaign kicked off on April 25, 1922, when students gathered in the college auditorium:

> Dr. H. H. King spoke. He spoke tersely but eloquently of the Aggie men who "paid the last full measure of devotion," and of the opportunity now to commemorate forever their deeds. Mike Ahearn forgot his fund of Irish jokes as he explained simply and earnestly how much the stadium is going to mean to K.S.A.C. in every way. Charles Bachman, who has coached the football team through the two most successful seasons it has known, came to the front of the stage and while he paced back and forth like a restless panther his words hurtled forth, flashing through the auditorium, and burning into the students' consciousness the fact that the stadium must be built.[12]

Memorial Stadium was the first World War I memorial on campus, with plaques commemorating deceased veterans located on the south end of the stadium. (Five of the forty-eight listed men have been mentioned in this book: Willis Comfort, Clede Keller, Willis Pearce, Eddie Wells, and George Wingate.) The first game held at the new stadium took place on October 6,

Photo 26.7: Kansas State Memorial Stadium, 1928. Courtesy of the Morse Department of Special Collectionsm, Kansas State University Libraries.

1922, with only the west wing in place. Ralph Nichols and Kansas State were victorious over Ted Blevins and Washburn, and the Aggies finished the season without a loss at home, defeating Iowa State and Texas Christian University and tying the Kansas Jayhawks. According to the *Manhattan Mercury*, the 7–7 homecoming game "was a victory for the Aggies in that it was a step closer to victory than the old order of score for the past 12 to 15 years which had almost invariably resulted in victories for K.U." Memorial Stadium served until 1967 as the home field for Kansas State football players. It is still used for lacrosse, rugby, and soccer, and as a practice field for the "Pride of the Wildcat Land," the K-State Marching Band.[13]

The David Booth Kansas Memorial Stadium, the seventh-oldest collegiate stadium in the nation, honors those who served in World War I. Kansas University history professor John H. McCool explains that the idea for a memorial stadium and athletic field was approved in April 1919 and endorsed by two KU legends: Dr. James Naismith told alumni they must support the project with "financial as well as moral support," and Director of Athletics Dr. Forrest C. "Phog" Allen exclaimed, "Rome had her Coliseum. Kansas must have a stadium!" As eloquently described by McCool, "on the four-year anniversary of when the guns fell silent in Europe, nearly 18,000 people packed the KU Memorial Stadium on Armistice Day, November 11, 1922, and fell silent themselves, if only briefly, to witness the stadium's formal dedication and the University's salute to the honored dead." Although

Photo 26.8: Kansas University Memorial Stadium, circa 1929. Courtesy of the Kenneth Spencer Research Library, University of Kansas.

the Jayhawks went down in defeat to the Nebraska Cornhuskers, the home team had prevailed in the first game played in the stadium the previous season, defeating Kansas State by the score of 21–7 on October 29, 1921.[14]

A few years later, on April 30, 1926, nearly three thousand people attended the ceremonial laying of the cornerstone of the Kansas Memorial Union. Sherman Grant Elliott, a politician and Kansas University law graduate, read the names of the 129 students and alumni who died during the Great War. "These 129 people paid the supreme price," Elliott declared. "We are endeavoring to show that we honor, love and claim them." Among the honored dead remembered then were William Fitzsimons, Jared Jackson, LaRue Kingsbury, and Lucy Catherine McLinden. Another person on the list, John Paul Slade of Clay Center, is also listed on the Kansas State memorial plaque. Slade attended Kansas State Agricultural College for two years, then went to Kansas University, where he studied electrical engineering before volunteering for service. He married Mildred Dyer in December 1917 just prior to departing for France. He died on September 17, 1918, succumbing to poison gas and pneumonia.[15]

As noted on the university's website, the "Grand Ballroom of the Kansas Union signified the official completion in 1934. The Union housed a cafeteria, ballroom, lounges, and the student activity office." Between 1947 and 1993, there were five major additions to the building, which now contains more than 250,000 square feet on six levels. The World War I memorial plaque is located on Level Four on the Jayhawk Walk.[16]

During and after the centennial of the armistice, the role of the Sunflower State in the Great War has been the subject of exhibits at museums and commemorative activities and events. The Kansas Museum of History in Topeka tells the story of the people of the state, including their role in World War I. In 1997 another museum in Topeka opened its doors: the Museum of the Kansas National Guard at the Forbes Field Air Force Base. The site is also the current home of the Kansas National Guard Hall of Fame, the Thirty-Fifth Division Museum, and the Thirty-Fifth Division Hall of Fame. Several World War I participants are in the Kansas National Guard Hall of Fame, including Erwin Bleckley, Frederick Funston, Perry Hoisington, Charles Martin, Wilder Metcalf, and Mahlon Weed. In 2019 James Naismith was inducted as a captain and chaplain of the First Kansas Infantry Regiment. Joining Naismith was Captain William A. Smith of Company B, 139th Regiment. After describing his heroics during the Meuse-Argonne offensive, the induction citation describes Smith's long and distinguished legal career, culminating in his appointment as the Chief Justice of the Supreme Court of Kansas.[17]

Although located across the state line in Missouri, the National WWI Museum and Memorial deserves mention. When the Liberty Memorial Tower was closed in 1994, the citizens of Kansas City agreed to a tax measure that would finance its restoration. At the same time, plans took shape to build a museum to showcase World War I artifacts and documents. Congress in 2004 designated the National WWI Museum and Memorial as the nation's official World War I museum, and in 2006 the Liberty Memorial was designated a National Historic Landmark. The museum and memorial, along with the Edward Jones Research Center, is home to one of the largest Great War collections in the world. The permanent exhibition includes original objects and documents, interactive maps, and recreated trenches, while temporary exhibits are frequently housed in Memory Hall and Exhibit Hall, the two buildings that flank the Liberty Memorial Tower. Among the museum's immense collection are documents donated by the family of Private William Davis, including letters, pictures, information about his death, and correspondence with the American Red Cross, the Kansas Compensation Board, the Bureau of War Risk Insurance, and the A.E.F. Graves Registration Service.[18]

Kansas has played a leading role in honoring men and women for their military service. During the presidency of Dwight D. Eisenhower (of Abilene), Congress heeded the suggestion of a shoe sales clerk from Emporia and changed Armistice Day to Veterans Day. The contribution of Alvin Jesse King is acknowledged in a 2003 concurrent resolution of the U.S. House of Representatives, which

> (1) encourages Americans to demonstrate their support for veterans on Veterans Day by treating that day as a special day of remembrance; (2) declares Emporia, Kansas, to be the founding city of Veterans Day; (3) recognizes Alvin J. King, of Emporia, Kansas, as the founder of Veterans Day; and (4) recognizes that Representative Ed Rees, of Emporia, Kansas, was instrumental in the efforts to enact into law the observance of Veterans Day.

When King—his stepson was killed in World War II—suggested that Armistice Day honor all veterans, the citizens of Emporia sent him and his wife to Washington, DC, where Representative Edward H. Rees transformed the notion into a bill. The legislation passed, and President Eisenhower signed the bill into law on June 1, 1954, in a White House ceremony attended by King, Rees, VFW commanders Wayne Richards (Arkansas City) and Richard Trombla (El Dorado), and American Legion commander John Nation of Chanute. According to King, he almost missed the event due to an untimely digestive mishap, but a "bottle of citrate of magnesia put my stomach back in order again in time to sit in when President Eisenhower affixed his name to the bill." Because of King's initiative, Emporia holds an annual multiday celebration, and part of the current school curriculum is to have students participate in a Veterans Day essay and poster contest.[19]

Starting in 2015, Kansans began to reflect on the meaning and legacy of the Great War and to focus on the upcoming armistice centenary. The Kansas World War I Centennial Committee was formed and—under the leadership of Mary Madden, director of the Kansas Museum of History—created a website providing a treasure trove of stories, documents, and photographs. In 2017, at the instigation of Kansas State alumni Jed Dunham, relatives of the "Fallen 48" were invited to a ceremony to rectify the fact that the official dedication of Memorial Stadium had never taken place. In 2018, in the months and days leading up to November 11, Kansans joined with citizens across the United States in commemorative activities and events. The Lyon County History Center in Emporia displayed World War I artifacts, including goblets crafted from artillery shells, a Victory Liberty Loan banner, and a panoramic photograph of Camp Funston. Residents of Lawrence gathered in the historic Memorial High School auditorium to hear middle school and high school choirs perform songs about the Great War. The students sang a choral rendition of the last stanza of "The King's Pilgrimage" by Rudyard Kipling, the words of which are set in stone above the stage. The poem pays homage to Allied soldiers—"All that they had they gave"—and commemorates King George V's visit in May 1922 to military cemeteries in France.[20]

In the nine days leading up to the armistice anniversary, the National WWI Museum and Memorial in Kansas City used a massive and moving light show to project war images and red poppies onto the memorial buildings and tower. On November 9, 2018, the student council in Axtell treated veterans to cookies, drinks, and a program, while Captain Lucas Osborn of the Thirty-Fifth Infantry Division was a guest speaker at Oskaloosa High School. Another member of the Thirty-Fifth Division, Major General Vic Braden, was the grand marshal on November 10 for the Sunflower Salute Veterans Parade in downtown Topeka. The actual anniversary of the armistice fell on Sunday, and churches tolled bells at the eleventh hour in remembrance of those who served and sacrificed. In Wichita the symphony orchestra played *The War Requiem* by Benjamin Britten, while in Manhattan a musical program entitled Voices on the Western Front was performed by faculty pianist Amanda Arrington and Bryan Pinkall, Grammy-winning soloist and Kansas State professor of music. In the small town of Ellinwood, citizens rang church bells and a fire bell, looked at binders with information about the sixty-five local men who were in the Great War, listened to a presentation at the American Legion, and then enjoyed a buffet dinner while listening to a selection of period songs. Similar events took place across Kansas, both on Sunday and on Monday, the federal holiday. For example, Emporia citizens braved chilly weather to view a parade that featured the high school and Emporia State University marching bands. Veterans Day in Manhattan likewise began with a parade in the morning, followed by a commemorative program at Peace Memorial Auditorium and a banquet at the Willis Pearce–Clede Keller American Legion Post.[21]

The armistice centennial has fueled a continuing interest in World War I. On November 11, 2019, the University of Kansas rededicated the Memorial Union and engraved 129 stars in the newly constructed arch canopy to honor the Jayhawk men and women who died while serving in the war. In addition to the stars, which are illuminated nightly, there is a bronze plaque outside the main entrance that reads, "In honor of the 129 WWI Fallen Jayhawks." After the ceremony, attendees were offered hot chocolate and cookies with frosting in the shape of red poppies. "It's something we wanted to bring to the forefront with the current generation of students on campus," said university employee Kara Stucky. "The archway is a symbolic place to remember that this is truly part of our history."[22]

* * *

Over one hundred years ago, in March 1919, Ted Blevins and Company B were still in France, stationed in the village of Vignot, some thirty miles south of Verdun. "The boys are sort of downhearted these days," he wrote to his parents. "Bill Smith went off to a law school yesterday and a Lieutenant is in command of the outfit." The man placed in charge of the company was Burr Davison of Montana, who had previously served in the Forty-First Division. Lieutenant Davison, on March 27, sent a memorandum to the commanding officer of the Thirty-Fifth Division recommending "1st Sgt. Theodore R. Blevins of Co. B 139th Infantry for [the] Distinguished Service Cross." The memorandum was copied from Captain Smith's letter, written in October 1918, recommending that Blevins receive an officer's commission. Smith had praised Blevins for his "fearlessness under fire and his leadership ability" during the September 28 attack on Montrebeau Wood.

Once again, however, the timing was not fortuitous: Company B was on its way home when Davison submitted his memorandum. Writing from Le Mans on March 28, 1919, Ted said, "the latest dope is that we sail soon after the 1st of April." He added, "I don't think I will ever get the D.S.C. as the recommendation went astray and didn't get to Hdqrs. in time." There is no indication that any action was taken on Lieutenant Davison's recommendation, and the sergeant came home without a medal.

Blevins never mentioned the nomination to his children, but his youngest child, Kathleen Pattee, found it nearly nine decades later and brought it to the attention of Senator Charles Grassley of Iowa. On June 10, 2005, Ted Blevins was posthumously awarded the Silver Star, the army's third-highest military decoration for valor in combat. The certificate, signed by Army Secretary Francis J. Harvey and Adjutant General Ernest E. Porter, states, "the President of the United States of America, authorized by Act of Congress July 9, 1918, has awarded THE SILVER STAR to (Then) First Sergeant Theodore R. Blevins United States Army for Gallantry in Action on 28 September 1918 in France."

Blevins Park is located on the west side of Fort Collins, Colorado, next to Blevins Middle School, which was formerly Blevins Junior High School. On January 17, 2006, students and Poudre School District employees packed

Photo 26.9: Blevins Park, Fort Collins, Colorado. Courtesy of Joseph Zappa.

Photo 26.10: Blevins Middle School, Fort Collins, Colorado. Courtesy of Joseph Zappa.

into the gymnasium to celebrate the life and accomplishments of the late Theodore Roosevelt "T. R." Blevins. In an emotional ceremony the Blevins family presented his Silver Star to the school, which remains on permanent display. As reported in the *Fort Collins Coloradoan*, students researched his life and what it takes to earn a Silver Star. Ted Blevins Jr., speaking on behalf of the family, told the audience, "if my dad were alive today, he would be very proud of this school, of the administrators and the staff, and particularly of these students." Tom Lopez, one of his former students who became a school principal, said T. R. Blevins was "what we strive to be." A teacher, Dawn Lauterbach, agreed: "I just really think it is inspirational for students to be a part of his legacy. I think they'll remember this day."[23]

* * *

World War I is sometimes called the "Forgotten War." The purpose of this book is to remember and commemorate Ted Blevins, his comrades in Company B, and all Kansans who stepped forward, both overseas and at home. They are not forgotten.

Acknowledgments

I am very grateful to Kathleen Blevins Pattee, daughter of Theodore Blevins, who graciously shared letters written by her father and diaries kept by her uncle, Jesse Blevins. These contemporaneous accounts of the Great War are invaluable primary sources. Kathleen Pattee received a draft version of this book before she passed away in 2022. Peter and Scott Pattee, her husband and son, have continued to provide assistance.

I have corresponded with relatives of William Davis, Samuel Gutschenritter, William Kimmel, Victor Segraves, and Bill Smith, and I appreciate the information and photographs provided by Rita Davis, Debbie Freeman, Jane Hoskinson, Geoffrey Kimmel, Sarah Barr, and Don Smith. Ardie Grimes of the Jefferson County Historical Society was very helpful, and I relied on Connie DiPasquale's research to better understand William Kimmel's participation in the "orphan train" relocation program. Liz Leech, originally from Jefferson County, is the source of the information regarding James Henry Irwin. Christine Hoffmark-Coffey (Andersonville National Historical Site) produced a still image of Melvin Dyson from his video interview with the National Prisoners of War Museum.

With regard to Kansans outside of Jefferson County, I obtained images with the help of Elisabeth and Jane Archer, Jane Buessing, Kelly and Toni Holzman, Andy and Jeff May, Laurie Millensifer, Patrick Murtha, Julie Stevens, Bob, Joel, and Diane Wagner, and Joseph Zappa. In addition, other images were provided by Kristine Schmucker (Harvey County Historical Museum), Lisa Soller (Lyon County History Center), Sharleen Wurm (Decatur County Museum), Jami Frazier Tracy (Wichita-Sedgwick County Historical Museum), Anna Grahlherr (Kirksville, Missouri, Museum of Osteopathic Medicine), and the libraries at Kansas State University (Ryan Leimkuhler), Pittsburg State University (Sara DeCaro), and the University of Kansas (Letha Johnson and Kathy Lafferty). My daughter, Anna Beatty, presented me with my own copy of the 1920 Shawnee County Honor Roll, which contains a multitude of military photographs.

Professor Steven Trout of the University of Alabama has written extensively on the cultural representation of war in literature, visual art, and public monuments. He received his doctorate from the University of Kansas and is the author of "Forgotten Reminders: Kansas World War I Memorials," a 2006 article published in *Kansas History*. His 2010 book, *On the Battlefield of Memory: The First World War and American Remembrance, 1919–1941*, includes an insightful critique of a John Steuart Curry painting that portrays the 1921 burial of William Davis in Winchester, Kansas. I am indebted to Professor Trout for his groundbreaking scholarship and for the help he gave me in the writing of this book.

The Kansas Historical Society has a sizeable collection of online materials related to World War I, and the National WWI Museum and Memorial is also a rich source of information about Kansas doughboys. I want to thank Lisa Keys, Jonathan Casey, and Tracy Dennis for providing images and copies of documents.

Ryan O'Grady, the digital projects manager for the University of Dayton Roesch Library, was always responsive to my numerous requests and helped enhance the quality of many images in this book.

Working with the University Press of Kansas has been a pleasure. In particular, I appreciate the contributions of Kevin Brock, Kelly Chrisman Jacques, Joyce Harrison, and Alec Loganbill.

Finally, I want to thank my wife, Pam, for her love, her support, and all that she does for our family.

Notes

Preface

1. Stephen L. Harris, *Rock of the Marne: The American Soldiers Who Turned the Tide against the Kaiser in World War I* (New York: Berkley Caliber, 2015), xvi.

2. Vova Pomortzeff, All Quiet on the Western Front: How the Places of the Bloody Battles of the First World War Look Like One Hundred Years Later, https://vova.pomortzeff.com/westfront (accessed August 2, 2023).

3. *Oskaloosa Independent*, January 3, 1919, 3. All newspapers cited are from Kansas unless otherwise indicated.

4. Adjutant General, State of Kansas, *Kansas Casualties in the World War, 1917–1919* (Topeka: Kansas State Printing Plant, 1921–1925); Kimberly J. Lamay Licursi, *Remembering World War I in America* (Lincoln: University of Nebraska Press, 2018), xiii.

5. *Oskaloosa Independent*, July 19, 1918, 1; Espionage Act, Public Law 65-24, 40 Stat. 217 (June 15, 1917); Sedition Act, Public Law 65-150, 40 Stat. 553 (May 16, 1918).

6. Brian Dexter Fowles, *A Guard in Peace and War: The History of the Kansas National Guard, 1854–1987* (Manhattan, KS: Sunflower University Press, 1989); Roger D. Cunningham, *The Black Citizen-Soldiers of Kansas, 1864–1901* (Columbia: University of Missouri Press, 2008).

7. John Whiteclay Chambers, *To Raise an Army: The Draft Comes to Modern America* (New York: Free Press, 1987), 116.

8. Robert H. Ferrell, *Collapse at Meuse-Argonne: The Failure of the Missouri-Kansas Division* (Columbia: University of Missouri Press, 2004), 3; John Patrick Finnegan, *Against the Specter of a Dragon: The Campaign for American Military Preparedness* (Westport, CT: Greenwood, 1974), 56.

9. John S. D. Eisenhower, *Yanks: The Epic Story of the American Army in World War I* (New York: Simon & Schuster, 2001), 307.

10. Chambers, *To Raise an Army*, 73.

11. *Topeka Plaindealer*, November 30, 1917, 1; Emmett J. Scott, *Scott's Official History of the American Negro in the World War* (New York, 1919), 98.

12. *Topeka Daily Capital*, December 16, 1918, 2; *Kansas City Advocate*, August 23, 1918, 1.

13. Chad L. Williams, *Torchbearers of Democracy: African American Soldiers in the World War I Era* (Chapel Hill: University of North Carolina Press, 2010), 201.

14. Lauren Fox, "In Remembrance of Fallen Jayhawks, 129 Stars Added under Archway of Kansas Memorial Union," *Lawrence Journal-World*, November 11, 2019.

1. The President Comes to Topeka

1. *Topeka State Journal*, January 22, 1916, 1. All newspapers cited are from Kansas unless otherwise indicated.

2. *Topeka State Journal*, January 27, 1916, 1; August Heckscher, *Woodrow Wilson* (New York: Scribner, 1991), 376.

3. Bureau of the Census, Department of Commerce and Labor, *Thirteenth Census of the United States Taken in the Year 1910, Statistics for Kansas* (Washington, DC: Government Printing Office, 1913), 568–593, 625, 634, 681; Robert W. Richmond, *Kansas: A Land of Contrasts* (St. Charles, MO: Forum, 1974), 214–215; Craig H. Miner, *Kansas: The History of the Sunflower State, 1854–2000* (Lawrence: University Press of Kansas, 2002), 214–216; Raquel Ramsey and Tricia Aurand, *Taking Flight: The Nadine Ramsey Story* (Lawrence: University Press of Kansas, 2022), 11–12.

4. Miner, *Kansas*, 191–199; Richmond, *Kansas*, 213–219; Anna E. Arnold, *A History of Kansas* (Topeka: State of Kansas Printing Plant, 1914), 172, 235–236.

5. Miner, *Kansas*, 187, 216, 222; Arnold, *History of Kansas*, 131, 137–138.

6. *Topeka Daily Capital*, September 13, 1913, 7; Leon H. Canfield, *The Presidency of Woodrow Wilson: Prelude to a World in Crisis* (Rutherford, NJ: Fairleigh Dickinson University Press, 1966), 22–37, 77.

7. Julie Irene Prieto, *The Mexican Expedition, 1916–1917* (Washington, DC: Center of Military History, U.S. Army, 2016), 8–11; Canfield, *Presidency of Woodrow Wilson*, 43–47 (1966); *Hutchinson Gazette*, March 27, 1914, 5.

8. Eisenhower, *Yanks*, 3; Canfield, *Presidency of Woodrow Wilson*, 59–60; Arthur Stanley Link, ed., *The Papers of Woodrow Wilson*, 69 vols. (Princeton, NJ: Princeton University Press, 1966–1994), 31:422; *Kansas City (MO) Star*, June 27, 1915, 1; *Kansas City (MO) Times*, November 30, 1973, 44.

9. *Topeka Daily Capital*, October 16, 1915, 1; Finnegan, *Against the Specter of a Dragon*, 53–54; Link, *Papers of Woodrow Wilson*, 35:299; *New York Times*, November 5, 1915, 1.

10. *Pittsburg Worker's Chronicle*, December 24, 1915, 3; *Topeka Daily Capital*, December 27, 1915, 3; *Topeka Capper's Weekly*, January 29, 1916, 4.

11. Miner, *Kansas*, 233; *Topeka Daily Capital*, February 13, 1915, 5; and January 15, 1916, 20.

12. *Topeka Daily Capital*, January 31, 1916, 1.

13. *Topeka Daily Capital*, December 27, 1915, 3; *Leavenworth Weekly Times*, December 2, 1915, 2.

14. Chambers, *To Raise an Army*, 107; U.S. Const., art. II, sec. 8; art. I, sec. 2; and amend. II.

15. Cunningham, *Black Citizen-Soldiers of Kansas*, x–xi; John Richard Stephens, *Commanding the Storm: Civil War Battles in the Words of the Generals Who Fought Them* (Guilford, CT: Lyons, 2012), 268.

16. Fowles, *Guard in Peace and War*, 15, 29–30, 42; *Topeka Daily Press*, February 16, 1893, 1; *Topeka Daily Capital*, August 8, 1893, 2; John D. Bright, *Kansas: The First Century*, vol. 1 (New York: Lewis Historical Publishing, 1956), 203; *Topeka State Journal*, May 1, 1899, 2.

17. *Topeka Daily Capital*, January 26, 1902, 14.

18. Michael Doubler, *I Am the Guard: A History of the Army National Guard, 1636–2000* (Darby, PA: Diane Publishing, 2001), 137; Finnegan, *Against the Specter of a Dragon*, 84.

19. John H. McCool, "Hello, I Must Be Going," President Woodrow Wilson and the First Lady Visiting Lawrence, Kansas, KU Memorial Union, https://kuhistory.ku.edu/articles/hello-i-must-be-going (accessed August 2, 2023); *Topeka Daily Capital*, February 3, 1916, 1; *Lawrence University Daily Kansan*, February 2, 1916, 1.

20. *Topeka State Journal*, February 2, 1916, 1; *Topeka Daily Capital*, February 3, 1916, 1.

21. *Oskaloosa Independent*, February 4, 1916, 1; *Oskaloosa Times*, February 3, 1916, 1; *Valley Falls New Era*, February 12, 1916, 1; *Perry Mirror*, February 17, 1916, 1.

22. *Leavenworth Post*, February 4, 1916, 3; *Leavenworth Times*, February 6, 1916, 1; *Olathe Register*, February 17, 1916, 10; *Harveyville Monitor*, June 1, 1916, 5.

23. Meirion Harries and Susie Harries, *The Last Days of Innocence: America at War, 1917–1918* (New York: Random House, 1997), 56–57; Chambers, *To Raise an Army*, 116; Finnegan, *Against the Specter of a Dragon*, 155, 185.

2. Oskaloosa Forms a National Guard Company

1. Alfred Theodore Andreas, *History of the State of Kansas*, vol. 1 (Chicago: A. T. Andreas, 1883), 505. The 1867 Jefferson County courthouse was the oldest in Kansas when it was destroyed by a tornado in 1960.

2. *Oskaloosa Independent*, August 7, 1875, 3; and January 3, 1908, 5; *Atchison Daily Globe*, August 3, 1911, 8; *Piedmont News*, May 18, 1908, 6; *Jefferson County Tribune* (Oskaloosa), May 5, 1916, 1; Andreas, *History of the State of Kansas*, 521; *Oskaloosa Independent*, April 21, 1888, 1; and March 26, 1987, 1.

3. Andreas, *History of the State of Kansas*, 503; Doubler, *I Am the Guard*, 107; *Valley Falls Daily Reporter*, March 30, 1916, 1.

4. *Lawrence Daily Journal*, March 2, 1899, 2; *Ottawa Herald*, February 19, 1903, 3; *Ottawa Republic*, February 14, 1903, 3; *Topeka Daily Capital*, January 4, 1916, 5; *Oskaloosa Independent*, February 18, 1916, 6.

5. *Oskaloosa Independent*, September 26, 1913, 5; *Perry Mirror*, February 17, 1916, 1; *Oskaloosa Times*, February 3, 1916, 4; *Oskaloosa Independent*, February 25, 1916, 5; *Oskaloosa Times*, February 17, 1916, 1; and March 2, 1916, 4.

6. *Grantville News*, November 30, 1901, 1; *Oskaloosa Independent*, March 17, 1905, 8; *Perry Mirror*, April 30, 1914, 5; *Valley Falls New Era*, November 15, 1915, 8; *Oskaloosa Independent*, October 9, 1914, 5; Reminiscence of T. R. Blevins, 1979, Blevins Papers.

7. *Oskaloosa Independent*, March 10, 1916, 2; *Valley Falls Daily Reporter*,

March 13, 1916, 1; *Oskaloosa Independent*, March 31, 1916, 5; *Valley Falls Daily Reporter*, March 30, 1916, 1; and April 1, 1916, 4.

8. *Valley Falls Daily Reporter,* April 1, 1916, 1; *Oskaloosa Times*, April 6, 1916, 4; *Jefferson County Tribune* (Oskaloosa), April 7, 1916, 5.

9. *Jefferson County Tribune* (Oskaloosa), July 12, 1918, 1; and June 12, 1908, 3; *Oskaloosa Times*, May 12, 1910, 1; September 9, 1915, 4; June 1, 1916, 3; and November 20, 1913, 4.

10. *Oskaloosa Times,* January 12, 1911, 1.

11. *Oskaloosa Times*, January 19, 1911, 5; Connie DiPasquale, "Riders on an Orphan Train to Kansas—1911: Anna May Potthoff Keeton, William James (Potthoff) Kimmel," Articles, Kansas Collection, n.d., http://www.kancoll.org/articles/orphans/orphan_t.htm (accessed August 2, 2023); *Oskaloosa Independent*, September 30, 1910, 4; and June 13, 1996, 3; *Jefferson County Tribune* (Oskaloosa), June 20, 1913, 5; and November 20, 1914, 5.

12. *Oskaloosa Independent*, April 20, 1916, 1; *Valley Falls Daily Reporter*, April 21, 1916, 1.

13. *Oskaloosa Times*, April 27, 1916, 4; *Oskaloosa Independent*, May 5, 1916, 5; and May 12, 1916, 8; and *Valley Falls Daily Reporter*, May 29, 1916, 1.

14. *Oskaloosa Independent*, May 5, 1916, 5; *Valley Falls Daily Reporter*, May 24, 1916, 2; *Oskaloosa Independent*, May 26, 1916, 5; *Jefferson County Tribune* (Oskaloosa), June 2, 1916, 4.

15. *Valley Falls New Era*, May 26, 1910, 8; *Washburn Review*, May 13, 1914, 6; *Valley Falls New Era*, June 25, 1914, 2; and October 29, 1914, 4.

16. *Valley Falls Daily Reporter*, January 12, 1916, 1; *Oskaloosa Times*, May 18, 1916, 4; and June 22, 1916, 1; *Valley Falls New Era*, June 15, 1916, 8.

17. *Oskaloosa Independent*, June 22, 1916, 1; *Oskaloosa Times*, June 22, 1916, 1; and June 29, 1916, 3; *Oskaloosa Independent*, June 23, 1916, 5; *Valley Falls Daily Reporter*, June 24, 1916, 4; *Oskaloosa Times*, July 6, 1916, 2; *Oskaloosa Independent*, July 7, 1916, 4; Reminiscence of T. R. Blevins, 1979, Blevins Papers.

3. The Kansas National Guard at the Mexican Border

1. *Oskaloosa Independent*, July 7, 1916, 4, 8; Fowles, *Guard in Peace and War*, 56; Lawrence Stallings, *The Doughboys: The Story of the AEF* (New York: Harper & Row, 1963), 5.

2. *Oskaloosa Independent*, July13, 1916, 3; T. R. Blevins, postcard from Eagle Pass, TX, July 11, 1916, Blevins Papers; *Oskaloosa Times*, July 13, 1916, 7; Jesse J. Blevins and Kathryn E. B. Bearman, *The Sergeant & Company B* (Privately printed, 1976), 31–32; *Winchester Star*, August 18, 1916, 2.

3. *Meriden Ledger*, July 20, 1916, 3; *Oskaloosa Times*, July 13, 1916, 3; *Jefferson County Tribune* (Oskaloosa), July 28, 1916, 5; *Topeka Daily Capital*, July 23, 1916, 20.

4. *Winchester Star*, August 18, 1916, 2.

5. Bernice Larson Webb, *The Basketball Man: James Naismith* (Lawrence: University Press of Kansas, 1973), 175–176; *Fredonia Daily Herald*, July 31, 1916, 1;

Topeka Daily Capital, August 6, 1916, 8; *Chanute Daily Tribune*, August 17, 1916, 5; Rob Rains, *James Naismith: The Man Who Invented Basketball* (Philadelphia: Temple University Press, 2009), 104; *Topeka Daily Capital*, September 11, 1916, 2; *Lawrence Daily Journal-World*, August 4, 1916, 2; and August 26, 1916, 20; Reminiscence of T. R. Blevins, 1979, Blevins Papers.

6. *Oskaloosa Independent*, September 1, 1916, 5; *Valley Falls New Era*, July 20, 1916, 1; and July 27, 1916, 12.

7. *Jefferson County Tribune* (Oskaloosa), September 8, 1916, 1; Fowles, *Guard in Peace and War*, 56; T. R. Blevins, letter from Eagle Pass, TX, September 6, 1916; and Blevins, postcard from Eagle Pass, TX, September 29, 1916, Blevins Papers; *Topeka State Journal*, September 12, 1916, 1; *Oskaloosa Independent*, September 29, 1916, 5.

8. *Oskaloosa Independent*, October 6, 1916, 3; *Topeka Daily Capital*, October 31, 1916, 5; Fowles, *Guard in Peace and War*, 56; *Valley Falls Vindicator*, November 6, 1916, 4; Reminiscence of T. R. Blevins, 1979, Blevins Papers.

9. *Topeka Daily Capital*, November 14, 1916, 3; *Jefferson County Tribune* (Oskaloosa), November 17, 1916, 4; *Oskaloosa Independent*, November 17, 1916, 5; *Valley Falls Daily Reporter*, December 22, 1916, 1; *Perry Mirror*, December 14, 1916, 5.

10. *Kansas City (MO) Star*, October 15, 1916, 1; *Oskaloosa Independent*, December 22, 1916, 2; December 29, 1916, 1; and July 21, 1916, 3; *Topeka Daily Capital*, November 14, 1916, 3.

11. Eisenhower, *Yanks*, 26–27; *Parsons Sun*, February 11, 1964, 6.

4. "Today We Stand behind the Nation's Chosen Leader"

1. Link, *Papers of Woodrow Wilson*, 30:393 (August 18, 1914); Harries and Harries, *Last Days of Innocence*, 32, 39; *Great Bend Tribune*, January 4, 1915, 3; Pearl James, "Citizen-Consumers in the American Iconosphere during World War I," in *World War I and American Art*, ed. Robert Cozzolino, Anne Classen Knutson, David M. Lubin (Philadelphia: Pennsylvania Academy of the Fine Arts, 2016), 46; *Topeka State Journal*, December 7, 1915, 8.

2. Keith Jeffrey, *1916: A Global History* (New York: Bloomsbury Publishing, 2016), 308; Clifford S. Griffin, *The University of Kansas: A History* (Lawrence: University Press of Kansas, 1974), 372.

3. Lewis L. Gould, *The First Modern Clash over Federal Power: Wilson versus Hughes in the Presidential Election of 1916* (Lawrence: University Press of Kansas, 2016), 66, 106, 121, 117, 129; Heckscher, *Woodrow Wilson*, 415; *Abilene Weekly Reflector*, November 16, 1916, 8.

4. Heckscher, *Woodrow Wilson*, 427, 440; Eisenhower, *Yanks*, 8; Frank Freidel, *Over There: The Story of America's First Great Overseas Crusade* (New York: Bramhall House, 1964), 6.

5. *Abilene Weekly Reflector*, April 12, 1917, 10; *Parsons Daily Republican*, April 14, 1917, 1.

6. *Topeka Daily Capital*, April 3, 1917, 4; *Chicago Tribune*, April 7, 1917, 2; Arnold

Krammer, *Undue Process: The Untold Story of America's German Alien Internees* (London: Rowman & Littlefield, 1997), 13–14.

7. Heckscher, *Woodrow Wilson*, 388; *Leavenworth Times*, July 18, 1916, 5; Jeffrey, *1916*, 329; *Salina Semi-Weekly Journal*, August 1, 1916, 1; Zachary Smith, *Age of Fear: Othering and American Identity during World War I* (Baltimore: Johns Hopkins University Press, 2019), 112.

8. *Wichita Eagle*, January 28, 1917, 1; *Perry Mirror*, March 29, 1917, 4; *Valley Falls Daily Reporter*, March 8, 1917, 1; *Ottawa Herald*, March 10, 1916, 10; *Wichita Daily Eagle*, June 1, 1916, 7. Beginning in 1948, the Atlantic and Pacific fleets have competed for the annual Marjorie Sterrett Battleship Fund Award, a stipend that supplements a ship's recreation fund.

9. *Newton Evening Kansan Republican*, April 6, 1917, 1; *Oskaloosa Independent*, April 13, 1917, 1; Alan Axelrod, *Selling the Great War: The Making of American Propaganda* (New York: Palgrave Macmillan, 2009), 75; Adam Hochschild, *American Midnight: The Great War, a Violent Peace, and Democracy's Forgotten Crisis* (New York: Mariner Books, 2022), 177; Richard Rubin, *The Last of the Doughboys* (Boston: Houghton Mifflin Harcourt, 2013), 174; Thomas Fleming, *The Illusion of Victory: America in World War I* (New York: Basic Books, 2003), 117, 247.

10. *Oskaloosa Independent*, May 25, 1917, 2; William Frank Zornow, *Kansas: A History of the Jayhawk State* (Norman: University of Oklahoma Press, 1957), 229–231; *Topeka Daily Capital*, March 14, 1918, 8; Herbert Pankratz, "The Suppression of Alleged Disloyalty in Kansas during World War I," *Kansas Historical Quarterly* 42, no. 3 (Autumn 1976): 277, 278–279.

11. George P. Morehouse, "Kansas as a State of Extremes, and Its Attitude during the World War," in *Collections of the Kansas Historical Society 1919–1922*, ed. William E. Connelley (Topeka: Kansas State Printing Plant, 1923), 21–26.

12. *Topeka Daily Capital*, June 16, 1917, 1; and September 12, 1918, 4; Debra Guiou Stufflebean, *At the Time, in This Place* (Bloomington: iUniverse, 2009), 154; *Topeka Daily Capital*, November 2, 1918, 4.

13. Webb, *Basketball Man*, 372; *Lawrence Daily Journal-World*, December 13, 1917, 4; Griffin, *University of Kansas*, 373; John H. McCool, "Chancellor Strong's About-Face," KU's Response to WW1, KU Memorial Union, n.d., https://union.ku.edu/chancellor-strongs-about-face (accessed August 2, 2023); McCool, "KU Women 'Do Their Bit,'" KU's Red Cross Course, KU Memorial Union, n.d., https://union.ku.edu/ku-women-do-their-bit (accessed August 2, 2023).

14. *Manhattan Mercury*, April 10, 1917, 1; *Manhattan Morning Chronicle*, April 11, 1917, 4; *Manhattan Weekly Mercury*, June 11, 1917, 1; *Concordia Blade-Empire*, June 28, 1918, 2–4; *Manhattan Morning Chronicle*, June 17, 1918, 1; and November 8, 1918, 1; *Concordia Blade-Empire*, June 23, 1919, 4.

15. Julius Terrass Willard, *History of the Kansas State College of Agriculture and Applied Science* (Manhattan: Kansas State College Press, 1940), 302–313.

16. *Jefferson County Tribune* (Oskaloosa), January 26, 1917, 3; *Oskaloosa Independent*, February 9, 1917, 5; March 9, 1917, 5; and March 30, 1917, 8.

17. *Valley Falls Vindicator*, April 13, 1; *Nortonville News*, April 20, 1917, 4; *Winchester Star*, April 27, 1917, 2; *Oskaloosa Independent*, April 5, 1917, 5.

18. *Oskaloosa Independent*, March 31, 1916, 7; *Oskaloosa Times*, May 19, 1916, 5.

19. *Oskaloosa Independent*, April 20, 1917, 5; *Jefferson County Tribune* (Oskaloosa), May 11, 1917, 1; *Oskaloosa Independent*, May 18, 1917, 5, 8.

5. The Army Draft and "Fatal Number 258"

1. Daniel Webster, *The Writings and Speeches of Daniel Webster*, vol. 14 (Boston: Little, Brown, 1903), 61; J. L. Bernstein, "Conscription and the Constitution: The Amazing Case of *Kneedler v. Lane*," *American Bar Association Journal* 53, no. 8 (August 1967): 708; Wesley Abney, *Random Destiny: How the Vietnam War Draft Lottery Shaped a Generation* (Wilmington, DE: Vernon, 2018), 1–2.

2. Chambers, *To Raise an Army*, 68, 138, 153–154, 160; *Leavenworth Times*, April 11, 1917, 1; *Coffeyville Sun*, April 29, 1917, 1; *Washington (DC) Herald*, April 29, 1917, 1; Link, *Papers of Woodrow Wilson*, 42:181 (May 19, 1917).

3. *Topeka Daily Capital*, May 22, 1917, 4; *Independence Daily Reporter*, June 6, 1917, 1; *Oskaloosa Independent*, May 18, 1917, 1.

4. *Topeka State Journal*, April 13, 1918, 5; Arlyn John Parish, *Kansas Mennonites during World War I* (Hays, KS: Fort Hays State University, 1968), 31; Governor Capper to Mr. W. H. Stanfield, May 6, 1918, Governor Arthur Capper's Slackers File, Kansas Memory, https://www.kansasmemory.org/item/212615/page/61 (accessed August 2, 2023); Arver v. United States, 245 U.S. 366 (1918) [seven lawsuits known as the Selective Draft Law Cases].

5. Gerald E. Shenk, *Work or Fight!: Race, Gender, and the Draft in World War One* (New York: Palgrave Macmillan, 2005), 4–5; *Baldwin Ledger*, June 8, 1917, 1; *Topeka Daily Capital*, June 6, 1917, 5; and June 6, 1917, 8; *Leavenworth Post*, June 6, 1917, 8.

6. *Washington (DC) Post*, July 21, 1917, 1; Chambers, *To Raise an Army*, 212.

7. *District of Columbia Evening Star* (Washington), July 21, 1917, 7; *Baltimore Sun*, July 27, 1917, 6; *Wilkes-Barre (PA) Record*, September 29, 1917, 8; *Reading (PA) Times*, August 16, 1917, 6; *Ottawa Herald*, August 1, 1917, 1; *Pine Bluff (AR) Daily Graphic*, September 9, 1917, 1; *Owensboro (KY) Messenger*, October 31, 1940, 5.

8. *Oskaloosa Independent*, August 3, 1917, 2; *Holyrood Banner*, July 27, 1917, 7.

9. *Topeka State Journal*, July 23, 1917, 5; Chambers, *To Raise an Army*, 191–196.

10. *Bonner Springs–Edwardsville Chieftain*, March 14, 1918, 4; *Topeka Daily Capital*, December 5, 1917, 4; January 2, 1918, 2; and July 2, 1917, 2; *Concordia Daily Blade*, August 21, 1917, 1; *Jamestown Optimist*, August 23, 1917, 2.

11. *Wichita Beacon*, July 20, 1917, 8; and August 6, 1917, 6; *Wellington Monitor-Press*, August 8, 1917, 3; *Wichita Beacon*, September 1, 1917, 5; and March 15, 1918, 11.

12. *Parsons Daily Republican*, August 30, 1917, 1; *Alma Enterprise*, June 28, 1918, 1; *Chanute Daily Tribune*, February 6, 1919, 1.

13. *Wichita Beacon*, August 10, 1917, 8; Chambers, *To Raise an Army*, 186, 200; Shenk, *Work or Fight!*, 34; Finnegan, *Against the Specter of a Dragon*, 190.

14. *Wellington Monitor-Press*, November 20, 1918, 3; *Wichita Beacon*, July 5, 1919, 9; August 30, 1920, 1; January 6, 1923, 3; January 11, 1923, 9; and January 21, 1923, 32; *Battle Creek (MI) Enquirer*, November 16, 1942, 12; *Wichita Beacon*, November 4,

1939, 3; Harry Scherman, foreword to *Balkan Journal*, by Laird Archer (New York: W. W. Norton, 1944), 9.

15. *Wichita Eagle*, December 18, 1924, 1; Julian Archer, foreword to *Balkan Tragedy*, by Laird Archer, rev. ed. (Manhattan, KS: MA/AH, 1983).

6. Kansas "Rainbow" Guardsmen

1. *Concordia Daily Kansan*, May 14, 1917, 4.

2. *Independence Daily Reporter*, June 12, 1917, 6; James J. Heiman, *Voices in Bronze and Stone: Kansas City's World War I Monuments and Memorials* (Kansas City, MO: Kansas City Star Books, 2013), 215–216; James J. Cooke, *The Rainbow Division in the Great War* (Westport, CT: Praeger, 1994), 9–10.

3. *Washington (DC) Post*, July 10, 1917, 1; *Oskaloosa Independent*, July 13, 1917, 2; *Kansas City Globe*, August 14, 1917, 1; Harries and Harries, *Last Days of Innocence*, 210.

4. *Manhattan Mercury*, August 18, 1917, 1; Cooke, *Rainbow Division*, 4, 14–15; *Topeka Daily Capital*, May 2, 1919, 1.

5. Harold Stanley Johnson, *Roster of the Rainbow Division (Forty-Second)* (New York: Eaton & Gettinger, 1917), 26–43; *Oskaloosa Independent*, August 10, 1917, 5; *Leavenworth Post*, August 29, 1917, 8; *Topeka Daily Capital*, April 30, 1919, 4.

6. Cooke, *Rainbow Division*, 34, 47, 75; *Manhattan Republic*, October 3, 1918, 1; *Garnett Review*, April 11, 1918, 4.

7. *Oskaloosa Independent*, June 21, 1918, 5; *Iola Register*, October 22, 1918, 4; *Dodge City Daily Globe*, July 12, 1917, 3; *Dodge City Globe*, August 15, 1918, 1; *Dodge City Daily Globe*, August 17, 1918, 1; *Kansas City (MO) Times*, September 16, 1918, 9; *Salina Evening Journal*, December 11, 1919, 11; Heiman, *Voices in Bronze and Stone*, 223.

8. *Jefferson County Tribune* (Oskaloosa), October 4, 1918, 1.

9. Cooke, *Rainbow Division*, 193, 201; Heiman, *Voices in Bronze and Stone*, 217; *Topeka Daily Capital*, May 2, 1919, 1; *Kansas City (MO) Times*, September 8, 1924, 3.

10. *Kansas City (MO) Star*, May 12, 1919, 1; *Topeka Daily Capital*, April 30, 1919, 4; *Oskaloosa Independent*, May 2, 1919, 5.

7. Camp Funston

1. Zornow, *Kansas*, 208; William E. Connelley, *History of Kansas*, vol. 2 (Chicago: American Historical Society, 1928), 903–904.

2. Jonathan Casey, "Training in Kansas for a World War: Camp Funston in Photographs," *Kansas History* 29, no. 3 (Autumn 2006): 165.

3. Leonard L. Lerwill, ed., *The Personnel Replacement System in the United States Army* (Washington, DC: Government Printing Office, 1954), 177–178; Casey, "Training in Kansas," 165–166; George H. English Jr., *History of the 89th Division, U.S.A.* (Denver, CO: Smith-Brooks, 1920), 19; *Topeka State Journal*, March 30, 1918, 10.

4. William M. Wright, *Meuse-Argonne Diary: A Division Commander in World War I*, ed. Robert H. Ferrell (Columbia: University of Missouri Press, 2004), 1; David Woodward, "'Black Jack' Pershing: The American Proconsul in Europe," in *Leadership in Conflict, 1914–1918*, ed. Matthew Hughes and Matthew Seligmann (Barnsley, UK: Leo Cooper, 1990), 142; Sandra Reddish, "An 'All Kansas' Regiment: The 353d Infantry Goes to War," *Kansas History* 29, no. 3 (Autumn 2006): 147, 149; English, *History of the 89th Division*, 21; *Independence Daily Reporter*, June 12, 1917, 6; Heiman, *Voices in Bronze and Stone*, 227.

5. *Sabetha Herald*, September 13, 1917, 1; *Seneca Courier-Tribune*, September 27, 1917, 1.

6. English, *History of the 89th Division*, 23; *Kansas City (MO) Times*, September 7, 1917, 3; Reddish, "'All Kansas' Regiment," 150.

7. Charles F. Dienst et al., *History of the 353rd Infantry Regiment, 89th Division, National Army* (Wichita, KS: Eagle, 1921), 8; John M. Barry, *The Great Influenza: The Epic Story of the Deadliest Plague in History* (New York: Penguin Books, 2005), 169; Casey, "Training in Kansas," 164, 167; Heiman, *Voices in Bronze and Stone*, 230.

8. English, *History of the 89th Division*, 27–28, 35; Reddish, "'All Kansas' Regiment," 151–152; *Kansas City Globe*, March 3, 1918, 1.

9. *Lawrence University Daily Kansan*, November 28, 1911, 4; *New York Tribune*, August 19, 1916, 12; *Topeka Daily Capital*, April 21, 1918, 18; Jim Leeke, *The Best Team Over There: The Untold Story of Grover Cleveland Alexander and the Great War* (Lincoln: University of Nebraska Press, 2021), 125.

10. Jim Leeke, *From the Dugouts to the Trenches: Baseball during the Great War* (Lincoln: University of Nebraska Press, 2017), 35, 84, 125, 148–151; *Manhattan Mercury*, May 9, 1918, 4.

11. Reddish, "'All Kansas' Regiment," 154; Dienst et al., *History of the 353rd Infantry Regiment*, 21.

12. *Manhattan Mercury*, September 1, 1917, 1; and September 12, 1917, 1; *Junction City Daily Union*, October 13, 1917, 1; *Fort Riley Trench and Camp*, October 20, 1917, 4.

13. Cunningham, *Black Citizen-Soldiers of Kansas*, xiii, xv, 96–102, 130; *New York Times*, November 19, 1862, 8; William A. Dobak, "Fort Riley's Black Soldiers and the Army's Changing Role in the West, 1867–1885," *Kansas History* 22, no. 3 (Autumn 1999): 216; Randall B. Woods, "Integration, Exclusion, or Segregation?: The 'Color Line' in Kansas, 1879–1900," *Western Historical Quarterly* 14, no. 2 (April 1983): 181–198.

14. Jami L. Bryan, "Fighting for Respect: African-American Soldiers in WWI," Army Historical Foundation, https://armyhistory.org/fighting-for-respect-african-american-soldiers-in-wwi/ (accessed August 2, 2023); Hayward Woody Farrar, "The Black Soldier in Two World Wars," in *A Companion to African American History*, ed. Alton Hornsby Jr. (Malden, MA: Blackwell Publishing, 2005), 350–351; Adam P. Wilson, *African American Army Officers of World War I* (Jefferson, NC: McFarland, 2015), 99.

15. Wilson, *African American Army Officers*, 44, 55, 67, 88, 99; Scott, *Official History of the American Negro in the World War*, 130–131, 378; *Topeka Plaindealer*, November 30, 1917, 1; J. A. Jamieson, *Complete History of the Colored Soldiers in the World War* (New York: Bennett & Churchill, 1919), 17.

16. Wilson, *African American Army Officers*, 5, 179; Scott, *Official History of the American Negro in the World War*, 471; Jack D. Foner, *Blacks and the Military in American History: A New Perspective* (New York: Praeger, 1974), 117–118.

17. *Topeka Daily Commonwealth*, April 17, 1879, 2; Woods, "Integration, Exclusion, or Segregation?," 197; Barbara A. Gannon, *The Won Cause: Black and White Comradeship in the Grand Army of the Republic* (Chapel Hill: University of North Carolina Press, 2011), 88; Gerald R. Butters Jr., "*The Birth of a Nation* and the Kansas Board of Review of Motion Pictures: A Censorship Struggle," *Kansas History* 14, no. 1 (Spring 1991): 3–7; James N. Leiker, "Race Relations in the Sunflower State," *Kansas History* 25, no. 3 (Autumn 2022): 223; Brent M. S. Campney, *This Is Not Dixie: Racist Violence in Kansas, 1861–1927* (Urbana: University of Illinois Press, 2015), 80, 141, 179–180, 209, 213; *Arkansas City Daily Traveler*, December 13, 1916, 3.

18. Wilson, *African American Army Officers*, 61; Scott, *Official History of the American Negro in the World War*, 97–98.

19. *Topeka Plaindealer*, April 12, 1918, 1; *New York Age*, April 13, 1918, 1; *Richmond (VA) Planet*, April 20, 1918, 5; *Kansas City (MO) Sun*, April 17, 1918, 1; and April 27, 1918, 5; *Kansas City Advocate*, April 26, 1918, 2; *Topeka Daily Capital*, April 22, 1918, 6.

20. Scott, *Official History of the American Negro in the World War*, 100–101; Wilson, *African American Army Officers*, 62–64; *New York Age*, May 4, 1918, 1; *Nashville Globe*, May 24, 1918, 1.

21. Scott, *Official History of the American Negro in the World War*, 50, 433–438; *New York Age*, May 4, 1918, 1.

8. Camp Doniphan

1. *Jefferson County Tribune* (Oskaloosa), May 25, 1917, 1; *Oskaloosa Independent*, June 8, 1917, 5; June 29, 1917, 5; July 13, 1917, 2; July 27, 1917, 5; and July 27, 1917, 5.

2. *Valley Falls Vindicator*, August 17, 1917, 1; *Jefferson County Tribune* (Oskaloosa), August 10, 1917, 1; *Oskaloosa Independent*, August 10, 1917, 5.

3. Thanks to a donation from the Davis family, the National WWI Museum and Memorial in Kansas City, Missouri, has several letters and documents relating to the war experiences of William Davis in its archival collections.

4. *Oskaloosa Independent*, February 16, 1917, 5; *Winchester Star*, April 3, 1914, 3; and June 10, 1921, 3; *Oskaloosa Independent*, September 28, 1917, 1; May 4, 1906, 8; September 20, 1907, 5; January 30, 1908, 4; July 2, 1909, 5; October 29, 1909, 5; and September 9, 1910, 4; *Topeka Daily Capital*, June 7, 1915, 5; and November 2, 1915, 12; *Jefferson County Tribune* (Oskaloosa), August 24, 1917, 1.

5. *Oskaloosa Independent*, September 7, 1917, 1; and September 21, 1917, 1; *Washburn Review*, March 29, 1918, 4; *Oskaloosa Independent*, September 21, 1917, 5; *Topeka State Journal*, September 24, 1917, 1; *Topeka Daily Capital*, September 26, 1917, 8.

6. *Oskaloosa Independent*, September 28, 1917, 4; *Valley Falls Vindicator*, September 28, 1917, 1; Reminiscence of T. R. Blevins, 1979, Blevins Papers.

7. T. R. Blevins, letter from Ft. Sill, OK, September 26, 1917, Blevins Papers; *Oskaloosa Independent*, November 2, 1917, 5; and March 22, 1918, 5; *Jefferson County Tribune* (Oskaloosa), November 30, 1917, 1; *Oskaloosa Independent*, February 15, 1918, 5; October 5, 1917, 4; and March 8, 1918, 5; T. R. Blevins, letters from Ft. Sill, OK, November 21, 1917, March 19, 1918, Blevins Papers.

8. Adjutant General, U.S. War Department, *Composition of National Guard Divisions and Disposition of Former National Guard Units, 1917* (Washington, DC: Government Printing Office, 1918); William Lee Miller, *Two Americans: Truman, Eisenhower, and a Dangerous World* (New York: Alfred A. Knopf, 2012), 19, 24.

9. Connelley, *History of Kansas*, 889–893; *Valley Falls Vindicator*, November 2, 1917, 1; *Topeka Daily Capital*, October 2, 1917, 3.

10. *Oskaloosa Independent*, October 5, 1917, 5; October 19, 1917, 5; and October 26, 1917, 1; *Jefferson County Tribune* (Oskaloosa), November 16, 1917, 1; T. R. Blevins, letter from Ft. Sill, OK, November 21, 1917, Blevins Papers.

11. Charles B. Hoyt, *Heroes of the Argonne: An Authentic History of the Thirty-Fifth Division* (Kansas City, MO: Franklin Hudson, 1919), 23; *Oskaloosa Independent*, October 26, 1917, 1; October 19, 1917, 5; March 8, 1918, 5; November 2, 1917, 5; and October 5, 1917, 4; Reminiscence of T. R. Blevins, 1979, Blevins Papers.

12. T. R. Blevins, letter from Ft. Sill, OK, November 18, 1917, Blevins Papers; William Davis to John Davis, January 22, 1918, William Louis Davis Papers, National WWI Museum and Memorial; *Jefferson County Tribune* (Oskaloosa), February 15, 1918, 1.

13. *Oskaloosa Independent*, January 18, 1918, 6; March 8, 1918, 1; and March 1, 1918, 5; William Davis to John Davis, January 22, 1918, Davis Papers; T. R. Blevins, letter from Ft. Sill, OK, November 2, 1917, Blevins Papers.

14. *Valley Falls Vindicator*, December 7, 1917, 5; *Oskaloosa Independent*, October 26, 1917, 5; January 4, 1918, 5; and January 18, 1918, 5; T. R. Blevins, letter from Ft. Sill, OK, December 22, 1917, Blevins Papers; *Winchester Star*, March 15, 1918, 1, 5; *Jefferson County Tribune* (Oskaloosa), February 1, 1918, 8; *Washburn Review*, March 29, 1918, 4; *Oskaloosa Independent*, February 8, 1918, 5.

15. T. R. Blevins, letter from Ft. Sill, OK, January 24, 1918, Blevins Papers; *Oskaloosa Independent*, February 1, 1918, 5; and February 15, 1918, 5; T. R. Blevins, letters from Ft. Sill, OK, February 25, March 1, 1918, Blevins Papers.

16. Ferrell, *Collapse at Meuse-Argonne*, 2–6; Dean Trickett, "The Story of Company A, Third Kansas Infantry, in World War I," *Kansas Historical Quarterly* 13, no. 6 (May 1945): 363; *Oskaloosa Independent*, November 2, 1917, 5; and October 12, 1917, 5; *Valley Falls Vindicator*, November 2, 1917, 1.

17. *Oskaloosa Independent*, February 8, 1918, 5; October 26, 1917, 1; and Jan-

uary 4, 1918, 5; T. R. Blevins, letters from Ft. Sill, OK, October 6, November 26, October 31, 1917, March 14, 1918, Blevins Papers.

18. William Davis, postcard, April 9, 1918, Davis Papers; *Oskaloosa Independent*, April 12, 1918, 5; T. R. Blevins, letters from Camp Mills, NY, April 13, April 17, 1918, Blevins Papers; William Davis, letter from Camp Mills, NY, April 17, 1918, Davis Papers.

19. *Oskaloosa Independent*, April 26, 1918, 5; Trickett, "Story of Company A," 13; *Oskaloosa Independent*, May 17, 1918, 5; and June 21, 1918, 5.

20. *Parsons Daily Sun*, October 6, 1917, 4; *Oskaloosa Independent*, July 22, 1921, 5; *Whitewater Independent*, February 10, 1921, 4; *Wichita Eagle-Beacon*, May 5, 1986, 24; *Wichita Eagle*, May 17, 1992, 43.

9. The Kansas Home Front, 1917

1. *Topeka State Journal*, March 15, 1917, 2; Frank W. Blackmar, ed., *History of the Kansas State Council of Defense* (Topeka: Kansas State Printing Plant, 1920), 46; *Wichita Eagle*, March 16, 1917, 9; *Topeka Daily Capital*, March 15, 1917, 1.

2. Blackmar, *History of the Kansas State Council of Defense*, 9–12, 17–24; *Topeka Daily Capital*, February 24, 1917, 1.

3. Blackmar, *History of the Kansas State Council of Defense*, 14, 36; *Wichita Beacon*, July 20, 1917, 4; *Leavenworth Post*, July 23, 1917, 2; W. M. Jardine, *How to Prepare Ground for Wheat, and Time to Sow*, Circular 6, Kansas State Council of Defense (Topeka: Kansas State Printing Plant, 1917), 4.

4. *Topeka Kansas Farmer*, June 1, 1918, 11; *Leavenworth Times*, June 5, 1918, 1; Blackmar, *History of the Kansas State Council of Defense*, 26–27.

5. *Topeka Daily Capital*, May 26, 1917, 1; *Gardner Gazette*, May 24, 1917, 1; *Topeka State Journal*, May 30, 1917, 8; *Concordia Daily Kansan*, June 2, 1917, 3; *Arkansas City Daily Traveler*, June 6, 1917, 2; *Wichita Beacon*, June 11, 1917, 1.

6. James J. Kimble, *Mobilizing the Home Front: War Bonds and Domestic Propaganda* (College Station: Texas A&M University Press, 2006), 17; *Topeka Daily Capital*, September 1, 1917, 1; *McLouth Times*, December 21, 1917, 4; *Wichita Daily Eagle*, June 17, 1917, 21; and September 9, 1917, 21; *Parsons Daily Sun*, August 25, 1917, 3; *Coffeyville Daily Journal*, October 24, 1917, 1.

7. Rubin, *Last of the Doughboys*, 29; *Williamstown News*, April 4, 1918, 6; Lamay Licursi, *Remembering World War I*, 50–51; *Independence Evening Star*, November 21, 1917, 3; *Topeka Daily Capital*, November 25, 1917, 3; Jeff Menne and Christian B. Long, eds., *Film and the American Presidency* (New York: Routledge, 2015), 87; *Parsons Daily Sun*, May 18, 1918, 8; *Pittsburg Sun*, June 2, 1918, 6.

8. Espionage Act, Pub. L. 65-24, 40 Stat. 217 (June 15, 1917); Pankratz, "Suppression of Alleged Disloyalty in Kansas," 291–293; *Topeka State Journal*, June 16, 1917, 1; Thom Rosenblum, "Liberty in the Line of Fire: The Topeka Antidraft Conspiracy during World War I," *Kansas History* 41, no. 2 (Summer 2018): 119–123; *Kansas City Globe*, January 22, 1918, 2; Miner, *Kansas*, 240.

9. *Topeka Daily Capital*, September 3, 1917, 4; *Oskaloosa Independent*, September 14, 1917, 1; H. W. Todd to Governor Arthur Capper, September 26, 1917, Governor Arthur Capper's Slackers File, https://www.kansasmemory.org/item/212615/page/24 (accessed August 2, 2023); *Topeka Daily Capital*, November 8, 1917, 3; and *Topeka Pink Rag*, November 23, 1917, 1.

10. Sara J. Keckeisen, "The Cost of Conscience Part 1: Coming of the Night," *Kansas Heritage* 12, no. 2 (Summer 2004): 8–9; Parish, *Kansas Mennonites during World War I*, 1–3; Walter Ebeling, *The Fruited Plain: The Story of American Agriculture* (Berkeley: University of California Press, 1979), 234; Arnold, *History of Kansas*, 155; James C. Juhnke, "Mob Violence and Kansas Mennonites in 1918," *Kansas Historical Quarterly* 43, no. 3 (Autumn 1977): 334.

11. *McPherson Daily Republican*, April 9, 1917, 1; *Topeka Daily Capital*, July 1, 1917, 12; and July 15, 1917, 15; *Hutchinson News*, August 2, 1917, 10.

12. Donald Eberle, "The Plain Mennonite Face of the World War One Conscientious Objector," *Journal of Amish and Plain Anabaptist Studies* 3, no. 2 (2015): 186–188; Parish, *Kansas Mennonites during World War I*, 37; *Topeka Daily Capital*, September 22, 1917, 3; English, *History of the 89th Division*, 31; Sara J. Keckeisen, "The Cost of Conscience Part 2: Henry's Story," *Kansas Heritage* 12, no. 4 (Winter 2004): 8–9; *McPherson Weekly Republican*, October 26, 1917, 4.

13. Keckeisen, "Cost of Conscience Part 2," 9; Eberle, "Plain Mennonite Face," 176; Chambers, *To Raise an Army*, 216.

14. *Leavenworth Times*, July 18, 1916, 5; *Great Bend Tribune*, July 21, 1916, 3; *Pittsburg Sun*, February 24, 1918, 1; *Tonganoxie Mirror*, April 11, 1918, 6; *Leavenworth Post*, June 30, 1918, 6; Frohwerk v. United States, 249 U.S. 204 (March 10, 1919); *Lawrence Democrat*, June 5, 1919, 1; *Leavenworth Times*, January 11, 1920, 7; *Larned Chronoscope*, November 15, 1917, 5.

15. *Topeka State Journal*, June 1, 1917, 1; and July 21, 1917, 1; *Topeka Daily Capital*, July 26, 1917, 8.

16. Blackmar, *History of the Kansas State Council of Defense*, 19; *Topeka Daily Capital*, June 3, 1917, 16.

17. William Allen White, *The Martial Adventures of Henry and Me* (New York: Macmillan, 1918), 5; Rubin, *Last of the Doughboys*, 183; *Howard Courant*, March 28, 1918, 1; *Oskaloosa Independent*, October 19, 1917, 1; *Independence Evening Star*, October 17, 1917, 1; *Meriden Ledger*, December 21, 1917, 4.

18. Governor Capper to Fred Robertson, April 13, 1917, Governor Arthur Capper's Slackers File, https://www.kansasmemory.org/item/212615/page/1; Otis Warrenburg to Governor Capper, April 30, 1917, Governor Arthur Capper's Slackers File, https://www.kansasmemory.org/item/212615/page/25; Charles Sessions, secretary to the governor, to Fred Robertson, July 6, 1917, Governor Arthur Capper's Slackers File, https://www.kansasmemory.org/item/212615/page/19.

19. *Hutchinson News*, November 25, 1917, 3; December 1, 1917, 2; December 4, 1917, 5; and December 10, 1917, 2; *Wichita Daily Eagle*, January 21, 1918, 5.

10. First in France

1. Nick Lloyd, *The Western Front: A History of the Great War, 1914–1918* (New York: W. W. Norton, 2021), 323, 356; Stallings, *Doughboys*, 12.

2. *Lyon Daily News*, November 5, 1917, 1.

3. *Stockton Review*, May 8, 1913, 1; *Salina Evening Journal*, March 21, 1; *Stockton Review and Rooks County Record*, November 22, 1917, 2; *Salina Evening Journal*, July 15, 1918, 5.

4. *Topeka Daily Capital*, March 5, 1915, 10; *Atchison Champion*, March 9, 1917, 1.

5. John J. Pershing, *My Experiences in the World War*, vol. 1 (New York: Frederick Stokes, 1931), 92; Stallings, *Doughboys*, 15–16.

6. *Salina Daily Union*, March 6, 1919, 6; *Stockton Review and Rooks County Record*, November 22, 1917, 2.

7. Society of the First Division, *History of the First Division during the World War, 1917–1919* (Philadelphia: John C. Winston, 1922), 27–30.

8. Lloyd, *Western Front*, 359; Stallings, *Doughboys*, 38–39; Harries and Harries, *Last Days of Innocence*, 3–5.

9. George Pattullo, "The First Raid," *Saturday Evening Post*, December 29, 1917, 42.

10. *Manhattan Nationalist*, August 22, 1918, 5; *Westmoreland Recorder*, October 17, 1918, 1; and July 28, 1921, 1.

11. *Stockton Review and Rooks County Record*, March 13, 1919, 1; *Independence Evening Star*, 1; Robert Jackson, *The Prisoners, 1914–18* (New York: Routledge, 1989), 7.

12. *St. Louis Star and Times*, November 17, 1917, 4; *Stockton Review*, November 29, 1917, 1; *Salina Evening Journal*, January 1, 1918, 2; Greg Eanes, *Captured Not Conquered: The American POW Experience in the First World War* (Crewe, VA: E&H Publishing, 2018), cover photograph.

13. *Stockton Review and Rooks County Record*, February 7, 1918, 3; *Junction City Daily Union*, February 20, 1918, 2; *Stockton Review and Rooks County Record*, March 13, 1919, 1.

14. *Topeka Daily Capital*, November 23, 1917, 5; *Mayetta Herald*, November 29, 1917, 1; *Holton Signal*, November 29, 1917, 6; *Topeka State Journal*, November 23, 1917, 6; *Atchison Daily Globe*, May 23, 1918, 4.

15. Kyle J. Hatzinger, "Democracy of Death: US Army Graves Registration and Its Burial of the World War I Dead" (PhD diss., University of North Texas, 2020), 347; *Chanute Daily Tribune*, December 3, 1917, 1; *Salina Daily Union*, December 3, 1917, 7; *Wichita Beacon*, December 3, 1917, 3; *Morland Monitor*, May 23, 1918, 2; Connelley, *History of Kansas*, 907; Zornow, *Kansas*, 233.

16. Hatzinger, "Democracy of Death," 340, 345–350; Joshua E. Kastenberg, *To Raise and Discipline an Army* (De Kalb: Northern Illinois University Press, 2017), 159; *Burlingame Enterprise*, January 10, 1918, 9. Kyle Hatzinger examines the formulation of the U.S. Army's policy governing the burial of soldiers who died overseas during the Great War. In chapter 5 he describes the return of Frank Cadue's body

to Kansas. As noted by Hatzinger, the misunderstanding of Cadue's military record has thus persisted: "In May of 2017, Jackson County, Kansas proudly unveiled its monument to all Purple Heart recipients from it and adjacent Holton County. Frank Cadue, the convicted child rapist who was executed by the United States Army and not a Purple Heart recipient, has his name inscribed amongst dozens of men who honorably earned their award through wounds or death caused by enemy action." Hatzinger, "Democracy of Death," 364–369.

17. Charles H. Browne and J. W. McManigal, *Our Part in the Great War: What the Horton Community Did* (Horton, KS: Headlight-Commercial, 1919), 20, 52, 215; *Horton Headlight-Commercial*, April 24, 1919, 8; *Hiawatha Kansas Democrat*, February 26, 1920, 8;

18. Thomas A. Britten, *American Indians in World War I* (Albuquerque: University of New Mexico Press, 1997), 52, 58–59, 178–179; An Act Granting Citizenship to Certain Indians, H.R. 5007, 41 Stat. 350 (November 6, 1919).

19. *Iola Register*, January 20, 1917, 1; *Atlanta Constitution*, March 26, 1917, 1; *Wichita Beacon*, July 6, 1917, 4; *Wichita Eagle*, February 24, 1918, 18; Carl P. Dennett, *Prisoners of the Great War: Authoritative Statement of Conditions in the Prison Camps of Germany* (New York: Houghton Mifflin, 1919), 79.

20. Carol Byerly, "William T. Fitzsimons," in *Builders of Trust: Biographical Profiles from the Medical Corps Coin*, ed. Sanders Marble (Fort Detrick, MD: Borden Institute, 2011), 99–105; Heiman, *Voices in Bronze and Stone*, 13–24; *Lawrence University Daily Kansan*, September 17, 1917, 6; *Kansas City (MO) Star*, September 17, 1917, 1.

21. Supplements Nos. 3 and 4, Adjutant General, *Kansas Casualties in the World War* (1922, 1925); *Kansas City Globe*, November 20, 1917, 1; *Kansas City (MO) Star*, November 19, 1917, 2; *Chanute Daily Tribune*, December 1, 1917, 1; and November 23, 1917, 1.

22. *New York Tribune*, August 25, 1918, 3; *Kansas City (MO) Times*, June 13, 1967, 11.

23. Adjutant General, *Kansas Casualties in the World War*; *Bisbee (AZ) Daily Review*, November 10, 1917, 4; *Chattanooga (TN) News*, February 13, 1918, 5; *Burlington Daily Republican*, May 1, 1919, 1, 4.

24. *Topeka Daily Capital*, September 29, 1920, 5; and January 16, 1921, 11; *Kansas City (MO) Times*, October 19, 1983, 1.

25. Heiman, *Voices in Bronze and Stone*, 31–32; *Olathe Mirror*, January 10, 1918, 4; *Paola Western Spirit*, January 11, 1918, 2.

11. Victory at Cantigny

1. *Emporia Gazette*, July 1, 1918, 4; Matthew J. Davenport, *First Over There: The Attack on Cantigny, America's First Battle of World War I* (New York: St. Martin's, 2015), 11–12; Mark E. Grotelueschen, *Into the Fight, April–June 1918: The U.S. Army Campaigns of World War I* (Washington, DC: Center of Military History, U.S. Army, 2018), 21.

2. Lloyd, *Western Front*, 430.

3. *Emporia Gazette*, November 1, 1915, 6; *Riley County Chronicle*, August 17, 1917, 2; *Manhattan Weekly Mercury*, June 10, 1918, 1; *Manhattan Morning Chronicle*, May 7, 1918, 1; *Emporia Gazette*, January 2, 1917, 3; and July 30, 1917, 4.

4. *Bushton News*, May 5, 1905, 1; Steven Flaig, "Clarence R. Huebner: An American Military Story of Achievement" (MA thesis, University of North Texas, 2006), 12–13, 16–17; *Lyons Daily News*, June 1, 1920, 4; *Kansas City (MO) Times*, May 19, 1949, 32; *Bushton News*, June 7, 1917, 5; Davenport, *First Over There*, 198.

5. *Bushton News*, December 6, 1917, 5; Davenport, *First Over There*, 78–80; Heckscher, *Woodrow Wilson*, 474; Freidel, *Over There*, 121; Stallings, *Doughboys*, 43; Harries and Harries, *Last Days of Innocence*, 229.

6. Flaig, "Clarence R. Huebner," 31; Grotelueschen, *Into the Fight*, 21; Harries and Harries, *Last Days of Innocence*, 229.

7. Grotelueschen, *Into the Fight*, 21–25; Stallings, *Doughboys*, 58; Lloyd, *Western Front*, 430.

8. *Manhattan Republic*, June 26, 1919, 6; *Manhattan Weekly Mercury*, July 5, 1918, 4.

9. *Emporia Gazette*, July 1, 1918, 6; *Manhattan Morning Chronicle*, May 12, 1919, 1; *Manhattan Weekly Mercury*, July 5, 1918, 4.

10. Davenport, *First Over There*, 150–151, Emporia Weekly Gazette, July 4, 1918, 6.

11. Freidel, *Over There*, 133; *Emporia Weekly Gazette*, July 4, 1918, 6.

12. Davenport, *First Over There*, 198, 203–204, 271, 274; Stallings, *Doughboys*, 65; Grotelueschen, *Into the Fight*, 30; Flaig, "Clarence R. Huebner," 41, 46.

13. *Manhattan Republic*, June 26, 1919, 6; *Junction City Daily Union*, January 12, 1920, 1; *Emporia Weekly Gazette*, June 19, 1919, 4.

14. *Lyon County News and Emporia Times*, August 8, 1918, 16; and February 27, 1919, 5; *Indianapolis News*, January 25, 1966, 6.

15. Flaig, "Clarence R. Huebner," 55, 66; Harries and Harries, *Last Days of Innocence*, 240; *Kansas City (MO) Times*, May 19, 1949, 32. Matthew Davenport states that Clarence Huebner was the only American to have fought in the battles at Cantigny, Meuse-Argonne, and Normandy, but at least one other soldier, Theodore Roosevelt Jr., participated in the three victories. See Davenport, *First Over There*, 289; and Robert W. Walker, *The Namesake: A Biography of Theodore Roosevelt, Jr.* (New York: Brick Tower, 2008), 97–100, 105–107, 292–319.

12. Belleau Wood

1. James G. Harbord, *Leaves from a War Diary* (New York: Dodd, Mead, 1925), 309.

2. *Manhattan Morning Chronicle*, December 23, 1919, 1.

3. *Holton Recorder*, September 26, 1918, 1.

4. Axelrod, *Miracle at Belleau Wood*, 145; *Holton Signal*, April 7, 1910, 1; *Robinson Index*, July 5, 1917, 1.

5. *Holton Signal*, April 26, 1917, 12; *Holton Tribune*, October 27, 1899, 5; *Topeka Daily Capital*, June 29, 1917, 1; *Atchison Daily Globe*, July 7, 1917, 9; *Robinson Index*, July 12, 1917, 3.

6. *Topeka Daily Capital*, June 29, 1917, 1; *Sabetha Herald*, July 5, 1917, 1; *Topeka Daily Capital*, July 15, 1917, 21; *Agra Sentinel*, July 25, 1917, 4; *Holton Recorder*, August 2, 1917, 7; *Holton Signal*, September 13, 1917, 5; *Hiawatha Kansas Democrat*, October 11, 1917, 5; and November 29, 1917, 1.

7. *Topeka Daily Capital*, December 2, 1917, 16; *Holton Recorder*, February 12, 1920, 13; February 19, 1920, 5; March 18, 1920, 5; and April 8, 1920, 5; *Sabetha Herald*, July 4, 1918, 4; *Clay Center Economist*, May 28, 1918, 7; *Holton Recorder*, June 3, 1920, 11.

8. Brian Fisher Neuman, "Pershing's Right Hand: General James G. Harbord and the American Expeditionary Forces in the First World War" (PhD diss., Texas A&M University, 2006), 11–12; *Topeka Daily Capital*, June 11, 1886, 5; *Manhattan Industrialist*, June 11, 1887, 5; James J. Cooke, *Pershing and His Generals* (Westport, CT: Praeger, 1997), 6.

9. Neuman, "Pershing's Right Hand," 4, 6, 126–127, 211–213, 254.

10. Neuman, 4, 6, 214–215, 251–264; Harbord, *Leaves from a War Diary*, 283; Stallings, *Doughboys*, 77–80.

11. *Holton Recorder*, June 3, 1920, 11; and June 10, 1920, 8. For an excellent account of the Battle of Belleau Wood, see Axelrod, *Miracle at Belleau Wood*.

12. *Holton Recorder*, June 10, 1920, 8; Stallings, *Doughboys*, 90; Neuman, "Pershing's Right Hand," 276, 280; Connelley, *History of Kansas*, 887; *Holton Signal*, January 30, 1919, 1.

13. Axelrod, *Miracle at Belleau Wood*, 200; *Holton Recorder*, June 10, 1920, 8; and June 17, 1920, 11; *Brown County World*, August 2, 1918, 2.

14. Axelrod, *Miracle at Belleau Wood*, 212–218; Richard S. Faulkner, *Pershing's Crusaders: The American Soldier in World War I* (Lawrence: University Press of Kansas, 2017), 465–466; *Hiawatha Daily World*, January 21, 1919, 1; *Holton Recorder*, January 9, 1919, 3; *Corning Gazette*, January 16, 1919, 1; *Holton Recorder*, June 17, 1920, 11; June 24, 1920, 18; and June 24, 1920, 18.

15. Axelrod, *Miracle at Belleau Wood*, 223–228; Neuman, "Pershing's Right Hand," 294–305; Harbord, *Leaves from a War Diary*, 297; *Sabetha Herald*, September 26, 1918, 2; *Holton Recorder*, July 1, 1920, 3.

16. *Horton Headlight-Commercial*, September 4, 1919, 4; *Hiawatha Daily World*, January 21, 1919, 1; *Fairview Enterprise*, August 24, 1961, 1; *Holton Signal*, January 2, 1919, 11; *Topeka State Journal*, March 27, 1972, 15; *Holton Recorder*, June 19, 1919, 1; and July 10, 1919, 8; *Sabetha Herald*, July 10, 1919, 6; *Holton Signal*, August 14, 1919, 9; *Washington (DC) Times*, August 13, 1919, 13; *Leavenworth Post*, June 24, 1920, 1; *Manhattan Mercury*, January 6, 1946, 2.

17. Neuman, "Pershing's Right Hand," 344–350; Harbord, *Leaves from a War Diary*, 329; Frederick Palmer, *Newton D. Baker: America at War*, vol. 2 (New York: Dodd, Mead, 1931), 369; Ira D. Graham, "Major General James Guthrie Harbord: An Appreciation," in *Collections of the Kansas State Historical Society, 1919–1922*,

ed. William E. Connelley, vol. 15 (Topeka: Kansas State Printing Plant, 1923), 11; *Wichita Eagle*, August 25, 1947, 4.

13. Rocks of the Marne

1. David John Ulbrich, "The Importance of the Battle of Belleau Wood," June 4, 2018, *War on the Rocks* (blog), Texas National Security Review, https://warontherocks.com/2018/06/the-importance-of-the-battle-of-belleau-wood/.

2. Harris, *Rock of the Marne*, xvi. For readers interested in a more comprehensive view, there are several outstanding accounts, including Michael S. Neiberg, *The Second Battle of the Marne* (Bloomington: Indiana University Press, 2008), and Harris, *Rock of the Marne*.

3. *McPherson Freeman*, July 6, 1883, 3; *McPherson Republican*, June 28, 1883, 3; Harris, *Rock of the Marne*, 30.

4. Jesse W. Wooldridge, *The Giants of the Marne: A Story of McAlexander and His Regiment* (Salt Lake City: Seagull, 1923), 14; *Corvallis (OR) Gazette-Times*, February 10, 1910, 1; and November 13, 1993, 7.

5. Wooldridge, *Giants of the Marne*, 14; Stallings, *Doughboys*, 83; Harris, *Rock of the Marne*, 28–29; Neiberg, *Second Battle of the Marne*, 202n36; *Corvallis (OR) Gazette-Times*, November 13, 1993, 7.

6. Harris, *Rock of the Marne*, 28–32.

7. *Cherokee County Democrat*, August 17, 1906, 7; *Grant City (MO) Times-Tribune*, February 27, 1935, 2; *Columbus Modern Light*, June 10, 1912, 1; and September 11, 1913, 1; *Columbus Daily Advocate*, January 29, 1917, 1; *Demopolis (AL) Times*, August 23, 1917, 1; and November 29, 1917, 8; *Columbus Weekly Advocate*, May 23, 1918, 3.

8. Freidel, *Over There*, 133; Harris, *Rock of the Marne*, 13; Stallings, *Doughboys*, 118, 161; Henry B. Davis, *Generals in Khaki* (Raleigh, NC: Pentland, 1998), 86–87.

9. Stallings, *Doughboys*, 128; Wooldridge, *Giants of the Marne*, 24; Harris, *Rock of the Marne*, 90–94, 101, 136, 189.

10. Harris, *Rock of the Marne*, 33, 48; Stallings, *Doughboys*, 127, 184–185.

11. Harris, *Rock of the Marne*, 229–231; *Wathena Times*, September 13, 1918, 1; Neiberg, *Second Battle of the Marne*, 112; *Leavenworth Times*, August 2, 1957, 3.

12. Stephen C. McGeorge and Mason W. Watson, *The Marne, 15 July–6 August 1918* (Washington, DC: Center of Military History, U.S. Army, 2018), 25; Harris, *Rock of the Marne*, 123, 251–254, 265.

13. Official report of Captain Reid, in Wooldridge, *Giants of the Marne*, 40–45; Harris, *Rock of the Marne*, 185, 214–215, 269–280.

14. McGeorge and Watson, *Marne*, 31; Wooldridge, *Giants of the Marne*, 44; Center of Military History, U.S. Army, *Organization of the American Expeditionary Forces* (Washington, DC: Government Printing Office, 1948), 25.

15. *Columbus Daily Modern Light*, August 22, 1918, 1; Harris, *Rock of the Marne*, 281, 304; Wooldridge, *Giants of the Marne*, 34, 39, 47, 61, 72.

16. Adjutant General, *Kansas Casualties in the World War* (1921–1925); *St. George News*, May 25, 1917, 1; and August 1, 1918, 1. *Kansas Casualties* lists as killed in action on July 15, 1918: John Barton of Chetopa, Dwight Cowles of Overland Park, William Cummings of Morrowville, David Deines of Russell, Frank Doerfer of Ruleton, John Emig of Goodland, William Fulton of Niotaze, Fred Harrington of Wamgeo, Charles Hoeb of Orion, Arthur Loomis of Graden Plain, John Luttjohan of Topeka, Fred Marten of Onaga, Clifford Monroe of Woodston, Charley Maxwell of Liberal, Clarence Prather of Leon, John Travis of Victor, Anton Vodraska of Black Wolf, John White of Hutchinson, and George Wingate of Ogden.

17. McGeorge and Watson, *Marne*, 33, 75–76; Edward G. Lengel, and James Lacey, "Background to the Meuse-Argonne," in *A Companion to the Argonne Campaign*, ed. Edward G. Lengel (Chichester, UK: John Wiley & Sons, 2014), 13; Harries and Harries, *Last Days of Innocence*, 322.

18. Davis, *Generals in Khaki*, 248; *Wichita Eagle*, September 19, 1936, 9.

19. *Demopolis (AL) Times*, June 4, 1959, 1; *Alabama Journal* (Montgomery), June 2, 1959, 9.

20. *Manchester Motor*, August 1, 1918, 1; *Stockton Review and Rooks County Record*, April 3, 1919, 1; *Marion Record*, October 17, 1918, 1.

21. *Topeka Daily Capital*, February 25, 1919, 4; *Beverly Tribune*, April 3, 1919, 1; and Thursday, August 10, 1921, 1.

22. *Nortonville News*, April 18, 1919, 2; *Emporia Gazette*, September 23, 1918, 4.

14. Death in the Trenches

1. T. R. Blevins to family, May 1918, Blevins Papers; William Davis to John Davis, May 16, 1918, Davis Papers; *Jefferson County Tribune* (Oskaloosa), January 3, 1919, 6; *Oskaloosa Independent*, June 28, 1918, 5.

2. T. R. Blevins to family, May 1918, Blevins Papers; *Jefferson County Tribune* (Oskaloosa), January 3, 1919, 6; *Oskaloosa Independent*, June 21, 1918, 5.

3. Trickett, "Story of Company A," 364–365; Hoyt, *Heroes of the Argonne*, 31; *Jefferson County Tribune* (Oskaloosa), January 3, 1919, 6; T. R. Blevins, letters from France, May 18, 27, 1918, Blevins Papers; *Winchester Star*, July 12, 1918, 5.

4. John W. Barry, *The Midwest Goes to War: The 32nd Division in the Great War* (Lanham, MD: Scarecrow, 2007), 47; *Jefferson County Tribune* (Oskaloosa), January 3, 1919, 6; T. R. Blevins, letter from France, June 13, 1918, Blevins Papers; *Oskaloosa Independent*, July 12, 1918, 5.

5. T. R. Blevins, letters from France, June 20, August 21, 1918, Blevins Papers; *Valley Falls Vindicator*, May 16, 1919, 3.

6. T. R. Blevins, letters from France, July 2, 7, 1918, Blevins Papers; *Kansas City (MO) Star*, August 8, 1918, 2; John Davis to William Davis, June 14, 1918, Davis Papers; *Valley Falls Vindicator*, May 16, 1919, 3.

7. *Ellsworth Messenger*, September 5, 1918, 7; *Winchester Star*, September 13, 1918, 5; *Oskaloosa Independent*, October 4, 1918, 4; and October 25, 1918, 5.

8. T. R. Blevins, letter from front line, August 3, 1918, Blevins Papers; *Winchester Star*, August 16, 1918, 5; *Oskaloosa Independent*, September 27, 1918, 4; *Winchester Star*, October 18, 1918, 8; *Nortonville News*, October 25, 1918, 4; *Winchester Star*, October 4, 1918, 8.

9. *Oskaloosa Independent*, October 4, 1918, 4; Hoyt, *Heroes of the Argonne*, 51.

10. *Valley Falls Vindicator*, October 4, 1918, 6; *Oskaloosa Independent*, October 4, 1918, 5; T. R. Blevins, letter to parents, August 21, 1918, Blevins Papers; *Oskaloosa Independent*, September 13, 1918, 5.

11. Ferrell, *Collapse at Meuse-Argonne*, 14.

12. William Davis to John Davis, May 16, 1918, Davis Papers.

15. Saint-Mihiel and the Eighty-Ninth Division

1. Harries and Harries, *Last Days of Innocence*, 340; Donald A. Carter, *St. Mihiel: 12–16 September 1918* (Washington, DC: Center of Military History, U.S. Army, 2018), 7, 60.

2. *Liberal News*, May 30, 1918, 12; *Kinsley Mercury*, May 30, 1918, 4; *Troy Kansas Chief*, May 30, 1918, 4; Dienst et al., *History of the 353rd Infantry Regiment*, ix, 21–22.

3. English, *History of the 89th Division*, 44–54; Reddish, "All Kansas' Regiment," 155–157; Dienst et al., *History of the 353rd Infantry Regiment*, 61–62; *Alma Enterprise*, October 4, 1918, 8.

4. Carter, *St. Mihiel*, 11–15; English, *History of the 89th Division*, 89, 96. The names of the three commanders—Wright, Wood, and Winn—served as the basis for the division's slogan, "Right Would Win."

5. Carter, *St. Mihiel*, 7, 21–22; Reddish, "All Kansas' Regiment," 158; English, *History of the 89th Division*, 89–91, 96–97, 260; Dienst et al., *History of the 353rd Infantry Regiment*, 257, 260.

6. Carter, *St. Mihiel*, 56–59; Wright, *Meuse-Argonne Diary*, 29.

7. *Barber County Index*, October 16, 1918, 1; and November 13, 1918, 1.

8. English, *History of the 89th Division*, 98–99, 105, 327, 392; *Little River Monitor*, December 5, 1918, 1; *Leavenworth Post*, May 28, 1918, 1; *Ottawa Herald*, March 16, 1955, 1.

9. *Winchester Star*, August 29, 1947, 1; *Jefferson County Tribune* (Oskaloosa), March 30, 1917, 3; *Perry Mirror*, September 26, 1918, 2; Andy May, "Oscar May in World War I," Climate Blog, Andy May Petrophysicist, November 5, 2018, https://andymaypetrophysicist.com/2018/11/05/oscar-may-in-world-war-I/.

10. *Topeka State Journal*, January 20, 1919, 8.

11. *Ogden (UT) Standard-Examiner*, May 9, 1920, 27; *Leavenworth Post*, September 24, 1918, 1; and October 18, 1920, 1.

12. *Salina Evening Journal*, April 13, 1909, 1; *Manhattan Morning Chronicle*, January 5, 1917, 1; *Wichita Messenger*, October 4, 1918, 1; *Manhattan Morning Chronicle*, May 12, 1917, 1; *Manhattan Republic*, October 3, 1918, 3; *Eagle*, August 6, 1918, 5; *Downs News and Times*, July 14, 1921, 1; and November 28, 1918, 7.

16. Meuse-Argonne and the Thirty-Fifth Division

1. Eisenhower, *Yanks*, 240; Richard S. Faulkner, *Meuse-Argonne, 26 September–11 November 1918* (Washington, DC: Center of Military History, U.S. Army, 2018), 7; David Reynolds, "America's 'Forgotten War' and the Long Twentieth Century," in *World War I and American Art*, ed. Robert Cozzolino, Anne Classen Knutson, David M. Lubin (Philadelphia: Pennsylvania Academy of the Fine Arts, 2016), 21; Stallings, *Doughboys*, 228, 237; Edward G. Lengel, *To Conquer Hell: The Meuse-Argonne, 1918* (New York: Henry Holt, 2008); Hoyt, *Heroes of the Argonne*; Clair Kenamore, *From Vauquois Hill to Exermont: A History of the Thirty-Fifth Division of the United States Army* (St. Louis: Guard Publishing, 1920); Ferrell, *Collapse at Meuse-Argonne*; Charles H. Browne, *A History of the 137th Infantry: An All-Kansas National Guard Regiment* (Horton, KS: Headlight Printshop, 1940); Clair Kenamore, *The Story of the 139th Infantry* (St. Louis: Guard Publishing, 1920).

2. Hoyt, *Heroes of the Argonne*, 57; Blevins and Bearman, *Sergeant & Company B*, 126–128; Eisenhower, *Yanks*, 187–188, 197–198; Faulkner, *Meuse-Argonne*, 7; Ferrell, *Collapse at Meuse-Argonne*, 17.

3. *St. Louis Post-Dispatch*, April 11, 1919, 26; Ferrell, *Collapse at Meuse-Argonne*, 21–24.

4. Harries and Harries, *Last Days of Innocence*, 353; Eisenhower, *Yanks*, 200–204; Faulkner, *Meuse-Argonne*, 12.

5. Hoyt, *Heroes of the Argonne*, 62; Eisenhower, *Yanks*, 212; Stallings, *Doughboys*, 228.

6. Heiman, *Voices in Bronze and Stone*, 152; *Kansas City (MO) Star*, April 9, 1919, 15; *Oskaloosa Independent*, January 3, 1919, 3; Robert Bryan Greene, World War I Soldier, Kansas Memory, https://www.kansasmemory.org/item/223847; *Ellsworth Messenger*, January 9, 1919, 2; Hoyt, *Heroes of the Argonne*, 15, 69.

7. *Oskaloosa Independent*, January 3, 1919, 3; Hoyt, *Heroes of the Argonne*, 71; Faulkner, *Meuse-Argonne*, 22; Eugene Prall, World War I Soldier, Kansas Memory, https://www.kansasmemory.org/item/225473.

8. Kenamore, *From Vauquois Hill to Exermont*, 94–95; *Oskaloosa Independent*, January 3, 1919, 3; Kenamore, *Story of the 139th Infantry*, 24; Reminiscence of T. R. Blevins, 1979, Blevins Papers; Eisenhower, *Yanks*, 213.

9. Ferrell, *Collapse at Meuse-Argonne*, 34, 39; Hoyt, *Heroes of the Argonne*, 80–82.

10. Ferrell, *Collapse at Meuse-Argonne*, 40–41; Clair Kenamore, "The 35th into Battle," *Kansas City (MO) Star*, April 9, 1919, 15.

11. *Oskaloosa Independent*, September 25, 1914, 4; *Neodesha Daily Sun*, May 13, 1919, 3; *Neodesha Register*, May 22, 1919, 5; Lengel, *To Conquer Hell*, 113; Carl E. Haterius, *Reminiscences of the 137th Infantry* (Topeka, KS: Crane, 1919), 42–44; Hoyt, *Heroes of the Argonne*, 74.

12. Fowles, *Guard in Peace and War*, 66; *Oskaloosa Independent*, September 25, 1914, 4; *Kansas City (MO) Star*, April 9, 1919, 15; *Ellsworth Messenger*, January 9, 1919, 2; Kenamore, *Story of the 139th Infantry*, 25.

13. Lengel, *To Conquer Hell*, 115; Ferrell, *Collapse at Meuse-Argonne*, 46; Eisenhower, *Yanks*, 233.

14. Adjutant General, *Kansas Casualties in the World War* (1921); 1st Lt. William Ellenburg to Commanding Officer, 139th Infantry, January 2, 1919, Paul Lloyd West, World War I Soldier, https://www.kansasmemory.org/item/224400/page/10.

15. Harries and Harries, *Last Days of Innocence*, 362; Ferrell, *Collapse at Meuse-Argonne*, 48–51; Hoyt, *Heroes of the Argonne*, 84; *Oskaloosa Independent*, January 3, 1919, 3; Robert H. Ferrell, "Angered to the Core: Henry J. Allen and the U.S. Army," *Kansas History* 29, no. 3 (Autumn 2006): 189; Kenamore quoted in *Kansas City (MO) Star*, April 10, 1919, 15; Lengel, *To Conquer Hell*, 137.

16. Kenamore, *Story of the 139th Infantry*, 29; Fowles, *Guard in Peace and War*, 67; Kenamore, *From Vauquois Hill to Exermont*, 154; *Newton Evening Kansan-Republican*, May 19, 1919, 3.

17. *Oskaloosa Independent*, January 3, 1919, 3; Company B, 3rd Kansas National Guard, 139th U.S. Infantry Regiment, *1955 Reunion* (Oskaloosa, KS, August 19, 1955); *Winchester Star*, November 8, 1918, 4; *Pemiscot (MO) Argus*, December 5, 1918, 1; *Jefferson County Tribune* (Oskaloosa), January 24, 1919, 1.

18. Clair Kenamore, "The 35th into Battle," *Kansas City (MO) Star*, April 10, 1919, 15; *Oskaloosa Independent*, October 25, 1918, 5; *Oskaloosa Independent*, April 11, 1919, 5; and November 8, 1918, 5; *Wichita Beacon*, January 8, 1944, 5.

19. Kenamore, *Story of the 139th Infantry*, 31; *Oskaloosa Independent*, January 3, 1919, 5; Blevins and Bearman, *Sergeant & Company B*, 134–135; Thomas M. McGinnis, "Unit Collapse: A Historical Analysis of Two Divisional Battles in 1918 and 1944" (MA thesis, U.S. Army Command and General Staff College, 1987), 51, https://apps.dtic.mil/dtic/tr/fulltext/u2/a184706.pdf; Fowles, *Guard in Peace and War*, 62.

20. Adjutant General, *Kansas Casualties in the World War* (1921); *Nortonville News*, April 18, 1919, 3; *Jefferson County Tribune* (Oskaloosa), February 28, 1919, 1.

17. Meuse-Argonne and the Thirty-Fifth Division: September 28–30, 1918

1. Adjutant General, *Kansas Casualties in the World War* (1921); *Kansas City (MO) Times*, November 19, 1918, 3; Ferrell, *Collapse at Meuse-Argonne*, 108; Hoyt, *Heroes of the Argonne*, 141.

2. Fowles, *Guard in Peace and War*, 68; Lengel, *To Conquer Hell*, 154; Ferrell, *Collapse at Meuse-Argonne*, 59–60; Clair Kenamore, "A Bloody Third Day," *Kansas City (MO) Star*, April 11, 1919, 4.

3. *Oskaloosa Independent*, January 3, 1919, 3; *Valley Falls Vindicator*, November 8, 1918, 6; *Winchester Star*, November 8, 1918, 1, 4; *Oskaloosa Independent*, November 1, 1918, 5; *Jefferson County Tribune* (Oskaloosa), December 27, 1918, 6; *Oskaloosa Independent*, November 29, 1918, 5; and November 8, 1918, 5; *Boston (MA) Globe*, June 27, 1924, 13.

4. William Smith's promotion recommendation for Sgt. Ted Blevins, October 10, 1918, Blevins Papers.

5. Fowles, *Guard in Peace and War*, 68; *Oskaloosa Independent*, November 1, 1918, 5; T. R. Blevins to parents, December 10, 1918, Blevins Papers; *Oskaloosa*

Independent, February 28, 1919, 5; *Jefferson County Tribune* (Oskaloosa), February 7, 1919, 1; *Emporia Gazette*, December 2, 1918, 4.

6. Hoyt, *Heroes of the Argonne*, 98; Harries and Harries, *Last Days of Innocence*, 363; Heiman, *Voices in Bronze and Stone*, 160; Blevins and Bearman, *Sergeant & Company B*, 136; *Linn County Republic*, November 28, 1918, 2.

7. Ferrell, *Collapse at Meuse-Argonne*, 83, 96–98; Clair Kenamore, "Bloody Third Day," *Kansas City (MO) Star*, April 11, 1919, 4; Kenamore, *Story of the 139th Infantry*, 40–44; Hoyt, *Heroes of the Argonne*, 103; Heiman, *Voices in Bronze and Stone*, 161–162; *Abilene Weekly Reflector*, July 28, 1917, 5.

8. *Oskaloosa Independent*, March 28, 1919, 5; and April 23, 1920, 5; Reminiscence of T. R. Blevins, 1979, Blevins Papers.

9. Joseph N. Rizzi, *Joe's War: Memoirs of a Doughboy* (Huntington, WV: Der Angriff, 1983), 106–107; Lengel, *To Conquer Hell*, 172–179; Ferrell, *Collapse at Meuse-Argonne*, 100; *St. Joseph (MO) Gazette*, August 15, 1935, 1; *Altoona Tribune*, February 6, 1919, 4; *Pomona Republican*, November 28, 1918, 1.

10. Ferrell, *Collapse at Meuse-Argonne*, 105; Heiman, *Voices in Bronze and Stone*, 166; *Jewell County Republican*, November 8, 1918, 1; *Valley Falls Vindicator*, November 8, 1918, 6.

11. *Oskaloosa Independent*, June 27, 1919, 5.

12. Steven Trout, "The Greatest Battle Ever Forgotten: The Meuse-Argonne Offensive and American Memory," in *A Companion to the Argonne Campaign*, ed. Edward G. Lengel (Chichester, UK: John Wiley & Sons, 2014): 510–511; Fowles, *Guard in Peace and War*, 69; Ferrell, *Collapse at Meuse-Argonne*, 111; Wilford Riegle, "Peck's Bad Boys: The Story of the 35th Infantry Division in World War I," *Kansas Historical Quarterly* 23, no. 1 (Spring 1957): 80.

13. *Oskaloosa Independent*, January 3, 1919, 5; and February 7, 1919, 5; Kenamore, *Story of the 139th Infantry*, 46; *Oskaloosa Independent*, November 29, 1918, 5.

14. T. R. Blevins, letter from France, January 11, 1919, Blevins Papers; *Corning Gazette*, January 16, 1919, 1; Blevins and Bearman, *Sergeant & Company B*, 143.

15. T. R. Blevins, letters from France, November 8, 1918, February 8, 1919, Blevins Papers; *Jefferson County Tribune* (Oskaloosa), January 24, 1919, 1; *Oskaloosa Independent*, December 27, 1918, 5; May 2, 1919, 5; and May 9, 1919, 5.

16. *Kansas City (MO) Star*, August 1, 1919, 1; *Kansas City Weekly Gazette Globe*, June 22, 1916, 1; *Kansas City News*, November 29, 1918, 5; *Kansas City (MO) Star*, January 10, 1919, 3; *Kansas City (MO) Times*, March 29, 1919, 4; and April 25, 1919, 6; *Huntsville (AR) Madison County Record*, November 11, 1926, 1.

18. Meuse-Argonne and the Eighty-Ninth Division: November 1–2, 1918

1. Robert Ferrell, editor's text, in Wright, *Meuse-Argonne Diary*, 135.

2. *Valley Falls Vindicator*, June 13, 1919, 3; *Perry Mirror*, January 2, 1919, 1; *Leavenworth Post*, March 17, 1919, 6; *Perry Mirror*, November 28, 1918, 2.

3. Faulkner, *Meuse-Argonne*, 22–70; English, *History of the 89th Division*, 195, 212–213.

4. English, *History of the 89th Division*, 156, 161, 164; *Smith County Journal*, February 20, 1919, 1; and November 28, 1918, 1; *Atchison Daily Globe*, February 21, 1919, 1; Rexmond C. Cochrane, *The 89th Division in the Bois de Bantheville, October 1918* (Washington, DC: U.S. Army Chemical Corps Historical Office, 1960), 55; *Barber County Index*, December 4, 1918, 4; *Medicine Lodge Republican*, November 8, 1918, 8.

5. Faulkner, *Meuse-Argonne*, 57; Wright, *Meuse-Argonne Diary*, 135; Stallings, *Doughboys*, 348.

6. Dienst et al., *History of the 353rd Infantry Regiment*, 264; English, *History of the 89th Division*, 185.

7. *Atchison Daily Globe*, November 26, 1918, 1; and February 21, 1919, 1; Adjutant General, *Kansas Casualties in the World War* (1921).

8. Wright, *Meuse-Argonne Diary*, 136–137, 140; Dienst et al., *History of the 353rd Infantry Regiment*, 179; English, *History of the 89th Division*, 208; *Liberal Democrat*, December 5, 1918, 1.

9. English, *History of the 89th Division*, 189–191; Dienst et al., *History of the 353rd Infantry Regiment*, 134–136; Wright, *Meuse-Argonne Diary*, 141.

10. Dienst et al., *History of the 353rd Infantry Regiment*, 134, 388, 391; *Wichita Eagle*, March 6, 1942, 5; *Oberlin Times*, July 14, 1921, 1.

11. English, *History of the 89th Division*, 195, 212–213; *Topeka Daily Capital*, February 23, 1919, 18; *Oskaloosa Independent*, January 3, 1919, 1; *Leavenworth Post*, March 17, 1919, 6.

12. *Valley Falls Vindicator*, June 13, 1919, 3; *Perry Mirror*, January 2, 1919, 1; *Winchester Star*, August 29, 1947, 1. George English says Oscar May won the French Croix de Guerre, but a picture of the medal confirms news accounts that it is the Belgian Croix de Guerre. English, *History of the 89th Division*, 390–391; May, "Oscar May in World War I," https://andymaypetrophysicist.com/2018/11/05/oscar-may-in-world-war-I/.

13. English, *History of the 89th Division*, 203, 226, 241–242; Wright, *Meuse-Argonne Diary*, 166.

14. Cochrane, *89th Division in the Bois de Bantheville*, 76; Doran L. Cart, "Kansas Football 'Over There,'" *Journal of the Central Plains* 29, no. 3 (Autumn 2006): 195–198.

15. *Topeka Daily Capital*, February 7, 1919, 8; Leeke, *From the Dugouts to the Trenches*, 123–124, 149, 184–185; John C. Skipper, *Wicked Curve: The Life and Troubled Times of Grover Cleveland Alexander* (Jefferson, NC: McFarland, 2006), 77; *Moran Herald*, May 30, 1919, 8; *Iola Register*, December 9, 1930, 1.

19. Black Kansas Soldiers: Fighting Germans and Segregation

1. *Salina Evening Journal*, June 8, 1917, 1; Jarret Bencks, "When World War I Ended, the Civil Rights Movement Was Just Getting Started," BrandeisNOW, November 13, 2018, https://www.brandeis.edu/now/2018/november/world-war-one-african-americans.html.

2. Gail L. Buckley, *American Patriots: The Story of Blacks in the Military from the Revolution to Desert Storm* (New York: Random House, 2002), 163; Wilson, *African American Army Officers*, 85; *Abilene Daily Reflector*, March 19, 1919, 3; *Lawrence Daily Journal–World*, January 21, 1919, 2.

3. Scott, *Official History of the American Negro in the World War*, 137–139; *Kansas City Advocate*, January 31, 1919, 2; *Highland Vidette*, January 23, 1919, 1.

4. Ferrell, *Collapse at Meuse-Argonne*, 26; Bryan, "Fighting for Respect" (accessed August 2, 2023); Farrar, "Black Soldier in Two World Wars," 352.

5. *Topeka Plaindealer*, December 29, 1916, 3; *Topeka Daily Capital*, October 14, 1917, 15; July 1, 1918, 3; and December 16, 1918, 2; *Topeka Plaindealer*, November 21, 1924, 1.

6. Bryan, "Fighting for Respect" (accessed August 2, 2023); *Salina Daily Union*, January 16, 1919, 5; *Leavenworth Post*, January 16, 1919, 3; *Leavenworth Times*, January 2, 1919, 6.

7. *Ottawa Herald*, October 24, 1917, 8; December 24, 1917, 4; December 3, 1918, 8; and October 3, 1921, 5.

8. Stallings, *Doughboys*, 311–313; Farrar, "Black Soldier in Two World Wars," 353; Foner, *Blacks and the Military*, 117–123; Arthur E. Barbeau and Florette Henri, *The Unknown Soldiers: African-American Troops in World War I* (Philadelphia: Temple University Press, 1974), 111–136.

9. Jamieson, *Complete History of the Colored Soldiers in the World War*, 106; *Pittsburg Sun*, December 21, 1918, 1.

10. *Fort Scott Daily Tribune and Daily Monitor*, July 17, 1915, 3; November 2, 1918, 1; June 20, 1918, 7; and July 13, 1918, 5; *Wichita Eagle*, June 28, 1983, 8; and March 8, 2006, 1.

11. *Lawrence Daily Gazette*, February 25, 1919, 2; *Lawrence Daily Journal–World*, February 5, 1919, 1.

12. *Kansas City Advocate*, August 23, 1918, 1; *Kansas City Kansan*, November 27, 1918, 1; *Kansas City Advocate*, February 14, 1919, 1.

13. *Kansas City (MO) Times*, February 7, 1976, 29; "Dr. Frank Scruggs: A Life of Community Service," February 13, 2014, https://theweeklychallenger.com/a-life-of-community-service/.

14. Foner, *Blacks and the Military*, 121; Farrar, "Black Soldier in Two World Wars," 351–352; Steven D. Smith and James A. Zeidler, *A Historic Context for the African American Military Experience* (Champaign, IL: U.S. Army Construction Engineering Research Laboratories, 1998), 293; Margaret M. McMahon, *A Guide to the U.S. Pioneer Infantry Regiments in WWI* (Monee, IL, 2018), 2–6, 81, 91, 93, 108, 110; *Oskaloosa Independent*, May 21, 1915, 8; and June 3, 1921, 5; Scott, *Official History of the American Negro in the World War*, 330.

15. Paul S. Bliss, *Victory: History of the 805th Pioneer Infantry* (St. Paul, MN: Privately printed, 1919), 11–14, 28, 54; Peter M. Lefferts, "Black US Army Bands and Their Bandmasters in World War I," Faculty Publications: School of Music. Digital Commons@University of Nebraska–Lincoln, March 2, 2018, https://digitalcommons.unl.edu/cgi/viewcontent.cgi?article=1069&context=musicfacpub.

16. Addie W. Hunton and Kathryn M. Johnson, *Two Colored Women with the American Expeditionary Forces* (Brooklyn, NY: Brooklyn Eagle, 1920), 235; Bryan Farwell, *Over There: The United States in the Great War, 1917–1918* (New York: W. W. Norton, 1999), 297.

17. *Iola Register*, July 15, 1912, 1; and August 12, 1912, 1; Mark E. Eberle, *Kansas Baseball, 1858–1941* (Lawrence: University Press of Kansas, 2017), 92–93; Williams, *Torchbearers of Democracy*, 201.

18. *Chanute Daily Tribune*, May 5, 1921, 1; *Humboldt Union*, October 13, 1921, 4; Eberle, *Kansas Baseball*, 93.

19. *Wichita Eagle*, February 3, 2012, C1; and October 2, 2016, D2.

20. Bliss, *Victory*, 41–42; *Kansas City Advocate*, July 11, 1919, 1; *Topeka Daily Capital*, July 5, 1919, 10; *Salina Daily Union*, July 26, 1919, 1; and August 13, 1919, 1.

20. Medals of Honor: John Balch, Erwin Bleckley, George Mallon, and George Robb

1. Statistics and FAQS, Congressional Medal of Honor Society, https://www.cmohs.org/medal/faqs.

2. *Syracuse Journal*, May 7, 1915, 1; *Lawrence University Daily Kansan*, September 28, 1915, 1.

3. *Edgerton Journal*, August 2, 1918, 1.

4. David Ulbrich, *Preparing for Victory: Thomas Holcomb and the Making of the Modern Marine Corps, 1936–1943* (Annapolis, MD: Naval Institute Press, 2013), 25.

5. *Miami News*, November 29, 1942, 27.

6. *South Bend (IN) Tribune*, May 29, 1942, 9; *Indianapolis (IN) Star*, December 18, 1944, 22.

7. *Wichita Eagle*, March 4, 1923, 13; and March 5, 1923, 5.

8. Beccy Tanner, "France to Honor Wichita Aviator," *Wichita Eagle*, October 4, 2009, 10A; *Wichita Eagle*, April 18, 1918, 5; Doug Jacobs, "2LT Erwin Russell Bleckley," Kansas National Guard Museum, January 30, 2013, https://ksngmuseum.wordpress.com/2013/01/30/2lt-erwin-russell-bleckley/.

9. Thomas M. Johnson and Fletcher Pratt, *The Lost Battalion* (Indianapolis: Bobbs-Merrill, 1936), 189; Rafael Garcia, "VFW Wants to Honor Medal Recipient on Centennial of Death," *Wichita Eagle*, August 15, 2018, 3DW; *Wichita Eagle*, March 4, 1923, 13; Tanner, "France to Honor Wichita Aviator," 10A.

10. *New York Tribune*, November 10, 1918, 9; *Wichita Beacon*, July 2, 1920, 2; *Wichita Eagle*, August 18, 1931, 2; and December 13, 1932, 5.

11. *Manhattan Morning Chronicle*, April 21, 1919, 4; "George Henry Mallon, 1877–1934," Minnesota Medal of Honor Memorial, https://www.minnesotamedalofhonormemorial.org/wp-content/uploads/2017/12/Mallon-George-Henry-Original-bio.pdf (accessed August 2, 2023); *Manhattan Nationalist*, January 20, 1899, 4; Stephen D. Chicoine, *Captain Mallon: Doughboy Hero* (Minneapolis: Freedom History Publishing, 2017), 17–25.

12. Chicoine, *Captain Mallon*, 29–37; *St. Louis Globe-Democrat*, March 1, 1905, 13; *St. Louis Post-Dispatch*, March 3, 1905, 7; *Fort Riley Guidon*, July 8, 1906, 1.

13. Chicoine, *Captain Mallon*, 58–59.

14. Chicoine, 61–67; Stallings, *Doughboys*, 231–232.

15. Chicoine, *Captain Mallon*, 69–77; "Putting Vim into the Victory Loan: An Advertising Campaign That Is Sure to Compel Attention," *Advertising and Selling* 28, no. 32 (Apr. 12, 1919): 10; *Manhattan Morning Chronicle*, April 21, 1919, 4.

16. *Salina Daily Union*, April 16, 1919, 1; "Who Was George Robb?," *Valor Magazine* 1, no. 1 (July 8, 2020): 5; Jeffrey T. Sammons and John H. Morrow Jr., *Harlem's Rattlers and the Great War: The Undaunted 369th Regiment and the African American Quest for Equality* (Lawrence: University Press of Kansas, 2015), 487; Stephen L. Harris, *Harlem's Hell Fighters: The African-American 369th Infantry in World War I* (Washington, DC: Potomac Books, 2003), 232.

17. *Salina Evening Journal*, November 13, 1918, 2; Harris, *Harlem's Hell Fighters*, 254; Sammons and Morrow, *Harlem's Rattlers*, 341–342; Arthur W. Little, *From Harlem to the Rhine: The Story of New York's Colored Volunteers* (New York: Covici Friede, 1936), 294.

18. *Salina Evening Journal*, November 13, 1918, 2; Little, *From Harlem to the Rhine*, 256–257; Sammons and Morrow, *Harlem's Rattlers*, 343–346.

19. *Topeka Daily Capital*, February 5, 1919, 1.

20. Sammons and Morrow, *Harlem's Rattlers*, 487–488; Chicoine, *Captain Mallon*, 83–85, 132, 136–137, 161; *Kansas City (MO) Star*, January 2, 1921, 1; *Manhattan Tribune*, January 20, 1921, 1; *Minneapolis (MN) Star*, November 9, 1922, 1.

21. The Kansas Home Front, 1918: Distrust, Coercion, and Influenza

1. *Topeka Daily Capital*, April 3, 1918, 4; *Topeka State Journal*, April 3, 1918, 6.

2. Dorothy Ann Pettit, "A Cruel Wind: America Experiences the Pandemic Influenza, 1918–1920: A Social History" (PhD diss., University of New Hampshire, 1976), 97; *Columbus Weekly Advocate*, April 25, 1918, 4.

3. *Junction City Daily Union*, September 15, 1917, 1; *Wichita Beacon*, October 31, 1917, 3; *Great Bend Tribune*, December 17, 1917, 1; *Leavenworth Times*, December 18, 1917, 8; *Topeka Daily Capital*, December 22, 1917, 1; *Leavenworth Chronicle*, December 28, 1917, 1; *Topeka State Journal*, December 29, 1917, 10.

4. *Oskaloosa Independent*, March 1, 1918, 2; *Topeka State Journal*, March 4, 1918, 8; *Topeka Daily Capital*, March 9, 1919, 1; *Leavenworth Times*, March 21, 1918, 5; *Salina Daily Union*, April 6, 1918, 8; *Topeka State Journal*, April 4, 1918, 6; *Coats Courant*, April 4, 1918, 3.

5. *Topeka Daily Capital*, April 4, 1918, 4, 10; and April 8, 1918, 1, 6; *Atchison Daily Globe*, April 24, 1918, 3; and April 27, 1918, 8; *Winfield Daily Courier*, June 1, 1918, 7; *Burden Times*, November 8, 1918, 2.

6. *Wichita Beacon*, April 6, 1917, 9; *Topeka Daily Capital*, January 1, 1918, 2; *Topeka State Journal*, January 3, 1918, 1; *Topeka Daily Capital*, January 6, 1918, 4.

7. *Washington (DC) Post*, November 20, 1917, 4; *Topeka State Journal*, January 3, 1918, 6; *Jefferson County Tribune* (Oskaloosa), January 25, 1918, 2; *Tampa (FL) Times*, May 31, 1918, 1.

8. John C. Gutschenritter affidavit, Enemy Alien Registration Affidavits, 1917–1921, Record Group 118, Records of U.S. Attorneys, 1821–2022, National Archives, NAID 288493, https://catalog.archives.gov/id/288493.

9. Kansas Registrations of Enemy Aliens, Enemy Alien Registration Affidavits, Record Group 118, National Archives, NAID 286181, https://catalog.archives.gov/id/286181; *Valley Falls Vindicator*, August 23, 1918, 4.

10. *Jefferson County Tribune* (Oskaloosa), February 1, 1918, 1; Pankratz, "Suppression of Alleged Disloyalty," 281, 290; *Jefferson County Tribune* (Oskaloosa), March 29, 1919, 2; *Emporia Gazette*, 4; *Wichita Beacon*, July 10, 1918, 6; *Altamont Journal*, November 7, 1918, 2.

11. *Harper Advocate*, April 18, 1918, 1; *Topeka Daily Capital*, June 3, 1918, 4; and June 17, 1918, 4; *Harper Advocate*, April 25, 1918, 1; and May 9, 1918, 1.

12. *Inman Review*, October 1, 1920, 4; Keckeisen, "Cost of Conscience Part 1," 11–12; *Kansas Heritage* 12, no. 4 (Winter 2004): 6–13. See also Keckeisen, "Cost of Conscience Part 2."

13. Juhnke, "Mob Violence and Kansas Mennonites," 334; *Great Bend Barton County Democrat*, April 18, 1918, 1; *Hoisington Dispatch*, April 18, 1918, 1; *Hutchinson Gazette*, April 19, 1918, 1; *Pratt Daily Tribune*, April 19, 1918, 4.

14. Keckeisen, "Cost of Conscience Part 1," 12–13; *Williamstown News*, May 2, 1918, 6.

15. Keckeisen, "Cost of Conscience Part 1," 13; *McPherson Freeman*, April 26, 1918, 1; *McPherson Daily Republican*, June 11, 1918, 1; Juhnke, "Mob Violence and Kansas Mennonites," 334; *McPherson Daily Republican*, June 7, 1918, 2; and June 10, 1918, 1.

16. *Lawrence Daily Journal–World*, May 9, 1918, 1; *Topeka Daily Capital*, June 6, 1918, 4; Katherine Lee Bates, "America the Beautiful," https://genius.com/Katharine-lee-bates-america-the-beautiful-lyrics; Juhnke, "Mob Violence and Kansas Mennonites," 334.

17. Eberle, "Plain Mennonite Face of the World War One Conscientious Objector," 193, 197; *Leavenworth Times*, June 4, 1918, 2; Parish, *Kansas Mennonites during World War I*, 41–42.

18. English, *History of the 89th Division*, 31; Keckeisen, "Cost of Conscience Part 1," 9–12.

19. Keckeisen, "Cost of Conscience Part 1," 12–13.

20. *Peabody Gazette-Herald*, June 27, 1918, 2; Toilet Paper, Kansas Memory, http://www.kansasmemory.org/item/313970; *Herington Times*, September 5, 1918, 1; *Winchester Star*, October 11, 1918, 7; *Perry Mirror*, January 10, 1918, 1.

21. Sedition Act of 1918, sec. 3, 40 U.S. Statutes at Large 553 (May 16, 1918); Pankratz, "Suppression of Alleged Disloyalty," 294, 298; *Dodge City Journal*, August 7, 1918, 3; *Ellsworth Messenger*, October 24, 1918, 1; *Manhattan Morning Chronicle*, July 30, 1918, 5; Grant Walter to Governor Capper, June 11, 1918, Governor

Arthur Capper's Slackers File, https://www.kansasmemory.org/item/212615/page/124.

22. Governor Capper to J. F. Fiegley, April 25, 1918, Governor Arthur Capper's Slackers File, https://www.kansasmemory.org/item/212615/page/44; *Horton Headlight-Commercial*, August 1, 1918, 1.

23. *Russell Informer*, April 8, 1918, 1; *Great Bend Barton County Democrat*, April 12, 1918, 1; *Coffeyville Daily Journal*, April 16, 1918, 1; *Cherryvale Weekly Republican*, April 18, 1918, 6; *Cherryvale Republican*, April 25, 1918, 8. A search for "yellow paint" in a digitized database of Kansas newspapers yielded 1,120 results for 1918, compared to 101 results for the following year. Newspapers.com (search for "yellow paint" on December 4, 2021).

24. *Natoma Independent*, May 2, 1918, 1; *Kansas Optimist* (Jamestown), May 2, 1918, 4; *Russell Record*, May 2, 1918, 8; *Norton Real Westerner*, June 1, 1918, 1; *Chetopa Clipper*, June 5, 1918, 1; *Winchester Star*, June 7, 1918, 7; *Atwood Square Deal*, June 27, 1918, 1; *Winchester Star*, September 20, 1918, 2.

25. Pankratz, "Suppression of Alleged Disloyalty," 286; *Atchison Globe*, November 12, 1918, 1; Juhnke, "Mob Violence and Kansas Mennonites," 334.

26. Barry, *Great Influenza*, 4, 96; *WaKeeny Western Kansas World*, March 21, 1918, 5; *Fort Riley Trench and Camp*, March 23, 1918, 2; Heiman, *Voices in Bronze and Stone*, 31–32.

27. *Lawrence University Daily Kansan*, October 8, 1918, 1; *Valley Falls Vindicator*, December 13, 1918, 3; Judith R. Johnson, "Kansas in the 'Grippe': The Spanish Influenza Epidemic of 1918," *Kansas History* 14, no. 1 (Spring 1992): 46–47.

28. *Burrton Graphic*, September 12, 1918, 8; Webb, *Basketball Man*, 218; *Manhattan Kansas Industrialist*, October 2, 1918, 1.

29. Webb, *Basketball Man*, 219; *Lawrence Daily University Kansan*, October 8, 1918, 1; *Marion Review*, November 21, 1918, 4; *Florence Bulletin*, November 14, 1918, 1; Griffin, *University of Kansas*, 377–378 (1974); Johnson, "Kansas in the 'Grippe,'" 49. The nineteen men honored by Kansas State who died from pneumonia or influenza are Henry C. Altman, Ralph V. Baker, George O. Beeler, Walter O. Brueckmann, MacArthur B. Brush, George Andrew Cunningham, Glenn W. Davis, Curtis V. Findley, Lester Hanawalt, Harry R. Heim, Carl F. Lasswell, Rollin H. Leedy, Walter T. McKinney, George W. McVicar, Delbert T. Pollock, John P. Slade, Frank E. Sullivan, Fred L. Taylor, and Ilo I. Taylor.

30. *Wichita Catholic Advance*, December 14, 1918, 45; Thomas Neville Bonner, *The Kansas Doctor: A Century of Pioneering* (Lawrence: University of Kansas Press, 1959), 161–163; *Oskaloosa Independent*, October 18, 1918, 2; *Topeka Daily Capital*, October 18, 1918, 8; Johnson, "Kansas in the 'Grippe,'" 55; "COVID-19 (2019 Novel Coronavirus) Summary," Kansas Department of Health and Environment, updated May 10, 2023, https://www.coronavirus.kdheks.gov/DocumentCenter/View/3097/2023-COVID-19-Summary-and-Historical-Binder-PDF?bidId= (accessed May 10, 2023).

31. *Jefferson County Tribune* (Oskaloosa), October 19, 1917, 3; *Oskaloosa Times*, May 27, 1909, 6; *Topeka Daily Capital*, December 25, 1918, 10.

22. Prisoners of War and the YMCA: Clyde Grimsley, Melvin Dyson, and Conrad Hoffman

1. Kenneth Steuer, *Pursuit of an "Unparalleled Opportunity"—The American YMCA and Prisoner of War Diplomacy among the Central Power Nations during World War I, 1914–1923* (New York: Columbia University Press, 2009), 1–4; Ed Dubin and Al Kugel, "WWI 100: Philately Tells the Story of U.S. Centennial in the Great War," *American Philatelist* 131, no. 4 (April 2017): 351; Eanes, *Captured Not Conquered*, preface.

Prisoners of war from Kansas were often reported in the newspapers. See *Wichita Beacon*, July 6, 1917, 4 (Walter Perkins, Wichita); *Salina Evening Journal*, November 16, 1917, 1 (Clyde Grimsley, Salina); *Ottawa Herald*, July 13, 1918, 5 (Emmet John Prosser, Minneapolis); *Topeka Daily Capital*, July 31, 1918, 1 (Harold G. Lawrence, Independence); *Kansas City (MO) Star*, August 20, 1918, 8 (Burt Cheesman, Parsons); *Enid (OK) Daily Eagle*, August 29, 1918, 6 (Homer Steele, Chanute); *Ottawa Herald*, October 24, 1918, 8 (Harry M. Hewitt, Mound City); *Manhattan Mercury*, October 21, 1918, 1 (Arthur Hayum, Holton); *Phillips County Post*, October 31, 1918, 1 (Roland Beaver, Portland, Oregon, and Kirwin, Kansas); *Chanute Daily Tribune*, November 1, 1918, 1 (Ernest C. Wood, Wilmore); *Topeka State Journal*, November 2, 1918, 8 (Herbert F. Gunther, Paxico); *Hartford Times*, November 8, 1918, 4 (Jennings Bryan Tatman, Hartford); *Topeka Daily Capital*, November 12, 1918, 2 (Charles Gefner, Olathe); *Lawrence Daily Journal-World*, November 13, 1918, 1 (Louis R. Davolt, Elkhart; Arthur A. Beck, Niles); *Coffeyville Daily Journal*, November 16, 1918, 1 (Earl Van Winkle, Coffeyville; John Francis Graves, Douglas); *Lawrence Daily Journal-World*, November 21, 1918, 1 (Hugh A. Garvie, Abilene; John L. Elliot, Wichita; Lafayette L. Troutman, Lewis); *Coffeyville Daily Journal*, December 3, 1918, 1 (Louis Jossi, Eldorado); *Leavenworth Times*, December 5, 1918, 3 (Edgar L. Jones, Coffeyville; Elmer W. Vail, Fort Scott; Melvin Dyson, Oskaloosa; Joseph P. Plante, Damar; Aubrey L. Ladow, Cawker City; Albert R. Sitz, Hays); *Wichita Eagle*, December 6, 1918, 2 (Herbert A. Green, Topeka; Lt. John B. Greever, Lansing; Herbert F. Stoffle, Morrowville; John O. Parson, Barnard; Carl L. Jewell, Burton; John F. Evers, Collyer); *Leavenworth Times*, December 8, 1918, 1 (Clyde T. Crocker, Coffeyville); *Topeka Daily Capital*, December 10, 1918, 8 (Roy B. Child, Auburn; John A. Harmon, Salina; Lloyd Gates, McPherson; Edward M. Horn, Hanston); *Atchison Daily Globe*, December 18, 1918, 1 (Alson Viles, Muscotah); *Topeka Daily Capital*, January 1, 1919, 2 (Andrew Loren, Anthony); *Coldwater Talisman*, January 9, 1919, 9 (Fay Tam, Coldwater); *Topeka Daily Capital*, January 21, 1919, 8 (Louis S. Covert, Glen Elder; Forrest H. Creamer, Portis; Paul Ward, Downs); *Beloit Gazette*, January 22, 1919, 2 (Lawrence E. Deal, Cawker City); *Independence Daily Reporter*, February 12, 1919, 1 (Clarence Brodie, Wichita); *Oskaloosa Independent*, March 21, 1919, 3 (Ben Brown, Iola); and *Horton Headlight-Commercial*, July 24, 1919, 7 (Earl W. Ross, Horton).

2. *Salina Daily Union*, December 18, 1918, 4; *Salina Evening Journal*, March 6,

1919, 1; *Stockton Review and Rooks County Record*, March 13, 1919, 1; *Salina Daily Union*, March 6, 1919, 6; Eanes, *Captured Not Conquered*, 59–60.

3. Edgar M. Halyburton, *Shoot and Be Damned* (New York: Covici Friede, 1932), 66; *Stockton Review and Rooks County Record*, March 13, 1919, 1; *Salina Daily Union*, March 6, 1919, 6; *Stockton Review and Rooks County Record*, February 21, 1918, 1; *Salina Daily Union*, April 16, 1919, 1.

4. *Salina Daily Union*, March 30, 1918, 1; *Salina Evening Journal*, June 29, 1918, 4; *Alton Empire*, March 20, 1919, 4; *Salina Daily Union*, March 6, 1919, 6; *Stockton Review and Rooks County Record*, March 13, 1919, 1.

5. Eanes, *Captured Not Conquered*, 240–242; Halyburton, *Shoot and Be Damned*, 75; *Salina Evening Journal*, March 6, 1919, 1; *Stockton Review and Rooks County Record*, March 13, 1919, 1; Steuer, *Pursuit of an 'Unparalleled Opportunity*,' 283; *Salina Daily Union*, January 18, 1919, 5.

6. *Stockton Review and Rooks County Record*, March 13, 1919, 1; Eanes, *Captured Not Conquered*, 54; *Salina Daily Union*, March 6, 1919, 6; *Salina Evening Journal*, June 29, 1918, 4; *Salina Daily Union*, January 18, 1919, 5.

7. *Madison (WI) State Journal*, June 1, 1913, 14; *Lawrence Daily Gazette*, April 16, 1913, 1; and May 14, 1915, 1.

8. Conrad Hoffman, *In the Prison Camps of Germany: A Narrative of "Y" Service among Prisoners of War* (New York: Association, 1920), 30; Jackson, *Prisoners*, 62; Webb, *Basketball Man*, 192–202; Lee Shippey, "It Kept Us from Going Mad: With the First Trainload of American Prisoners Brought Out of Germany through Switzerland, Came a Cargo of Praise for the Red Triangle and for Conrad Hoffman, Who Had Supplied the Men with Athletic Goods, Books, and Other Comforts," *YMCA Association Men* 44, no. 7 (March 1919): 520.

9. Richard C. Lancaster, *Serving the U.S. Armed Forces, 1861–1986: The Story of the YMCA's Ministry to Military Personnel for 125 Years* (Schaumburg, IL: Armed Services YMCA of the USA, 1987), 42–43; Hoffman, *In the Prison Camps of Germany*, 146–148; Halyburton, *Shoot and Be Damned*, 245–246; Eanes, *Captured Not Conquered*, 40.

10. *Oskaloosa Independent*, January 3, 1919, 3; *Leavenworth Post*, May 13, 1919, 2; Eanes, *Captured Not Conquered*, 51–52. Excerpts from an interview with Melvin Dyson were shown in 2003 on C-Span. See Melvin Dyson, interview (June 1996), *Prisoner of War Interviews*, C-Span, broadcast May 14, 2003, https://www.c-span.org/video/?176624-3/world-war-pow-private-melvin-dyson.

11. *Leavenworth Post*, May 13, 1919, 2.

12. Eanes, *Captured Not Conquered*, 8; Hoffman, *In the Prison Camps of Germany*, 159–170; Halyburton, *Shoot and Be Damned*, 338–339, 411; Steuer, *Pursuit of an 'Unparalleled Opportunity*,' 285–288; *Stockton Review and Rooks County Record*, March 13, 1919, 1.

13. Steuer, *Pursuit of an 'Unparalleled Opportunity*,' app. 14b, 286; *Salina Daily Union*, March 6, 1919, 6; Hoffman, *In the Prison Camps of Germany*, 168, 179–180; Halyburton, *Shoot and Be Damned*, 342–343.

14. *Norton Champion*, April 3, 1919, 3; *Jetmore Republican*, December 13, 1918, 3; and January 24, 1918, 1; *Salina Evening Journal*, March 6, 1919, 1.

15. Frank Ward O'Malley, "Published in a German Prison," *Red Cross Magazine* 14, no. 6 (June 1919), 6; Richard van Emden, *Prisoners of the Kaiser: The Last POWs of the Great War* (Barnsley, UK: Pen & Sword Books, 2009), 157; *Oskaloosa Independent*, January 3, 1919, 3.

16. *Salina Evening Journal*, March 6, 1919, 1; *Stockton Review*, January 9, 1919, 1; *Stockton Review and Rooks County Record*, March 13, 1919, 1.

17. *Ottawa Herald*, April 1, 1919, 6; *Salina Daily Union*, April 16, 1919, 1; *Stockton Review*, May 1, 1919, 4; *Salina Evening Journal*, January 24, 1922, 4.

18. Marc L. Greenberg, "Hoffman's Hawk: A University of Kansas Jayhawk Carved during the Russian Revolution of 1917 Reappears at KU in the Twenty-First Century," KU Scholar Works, November 24, 2010, https://kuscholarworks.ku.edu/bitstream/handle/1808/6896/Russian_Jayhawk_history_2010Nov24_MLGreenberg.pdf?sequence=1&isAllowed=y; Hoffman, *In the Prison Camps of Germany*, 40; *Lawrence University Daily Kansan*, October 13, 1920, 4; *Bridgewater (NJ) Courier-News*, September 26, 1936, 2; Clarence Prouty Shedd, *History of the World's Alliance of Young Men's Christian Associations* (London: SPCK Publishing, 1955), 565.

23. The Kansas Home Front after the War

1. *Kansas City Advocate*, March 7, 1919, 1; *Kansas City (MO) Sun*, March 15, 1919, 1; *Kansas City Advocate*, March 21, 1919, 3; *Kansas City (MO) Sun*, March 22, 1919, 1; *La Crosse Chieftain*, March 27, 1919, 6; *Topeka Daily Plaindealer*, March 28, 1919, 1; *Topeka Daily Capital*, July 30, 1919, 1.

2. *Topeka Daily Capital*, May 6, 1919, 1; *Topeka State Journal*, May 5, 1919, 1.

3. *Topeka State Journal*, May 8, 1919, 1; *Topeka Daily Capital*, May 9, 1919, 1; *Hutchinson Gazette*, May 8, 1919, 1; *Independence South Kansas Tribune*, May 7, 1919, 1; *Kansas City Kansan*, May 7, 1919, 1; *Lawrence Daily Journal–World*, May 8, 1919, 1; *Wichita Daily Eagle*, May 9, 1919, 1.

4. *Pratt Daily Tribune*, May 22, 1919, 1.

5. *Kansas City (MO) Star*, May 30, 1919, 1; *Topeka State Journal*, May 30, 1919, 1; and May 31, 1919, 2; *Topeka Daily Capital*, May 31, 1919, 1; *Emporia Gazette*, May 31, 1919, 1; *Atchison Weekly Globe*, June 5, 1919, 3.

6. *Jamestown Optimist*, September 12, 1918, 1; September 26, 1918, 1; May 8, 1919, 1; and October 6, 1921, 1.

7. *Atchison Weekly Globe*, December 5, 1918, 1; *Oskaloosa Independent*, December 27, 1918, 2; *Perry Mirror*, January 30, 1919, 1.

8. *Nortonville News*, January 10, 1919, 1; February 7, 1919, 1; and February 28, 1919, 1; *Irving Leader*, January 31, 1919, 1; and March 14, 1919, 4.

9. *Oskaloosa Independent*, November 8, 1918, 5; T. R. Blevins to parents, December 10, 1918, Blevins Papers; *Topeka Daily Capital*, November 4, 1918, 6; *Oskaloosa Independent*, November 29, 1918, 5.

10. T. R. Blevins to his parents, March 1, December 10, 1918, Blevins Papers;

Katie Lange, "Dog Tag History: How the Tradition & Nickname Started," DOD News, September 9, 2020, https://www.defense.gov/News/Inside-DOD/Blog/Article/2340760/dog-tag-history-how-the-tradition-nickname-started/; *Carson City (NV) Daily Appeal*, March 9, 1918, 4; *Hiawatha Daily World*, February 5, 1918, 1; *Hiawatha Brown County World*, February 5, 1918, 1.

11. *Oskaloosa Independent*, January 24, 1919, 5; *Jefferson County Tribune* (Oskaloosa), February 7, 1919, 1; and May 9, 1919, 4.

12. White, *Martial Adventures of Henry and Me*, 83; *Manhattan Tribune*, August 1, 1918, 1; *Topeka State Journal*, January 13, 1919, 1; *Topeka Daily Capital*, January 14, 1919, 1; Ferrell, "Angered to the Core," 185.

13. *Topeka State Journal*, January 15, 1919, 6; *Topeka Daily Capital*, January 23, 1919, 1; Ferrell, *Collapse at Meuse-Argonne*, 117; Ferrell, "Angered to the Core," 189–193; *Oskaloosa Independent*, May 9, 1919, 1; and June 6, 1919, 1; T. R. Blevins to parents, France, February 8, 1919, Blevins Papers.

14. *Brooklyn (NY) Daily Eagle*, September 18, 1937, 2; *Augusta Gazette*, May 6, 1919, 3; Thomas A. Rumer, *The American Legion: An Official History, 1919–1989* (New York: M. Evans, 1990), 28; Steven Trout, "Forgotten Reminders: Kansas World War I Memorials," *Kansas History* 29, no. 3 (Autumn 2006): 209.

15. *Oskaloosa Independent*, September 5, 1919; *Atchison Daily Globe*, December 2, 1946, 1; *Newton Evening Kansan–Republican*, May 23, 1919; *Hutchinson News*, December 20, 1919, 15; *Olathe Mirror*, June 29, 1922, 10; *Hutchinson News*, August 5, 1918, 8; *Salina Journal*, August 25, 1998, 9.

16. *WaKeeney Western Kansas World*, November 7, 1918, 1; February 6, 1919, 1; February 20, 1919, 1; and August 25, 1921, 1.

17. *Oswego Democrat*, January 4, 1918, 5; *Ottawa Herald*, January 4, 1918, 1; *Arkansas City Daily News*, May 30, 1919, 1; Sledge, *Soldier Dead*, 176; Heiman, *Voices in Bronze and Stone*, 46–48; *Kansas City (MO) Star*, July 6, 1930, 1; *Manhattan Mercury*, March 10, 1930, 1.

18. *Hutchinson News*, February 18, 1930, 5; *Abilene Daily Chronicle*, September 30, 1907, 4; *Abilene Daily Reflector*, February 14, 1905, 3; and April 20, 1911, 3; *Abilene Daily Chronicle*, June 17, 1912, 4; and April 10, 1919, 1.

19. *Manhattan Mercury*, December 18, 2021, C1; and May 21, 1930, 1; *Manhattan Chronicle*, July 27, 1930, 1; *Wichita Eagle*, September 13, 1930, 11; *Wichita Beacon*, September 12, 1930, 13; *Pittsburg Booster*, September 18, 1930, 2.

24. The Boys of Company B: William Davis, Victor Segraves, Ralph Nichols, and Samuel Gutschenritter

1. Samuel Gutschenritter obituary, *Oskaloosa Independent*, November 4, 1954.

2. American Red Cross to John Davis, April 5, 1919, Davis Papers; *Winchester Star*, June 10, 1921, 3; *Oskaloosa Independent*, June 10, 1921, 5.

3. Samuel McCune Lindsay, "Purpose and Scope of War Risk Insurance," *Annals of the American Academy of Political and Social Science* 79, no. 1 (September 1918): 65–68; *Abilene Weekly Chronicle*, October 10, 1917, 2; Bureau of War Risk Insurance

to John Davis, November 26, 1918, Davis Papers; *Manhattan Weekly Mercury*, March 6, 1923, 1; Kansas Compensation Board to John Davis, November 22, 1923, Davis Papers.

4. See M. Sue Kendall, *Rethinking Regionalism: John Steuart Curry and the Kansas Mural Controversy* (Washington, DC: Smithsonian Institution Press, 1986); Marjorie Swann and William M. Tsutsui, "John Steuart Curry: A Portrait of the Artist as a Kansan," in *John Brown to Bob Dole: Movers and Shakers in Kansas History*, ed. Virgil W. Dean (Lawrence: University Press of Kansas): 244–247.

5. Steven Trout, *On the Battlefield of Memory: The First World War and American Remembrance, 1919–1941* (Tuscaloosa: University of Alabama Press, 2010), 198–199, 209, 213.

6. Trout, *On the Battlefield of Memory*, 199, 205–207.

7. *Emporia Gazette*, January 12, 1938, 3.

8. *Jefferson County Tribune* (Oskaloosa), February 7, 1919, 1; *Oskaloosa Independent*, September 13, 1918, 5; Reminiscences of T. R. Blevins, 1979, Blevins Papers.

9. *Topeka State Journal*, April 23, 1919, 2; *Jefferson County Tribune* (Oskaloosa), June 20, 1919, 1; *Oskaloosa Independent*, June 20, 1919, 5; and September 19, 1919, 5.

10. *Meridan Message*, October 26, 1923, 8; *McLouth Times*, December 27, 1923, 4.

11. *Oskaloosa Independent*, May 16, 1919, 5; *Jefferson County Tribune* (Oskaloosa), January 17, 1919, 4; and June 20, 1919, 4; *Oskaloosa Independent*, June 6, 1919, 5; *Jefferson County Tribune* (Oskaloosa), September 12, 1919, 5; and November 14, 1919, 1.

12. *Oskaloosa Independent*, May 14, 1920, 7; May 21, 1920, 1; September 10, 1920, 5; and November 5, 1920, 5; *The Royal Purple 1924* (Manhattan: Kansas State Agricultural College, 1924), 132, available at Archive.org, https://archive.org/details/RoyalPurple_20121207_1737/page/n141/mode/1up.

13. *Manhattan Daily Nationalist*, December 12, 1922, 1; *Manhattan Morning Chronicle*, December 8, 1923, 5; and April 8, 1924, 2; *Hartford (CT) Courant*, November 1, 1926, 13; and November 8, 1926, 12.

14. *Amarillo (TX) Globe Times*, January 22, 1929, 7; *Manhattan Kansas Industrialist*, February 6, 1929, 3; and January 23, 1929, 4.

15. *Oskaloosa Independent*, April 18, 1919, 5; *Jefferson County Tribune* (Oskaloosa), January 24, 1919, 1; *Oskaloosa Independent*, December 27, 1918, 5; Claude McNeal, *Miracle in Springs Valley: The Amazing Story of Two Grand Hotels* (Indianapolis: CMcN Books, 2010), 77.

16. *Oskaloosa Independent*, April 18, 1919; January 9, 1920, 4; and February 27, 1920, 5; *Winchester Star*, May 5, 1939, 2; Samuel Gutschenritter obituary, *Oskaloosa Independent*, November 4, 1954.

25. The Boys of Company B: William Smith, William Kimmel, Theodore Blevins, and Melvin Dyson

1. Charles William Sloan Jr., "Kansas Battles the Invisible Empire: The Legal Ouster of the KKK from Kansas, 1922–1927," *Kansas Historical Quarterly* 40, 3 (Autumn 1974): 400–401.

2. *Topeka Kansas State News*, September 18, 1924, 2; Sloan, "Kansas Battles the Invisible Empire," 393; *Emporia Gazette*, June 12, 1926, 6; Duane Roy Perkins, "The Ku Klux Klan in Lyon County, Kansas, in the 1920s" (MA thesis, Emporia State University, 1981), 45–47, https://esirc.emporia.edu/bitstream/handle/123456789/2221/Perkins%201981.pdf?sequence=1; *Emporia State Bugle*, June 25, 1926, 1; *Emporia Gazette*, July 2, 1926, 2; *Mulberry Independent*, July 2, 1926, 3; *Hutchinson News*, November 20, 1926, 1; Knights of Ku Klux Klan v. State of Kansas ex rel. Griffith, 273 U.S. 664 (February 28, 1927).

3. *Kansas City (MO) Times*, September 17, 1930, 1; Webb v. School Dist. No. 90, Johnson County, 206 P.2d 1066, 1068, 1073 (Kan. Sup. Ct. 1949); *Topeka Capital-Journal*, December 15, 2016.

4. *Emporia Gazette*, July 22, 1968, 10; Kansas Reports, 188:xiv (1961); Company B, *1955 Reunion*.

5. *Topeka Daily Capital*, May 6, 1919, 1, 6; *Oskaloosa Independent*, May 9, 1919, 5.

6. *Manhattan Republic*, August 4, 1954, 2; *St. Louis Post-Dispatch*, November 17, 1967, 20.

7. *Leavenworth Times*, September 30, 1962, 5; Geoffrey Kimmel to Blake Watson, email, February 28, 2022.

8. *Jefferson County Tribune* (Oskaloosa), November 8, 1918, 6; *Atlanta Constitution*, May 25, 1934, 1.

9. *Oskaloosa Independent*, February 21, 1919, 5; T. R. Blevins to parents, France, March 28, 1919, Blevins Papers.

10. *Oskaloosa Independent*, September 19, 1919, 5; *Fort Collins (CO) Coloradoan*, July 26, 1925, 5; April 28, 1965, 3; and November 26, 1989, *Valley Falls Vindicator*, February 2, 1923, 1; *Fort Collins (CO) Coloradoan*, May 9, 1965, 25; T. R. Blevins, interview in *Spilled Ink* (Fort Collins High School newspaper), December 16, 1926, Blevins Papers.

11. *Fort Collins (CO) Coloradoan*, April 28, 1965, 3; March 14, 1967, 1; November 24, 1968, 15; and June 11, 1973, 11.

12. *Fort Collins (CO) Coloradoan*, August 8, 1975, 1; Theodore Blevins obituary, *Fort Collins (CO) Coloradoan*, November 26, 1989.

13. *Oskaloosa Independent*, April 7, 1922, 5; *Siskiyou (CA) Daily News*, October 7, 1926, 1.

14. *Portland Oregonian*, January 26, 1996, C10; and December 26, 1979, 35.

15. *St. George (UT) Daily Spectrum*, July 22, 1984, 17; *Los Angeles Times*, September 19, 1986, 25; *Salem (OR) Statesman*, August 13, 1990, 1; Melvin Dyson, interview (June 1996), *Prisoner of War Interviews*, C-Span, broadcast May 14, 2003, https://www.c-span.org/video/?176624-3/world-war-pow-private-melvin-dyson.

16. *Topeka Daily Capital*, July 29, 1918, 3; *Wichita Eagle*, January 25, 2007, 9.

Conclusion

1. Trout, "Forgotten Reminders," 202; Heiman, *Voices in Bronze and Stone*, 173; American Memorials Directory, https://www.americanmemorialsdirectory.com.

2. "Kansas Casualties in the World War, 1917–1919: Grouped by Towns Shown as Being Residence of Deceased Soldiers, Kansas Casualties," KSGenWeb Project, https://www.ksgenweb.org/archives/statewide/military/wwI/casualty/.

3. Trout, "Forgotten Reminders," 203.

4. *Oakley Graphic*, May 4, 1923, 1; and May 18, 1923, 6; *Frankfort Index*, April 20, 1925, 3; *Axtell Standard*, August 29, 1918, 1; James Patton, "The Centennial at the Grass Roots: Finding WWI in Rural Kansas," *Roads to the Great War* (blog), October 9, 2017, http://roadstothegreatwar-ww1.blogspot.com/2017/10/the-centennial-at-grass-roots-finding.html.

5. *Parsons Sun*, November 12, 1930, 10.

6. *Wichita Beacon*, May 17, 1919, 7; *Wichita Eagle*, January 2, 1920, 5; *Wichita Catholic Advance*, May 12, 1923, 1; *Iola Register*, October 29, 1926, 1; St. Mary's World War I Memorial Arch Fund, https://www.ccfks.org/cause/st-marys-world-war-i-memorial-arch-fund/.

7. "Haskell Stadium Memorial Arch," Historical Marker Database, last revised September 20, 2022, https://www.hmdb.org/m.asp?m=77316; Clarence Dennis, "What Is the History of the Rosedale Arch?," CuriousKC, Flatland, November 16, 2020, https://www.flatlandkc.org/curiouskc/question-everything/questions-answered/curiouskc-what-is-the-history-of-the-rosedale-arch/; Suzanne Hogan, "How Kansas City Became Home to the Nation's Official World War I Memorial," KCUR, NPR in Kansas City, November 9, 2018, https://www.kcur.org/arts-life/2018-11-09/how-kansas-city-became-home-to-the-nations-official-world-war-i-memorial.

8. Hogan, "How Kansas City Became Home to the Nation's Official World War I Memorial"; *Kansas City (MO) Star*, November 11, 1926, 27; and November 3, 1926, 1.

9. Trout, "Forgotten Reminders," 209–210; *Kansas City (MO) Star*, March 6, 1963, 1.

10. *Wichita Eagle*, April 7, 1919, 3; *Lawrence Daily Gazette*, October 31, 1918, 1; "Liberty Memorial Central Middle School," United States World War One Centennial Commission, November 14, 2016, https://www.worldwar1centennial.org/index.php/component/gmapfp/916:liberty-memorial-central-middle-school.html?view=gmapfp.

11. *Topeka Daily Capital*, June 12, 1919, 1; *Topeka State Journal*, January 26, 1921, 8; *Topeka Capper's Weekly*, June 16, 1923, 8; Madison Dean, "Then and Now: Washburn's Campus," Washburn Review, June 22, 2012, https://washburnreview.org/30662/news/then-and-now-washburns-campus/; "Veteran Memorials," Washburn University, https://www.washburn.edu/about/community/attractions/veteran-memorials.html. Benton Hall was the first-year residence of Barbara Nichols Watson, the author's mother, who received two demerits for noise on April 19, 1950.

12. *The Royal Purple 1923* (Manhattan: Kansas State Agricultural College, 1923), dedication, available at Archive.org, https://archive.org/details/RoyalPurple_20121207_1627/page/n9/mode/1up; *Manhattan Kansas Industrialist*, December 6, 1922, 2.

13. *Manhattan Kansas Industrialist*, December 6, 1922, 2; *Manhattan Mercury*,

October 30, 1922, 1. John Watson, the author's father, played football at Memorial Stadium for Kansas State in 1945.

14. John McCool, "' . . . Kansas Must Have a Stadium!,'" Memorial Stadium. KU Memorial Union, https://union.ku.edu/kansas-must-have-stadium (accessed August 2, 2023); 1921 Kansas Jayhawks Schedule and Results, https://www.sports-reference.com/cfb/schools/kansas/1921-schedule.html.

15. Ceremonial Laying of the Cornerstone, KU Memorial Union, https://union.ku.edu/ceremonial-laying-cornerstone; *University Daily Kansan*, January 17, 1919, 1.

16. "Heart of Campus," KU Memorial Union, https://union.ku.edu/kansas-union.

17. Kansas Museum of History, https://www.kshs.org/p/kansas-museum-of-history/19578; "Kansas National Guard Hall of Fame," Museum of the Kansas National Guard, https://www.kansasguardmuseum.com/hall-of-fame/.

18. "Built by Kansas Citizens, Embraced by the Nation," Our Story, The National WW1 Museum and Memorial, https://www.theworldwar.org/explore/our-story.

19. "Emporia, Kansas, Founding City of Veterans Day," H.R. Concurrent Resolution 159, 117 U.S. Statutes at Large 2958 (October 31, 2003); *Wichita Eagle*, June 2, 1954, 1; *Emporia Gazette*, October 23, 1971, 3 (reprint of story dated June 18, 1954).

20. Kansas World War I Centennial Committee, http://www.kansasww1.org/ (site discontinued); *Emporia Gazette*, October 30, 2018.

21. *Wichita Eagle*, November 4, 1918, B1; Sarah Moyer, "Manhattan Observes Armistice Day Centennial with Concert and More," *Kansas State Collegian*, November 12, 2018, https://www.kstatecollegian.com/2018/11/12/manhattan-observes-armistice-day-centennial-with-concert-and-more/; *Manhattan Mercury*, November 8, 2018, A3.

22. *Lawrence Journal-World*, November 11, 2019.

23. T. R. Blevins, letters from France, March 6, 28, 1919, Blevins Papers; *Fort Collins Coloradoan*, January 18, 2006, B9; Jennifer D. Keene, "Remembering the 'Forgotten War': American Historiography on World War I," *Historian* 78, no. 3 (2016): 439.

Bibliography

Unpublished Primary Sources

Letters and Recollections of Theodore Blevins. Theodore Blevins Papers. Pattee Family Collection. In author's possession.

William Louis Davis Papers. National WWI Museum and Memorial, Kansas City, MO.

Published Primary Sources

Adjutant General, State of Kansas. *Kansas Casualties in the World War, 1917–1919*. Topeka: Kansas State Printing Plant, 1921–1925.

Adjutant General, U.S. War Department. *Composition of National Guard Divisions and Disposition of Former National Guard Units, 1917*. Washington, DC: Government Printing Office, 1918.

Arnold, Anna E. *A History of Kansas*. Topeka: State of Kansas Printing Plant, 1914.

Blackmar, Frank W., ed. *History of the Kansas State Council of Defense*. Topeka: Kansas State Printing Plant, 1920.

Blevins, Jesse J., and Kathryn E. B. Bearman. *The Sergeant & Company B*. Privately printed, 1976.

Bliss, Paul S. *Victory: History of the 805th Pioneer Infantry*. St. Paul, MN: Privately printed, 1919.

Browne, Charles H. *A History of the 137th Infantry: An All-Kansas National Guard Regiment*. Horton, KS: Headlight Printshop, 1940.

Browne, Charles H., and J. W. McManigal. *Our Part in the Great War: What the Horton Community Did*. Horton, KS: Headlight-Commercial, 1919.

Bureau of the Census, Department of Commerce and Labor. *Thirteenth Census of the United States Taken in the Year 1910, Statistics for Kansas*. Washington, DC: Government Printing Office, 1913.

Company B, 3rd Kansas National Guard, 139th U.S. Infantry Regiment. *1955 Reunion*. Oskaloosa, KS, August 19, 1955.

Dennett, Carl P. *Prisoners of the Great War: Authoritative Statement of Conditions in the Prison Camps of Germany*. New York: Houghton Mifflin, 1919.

Dienst, Charles F., et al., *History of the 353rd Infantry Regiment, 89th Division, National Army*. Wichita, KS: Eagle, 1921.

English, George H., Jr. *History of the 89th Division, U.S.A.* Denver, CO: Smith-Brooks, 1920.

Graham, Ira D. "Major General James Guthrie Harbord: An Appreciation." In *Collections of the Kansas State Historical Society, 1919–1922,* edited by William E. Connelley, 15:7–13. Topeka: Kansas State Printing Plant, 1923.

Halyburton, Edgar M. *Shoot and Be Damned.* New York: Covici Friede, 1932.

Harbord, James G. *Leaves from a War Diary.* New York: Dodd, Mead, 1925.

Haterius, Carl E. *Reminiscences of the 137th Infantry.* Topeka, KS: Crane, 1919.

Hoffman, Conrad. *In the Prison Camps of Germany: A Narrative of "Y" Service among Prisoners of War.* New York: Association, 1920.

Honor Roll, Shawnee County Kansas. Kansas City, MO: Burger Engraving, 1920.

Hoyt, Charles B. *Heroes of the Argonne: An Authentic History of the Thirty-Fifth Division.* Kansas City, MO: Franklin Hudson, 1919.

Hunton, Addie W., and Kathryn M. Johnson. *Two Colored Women with the American Expeditionary Forces.* Brooklyn, NY: Brooklyn Eagle, 1920.

Jamieson, J. A. *Complete History of the Colored Soldiers in the World War.* New York: Bennett & Churchill, 1919.

Jardine, W. M. *How to Prepare Ground for Wheat, and Time to Sow.* Circular 6, Kansas State Council of Defense. Topeka: Kansas State Printing Plant, 1917.

Johnson, Harold Stanley. *Roster of the Rainbow Division (Forty-Second).* New York: Eaton & Gettinger, 1917.

Johnson, Thomas M., and Fletcher Pratt. *The Lost Battalion.* Indianapolis: Bobbs-Merrill, 1936.

Kenamore, Clair. *From Vauquois Hill to Exermont: A History of the Thirty-Fifth Division of the United States Army.* St. Louis: Guard Publishing, 1919.

———. *The Story of the 139th Infantry.* St. Louis: Guard Publishing, 1920.

Lindsay, Samuel McCune. "Purpose and Scope of War Risk Insurance." *Annals of the American Academy of Political and Social Science* 79, no. 1 (September 1918): 52–68.

Link, Arthur Stanley, ed. *The Papers of Woodrow Wilson.* 69 vols. Princeton, NJ: Princeton University Press, 1966–1994.

Little, Arthur W. *From Harlem to the Rhine: The Story of New York's Colored Volunteers.* New York: Covici Friede, 1936.

Morehouse, George P. "Kansas as a State of Extremes, and Its Attitude during This World War." In *Collections of the Kansas Historical Society, 1919–1922,* edited by William E. Connelley, 15:15–28. Topeka: Kansas State Printing Plant, 1923.

O'Malley, Frank Ward. "Published in a German Prison: The Story of an American Newspaper." *Red Cross Magazine* 14, no. 6 (June 1919): 52–57.

Palmer, Frederick. *Newton D. Baker: America at War.* Vol. 2. New York: Dodd, Mead, 1931.

Pattullo, George. "The First Raid." *Saturday Evening Post*, December 29, 1917.

Pershing, John J. *My Experiences in the World War.* Vol. 1. New York: Frederick Stokes, 1931.

"Putting Vim into the Victory Loan: An Advertising Campaign That Is Sure to Compel Attention." *Advertising and Selling*, no. 32 (April 12, 1919):10–11.

Rizzi, Joseph N. *Joe's War: Memoirs of a Doughboy*. Edited by Richard A. Baumgartner. Huntington, WV: Der Angriff, 1983.
Scott, Emmett J. *Scott's Official History of the American Negro in the World War*. New York, 1919.
Shippey, Lee. "It Kept Us from Going Mad: With the First Trainload of American Prisoners Brought Out of Germany through Switzerland, Came a Cargo of Praise for the Red Triangle and for Conrad Hoffman, Who Had Supplied the Men with Athletic Goods, Books, and Other Comforts." *YMCA Association Men* 44, no. 7 (March 1919): 520, 566–567.
Society of the First Division. *History of the First Division during the World War, 1917–1919*. Philadelphia: John C. Winston, 1922.
Trickett, Dean. "The Story of Company A, Third Kansas Infantry, in World War I." *Kansas Historical Quarterly* 13, no. 6 (May 1945): 358–366.
Webster, Daniel. *The Writings and Speeches of Daniel Webster*. Vol. 14. Boston: Little, Brown, 1903.
White, William Allen. *The Martial Adventures of Henry and Me*. New York: Macmillan, 1918.
Wooldridge, Jesse W. *The Giants of the Marne: A Story of McAlexander and His Regiment*. Salt Lake City: Seagull, 1923.
Wright, William M. *Meuse-Argonne Diary: A Division Commander in World War I*. Edited by Robert H. Ferrell. Columbia: University of Missouri Press, 2004.

Published Secondary Sources

Abney, Wesley. *Random Destiny: How the Vietnam War Draft Lottery Shaped a Generation*. Wilmington, DE: Vernon, 2018.
American Battle Monuments Commission. *American Armies and Battlefields in Europe*. Washington, DC: Government Printing Office, 1938.
Andreas, Alfred Theodore. *History of the State of Kansas*. Vol. 1. Chicago: A. T. Andreas, 1883.
Archer, Laird. *Balkan Journal*. New York: W. W. Norton, 1944.
———. *Balkan Tragedy*. Rev. ed. Manhattan, KS: MA/AH, 1983.
Axelrod, Alan. *Miracle at Belleau Wood: The Birth of the Modern U.S. Marine Corps*. Guilford, CT: Lyons, 2007.
———. *Selling the Great War: The Making of American Propaganda*. New York: Palgrave Macmillan, 2009.
Barbeau, Arthur E., and Florette Henri. *The Unknown Soldiers: African-American Troops in World War I*. Philadelphia: Temple University Press, 1974.
Barry, John M. *The Great Influenza: The Epic Story of the Deadliest Plague in History*. New York: Penguin Books, 2005.
Barry, John W. *The Midwest Goes to War: The 32nd Division in the Great War*. Lanham, MD: Scarecrow, 2007.
Bernstein, J. L. "Conscription and the Constitution: The Amazing Case of

Kneedler v. Lane." *American Bar Association Journal* 53, no. 8 (August 1967): 708–712.

Bonner, Thomas Neville. *The Kansas Doctor: A Century of Pioneering*. Lawrence: University of Kansas Press, 1959.

Bright, John D. *Kansas: The First Century*. Vol. 1. New York: Lewis Historical Publishing, 1956.

Britten, Thomas A. *American Indians in World War I: At War and at Home*. Albuquerque: University of New Mexico Press, 1997.

Buckley, Gail L. *American Patriots: The Story of Blacks in the Military from the Revolution to Desert Storm*. New York: Random House, 2002.

Butters, Gerald R. "*The Birth of a Nation* and the Kansas Board of Review of Motion Pictures: A Censorship Struggle." *Kansas History* 14, no. 1 (Spring 1991): 2–14.

Byerly, Carol. "William T. Fitzsimons." In *Builders of Trust: Biographical Profiles from the Medical Corps Coin*, edited by Sanders Marble, 99–107. Fort Detrick, MD: Borden Institute, 2011.

Campney, Brent M. S. *This Is Not Dixie: Racist Violence in Kansas, 1861–1927*. Urbana: University of Illinois Press, 2015.

Canfield, Leon H. *The Presidency of Woodrow Wilson: Prelude to a World in Crisis*. Rutherford, NJ: Fairleigh Dickinson University Press, 1966.

Cart, Doran L. "Kansas Football 'Over There.'" *Journal of the Central Plains* 29, no. 3 (Autumn 2006): 194–199.

Carter, Donald A. *St. Mihiel: 12–16 September 1918*. Washington, DC: Center of Military History, U.S. Army, 2018.

Casey, Jonathan. "Training in Kansas for a World War: Camp Funston in Photographs." *Kansas History* 29, no. 3 (Autumn 2006): 164–171.

Center of Military History, U.S. Army. *Organization of the American Expeditionary Forces*. Washington, DC: Government Printing Office, 1948.

Chambers, John Whiteclay. *To Raise an Army: The Draft Comes to Modern America*. New York: Free Press, 1987.

Chicoine, Stephen D. *Captain Mallon: Doughboy Hero*. Minneapolis: Freedom History Publishing, 2017.

Cochrane, Rexmond C. *The 89th Division in the Bois de Bantheville, October 1918*. Washington, DC: U.S. Army Chemical Corps Historical Office, 1960.

Connelley, William E. *History of Kansas*. Vol. 2. Chicago: American Historical Society, 1928.

Cooke, James J. *Pershing and His Generals: Command and Staff in the AEF*. Westport, CT: Praeger, 1997.

———. *The Rainbow Division in the Great War, 1917–1919*. Westport, CT: Praeger, 1994.

Cunningham, Roger D. *The Black Citizen-Soldiers of Kansas, 1864–1901*. Columbia: University of Missouri Press, 2008.

Davenport, Matthew J. *First Over There: The Attack on Cantigny, America's First Battle of World War I*. New York: St. Martin's, 2015.

Davis, Henry B. *Generals in Khaki*. Raleigh, NC: Pentland, 1998.

Dobak, William A. "Fort Riley's Black Soldiers and the Army's Changing Role in the West, 1867–1885." *Kansas History* 22, no. 3 (Autumn 1999): 214–227.

Doubler, Michael. *I Am the Guard: A History of the Army National Guard, 1636–2000*. Darby, PA: Diane Publishing, 2001.

Dubin, Ed, and Al Kugel. "WWI 100: Philately Tells the Story of U.S. Centennial in the Great War." *American Philatelist* 131, no. 4 (April 2017): 328–359.

Eanes, Greg. *Captured Not Conquered: The American POW Experience in the First World War*. Crewe, VA: E&H Publishing, 2018.

Ebeling, Walter. *The Fruited Plain: The Story of American Agriculture*. Berkeley: University of California Press, 1979.

Eberle, Donald. "The Plain Mennonite Face of the World War One Conscientious Objector." *Journal of Amish and Plain Anabaptist Studies* 3, no. 2 (2015): 175–201.

Eberle, Mark E. *Kansas Baseball, 1858–1941*. Lawrence: University Press of Kansas, 2017.

Eisenhower, John S. D. *Yanks: The Epic Story of the American Army in World War I*. New York: Simon & Schuster, 2001.

Farrar, Hayward Woody. "The Black Soldier in Two World Wars." In *A Companion to African American History*, edited by Alton Hornsby Jr., 349–363. Malden, MA: Blackwell Publishing, 2005.

Farwell, Bryan. *Over There: The United States in the Great War, 1917–1918*. New York: W. W. Norton, 1999.

Faulkner, Richard S. *Meuse-Argonne, 26 September–11 November 1918*. Washington, DC: Center of Military History, U.S. Army, 2018.

———. *Pershing's Crusaders: The American Soldier in World War I*. Lawrence: University Press of Kansas, 2017.

Ferrell, Robert H. "Angered to the Core: Henry J. Allen and the U.S. Army." *Kansas History* 29, no. 3 (Autumn 2006): 184–193.

———. *Collapse at Meuse-Argonne: The Failure of the Missouri-Kansas Division*. Columbia: University of Missouri Press, 2004.

Finnegan, John Patrick. *Against the Specter of a Dragon: The Campaign for American Military Preparedness*. Westport, CT: Greenwood, 1974.

Fleming, Thomas. *The Illusion of Victory: America in World War I*. New York: Basic Books, 2003.

Foner, Jack D. *Blacks and the Military in American History: A New Perspective*. New York: Praeger, 1974.

Fowles, Brian Dexter. *A Guard in Peace and War: The History of the Kansas National Guard, 1854–1987*. Manhattan, KS: Sunflower University Press, 1989.

Freidel, Frank. *Over There: The Story of America's First Great Overseas Crusade*. New York: Bramhall House, 1964.

Gannon, Barbara A. *The Won Cause: Black and White Comradeship in the Grand Army of the Republic*. Chapel Hill: University of North Carolina Press, 2011.

Gould, Lewis L. *The First Modern Clash over Federal Power: Wilson versus Hughes in the Presidential Election of 1916*. Lawrence: University Press of Kansas, 2016.

Griffin, Clifford S. *The University of Kansas: A History*. Lawrence: University Press of Kansas, 1974.

Grotelueschen, Mark E. *Into the Fight, April–June 1918: The U.S. Army Campaigns of World War I*. Washington, DC: Center of Military History, U.S. Army, 2018.

Harries, Meirion, and Susie Harries. *The Last Days of Innocence: America at War, 1917–1918*. New York: Random House, 1997.

Harris, Stephen L. *Harlem's Hell Fighters: The African-American 369th Infantry in World War I*. Washington, DC: Potomac Books, 2003.

———. *Rock of the Marne: The American Soldiers Who Turned the Tide against the Kaiser in World War I*. New York: Berkley Caliber, 2015.

Heckscher, August. *Woodrow Wilson*. New York: Scribner, 1991.

Heiman, James J. *Voices in Bronze and Stone: Kansas City's World War I Monuments and Memorials*. Kansas City, MO: Kansas City Star Books, 2013.

Hochschild, Adam. *American Midnight: The Great War, a Violent Peace, and Democracy's Forgotten Crisis*. New York: Mariner Books, 2022.

Jackson, Robert. *The Prisoners, 1914–18*. New York: Routledge, 1989.

James, Pearl. "Citizen-Consumers in the American Iconosphere during World War I." In *World War I and American Art*, edited by Robert Cozzolino, Anne Classen Knutson, and David M. Lubin, 45–55. Philadelphia: Pennsylvania Academy of the Fine Arts, 2016.

Jeffrey, Keith. *1916: A Global History*. New York: Bloomsbury Publishing, 2016.

Johnson, Judith R. "Kansas in the 'Grippe': The Spanish Influenza Epidemic of 1918." *Kansas History* 14, no. 1 (Spring 1992): 44–55.

Juhnke, James C. "Mob Violence and Kansas Mennonites in 1918." *Kansas Historical Quarterly* 43, no. 3 (Autumn 1977): 334–350.

Kastenberg, Joshua E. *To Raise and Discipline an Army*. De Kalb: Northern Illinois University Press, 2017.

Keckeisen, Sara J. "The Cost of Conscience Part 1: Coming of the Night." *Kansas Heritage* 12, no. 2 (Summer 2004): 6–13.

———. "The Cost of Conscience Part 2: Henry's Story." *Kansas Heritage* 12, no. 4 (Winter 2004): 6–13.

Keene, Jennifer D. "Remembering the 'Forgotten War': American Historiography on World War I." *Historian* 78, no. 3 (2016): 439–468.

Kendall, M. Sue. *Rethinking Regionalism: John Steuart Curry and the Kansas Mural Controversy*. Washington DC: Smithsonian Institution Press, 1986.

Kimble, James J. *Mobilizing the Home Front: War Bonds and Domestic Propaganda*. College Station: Texas A&M University Press, 2006.

Krammer, Arnold. *Undue Process: The Untold Story of America's German Alien Internees*. London: Rowman & Littlefield, 1997.

Lamay Licursi, Kimberly J. *Remembering World War I in America*. Lincoln: University of Nebraska Press, 2018.

Lancaster, Richard C. *Serving the U.S. Armed Forces, 1861–1986: The Story of the YMCA's Ministry to Military Personnel for 125 Years*. Schaumburg, IL: Armed Services YMCA of the USA, 1987.

Leeke, Jim. *The Best Team Over There: The Untold Story of Grover Cleveland Alexander and the Great War*. Lincoln: University of Nebraska Press, 2021.

———. *From the Dugouts to the Trenches: Baseball during the Great War*. Lincoln: University of Nebraska Press, 2017.

Leiker, James N. "Race Relations in the Sunflower State." *Kansas History* 25, no. 3 (Autumn 2002): 214–236.

Lengel, Edward G. *To Conquer Hell: The Meuse-Argonne, 1918*. New York: Henry Holt, 2008.

Lengel, Edward G., and James Lacey. "Background to the Meuse-Argonne." In *A Companion to the Argonne Campaign*, edited by Edward G. Lengel, 7–20. Chichester, UK: John Wiley & Sons, 2014.

Lerwill, Leonard L., ed. *The Personnel Replacement System in the United States Army*. Washington DC: Government Printing Office, 1954.

Lloyd, Nick. *The Western Front: A History of the Great War, 1914–1918*. New York: W. W. Norton, 2021.

McGeorge, Stephen C., and Mason W. Watson. *The Marne, 15 July–6 August 1918*. Washington, DC: Center of Military History, U.S. Army, 2018.

McMahon, Margaret M. *A Guide to the U.S. Pioneer Infantry Regiments in WWI*. Monee, IL, 2018.

McNeal, Claude. *Miracle in Springs Valley: The Amazing Story of Two Grand Hotels*. Indianapolis: CMcN Books, 2010.

Menne, Jeff, and Christian B. Long, eds. *Film and the American Presidency*. New York: Routledge, 2015.

Miller, William Lee. *Two Americans: Truman, Eisenhower, and a Dangerous World*. New York: Alfred A. Knopf, 2012.

Miner, Craig H. *Kansas: The History of the Sunflower State, 1854–2000*. Lawrence: University Press of Kansas, 2002.

Neiberg, Michael S. *The Second Battle of the Marne*. Bloomington: Indiana University Press, 2008.

Pankratz, Herbert. "The Suppression of Alleged Disloyalty in Kansas during World War I." *Kansas Historical Quarterly* 42, no. 3 (Autumn 1976): 277–307.

Parish, Arlyn John. *Kansas Mennonites during World War I*. Hays, KS: Fort Hays State University, 1968.

Prieto, Julie Irene. *The Mexican Expedition, 1916–1917*. Washington, DC: Center of Military History, U.S. Army, 2016.

Rains, Rob. *James Naismith: The Man Who Invented Basketball*. Philadelphia: Temple University Press, 2009.

Ramsey, Raquel, and Tricia Aurand. *Taking Flight: The Nadine Ramsey Story*. Lawrence: University Press of Kansas, 2022.

Reddish, Sandra. "An 'All Kansas' Regiment: The 353d Infantry Goes to War." *Kansas History* 29, no. 3 (Autumn 2006): 146–163.

Reynolds, David. "America's 'Forgotten War' and the Long Twentieth Century." In *World War I and American Art*, edited by Robert Cozzolino, Anne Classen

Knutson, and David M. Lubin, 19–29. Philadelphia: Pennsylvania Academy of the Fine Arts, 2016.

Richmond, Robert W. *Kansas: A Land of Contrasts*. St. Charles, MO: Forum, 1974.

Riegle, Wilford. "Peck's Bad Boys: The Story of the 35th Infantry Division in World War I." *Kansas Historical Quarterly* 23, no. 1 (Spring 1957): 70–81.

Rosenblum, Thomas. "Liberty in the Line of Fire: The Topeka Antidraft Conspiracy during World War I." *Kansas History* 41, no. 2 (Summer 2018): 106–123.

Rubin, Richard. *The Last of the Doughboys: The Forgotten Generation and Their Forgotten World War*. Boston: Houghton Mifflin Harcourt, 2013.

Rumer, Thomas A. *The American Legion: An Official History, 1919–1989*. New York: M. Evans, 1990.

Sammons, Jeffrey T., and John H. Morrow Jr. *Harlem's Rattlers and the Great War: The Undaunted 369th Regiment and the African American Quest for Equality*. Lawrence: University Press of Kansas, 2015.

Shedd, Clarence Prouty. *History of the World's Alliance of Young Men's Christian Associations*. London: SPCK Publishing, 1955.

Shenk, Gerald E. *Work or Fight!: Race, Gender, and the Draft in World War One*. New York: Palgrave Macmillan, 2005.

Skipper, John C. *Wicked Curve: The Life and Troubled Times of Grover Cleveland Alexander*. Jefferson, NC: McFarland, 2006.

Sledge, Michael. *Soldier Dead: How We Recover, Identify, Bury, and Honor Our Military Fallen*. New York: Columbia University Press, 2005.

Sloan, Charles William, Jr. "Kansas Battles the Invisible Empire: The Legal Ouster of the KKK from Kansas, 1922–1927." *Kansas Historical Quarterly* 40, no. 3 (Autumn 1974): 393–409.

Smith, Steven D., and James A. Zeidler. *A Historic Context for the African American Military Experience*. Champaign, IL: U.S. Army Construction Engineering Research Laboratories, 1998.

Smith, Zachary. *Age of Fear: Othering and American Identity during World War I*. Baltimore: Johns Hopkins University Press, 2019.

Stallings, Laurence. *The Doughboys: The Story of the AEF*. New York: Harper & Row, 1963.

Stephens, John Richard. *Commanding the Storm: Civil War Battles in the Words of the Generals Who Fought Them*. Guilford, CT: Lyons, 2012.

Steuer, Kenneth. *Pursuit of an 'Unparalleled Opportunity'—The American YMCA and Prisoner of War Diplomacy among the Central Power Nations during World War I, 1914–1923*. New York: Columbia University Press, 2009.

Stufflebean, Debra Guiou. *At the Time, in This Place*. Bloomington: iUniverse, 2009.

Swann, Marjorie, and William M. Tsutsui. "John Steuart Curry: A Portrait of the Artist as a Kansan." In *John Brown to Bob Dole: Movers and Shakers in Kansas History*, edited by Virgil W. Dean, 241–252. Lawrence: University Press of Kansas, 2006.

Trout, Steven. "Forgotten Reminders: Kansas World War I Memorials." *Kansas History* 29, no. 3 (Autumn 2006): 200–215.

———. "The Greatest Battle Ever Forgotten: The Meuse-Argonne Offensive and American Memory." In *A Companion to the Argonne Campaign*, edited by Edward G. Lengel, 496–514. Chichester, UK: John Wiley & Sons, 2014.

———. *On the Battlefield of Memory: The First World War and American Remembrance, 1919–1941*. Tuscaloosa: University of Alabama Press, 2010.

Ulbrich, David John. *Preparing for Victory: Thomas Holcomb and the Making of the Modern Marine Corps, 1936–1943*. Annapolis, MD: Naval Institute Press, 2013.

Van Emden, Richard. *Prisoners of the Kaiser: The Last POWs of the Great War*. Barnsley, UK: Pen & Sword Books, 2009.

Walker, Robert W. *The Namesake: A Biography of Theodore Roosevelt, Jr.* New York: Brick Tower, 2008.

Webb, Bernice Larson. *The Basketball Man: James Naismith*. Lawrence: University Press of Kansas, 1973.

"Who Was George Robb?" *Valor Magazine* 1, no. 1 (July 8, 2020): 5.

Willard, Julius Terrass. *History of the Kansas State College of Agriculture and Applied Science*. Manhattan: Kansas State College Press, 1940.

Williams, Chad L. *Torchbearers of Democracy: African American Soldiers in the World War I Era*. Chapel Hill: University of North Carolina Press, 2010.

Wilson, Adam P. *African American Army Officers of World War I: A Vanguard of Equality in War and Beyond*. Jefferson, NC: McFarland, 2015.

Woods, Randall B. "Integration, Exclusion, or Segregation?: The 'Color Line' in Kansas, 1879–1900." *Western Historical Quarterly* 14, no. 2 (April 1983): 181–198.

Woodward, David. "'Black Jack' Pershing: The American Proconsul in Europe." In *Leadership in Conflict, 1914–1918*, edited by Matthew Hughes and Matthew Seligmann, 141–157. Barnsley, UK: Leo Cooper, 1990.

Zornow, William Frank. *Kansas: A History of the Jayhawk State*. Norman: University of Oklahoma Press, 1957.

Unpublished Secondary Sources

Allen, Benjamin H. "The Greatest Battle Never Told: The Meuse-Argonne Offensive, 1918." Unpublished paper, November 9, 2015. Meuse-Argonne. http://meuseargonnerg.wpengine.com/wp-content/uploads/2016/01/The_Greatest_Battle_Never_Told_The_Meuse.pdf.

Bencks, Jarret. "When World War I Ended, the Civil Rights Movement Was Just Getting Started." BrandeisNOW, November 13, 2018. https://www.brandeis.edu/now/2018/november/world-war-one-african-americans.html.

Bryan, Jami L. "Fighting for Respect: African-American Soldiers in WWI." Army Historical Foundation. https://armyhistory.org/fighting-for-respect-african-american-soldiers-in-wwi/.

Carpenter, W. R. "Company M, 139th Infantry, 35th Division, A.E.F." Kansas History and Heritage Project. https://sites.rootsweb.com/~ksmarihp/military/historyof35thdivision.html.

Dean, Madison. "Then and Now: Washburn's Campus." Washburn Review, June

22, 2012. https://washburnreview.org/30662/news/then-and-now-washburns-campus/.

Dennis, Clarence. "What Is the History of the Rosedale Arch?" CuriousKC. Flatland, November 16, 2020. https://www.flatlandkc.org/curiouskc/question-everything/questions-answered/curiouskc-what-is-the-history-of-the-rosedale-arch/.

DiPasquale, Connie. "Riders on an Orphan Train to Kansas—1911: Anna May Potthoff Keeton, William James (Potthoff) Kimmel." Articles. Kansas Collection. http://www.kancoll.org/articles/orphans/orphan_t.htm.

Dyson, Melvin. Interview (June 1996). *Prisoner of War Interviews*. C-Span, broadcast May 14, 2003. https://www.c-span.org/video/?176624-3/world-war-pow-private-melvin-dyson.

Flaig, Steven. "Clarence R. Huebner: An American Military Story of Achievement." M.S. thesis, University of North Texas, 2006.

"George Henry Mallon, 1877–1934." Minnesota Medal of Honor Memorial. https://www.minnesotamedalofhonormemorial.org/wp-content/uploads/2017/12/Mallon-George-Henry-Original-bio.pdf.

Governor Arthur Capper's Slackers File. Kansas Memory. https://www.kansasmemory.org/item/212615.

Greenberg, Marc L. "Hoffman's Hawk: A University of Kansas Jayhawk Carved during the Russian Revolution of 1917 Reappears at KU in the Twenty-First Century." KU Scholar Works. November 24, 2010. https://kuscholarworks.ku.edu/bitstream/handle/1808/6896/Russian_Jayhawk_history_2010Nov24_MLGreenberg.pdf?sequence=1&isAllowed=y.

Hatzinger, Kyle J. "Democracy of Death: US Army Graves Registration and Its Burial of the World War I Dead." PhD diss., University of North Texas, 2020.

Hogan, Suzanne. "How Kansas City Became Home to the Nation's Official World War I Memorial." KCUR, NPR in Kansas City. November 9, 2018. https://www.kcur.org/arts-life/2018-11-09/how-kansas-city-became-home-to-the-nations-official-world-war-i-memorial.

Jacobs, Doug. "2LT Erwin Russell Bleckley." Kansas National Guard Museum. January 30, 2013. https://ksngmuseum.wordpress.com/2013/01/30/2lt-erwin-russell-bleckley/.

"K-State's 48 Fallen." World War I Memorial Stadium. Kansas State Alumni Association. https://www.k-state.com/about/wwi/indexwwi/service.php.

Lange, Katie. "Dog Tag History: How the Tradition & Nickname Started." DOD News, September 9, 2020. https://www.defense.gov/News/Inside-DOD/Blog/Article/2340760/dog-tag-history-how-the-tradition-nickname-started/.

Lefferts, Peter M. "Black US Army Bands and Their Bandmasters in World War I." Faculty Publications: School of Music. Digital Commons@University of Nebraska–Lincoln, March 2, 2018. https://digitalcommons.unl.edu/cgi/viewcontent.cgi?article=1069&context=musicfacpub.

May, Andy. "Oscar May in World War I." Climate Blog. Andy May Petrophysicist,

November 5, 2018. https://andymaypetrophysicist.com/2018/11/05/oscar-may-in-world-war-I/.
McCool, John H. "Chancellor Strong's About-Face." KU's Response to WW1. KU Memorial Union. https://union.ku.edu/chancellor-strongs-about-face.
———. "Hello, I Must Be Going." President Woodrow Wilson and the First Lady Visiting Lawrence, Kansas. KU Memorial Union. https://union.ku.edu/president-woodrow-wilson-and-first-lady-visiting-lawrence-kansas.
———. "' . . . Kansas Must Have a Stadium!'" Memorial Stadium. KU Memorial Union. https://union.ku.edu/kansas-must-have-stadium.
———. "KU Women Do Their Bit." KU's Red Cross Course. KU Memorial Union. https://union.ku.edu/ku-women-do-their-bit.
McGinnis, Thomas Michael. "Unit Collapse: A Historical Analysis of Two Divisional Battles in 1918 and 1944." MA thesis, U.S. Army Command and General Staff College, 1987. https://apps.dtic.mil/dtic/tr/fulltext/u2/a184706.pdf.
Moyer, Sarah. "Manhattan Observes Armistice Day Centennial with Concert and More." *Kansas State Collegian*, November 12, 2018. https://www.kstatecollegian.com/2018/11/12/manhattan-observes-armistice-day-centennial-with-concert-and-more/.
Neuman, Brian Fisher. "Pershing's Right Hand: General James G. Harbord and the American Expeditionary Forces in the First World War." PhD diss., Texas A&M University, 2006.
Patton, James. "The Centennial at the Grass Roots: Finding WWI in Rural Kansas." *Roads to the Great War* (blog), October 9, 2017. http://roadstothegreatwar-ww1.blogspot.com/2017/10/the-centennial-at-grass-roots-finding.html.
Perkins, Duane Roy. "The Ku Klux Klan in Lyon County, Kansas, in the 1920s." MA thesis, Emporia State University, 1981. https://esirc.emporia.edu/bitstream/handle/123456789/2221/Perkins%201981.pdf?sequence=1.
Pettit, Dorothy Ann. "A Cruel Wind: America Experiences the Pandemic Influenza, 1918–1920: A Social History." Ph.D. diss., University of New Hampshire, 1976.
Pomortzeff, Vova. All Quiet on the Western Front: How the Places of the Bloody Battles of the First World War Look like One Hundred Years Later. 2018. https://pomortzeff.com/eng/westfront.
Ulbrick, David John. "The Importance of the Battle of Belleau Wood." June 4, 2018. *War on the Rocks* (blog), Texas National Security Review. https://warontherocks.com/2018/06/the-importance-of-the-battle-of-belleau-wood/.
"Veteran Memorials." Washburn University. https://www.washburn.edu/about/community/attractions/veteran-memorials.html.

Index